ANCIENT INDIAN SOCIAL HISTORY
SOME INTERPRETATIONS

Ancient Indian Social History
Some Interpretations

Second Edition

ROMILA THAPAR

Orient BlackSwan

ANCIENT INDIAN SOCIAL HISTORY

ORIENT BLACKSWAN PRIVATE LIMITED

Registered Office
3-6-752 Himayatnagar, Hyderabad 500 029 (Telangana), INDIA
e-mail: centraloffice@orientblackswan.com

Other Offices
Bengaluru, Bhopal, Chennai, Ernakulam, Guwahati, Hyderabad,
Jaipur, Kolkata, Lucknow, Mumbai, New Delhi, Noida, Patna, Vijayawada

First published by Orient Blackswan Private Limited 1978
Reissued 1984
Reprinted 1987, 1990, 1996, 2004, 2006
First Orient Blackswan impression 2009
Second edition, Orient Blackswan Pvt. Ltd. 2010
Reprinted 2011, 2012, 2013, 2014, 2015, 2016

ISBN: 978 81 250 3962 4

Typeset by
InoSoft Systems
Noida

Printed in India at
Glorious Printers
Delhi

Published by
Orient Blackswan Private Limited
1/24 Asaf Ali Road, New Delhi 110 002
e-mail: delhi@orientblackswan.com

Contents

Acknowledgements

The author and the publishers would like to thank the editors and publishers of the journals and books listed below for permission granted for inclusion in this volume of the material cited:

For 'Interpretations of Ancient Indian History' from *History and Theory,* (1968), Wesleyan University, Connecticut, USA.

For 'Society and Law in the Hindu and Buddhist Traditions' from *International Social Science Journal* (1966), Paris, France.

For 'Ethics, Religion and Social Protest in the First Millennium B.C. in Northern India' from *Daedalus,* Journal of the American Academy of Arts and Science, Boston, Massachusetts, USA, Spring 1975, *Wisdom, Revelation and Doubt.*

For 'Renunciation: The Making of a Counter-culture?' from *Homage to a Historian,* Dr. N. Subrahmanian Felecitation Volume, N. Jagadesan and J. Jeyapragasan (eds.).

For '*Dāna* and *Dakṣiṇā* as forms of Exchange' from *Indica* (1976), St. Xavier's College, Bombay.

For 'Social Mobility in Ancient India with Special Reference to Elite Groups' from *Indian Society: Historical Probings (Essays in memory of D.D. Kosambi)* R.S. Sharma and D.N. Jha (eds.) (1974), Indian Council of Historical Research, New Delhi.

For 'Image of the Barbarian in Early India' from *Comparative Studies in Society and History* (1970), Cambridge University Press, London, England.

For 'The Historian and Archaeological Data' from *Radiocarbon and Indian Archaeology* D.P. Agarwal and A.C. Ghosh (eds.) (1973), Tata Institute of Fundamental Research, Bombay.

For 'The Study of Society in Ancient India' from Proceedings of XXXI Indian History Congress (1969), Varanasi.

For 'Puranic Lineages and Archaeological Data' from *Puratattva* (1975), The Archaeological Survey of India, New Delhi.

For 'The Tradition of Historical Writing in Early India' for *Indian Church History Review* (1972), Church History Association of India, Bangalore.

For 'Origin Myths and the Early Indian Historical Tradition' from *History and Society: Essays in Honour of Professor Niharrajan Ray*, D. Chattopadhyaya (ed.) (Calcutta, 1978).

For 'Genealogy as Source of Social History' from the *Indian Historical Review* (1976), Indian Council of Historical Research, New Delhi.

For 'The Scope and Significance of Regional History', Address to the Punjab History Conference, 1976, Punjab University, Patiala.

For 'Great Eastern Trade: Other Times, Other places' (Maritime Trade in the First Millennium A.D.), by Romila Thapar, The Fourth Vasant J. Sheth Memorial. Lecture, delivered in Mumbai on 10 January 2002. Grateful acknowledgement is made for permission to reprint the lecture from the Vasant J. Sheth Memorial Foundation, Mumbai.

For 'The Future of the Indian Past; The Seventh D.T. Lakdawala Memorial Lecture, 21 February 2004, Institute of Social Science, New Delhi.

For 'Recognizing Historical Traditions of Early India', Yoda Press, New Delhi.

Introduction to the Second Edition

Reading these essays, some written forty years ago, means thinking of reformulations. To rewrite them would be a major enterprise and not necessary as I have little disagreement with what I said when the essays were first published. I still endorse what I have said earlier although some nuances may be less or more emphatic. I shall therefore just draw attention to what I would now tend to emphasize as and where I think such emphasis is necessary.

The notion of 'law' can be misunderstood if treated in its modern sense as regulations binding on a society backed by the state. The *dharmaśāstra* works are more in the nature of coding social observances so as to give a structure to *varṇa* based society.

The broad-based term 'tribe' which covers a range of community patterns in its current usage, is now being replaced for references to earlier periods with more specific terms. This includes 'clan' or (my preference) lineage-based societies. This also makes it easier to differentiate a clan from a caste society.

Much of the social history of India focuses on elite groups as are most of these essays. This is in part because the surviving texts from that period are from these sections of society and partly because historians have not searched sufficiently in these texts for reflections of the lower strata. Thus in the notion of tolerance the noticeable fact is that whereas caste permitted the co-existence of multiple religious sects in a relatively tolerant acceptance of difference, the impact of intolerance was fully felt and applied to hierarchies within the caste structure. There was no equivalent of an ecclesiastical ban on divergence in religious practice and belief where such divergences often took the form of a breakaway caste. But there was a rigid concern, in theory at least, with disallowing deviation within the practices of a caste.

We know of course that such deviations from the *dharmaśāstra* norms were frequent and were papered over. However the distance between high caste, especially *brāhmaṇ* and untouchable was fiercely insisted upon by the high caste. Under the guise of ritual purity and impurity this became the mechanism of caste society maintaining a permanent labour force, perpetuated by insisting that such powers were segregated by marriage, location, religious practice, language and social custom. It was virtually a different society but kept suppressed. Indian civilization may have been relatively tolerant in matters of religious codes but was largely intolerant in its social codes.

This is also reflected in attitudes to social ethic. The brahmanical ethic required the observance of the *varṇa-āśrama-dharma* where the ethic was determined by the *varṇa.* Kṛśṇa's teaching in the *Bhāgvad Gītā* states in no uncertain terms that the *kṣatriya's dharma* is to destroy evil and to kill where necessary. The Buddhist ethic on the contrary opposed violence and preferred persuasion as a means of overcoming evil. Furthermore, it posed a universal social ethic of tolerance and non-violence with an emphasis on amicable social behaviour between people. This ethic was applicable uniformly to all and to be observed by all, irrespective of caste.

It has recently been argued that there was a widespread debate about the social ethic and governance after the reign of Aśoka who had tried to implement the universally applicable ethic. In this connection the *rājadharma* section of the Śāntiparvan in the *Mahābhārata* is an attempt to counter this ethic and give primacy to the *varṇa-āśrama-dharma.* Yudhiṣṭhira's wish to renounce kingship and become an ascetic was not unconnected with this debate. From the *dharma-śāstra* perspective only renouncers could observe a universally applicable ethic.

Social distancing within the functioning of caste was not limited to untouchables and lower castes. It also applied to elite groups who were outside the caste and culture boundaries. These were the *mlecchas* who did not speak Sanskrit and who did not observe the norms of caste. Interestingly, few references are made to differences in belief systems among such groups.

Those called *mleccha* range over various categories. Some

are local but like the Śabara, Niṣada and Pulinda, they do not observe caste culture and are generally the people of the forest who are treated with contempt. This is illustrated in a founding myth where the *brāhmaṇs* kill Vena and banish his first born to the forest where he becomes the proto-type of the forest dwellers. Such groups which are many, are only slightly better off than the untouchable since they can move freely through the forests.

Another category of *mleccha* are 'foreigners'—mainly those that enter through the north-west or the western sea-board. The latter often married locally thus establishing new communities and castes in which their foreignness was subsumed. Where they retained their language and custom they remained *mleccha.* The essay on trade between west Asia and India illustrates these points. The politically powerful such as the Sultans of medieval India, are sometimes referred to as *mleccha* in local inscriptions. The label was obviously not being used as a term of contempt but rather as a reference to their being culturally distinct.

The incorporation of originally *mleccha* groups into caste society was known. It required a change to speaking the language of the administration, generally Sanskrit, and giving up the relatively more egalitarian clan system for the hierarchies of caste status. The adoption of Puranic Hinduism was another feature of this change. This process can be seen in the claims to the status of *ksatriya* of some ruling families in the post-Gupta period. The construction of genealogies or even their fabrication in most cases, was an essential requirement for the change of status. This was provided by willing *brāhmaṇs* delving back into the Puranic descent lists and selecting generational links. The sanction was sealed by the performance of Vedic *śrauta* rituals. The recompense was often a handsome grant of land. A stock of myths was available and appropriate ones were selected to further the narrative of the connections. These processes are now becoming clearer with research into regional history which reveals varieties of new sources permitting a more detailed investigation.

The tradition of historical writing in India has been treated in a variety of new ways and has resulted in new theories of historiography that refer to texts of the sixteenth century and later. Similar writing in early India is beginning to be explored but not sufficiently as yet. The essay published in this collection is an early foray into the subject as will be clear when comparing it to the more recent one newly added. The cliché that Indian civilization lacked a sense of history is open to discussion. The mutation in our present-day understanding of history as a discipline, so different from the way it was understood a couple of centuries ago, has also challenged the dismissal of historical traditions in early India. More importantly there is a need to demonstrate how we can search for such traditions from the varied genres of texts that we work with.

Two essays focus on contemporary problems relating to how early history is presented and interpreted either by institutions such as museums or by the political exploitation of history. Museums should not be treated as 'curiosity houses' where objects from the past are collected and some are displayed. The method and the intellectual and aesthetic direction behind the display are of fundamental importance.

The final essay was written at a time when history as a social science discipline was under attack by those who preferred to use it as the ideological mythology of a particular political programme. That condition one hopes has ended. But it would be as well to remind ourselves of the debate at the time. Being aware of the debate is part of the process of protecting the right to historical interpretation.

New Delhi 2009 Romila Thapar

Interpretations of Ancient Indian History

Despite the stereotypes of 'unchanging India' and her 'unhistorical' religions and peoples, the historical writing on ancient India goes back for more than two centuries and exhibits an instructive series of changes in interpretation. The historical writings produced by European scholars, beginning in the eighteenth century, were formulated in terms of the ideological attitudes then dominant in Europe, and naturally these were significantly different from the indigenous tradition of ancient India. European ideologies entailed a set of attitudes toward India which were for the most part highly critical, though there were also some sympathetic historians. These ideologies continued to be influential even after Indian scholars began to write, since they often wrote in reply to earlier interpretations and were therefore still moulded by them. It has been only in recent years that the influence of ideologies on the interpretation of Indian history has been recognized; perhaps now for the first time a history of the changing interpretations of ancient India can be written.

India was by no means a country unknown to Europe. In the post-Renaissance period knowledge of and familiarity with things Indian grew with the visits of merchants, ambassadors, and missionaries from various parts of Europe to the Indian sub-continent. The accounts written by some of these visitors—such as those of Sir Thomas Roe, the ambassador of James I to the Mughal court of the emperor Jahangir,[1] or Francois Bernier who visited India in 1668 and was associated with the court of Louis XIV[2]—became the basic European source of information on India in the seventeenth and eighteenth centuries. Some of these accounts were fairly reliable; others were a mixture of observation and a large amount of fantasy.

The first serious study of India and its past began in the late eighteenth century with the work of scholars who have since been

From *History and Theory*, 1968, VII; no. 3, pp. 318-35.

described as the Orientalists or Indologists.[3] This study arose principally because the East India Company required that its officers, in order to administer properly the territories which it had acquired, become familiar with the laws, habits and history of the people they were governing. Thus William Jones as a judge in the Presidency of Bengal was able to devote time to the study of Sanskrit and philology of the Indo-European languages and to work on the pre-British legal systems. Nevertheless, scholars such as William Jones, Charles Wilkins, H.T. Colebrooke, and H.H. Wilson did also have a genuine interest in the culture of India and would probably have sustained this interest without the incentive of being administrators in India. Because of this their work took them beyond the codification of laws and into the realms of classical Sanskrit literature and the study of religion and philosophy. In order to encourage this research and provide a focus for it, the Asiatic Society was founded in 1784. By the middle of the nineteenth century Orientalists were no longer merely the people who had direct contact with India through the East India Company. Interest in the ancient past of India had by then spread to a number of universities in Europe, with scholars working on Sanskrit and related subjects. Some of the best known of such so-called Orientalists and Indologists had never even visited India, a case in point being Max Müller.

For the Orientalists, the most significant discovery was that of the relationship between Sanskrit and certain European languages, which led to subsequent work on the common Indo-European heritage. The ancient Indian past was seen almost as a lost wing of early European culture, and the Āryans of India were regarded as the nearest intellectual relatives of the Europeans. There was an emphasis on the study of Sanskrit, since it was believed to belong to a period earlier than that of Greek and thus to be in a purer state of preservation; it therefore provided a better understanding of all Indo-European languages. A sharp distinction was made between the speakers of Āryan and non-Āryan languages in the sub-continent, and a variety of noble virtues were attributed to the Āryans. This, incidentally, strengthened the indigenous tradition of acclaiming the Sanskritic traits of Indian culture, and not surprisingly the writings of the Orientalists are frequently quoted by members of various nineteenth century socio-religious reform movements such as the Arya Samaj. The heritage of Sanskrit literature was the emphasis upon a totally different set of values from those current in Europe. As Max Müller put it: 'not the active, combative and acquisitive, but the passive, meditative and reflective.'[4] The Indian past was seen as an unchanging society where the village community was the idyllic centre of Indian life and was, in fact, the natural background for the qualities of gentleness, passivity, truthfulness, and other worldliness qualities associated by Westerners with Indians. If the Orientalists tended to exaggerate the virtues they saw in Indian society, it was in part because they were searching for a distant Utopia to escape from the bewildering changes taking place in nineteenth century Europe, and in part to counteract the highly critical attitudes current among Utilitarian thinkers in Britain, from whose ranks came more influential writing on India.

No sustained attempt was made to place the source material in the context of its contemporary background. The sources, particularly those in Sanskrit, were in the main the works of the *brahmaṇs*, as keepers of the ancient classical tradition, and expressed the brahmanical *Weltanschauung*. The fact that these were texts emanating from and relating to a particular segment of society was often overlooked, though in fairness to the Orientalists it must be said that the critical and analytical study of literature from other classical cultures was still in its infancy. The reliance on 'pandits', those learned in Sanskrit and supposedly the guardians of the ancient tradition, was not the most reliable—although undoubtedly the most convenient—access to ancient history. Many of the contemporary ideological prejudices of the pandits were often incorporated into what was believed to be the interpretation of the ancient tradition. This vitiated the study of 'ancient culture', particularly the section of it which was concerned with the law-books and legal codes, the *dharmaśāstras*.

It was largely due to the enthusiasm of the Orientalists that translations of Indian literature and of philosophical works became popular with intellectuals in Europe and even America. As early as 1791 Thomas Jefferson, who had known William Jones in Paris, sent a copy of Kalidasa's play *Shakuntala* (which had been recently translated into English by Jones) to his daughter, to introduce her to classical Indian literature which he so greatly admired in what was available in translation at the time. The admiration of the poets of the German Romantic movement was even greater, as is evident from the remarks of Frederick Schlegel.[5] Goethe's eulogy on *Shakuntala* can hardly bear quoting again, it is quoted so often. Schopenhauer's interest in the philosophy of the *Upaniṣads* is equally well known. Much of this enthusiasm was, however, limited to literary circles and did not make the required impact on historians. Philosophers of history such as Hegel took little notice of this literature.

The first important history of India did not come from the Orientalists, but from a totally different source. In 1817, James Mill published his *History of British India*, a lengthy work divided into three major sections: Hindu civilization, Muslim civilization and the British period. For Mill the principal value of a culture was the degree to which it contributed to the furtherance of rationalism and individualism. He saw neither of these two values in Hindu civilization and therefore condemned it severely. He was unwilling to make any of the concessions which the Orientalists had made and continued to make. He also maintained that Indian society had remained substantially unchanged from the period of its origin, the coming of the Aryans, until the arrival of the British. Furthermore, Indian civilization showed no great concern for political values, for the Indian people had been ruled by a series of despotic and tyrannical rulers until the coming of the British. His division of Indian history into three periods—the Hindu, the Muslim and the British—became the accepted periodization of Indian history and has remained so, with marginal modification, to the present day.[6] Mill was a firm believer in the Utilitarian principle that legislation can improve society. In the Indian context this belief implied that British administrators in applying legislation could change India from a traditional, unchanging society to a progressive and dynamic society, 'tradition' and 'progress' being defined in Utilitarian terms. That the new legislation was totally without roots in the Indian social system and would be regarded as an imposition did not unduly disturb Mill.

Mill's history became the standard work on India and remained so for many decades. Even H.H. Wilson, who was generally much more sympathetic to the early period of Indian history, was content to add a critical commentary in the form of footnotes to a later edition of Mill's *History* and did not think it necessary to write a fresh work contradicting some of Mill's out-of-date statements. Mill was a radical in the British context, and, as was the case with quite a few other radicals of this period, he tended to exaggerate the conservatism and backwardness of India in order to accentuate his own radicalism.

The Utilitarians were not the only group who saw pre-British Indian history as being almost totally without virtue. A similar position had been taken by the Evangelicals, as for example in the writings of Charles Grant,[7] although their motives for this position were different from those of the Utilitarians. Whereas Mill was concerned with changing India through legislation, the Evangelicals wished to do it through conversion to Christianity. Not unexpectedly, the Evangelicals concentrated on trying to prove that the essential backwardness of India, as they saw it, was due to the Hindu religion.

Mill's assertion that the Indian past had been that of an unchanging, static society dominated by despotic rulers was reflected in various philosophies of histroy current in the nineteenth century. The most influential of these with respect to Indian history were the works of Hegel.[8] For Hegel, of course, true history involved dialectical change and development. Indian history remained stationary and fixed and therefore outside the stream of world history. The basis of Indian society was the immutable pattern of the Indian village, inhabited by a people totally unconcerned with political relationships. This permitted not only despotic rulers but also frequent conquests and continual subjugation. The static character of Indian society with its concomitant despotic rulers became an accepted truth of Indian history. The concept of Oriental Despotism began to take shape.

This concept was not new to European thinking on Asia. Its roots can perhaps be traced to the writings of Herodotus, to the Greco-Persian antagonism in the ancient world, and to the pronouncements of Aristotle on the nature of kingship and political systems in Asia. It was taken up and developed into a political theory by Montesquieu in *L'Esprit des lois*, and this theory was debated by the French physiocrats and by Voltaire, who found it unacceptable. But the concept became established in the nineteenth century when it was introduced into various philosophies of history and was thus given intellectual legitimacy. In the case of India the primary reason given for the rise of Oriental Despotism was the belief that there was no private property in land in pre-British India. This belief was based on a misunderstanding of the agrarian system of the Mughal empire by both Thomas Roe and Francois Bernier.[9]

Hegel's philosophy of history influenced yet another interpretation of Indian history. Christian Lassen, writing in the mid-nineteenth century, applied the dialectic of thesis, antithesis, and synthesis—applied by Hegel to the phases of Greek, Roman and Christian civilization in Europe—to India, where the three phases became Hindu, Muslim and Christian civilization.[10] Lassen tried in this way to connect Indian history with the general stream of world history in the common synthesis of Christian civilization. In addition, this idea further strengthened Mill's original periodization.

In spite of applying the Hegelian dialectic to his interpretation of Indian history, Lassen was unable to refute Hegel's assumption concerning the unchanging nature of India's past. This assumption was taken up by Marx and worked into the thesis on the Asiatic Mode of Production.[11] Marx used as sources the information supplied by administrators and other officers employed by the British Indian government and the Parliamentary Reports. Unfortunately neither he nor Engels worked on this theory in great detail; the Asiatic Mode of Production was marginal to their main concern, which was the dialectic of European history. The sources were not only scanty but also not altogether reliable, since many of the administrators had preconceived ideas about the Indian past based on the writings of James Mill, Richard Jones, and others which were prescribed texts at Haileybury College and other such institutions where these administrators were trained. The characteristics of the Asiatic Mode of Production were: the absence of privately owned land, since all land was state-owned; the predominantly village economy, the occasional town functioning more as a military camp than as a commercial centre; the nearly self-sufficient nature of this village economy with each isolated village meeting its agricultural needs and manufacturing essentail goods; the lack of much surplus for exchange after the collection of a large percentage of the surplus by the State; the complete subjugation of the village communities to the State, made possible by state control of major public works, most importantly irrigation. The extraction of a maximum percentage of the surplus from the village communities enabled the despotic ruler to live in considerable luxury.

The emphasis on village communities and despotic rulers continued to haunt the writing of Indian history in the late nineteenth and early twentieth centuries. Many of the historians of this period were administrators who were convinced that the pattern of British administration was acting as a catalyst in changing Indian society for the better.[12] Source material pertaining to the ancient period of Indian history was now interpreted to fit these preconceptions, as, for example, in the writings of Henry Maine on ancient law and on early village communities in India.[13] In analyzing the reasons for the static quality of Indian society, historians generally criticized the institution of caste. The theoretical ideal of the caste system as a rigid social system, as implied in the ancient law-books, *dharmaśāstras*, was accepted as an actual description of a caste society, in spite of the fact that many of these writers were intimately concerned with rural administration, where discrepancies between the theoretical description of the caste system and its actual working were obvious.[14] The disinclination to look for change in the Indian past was also strengthened by the thinking of social and cultural evolutionists, for whom unfamiliar societies were rejects of the linear movement toward progress. Attempts were therefore made to fit Indian society into the uniform scheme of evolution which was current in the late nineteenth century. Obviously, it would be easier to fit an atypical society into such a scheme if it could be assumed that such a society had always been static.

An interesting contrast to British historiography of India can be seen in German and French writing on India. These scholars were not writing under the shadow of administrative duties and governmental policy, and their comprehension of the Indian past was significantly different. The keynote to this understanding was struck by Auguste Comte, who was generally sympathetic to the early Indian tradition[15] partially due to the influence of the Orientalists but also due to the interest of French and German sociological thought in the nature of industrialization and its relation to social organization. One expression of this interest was the study of societies with an ideological base believed to be totally different from that of contemporary Europe, exemplified by Max Weber's work on India.[16] The culmination of this avenue of thought can be seen in the presuppositions of a recent French study of Indian society and culture, Louis Dumont's *Homo Hierarchicus*. Dumont maintains that the basic misunderstanding of Indian culture arose from the fact that an essentially hierarchically ordered culture was studied by persons committed to an egalitarian ordering of society, who were consequently unable to comprehend the society they were studying. Dumont's contention is open to question. What is interesting, however, is that this kind of conceptual framework for the study of Indian culture and history did not emerge from British writing on early India. Not only was British sociological thinking different, but in the specific case of India the exigencies of administration impinged on historical understanding. What the French made of the history of their own colonies is quite another story.[17]

The idea that the British administration brought to an end the tradition of oppressive despots is a basic belief in the writings of perhaps the best known of the administrator historians, Vincent Smith.[18] He devoted himself especially to the study of ancient India and combined in his scholarship both more advanced techniques of historical reconstruction and a clearly defined interpretation. Smith's historical training was in European classical scholarship. He was enthusiastic about the activities of the ancient Greeks and took their achievements to be the yardstick by which to measure all civilizations. His pro-Greek bias is shown in attempts to suggest that the finer qualities of Indian civilization were derived from Greece.[19] He was equally impressed by the grand sweep of Roman history as presented by Gibbon. Heroes and empires were the subject matter of history; and, furthermore, only those who had survived successfully were worth consideration. Thus Aśoka's Chandragupta II, and Akbar became his heroes and their reigns the glorious periods of Indian history. The intervening periods of small kingdoms he saw as periods of anarchy and misrule, since they failed to produce emperors; and in his interpretation of Indian history, these became the dark ages. Smith's depiction of the rise and fall of empires and the intervening dark ages did weaken the idea of a totally unchanging society, even if the change was largely limited to the upper sections of society.

Vincent Smith and his contemporaries writing on India were in a sense reflecting the main trend of British historical writing of the time. It is perhaps as well to remember that in the late nineteenth century British historians studying Britain also were focusing attention on 'great men'. As has been recently observed: 'History was more conveniently interpreted as the interaction between great men and the institutions they created, modified or restored.'[20] Charles Kingsley in his inaugural lecture as professor of history at Cambridge in 1861 had stated that: 'the new science of little men can be no science at all; because the average man is not the normal man, and never yet has been; because the great man is rather the normal man, as approaching more nearly than his fellows to the true "norma" and standard of a complete human character to turn to the mob for your theory of humanity is (I think) about as wise as to ignore the Apollo and the Theseus and to determine the proportions of the human figure from a crowd of dwarfs and cripples.' This sentiment was pre-eminent for many decades in British historical writing.

Smith's studies of ancient Indian history present, nevertheless, a considerable advance over earlier writings on the same subject, because a significant new body of evidence was available. Apart from the work on the literary sources, there developed in the later nineteenth century an interest in the antiquities of India. The objects and the information collected constituted the beginnings of archaeology in India. James Prinsep had deciphered the *brahmi* script in 1837, thus opening up the epigraphical sources. Alexander Cunningham began a systematic study of monuments, which became the nucleus of art-history. The exploration of archaeological sites laid the foundation not only for archaeological work but also for an interest in historical geography, which in turn encouraged local history. The study of numismatics, originally inspired by the extension of the study of Greek coins to those in India, became a source of fresh evidence. Surveys of local castes, customs, religious practices, and languages served to advance the cause of antiquarian interests. By the early twentieth century, there was a sizeable amount of non-literary evidence to complement the written sources.[21] But the former tradition of antiquarian writing continued, and these new sources were used largely to increase the quantum of evidence, with few attempts at analyzing the material. The main concern of historians writing on ancient India was still with political and dynastic history for which fresh information was available from the epigraphic and numismatic evidence.

It was also about this time that Indian historians first began writing on ancient Indian history, the most eminent among them being R.G. Bhandarkar.[22] At this stage they did not have any new perspective on Indian history, but followed the models set by British historians. Historical writing was mainly a narrative of dynastic and political history or else work of a largely antiquarian interest in fact-finding. Bhandarkar, though recognizing the deficiencies of the sources as historical material, was also aware of the more obvious prejudices of contemporary historians writing on the Indian past. Incidentally, it is interesting to observe that many of the early writers came from *brāhmaṇ* and *kayastha* families, largely because they were the ones who had the quickest access to a knowledge of the required classical language. The cultural background of Indian historians tended to inhibit a critical or analytical study of the sources. However, their hesitation to question the model put forward by British historians is linked with the larger question of sociology of education in modern India. Subsequently the challenge arose out of nationalism and gradually acquired intellectual formulations within the discipline of history.

The following generation of Indian historians, however, differed from their elders in one fundamental assumption. Historians writing in the 1920s and 1930s felt the impact of the national movement, and this was reflected in their historical thinking. Historians such as H.C. Raychaudhuri, K.P. Jayaswal, R.C. Majumdar, R.K. Mookerjee and H.C. Ojha, among others, continued to write political and dynastic history in the main, but their interpretations were based on a clearly nationalistic point of view.[23] There was an unashamed glorification of the ancient Indian past. This was in part a reaction to the criticism of Mill and other writers and in part a necessary step in the building of national self-respect. The glorious past was also a compensation for the humiliating present. To some extent the glorification of the past represented a revival of interest in the writings of the more sympathetic Orientalists; and, not surprisingly, eulogistic quotations from Max Müller, for instance, were given as proof of disinterested European opinion of India's past.

Ancient Indian society was visualized by these writers as a comparatively unchanging society over the period from 1000 B.C. to A.D.1000 with a uniformly high quality of achievement; the basis of this stability was the ancient Āryan culture. It was felt that nineteenth-century historians had belittled the achievements of anceint India by, among other things, denying its antiquity and by suggesting that its achievements were borrowed mainly from Greece. There was an attempt, therefore, to place literary sources as early in time as was reasonably feasible and to prove that the more worthwhile aspects of Indian culture were entirely indigenous.[24] To counter the argument that the Indian tradition lacked a concern for the rational and the pragmatic, it was maintained that Indian culture had an essentially spiritual quality which was totally opposed to that of the essentially materialistic Western civilization. It followed that in essence Indian culture was superior.

Another characteristic of historical interpretation influenced by nationalism was the desire to stress the political unity of the country from earliest times. Thus the rise of the Mauryan empire in the third century B.C. and its extension over almost the entire sub-continent was seen as an expression of an all-India consciousness.[25] The earlier emphasis of Smith on empires as the relevant periods of study was therefore continued, but for different reasons. References to imperial glory gave rise to a sense of pride in the past and strengthened the ideology of nationhood. The term 'empire' continued to be applied to the large north Indian kingdoms, and the geographical perspective was that of the Ganges heartland. In spite of this geographical focus there was no lack of generalization embracing the entire sub-continent.

Some of the generalizations now appear to be self-contradictory, but clearly they were not so regarded at the time. For example, whereas on the one hand non-violence was regarded as a distinguishing feature of Indian culture, there was at the same time a glorification of military power. For some, Aśoka's policy of non-violence was his greatest achievement; other historians found this the major criticism of him, arguing that he so weakened the defence of India that the northwestern part of the sub-continent was conquered with ease by foreign invaders.[26] The adulation of Chandragupta Maurya or the flattering comparisons of Samudragupta with Napoleon were all based on pride in the military prowess of these rulers.

Historians such as Vincent Smith, W. W. Tarn and others came under attack because of their theories concerning the widespread influence of Greek culture on Indian culture.[27] A determined attempt was made to prove that Indian civilization did not lack any of the laudable qualities ascribed to the Greeks. Thus Jayaswal maintained that the political life of the ancient Indian republics had been based on the concepts of democracy and representative government to the same degree as had the political life of the Greek city-states.[28] Alternatively, A.K. Coomaraswami argued against the aesthetic superiority of Greek art, since the Greeks were obsessed with physical beauty whereas the Indian artists sought to express higher spiritual values in their work.[29] It was this quality in Indian art which made it aesthetically unappealing to the Western viewers.

The nationalist historians were writing at a time when the leaders of the national movement were demanding political rights and political representation in the government. Understandably, therefore, the political life and institutions of the past were probably the most sensitive areas of disagreement with earlier historians. The discovery and interpretation of the *Arthaśastra*, a work on political economy, was, for instance, a form of exoneration from the charge that Indian society was unconcerned with political relationships.[30] Hence the frequent comparisons of the text with the writings of Machiavelli and the ideas of Bismarck, or, for that matter, the comparison of the *mantripariṣad* as described by Kauṭalya with the Privy Council of Britain,[31] and the suggestion that the Kauṭalyan monarch was similar to the constitutional monarch of Britain.[32] It would seem that in matters relating to political history and institutions the values current in European thought were accepted and their equivalents sought in the Indian past.

In spite of such weaknesses the nationalist historians played a very significant role in the interpretation of ancient Indian history. Because they wrote in conscious opposition to the earlier writing, they forced historians to take a fresh look at the sources. They raised controversies, and a debate began. The recognition of an historian's conceptual framework became meaningful. The interpretation of Indian history was no longer based on a monolithic ideology deriving authority from the concept of Oriental Despotism. Furthermore, the study of the ancient past began to have relevance for the present, and historical writing had to be more than the antiquarian's collection of facts. Although most of the historical writing was still confined to dynastic history, the debate on ancient political and cultural life necessitated the study of social and economic history.[33] Interestingly enough, although a fair amount of work had been done by this time on, for example, caste and religious groups, historians rarely integrated the results of this work into their histories; thus bibliographies of sections entitled 'Society' in most standard histories would refer to Altekar's book *The Position of Women in Ancient India* or N.K. Dutta's *Origin and Growth of Caste in India*, both merely compilations of references to the subject from the literary source material, but would rarely mention any of the standard works on the study of caste or social institutions. (That the system of placing various facets of history in water-tight compartments neatly labelled Political History, Economic History, Society, Religion and Philosophy, Language and Literature, the Arts, etc., continues to this day can be seen in the most standard of all standard histories, the series entitled, 'The History and Culture of the Indian People'.)

There was a tendency to regard the ancient period as one of considerable prosperity and general contentment, in fact a period of which the Indian people could justifiably be proud. This was legitimate for its purposes except on occasions when there was a reluctance to admit to blemishes on the culture. Mill's periodization was accepted without much questioning, and a very sharp distinction was drawn between the Hindu/Ancient and the Muslim/Medieval periods. This distinction was emphasized by the rather arbitrary association of the most acceptable achievements of the Indian past with Hindu culture. Not surprisingly, nationalism was replaced by a form of militant Hinduism, and the communal atmosphere in Indian politics in the late 1930s and the 1940s tended to vitiate the study of ancient and medieval history. The Gupta period became the 'Golden Age' largely because it was the period of renascent Hinduism. Many of the ills of India were ascribed to 'the Muslim invasions and rule'. It was maintained that Hinduism in its Sanskritic form was the essential culture of India, and other forces were in a sense an intrusion. The identification of ancient India with Hindu culture became so marked that even the Buddhists were regarded with some suspicion. Earlier attempts at proving the indigenous origin of all things Indian were accentuated, a trend which continues to be supported by certain historians to this day. At another level, it was believed that the dynamics of many Asian cultures, particularly those of Southeast Asia, arose from Hindu culture, and the theory of Greater India derived sustenance from Pan-Hinduism. A curious pride was taken in the supposed imperialist past of India, as expressed in sentiments such as these: 'The art of Java and Kambuja was no doubt derived from India and fostered by the Indian *rulers* of these *colonies*.'[34] (Italics mine.) This form of historical interpretation, which can perhaps best be described as being inspired by Hindu nationalism, remains an influential school of thinking in present historical writings.[35]

From the historical point of view a more valuable offshoot of the nationalist school was the growth of interest in regional and local histories. Studies of regional histories of smaller geographical areas and states—such as histories of Bengal, Maharashtra and various parts of the peninsula—became more common.[36] This was a useful departure because it corrected the tendency to generalize about the entire Indian sub-continent on the basis of the history of the Ganges heartland. It led to the discovery of new source material in local archives and to greater archaeological work in the region. The results of these studies not only filled many lacunae in historical knowledge of the early period but also acted as a corrective to some of the earlier generalizations. It also led to the recognition of the fact that an area as large as the Indian sub-continent will show evidence of regional variations in the cultural pattern and this historical change in the sub-continent need not be identical nor occur simultaneously. Nilakantha Sastri's work on south Indian history created a new awareness of the history of the sub-continent by bringing the history of the south into perspective.[37]

Another trend which was also rooted in the writings of the nationalist school, but which developed more extensively in the post-independence period, began in a marginal way with an interest in the systematic study of social organization and political and economic institutions. Some writers came to it through an interest in Marxism, as is exemplified in the work of D.D. Kosambi. For others it resulted from a recognition that history, and particularly ancient history, can best be studied within the framework of a social science discipline. The Marxists did not accept the scheme implicit in the theory of the Asiatic Mode of Production; their interpretations derived more from the understanding of the principles of dialectical materialism and the historical philosophy of Marx, as has frequently been the case with Asian Marxists writing their own history.[38] This trend has led to the study of the relationship between social and economic organization and its effect on historical events, and the development of the idea that it is the interrelation of a variety of forces which determines historical events. Kosambi stated in the *Introduction to the Study of Indian History* that he saw the means of production as the key to historical events, and his analysis of ancient Indian history is based on this. For him dynastic history had no meaning, because, apart from everything else, our information on it is of such an uncertain character. It was more important, therefore, to investigate the workings of social and economic forces. The importance of his work, however, lies not so much in the historical totality which he presented, but in the fact that it raised a number of new ideas and revealed new questions to be put to the sources, such as: To what extent can archaeological evidence provide a background to developments in historical times? Can archaeology and literary sources give us the clues to technological change? Was the economy in fact the base to the super-structure of other forces in Indian society? Can religious activities in India be studied in either Marxist or Weberian terms, or, for that matter, on the basis of any other model? Most important of all, what are the variables in the Indian tradition which distinguish it from other traditions?

Kosambi's writings became a focus and served to emphasize the validity of such questions and the need for further questions and the answers to them. This does not require a search for new evidence so much as a re-reading of the sources, with a different set of questions in mind. It also requires fresh annotations of existing texts, particularly the law-books, *dharmaśāstras*. It requires not merely a familiarity with existing models but, even more important, an awareness and understanding of analytical methods. To this extent the problems in the interpretation of ancient Indian history are not totally dissimilar to problems faced by contemporary historians of other ancient cultures.

These ideas coincided with the realization that the major part of the dynastic history of ancient India had already been written and that other aspects of the historical past would now have to be investigated, not merely by compilation of more information, but also by analysis of the facts with a view to establishing causal relationships. The paucity of fresh literary source material would inevitably have led to a shift from the antiquarian interest in the ancient past to a more analytical comprehension of it. The increasing relevance of the methodology of the social sciences facilitated this shift. Not surprisingly, the intensification of work in archaeology and anthropology has coincided with this new emphasis in ancient history.

Archaeology is now the major source of fresh evidence, since it is unlikely that large numbers of literary sources still remain to be discovered. It not only provides new evidence in the form of the material remains of past culture, but, precisely because this evidence is tangible, it allows of a more accurate reconstruction of the past. From the results of investigation into pre-history and proto-history a picture of the evolution of cultures in India is emerging.

It is now possible to trace the successive phases of cultures relating to the Palaeolithic, the Neolithic, and the Chalcolithic types. The work on the Neolithic has enabled us to map the major areas of early agriculture in the last three millennia B.C. and to trace communication links. Work on the Chalcolithic in the northern half of India has been somewhat concentrated on extensive excavations relating to the Harappa culture or the Indus Valley Civilization, as it was called until recently. The discovery of new towns and fresh evidence about the chronology and the decline of the Harappa culture necessitates a reconsideration of Mortimer Wheeler's theory that the invading Āryans destroyed the cities of the Harappans. In the Deccan, Chalcolithic traces have provided evidence of trade routes and contact between the Ganges valley and the northwest Deccan and the routes across the Deccan in the beginning of the first millennium B.C. The continued use of these routes well into the historical period opens up new possibilities of historical analyses of the early history of the Deccan. Detailed studies on the Iron Age and iron technology from various sites in the sub-continent provide interesting insights into the use and expansion of this technology. Recent carbon-14 analyses have suggested *c*. 1100 B.C. as the date for the use of iron, which is 300 years earlier than previous dates. For the far south of India there is now archaeological evidence for the period from *c*. 500 B.C. to A.D. 150, beginning with the Megalithic culture and continuing with a fairly highly developed Roman trade with south India. In both cases the contact is with the western end of what has been described as the 'Indian Ocean Arc'. The economics of the Roman trade which is now being studied on the basis of archaeological remains, coins, and literary source in Greek, Latin, and Tamil are likely to provide some useful information on the growth of the south Indian kingdoms. The material evidence from the excavations of urban centres can corroborate or act as a corrective to literary evidence. Epigraphical evidence has illuminated many areas of post-Gupta history from the fifth century A.D. onward, particularly in the Deccan and south India. Material remains can also provide statistical evidence. Thus the quantity and distribution of the characteristic pottery of the period—the northern-black polished ware—very relevant to the study of communication and trade in the pre-Mauryan and Mauryan periods, the fifth to third centuries B.C.

Studies in economic and social history in recent years have attempted to determine not only the periods of change but the nature of change. In economic history this has resulted in an intensive study of the agrarian system. It can now be said that not only is there evidence to prove the existence of private property in land but also that the rule of property changed significantly over the centuries. This disproves the basic premise of the argument in support of the theory of Oriental Despotism as applied to India. The major contribution in this area has been the study of land grants reconstructed from epigraphical sources, on the basis of which it has been suggested that a gradual change took place in the agrarian system from the fourth century A.D. onward, resulting in what has been called a feudal society by about the seventh to the eighth century A.D.[39] Related to this is the question of the changing forms of land-ownership and the varieties of private property. Various aspects of the revenue system have also been reconsidered in the light of new interpretations of forms of ownership. These studies have a bearing on the nature of the bureaucracy. Epigraphical material is frequently used as a means of checking the evidence from literary sources. The use of inscriptions for such studies is comparatively new, since earlier historians tended to use inscriptions largely for information on dynastic history. Archaeology provides evidence for the study of trade and the growth of towns in the context of a well-developed commercial economy, and here again the material remains have been used effectively in correlation with literary sources. This is an area of study for which there is immense scope with fresh excavations of trade centres and townsites.

Indian social history at the moment has one basic preoccupation: an inquiry into the precise nature of social relationships in the structure of early Indian society.[40] Such an inquiry meets with obvious problems because of the nature of the literary source material. Attempts are being made at re-examining the texts in the light of our contemporary understanding of theoretical model of the caste system, *varna*. These inquiries have taken the form of investigating a particular social group, for example the studies on the Śūdras on the Vratyas, or the interrelationships of groups in a particular period, or the nature of an institution known to other societies as well, for example, slavery. The social and economic underpinnings of religious institutions provide yet another avenue of related interest, the studies of the Chola temples being a case in point.

The nationalist phase also saw considerable interest in the study of ancient Indian political theory. The dominant themes were the status and role of the king, the channels of political representation, the function of the bureaucracy, and the distribution of power. The understanding of the theory of kingship in ancient India had been coloured in the nineteenth century by the concept of the divinity of kingship, based on the evidence from the Ancient Near East. This concept was rather arbitrarily extended to Indian kingship, together with the political corollary of a lack of representative institutions and the concentration of power with the king. Although the nationalist historians did attempt to refute the latter, they rather overlooked the question of the divinity of the king. This theme has come into prominence in recent work on the nature of kingship and the distribution of political power and status in early Indian society.[41] The question of the distribution of political power is being re-examined in the framework of the functioning of a caste society, and with reference to the existing evidence on institutions of local control, such as village councils. The work on the land-grants, particularly from the sixth century onward, suggests a different type of power structure for the bureaucracy than was previously assumed on the basis of the theory of despotism. The exclusion of straight political history is not for all time. There are indications of a more meaningful return to political history now that the background of social and economic history is being gradually filled in.

The nationalist phase of historical interpretation led for obvious reasons to the overwhelming participation of Indian historians in writing their own history. This seemed to coincide with an appreciable decline of interest in ancient Indian history by European Indologists, except in France. The more recent interpretations of ancient Indian history have suggested methods of analysis which can be used by historians of any nationality and can circumvent national and ideological bias, and by the use of which a greater degree of objectivity in interpretation can be achieved.[42] Even if history is based on selected data, the data selected need not be entirely arbitrary. These methods work within the framework of certain hypotheses. They assume that all societies change and that in a period stretching from 2500 B.C. to A.D. 1000 Indian society and its institutions must have undergone change; it is the work of the historian to study the nature of this change. The idea of a static society is cleary no longer tenable.[43]

This raises the crucial question of periodization in Indian history. Clearly there is a need to redefine the various periods of Indian history, if periodization is necessary, or else to dispense with such divisions altogether. The earliest pattern of periodization, that of the Hindu-Muslim-British periods of Indian history, gives undue importance to ruling dynasties and foreign invasions and is based, presumably, on the professed religions of the dynasties of northern India. In many cases it was merely the dynasty which changed, for the major historical characteristics of one period continued into the next. The change in terminology to Ancient-Medieval-Modern does not clarify the problem if the basis for the division remains the same. The Ancient/Hindu period is traditionally accepted as terminating with the Muslim conquest. Yet 'the Muslims' conquered various parts of India at different periods in time. The Arabs conquered Sind in the eighth century; the Turks and Afghans conquered the Punjab at the end of the tenth, northern India in the thirteenth, and the Deccan in the fourteenth century. The history of the area further south, with its alternating Hindu and Muslim dynasties, does not fit this pattern of periodization in any case. The arbitrary choice of A.D. 1000 seeks to impose a pattern which the evidence does not permit. If the basis of periodization were to be significant social and economic changes, then the ancient period would end roughly in the eighth century A.D., or possibly a little earlier, since the more significant changes did not coincide with dynastic changes and the conquests of 'the Muslims'. Although an improvement on the earlier pattern in historical terms, even this pattern of periodization could not be applied to every part of the sub-continent.

Perhaps the most significant result of the work done on ancient Indian history so far is the realization that well-defined phases of historical development are not uniformly applicable to the history of every society, and that the historian's interpretation should be the outcome of a search for the phases of historical development within a given society, which can then be analytically compared with other phases in other societies. This is not to deny the legitimacy of historical generalizations, but to recognize the variable factors and to demand a more precise definition of historical formulations.

Lady Margaret Hall, Oxford

REFERENCES AND NOTES

1. Thomas Roe, *The Embassy of Sir Thomas Roe to India 1615-1619*, ed. W. Foster (London, 1926).
2. *Voyages de F. Bernier* . . . (Amsterdam, 1699).
3. The term Orientalist was used in the wider sense of scholars interested in Asia, and the term Indologist referred to those interested only in India. However, the more generally used term even for the latter was 'Orientalists', and it has been used in this sense here.
4. *India, What Can It Teach Us?* (London, 1883), p. 101.
5. E.g., "Im Orient müssen wir das Höchste Romantische suchen."
6. The periodization of Ancient, Medieval, and Modern, which is generally accepted by most historians of India and by most universities teaching Indian history, is basically the same as that of Mill, since the Ancient period usually ends with the establishment of Muslim dynasties and the Medieval period with the acquisition of political power by the East India Company.
7. Charles Grant, *Observations on the State of Society* . . (London, 1813).
8. *Lectures on the Philosophy of History* (1837).
9. G. Lichtheim, 'Marx and the Asiatic Mode of Production', *St. Antony's Papers*, 14 (1963).
10. *Indische Alterthumskunde*, 4 vols. (Bonn, Leipzig, 1847-1862).

11. *Capital,* vol. I; *The Communist Manifesto; Pre-Capitalist Economic Formations,* ed. E.J. Hobsbawm. London, 1964.
12. E.g., in the works of F.J. Stephen, J. Strachey, A. Lyall.
13. H. Maine, *Ancient Law* (London, 1861); *Village Communities East and West* (London, 1871).
14. This is best seen in the works of W.W. Hunter and J. Talboys Wheeler.
15. Comte, *The Positive Philosophy of Auguste Comte,* ed. H. Martineau (n.p., 1853) II, p. 238. Comte was greatly appreciated by nineteenth century Indian intellectuals, and his writing was a formative element in some aspects of Indian thinking during this period. An interesting analysis of this has recently been made by S. Gopal in a course of lectures delivered at Oxford (1968) on 'The Intellectual Origins of Indian Nationalism.'
16. *The Religion of India* (English trans. Glencoe, 1958).
17. J. Chesneaux, 'French Historiography and the Evolution of Colonial Viet-nam,' in *Historians of South East Asia,* ed. D.G.E. Hall (London, 1961), pp. 235 ff.
18. *Early History of India* (Oxford, 1904); *Oxford History of India* (Oxford, 1919).
19. E.h., *Early History of India* (4th ed., Oxford, 1924), p. 442.
20. G. Stedman-Jones, 'The Pathology of English History', in *The New Left Review,* p. 46 (1967).
21. Cunningham was appointed Archaeological Surveyor in 1892. It was, however, not until 1901 that the Archaeological Survey of India received a real boost owing to the interest of the then viceroy, Lord Curzon.
22. *The Early History of the Dekkan* ([Bombay], 1894); *A Peep into the Early History of India* (Bombay, 1920).
23. H.C. Raychaudhuri, *The Political History of Ancient India* (Calcutta, 1923); K.P. Jayaswal, *Hindu Polity* (Calcutta, 1924); R.K. Mookerji, *Harsha* (London, 1926); H.C. Ojha, *Rajputānākāitihāsa* (Banaras, 1925-1941).
24. It was suggested that perhaps the Āryans did not migrate from an Indo-European homeland but were in fact of Indian origin and therefore by extension the Indo-European homeland may have been in India. In view of the cultural importance of the revival of interest in Vedic culture during the nineteenth and twentieth centuries in India, this theory was extremely popular. It has since been taken up by some recent historians who maintain that not only were the Aryans and their culture entirely indigenous to India and therefore spread from South Asia to West Asia, but that the Vedic period is pre-Harappan.
25. *The Age of the Nandas and Mauryas,* ed. Nilakanta Sastri (Banaras, 1952).
26. Raychaudhuri, *Political History of Ancient India,* p. 363.
27. Theories regarding Greek influences on Indian culture have been challenged by Indians from the 1870s onward, but in a rather sporadic way. Now the challenge was formulated in the more academic form of historical argument.
28. This is maintained in his *Hindu Polity.*
29. *History of Indian and Indonesian Art* (London, 1927); *The Dance of Siva* (New York, 1918).
30. H. Voigt, *St. Antony's Papers,* p. 8.
31. R.C. Majumdar, *Corporate Life in Ancient India* (Poona, 1966), pp. 126-27.
32. Jayaswal, *Hindu Polity* II, pp. 60 ff.

33. Beni Prasad, *The State in Ancient India* (Allahabad, 1928); A.S. Altekar, *A History of Village Communities in Western India* (Bombay, 1927); U.N. Ghoshal, *History of Hindu Political Theories* (London, 1927); *The Agrarian System in Ancient India* (Calcutta, 1930); P.V. Kane, *History of Dharmashastra* (Poona, 1930).
34. R.C. Majumdar, *Advanced History of India* (2nd. ed., London, 1950), p. 221.
35. This perspective is supported by certain sections of "The History and Culture of the Indian People" series, published by the Bharatiya Vidya Bhavan.
36. R.C. Majumdar, *The Early History of Bengal* (London, 1925); A.S. Altekar, *The Rashtrakutas and Their Times* (Poona, 1934); V.R.R. Dikshitar, *Studies in Tamil Literature and History* (London, 1930).
37. *The Pandyan Kingdom* (London, 1929); *The Cholas* (Madras, 1935); *A History of South India* (Madras, 1955).
38. D.D. Kosambi, *An Introduction to the Study of Indian History* (Bombay, 1956); R.S. Sharma, *Shudras in Ancient India* (Delhi, 1958); Deva Raj Chanana, *Slavery in Ancient India* (New Delhi, 1960).
39. R.S. Sharma, *Indian Feudalism* (Calcutta, 1965).
40. Sociological studies such as I. Karve, *Hindu Society—an Interpretation* (Poona, 1961); and M.N. Srinivas, *Caste in Modern India and Other Essays* (Bombay, 1962) have helped to create an interest in this kind of investigation.
41. C. Drekmeier, *Kingship and Community in Early India* (Stanford, 1962).
42. The work of non-Indian scholars such as A.L. Basham, *The Wonder That Was India* (London, 1954) is widely accepted in Indian historical circles. During the 1930s and the 1940s the major contributions of non-Indian scholars to the early history of India came from France in the work of Louis de le Valle Poussin, *L'Inde aux temps des Mauryas* . . . ([Paris], 1930); *Dynasties et histoire de l'Inde* . . . ([Paris], 1935); and L. Renou, *La Civilisation de L'Inde ancienne* (Paris, 1950); and L. Renou and J. Filliozat, *L'Inde classique* (Paris, 1947).
43. A recent attempt to revive this thesis has been made by K. Wittfogel, *Oriental Despotism* (New Haven, 1957).

Society and Law in the Hindu and Buddhist Traditions

The relationship between law and society involves both the actual and the ideal. To the extent that particular laws are related to a particular society they can be regarded as a reflection of its value system. But law (both customary and codified) is also seen as a means of controlling societal function and, as such, an attempt is made to perfect the legal framework, which then becomes a reflection of the aspiration of that society. The Universal Declaration of Human Rights reflects the values of modern man but the implementation of these rights in full demands a society which has yet to emerge. Article I states: 'All human beings are born free and equal in dignity and rights.' This in itself indicates the large degree of idealism manifested in such documents. Despite the fact that the declaration is acceptable to a large number of nations it would be difficult to find amongst them a single nation where this article is adhered to, implicitly and in practice, outside the strictly legal context.

The problem of sifting ideals from actuality becomes increasingly difficult when the period under study is considerably removed from the present. Both time and environment lead to changes in the concept of law. Even within a single tradition there can be apparently divergent and contradictory attitudes at various levels for which there is little or no precise explanation; in such cases one has to search for detailed, accurate information in order to understand the contradictions. Such information is difficult to establish if the society is one which existed two thousand years ago. Keeping these problems in mind we can at best concern ourselves with the broad framework in which these laws were evolved. In the Hindu and Buddhist tradition this framework can be deduced from a number of texts and documents, most of which were composed

From *International Social Science Journal,* XVIII, I, 1966, pp. 32-40.

in the period between 400 B.C. and A.D. 500. Much of the later literature is in the nature of commentaries on the earlier works, which reflect relevant changes in both society and its laws.[1]

There are two approaches to an attempt at understanding the rights of the human being in the Hindu and Buddhist tradition. First of all, the metaphysical aspect provides a framework of a rather generalized kind emanating from a small group of thinkers. Metaphysical thought certainly contributes to the ethos of a society, but this contribution becomes fairly diluted by the time it reaches the concrete reality of a legal code. The second and more significant aspect of the study is provided by the Law Books themselves which draw a more distinct picture of the legal framework. However, reliance even on such definite sources is not without its dangers. The Law Books are both a reflection of early Indian society as well as attempts at working out what was believed to be a perfect social system. Therefore the aspirations of the law-makers are also to be considered. Nevertheless, the danger can be mitigated somewhat by testing from historical sources the actual validity of the legal systems codified by the law-givers.

At the metaphysical level both Hindu and Buddhist thought are concerned primarily with the ultimate destiny of man—a transcendent, spiritual state where the soul finds salvation or the individual consciousness attains extinction. At this level of thinking the necessities and requirements of social life have at most a transitory value. Considerable emphasis is placed on the universal quality of all human beings, on the values of tolerance and compassion, and on the need for harmony between man and nature through recognition of the rights of each—all of which would lead to spiritual peace. There has been no dearth of modern philosophers who maintain that the Indian moral consciousness has been concerned almost solely with a quest for spiritual peace. Perhaps it was this concern with the ultimate quest for peace which led to a dichotomy between metaphysical thinking which encouraged a withdrawal from life and the actual social institutions which were almost obsessed with the idea of a purposeful ordering of life. A perusal of the social and legal literature suggests that the metaphysical attitude was an ideal to which many have aspired but which few achieved. Nor was this ideal allowed to interfere too frequently in the organization of society.

Metaphysical values apart, it must be remembered that the Hindu and Buddhist traditions arose out of two disparate socio-economic backgrounds: a fact which is reflected in their differing attitudes to human rights. Hindu law was first formulated in a tribal society and it was based largely on customary practices and relationships. As is frequent in kin-societies, social controls had the force of laws. The central problem at this stage was to maintain peace between the tribes rather than to protect the rights of the individual. The acceptance of a monarchical system by these tribes introduced two new features. The political structure required by kingship encouraged an element of authoritarianism amongst the law-makers. The close association of kingship with divinity was projected into the realm of laws and provided a supernatural sanction for the laws whenever necessary. The status of the individual in society came to be conditioned by these new factors.

The Buddhist tradition originated at a time when tribal loyalty was changing into territorial loyalty and there was a sharper awareness of political organization. Buddhism began as one of a number of heterodox sects whose common feature was their breaking away from brahmanical orthodoxy. The Buddhists and the Jainas had their origin in, and found their earliest supporters amongst, the republican tribes of northern India, and the republican tradition found its echo in the teachings of both Mahavira and the Buddha. Absence of monarchical authoritarianism and close association with the idea of divinity in the political sphere both led to a stress on the rights of the individual in society. This was further emphasized when in the early stages Buddhism became popular amongst the emergent commercial classes who, in a period of expanding trade, gave it more than lip-service. In this milieu, not only was the individual increasingly regarded as the social unit, but even in institutional matters emphasis was laid on contractual arrangements, free from the interference of divine agencies.

The differences in the two traditions are significantly demonstrated in the respective theories on the origin of government. According to the Hindu tradition, men, in a state of defencelessness and social disorder, appealed to the gods and the latter appointed a king in their own image, who would protect the people and maintain law and order and in return take a share of one-sixth of the produce.[2]

The social order of castes also emerged from a divine source.[3] The Buddhist theory relates a different sequence of events. It postulates a golden age which gradually decayed through the institution of private property and other social evils. Finally the people gathered together and elected one from amongst themselves to rule over them and maintain an orderly society. He was given a sixth of the produce as wages.[4] In the Buddhist theory the emphasis is on the quasi-contractual nature of the beginnings of government and on the sovereignty of the people. The latter idea remained central to Buddhist political thinking but it was never taken a step further and developed into a theory of the rights of the people. There was no attempt to provide a divine origin for the evolution of the social structure in Buddhist thought. We are told that people tended to keep together in groups based on their occupations and these occupational groups gradually crystallized into castes.[5]

At the root of the social and legal thinking of both traditions was the belief that government is an unfortunate necessicity in an age of decay. Such a belief implied that society existed prior to any governmental organization and, furthermore, that in effect society is more important than any form of government. The Indian mind therefore concerned itself with the quest for a perfect social system.

In the Hindu tradition individual salvation *(mokṣa)* lies in co-ordinating in a balanced manner the three pursuits of human existence, which are *dharma* (the laws of the social order), *artha* (prosperity) and *kāma* (pleasure). *Dharma* is the most important of these.[6] Briefly, *dharma* refers to the norm of conduct and of duties incumbent on each man in accordance with his caste. It derives from both the legal treatises of the past (often regarded as sacred texts) and from approved custom, particularly that which is not opposed to the sacred texts. The idea of *dharma* is fully articulated in the theory of *varṇa-āśrama-dharma,*[7] where the definition of one's duty has reference not only to one's caste, but also to the particular stage in one's life, i.e., student, householder, ascetic, etc. Gradually *dharma* became the most significant concept in the Hindu tradition and the very basis of the status of the individual in Hindu society. The proper working of *dharma* was dependent on the fact that every individual must recognize the duties he was expected to perform and act accordingly.[8] The message of the *Bhagavad Gītā* was precisely this: one must act according to the rules of one's *dharma*—one's own duty even if poorly done is better than doing another's duty no matter how perfectly.[9] To act according to the rules of his *dharma* meant that a man must accept his position and role in society on the basis of the caste into which he was born and the norms which had been enunciated for that caste by the authors of the Law Books. Duties implied obligations and the stress was far more on obligations than on rights. This tendency was further emphasized by the strongly patriarchal character of the family unit.

Dharma was essential because it promoted individual security and happiness as well as the stability of the social order. Each man's *dharma* had its own role in the larger and more complex network of the social structure. Therefore by observing the rule of his own *dharma* a man was showing an awareness of others in society as well. If individual members of society tried to formulate their own rules of *dharma* the result would be a chaotic society. *Dharma* was the foundation of individual and collective security since a state of nature without law was equivalent to anarchy.[10] The fear of anarchy led to the elevation of *dharma* to divine status and this in turn gave it even higher status than the king and the government.[11] To further safeguard the position of *dharma* another concept was introduced that *dharma* is protected by *daṇḍa* (literally a rod or staff, signifying punishment).[12]

The rules of *dharma* were formulated by the law-makers who were by and large members of the brāhmaṇ caste and who naturally tried to maintain the superiority of their caste. Inevitably, since they were the ones who gave definition to *dharma,* the innate superiority of the *brāhmaṇ* was expounded. As a complement to this it was necessary to formulate a system of social hierarchies. Social (and often economic) and legal privileges decreased with each descending step in the social hierarchy.[13] Certain categories of *brāhmaṇs* were immune from the more exacting labours of routine living such as paying taxes, and could on occasion be regarded as above the law. The concept of *dharma* rooted in caste was extended to every aspect of human activity. It was logical therefore that the equality of all before the law was not recognized. According to the Law Books, judicial punishments were required to take into consideration the caste of the offender.[14] Rights were extended primarily to the privileged upper castes. The lower orders had only obligations. The burden of society fell most heavily on the shoulders of the *śūdras* and the untouchables who could claim hardly any privileges or rights.

An important characteristic of caste is that an individual is born into a particular caste and cannot acquire the status of any other caste. This resulted in a check on individual social mobility. It also came to be associated with a basic religio-philosophical concept of Hinduism, that of *karma,* which maintains that one's deeds and activities in one's present incarnation determine one's status and happiness in the life to follow. Thus a man's caste status was entirely of his own making and he was in a position to improve it by conforming to *dharma* and being reborn at a higher status in his next incarnation.[15] This was an excellent answer to those who queried the justice of the caste system. It also acted as a powerful check on non-conformity through the fear of worsening one's condition in future incarnations.

Among the various means of maintaining the purity of the caste two are specially stressed: the ban on commensality among members of various castes and the strict observance of rules of endogamy and exogamy as applied with reference to caste. The rules of marriage were rigidly enforced and marriage was primarily a social institution.[16] The lower the status of women the stronger was the legal tie of marriage. The patriarchal system tended to keep the status of women at a low level, and the emergence of the joint family with special property rights for the male members reinforced male dominance.[17] The family was recognized as a basic unit of society and enjoyed the right to protection by society and the state. This was accentuated in the case of families who owned land and who worked on the land. The concept of property in the Hindu tradition was usually associated with the ownership of land. The right to own property was granted to those who could afford it. The Law Books maintain that property is founded on virtue and that the king has a right to confiscate the property of the wicked,[18] of which, however, there is no record in historical sources.

Yet another aspect of community living where caste discrimination applied was in education. The Law Books are very clear on the point that only the three upper castes are entitled to education.[19]

Frequently it was only the *brāhmans* and the aristocracy who received formal education. Caste discrimination kept the *śūdras* away and the nature and content of the formal training kept the other non-*brāhmans* away. Here the Buddhist tradition was in striking contrast. Not only were Buddhist monasteries open to persons of any caste, but even the syllabuses had a wider range and included disciplines of more practical interest.

The Buddhist tradition protested against the institution of caste. It recognized that in the routine working of society there were bound to be social distinctions, but maintained that these should not be exploited to the point of rejecting the concept that all human beings are equal. The Buddha was frequently asked about the relative purity of the four castes and invariably replied that all castes were equally pure. Buddhism was in favour of the equality of all before the law. An offender brought before justice must be judged and punished according to his offence and without any concession to immunities or privileges relating to his caste.[20]

Arising out of its stern and unwavering ethical code, the Buddhist tradition supported the unqualified supremacy of moral law over politics. Law is for the welfare of all mankind. It saw in brahmanical law the conditioning of society according to the requirements of a powerful elite. The same idea of the application of a moral law and the equality of human beings was extended to all created beings, and this was to result in the concept of *ahimsa* (non-violence). Everything that has life has a right to live; and to destroy life, no matter what its form, is a crime. It may be argued that the Buddhists (and more than the Buddhists, the Jainas) made a fetish of non-violence, yet the intellectual and moral assumptions of the concept arose from a healthy tradition.

Whereas Buddhism preached non-attachment to worldly possessions, and property as we have seen was regarded as an evil (precipitating the decay of the world in the days of its pristine purity), in actual practice the acquisition of property was regarded as a normal activity. Entrepreneurial activities in particular were encouraged and were open to anyone with sufficient foresight and resourcefulness.[21] In its attitude to women, the Buddhist tradition showed greater liberality than the Hindu tradition, as for instance in permitting women to become nuns.

Historical evidence sheds interesting light on the literary tradition.

Among the more meaningful historical documents are the edicts of the Emperor Aśoka (third century B.C.) which reflect a familiarity with both the Hindu and the Buddhist traditions.[22] The edicts are meaningful in the present context since they are the attempts of a ruler at solving the problem of the human being in a complex society. The norm of conduct suggested by the emperor carries a deep conviction of faith in humanity. Within the existing framework of social and economic relations, Aśoka makes a powerful plea for social responsibility, for dignity and justice in the behaviour of one man towards another, for tolerance and kindness in human relationships and for non-violence.

That the imposition of the brahmanical pattern in its totality was rarely a historical reality can be deduced from the fact that the heterodox tradition throughout the centuries was opposed to it in greater or lesser degree.[23] The heterodox sects often drew their following from the lower castes who were numerically larger than the upper castes. The heterodox tradition emphasized the equality of human beings, the equality of all before the law, disapproved of slavery, encouraged the acceptance of a higher status for women and placed greater value on empirical thinking and education than on the formalism of the brahmanical system. That the heterodox tradition failed to overthrow the brahmanical tradition was due partly to historical reasons[24] and partly to the very nature of caste society.

The origin and development of caste was not controlled by the *brāhmaṇs*. The latter were merely shrewd enough to realize that they could use the existing system to their own benefit. In accordance with their own vision of society they enunciated laws on caste. These laws were by and large observed by the upper castes and were familiar in areas where orthodoxy played an authoritarian role. Elsewhere and amongst the lower castes, custom and usage made a substantial contribution to the formulation of laws. The fact that caste was never confronted with the shadow of its decline can be traced to the structure of the institution itself. Each caste or sub-caste formed its own independent social unit, with its own laws of survival based on the economic possibilities to which it could aspire. As long as the *brāhmaṇs* could maintain their position as the pre-eminent unit—which they did by appropriating the administrative, educational and religious functions—their ascendancy was assured. To perpetuate their ascendancy they worked out the complicated and, what seemed to them, almost foolproof concept of *dharma*. But the actual working of society was not strictly in accordance with this plan. Castes and sub-castes as social units did have some mobility and frequently sought to better their status, even if such improvement was denied to the individual member. Economic necessities for instance could lead to a change in the status of a particular caste.[25] Invading foreigners had also to be accommodated and their caste status defined. The objection of the heterodox groups was thus not to the system (which was a workable, socio-economic system) but to the brahmanical interpretation of it.

It is against this background that we must view the development of the Hindu and Buddhist traditions. The framework within which the Buddhist tradition functioned is not available in a single code of laws. Much of it consisted of regulations which grew out of custom and usage and which were conditioned by the professions of those who supported Buddhism. The republican background nurtured an individualistic tradition in Buddhism with a strong support for the kind of social and moral attitudes implicit in human rights. Despite the tradition having to contend with a caste society, the rights of the individual are given due stress.

The Hindu tradition is in comparison far more complicated. This is due in part to the fact that it has to be analyzed from two perspectives. There is firstly the overall framework of Hindu society where the emphasis is on duties and, judging by the Law Books, access to rights is limited to the privileged classes. The second perspective is that of the localized group as caste where the concept.of rights did exist although to a limited extent. The functioning of each small unit was controlled by its own mechanism and within this unit the individual member could claim rights of equality and self-expression.[26] The balance of rights and duties was fairly equal. Rights within such a group were not thought of in any total or irrevocable sense. The member of a sub-caste for instance could claim economic and social security from his sub-caste and the right to equality and to protection from violence, provided he observed the rules of that particular group. This is in a sense the key to the functioning of the Hindu tradition. Freedom lies in belonging to a group because the group can claim rights, as for example the rights of the caste, the rights of the family, the rights of the guild, etc.; the individual as an individual has no identity in a societal sense.

The Hindu pattern did not see man and society as antagonistic to each other. The two entities had mutual obligations and a commitment to these obligations would ensure the welfare of all. The Hindu vision was that of an orderly society with each man attending to his appointed task, which would infuse a people with a sense of community and which with its intense loyalty to the social group, i.e., caste, would provide both economic and psychological security. The careful classifying of all degrees of social relationships into a well-ordered system was partly to meet the requirements of this vision, and partly due to the normal tendency of Hindu theorists to classify everything down to the minutest detail (this was applied to matters as diverse as tax collection on the one hand and the art of love on the other). This carefully worked out socio-legal framework reflected the brahmanical vision of the perfect society. Those who were opposed to such a vision could take a non-conformist stand by opting out of society, perhaps by becoming ascetics or mendicants, or by joining a dissident group.

The Hindu tradition managed to maintain a considerable degree of social harmony by a careful balancing of over-all authoritarianism with local autonomy. New ethnic groups or occupational groups tended to become sub-castes and maintained their own system of rights and duties. Dissident groups which began with the support of a cross-section of society ended up by being identified as a separate sub-caste. Thus, where the dissident element could not be absorbed in the existing structure, a compromise was worked out and it was allowed a separate identity. This was both independent within its own terms and yet a part of society. Sometimes the brahmanical tradition would even appropriate some of the rituals and customs of such a group in order to avoid open conflict. Social tensions arose at the birth of a dissident group, but they rarely took an acutely antagonistic form. The marginal relationships of the various sub-castes kept them from face-to-face confrontations.

In fact the system was conducive to the co-existence of various groups. The high value placed on tolerance in Indian thought was not just a pious wish, since, given this social structure, a little bit of tolerance could go a long way in preserving social harmony; more so perhaps than in other societies. In allowing these concessions in the working of society, the legal and social iniquities of the caste structure and the implications of the Hindu code were somewhat modified. This would also largely explain the striking absence of fanaticism in the Hindu tradition.

The guardians of law are, in the nature of things, persons belonging to elite groups. Consequently legal codes conform to their world view. It is premature to look for well-articulated legal codes in the cultures of two thousand years ago which might reflect human rights as we know them and desire them today. In the ancient past there were moments when societies incorporated the metaphysical ideals of human rights into their legal and social functioning. Even in such moments the rights were extended only to elite groups: the slaves, the *śūdras,* the serfs were all beyond the pale. The concept of human rights is essentially a modern phenomenon. For the first time in the history of many cultures it has ceased to be a metaphysical concept. The implementation of human rights demands a certain socio-economic ethos which is becoming increasingly feasible in most parts of the world. For various reasons, a society is no longer regarded as an aggregate of families or groups as in the past, but as an aggregate of individuals. With a shift in emphasis from the welfare of the group to the welfare of the individual, the rights of the individual have been conceded. What this implies, both for the individual and for the future of society, raises another set of metaphysical questions.

REFERENCES AND NOTES

1. Hindu law has been codified in the *Dharmaśāstra* literature, frequently referred to as the Law Books. Of these the most significant for our purposes are the *Dharmaśāstras* of Manu, Yajñavalkya and Nārada. Buddhist concepts on law were never codified in any single source. Legal ideals are, however, found in the Buddhist Canon, particularly in the *Vinaya-piṭaka.*
2. *Rg Veda,* VIII, 35; *Taittirīya Brāhmaṇa,* I, 5, 9.
3. *Rg Veda,* X, 90; *Taittirīya Saṃhitā,* VII, I, I, 4-6.

4. *Dīgha Nikāya,* III, 61-77; Āryadeva, *Chatuṣaṭaka,* IV, 76.
5 Vasubandhu, *Abhidharmakoṣa,* III, 98.
6. *Manu,* VII, 151-2; *Vasiṣṭha,* I, 4-5; *Gautama,* XI, 19.
7. *Varṇa,* the literal meaning of which is colour, refers to castes, of which there were four major ones, i.e., *brāhmaṇa* (priest), *kṣatriya* (warrior), *vaiśya* (trader) and *śūdra* (the agriculturalist or any low profession). To these four were later added the untouchable, who was in fact outside the caste framework. The literal meaning of *āśrama* is refuge. In this context the reference is to the four stages into which a man's life was divided, i.e., student, householder, retirement from professional and domestic duties, and finally, ascetic.
8. The king's duty was to protect his people and if a king failed to do so, then the people were justified in deserting him *(Mahābhārata,* XII, 57). However, the right to revolt in the Hindu tradition was whittled down to a moral right with the merest of legal sanction, probably arising out of a fear of anarchy. The *brāhmaṇs* were permitted to express their disapproval of an oppressive ruler, and on occasion this expression could be extended to the populace. The justification for such action did not emerge from an anxiety to protect civil rights, but rather to oppose the abuse of power on the part of the ruler (*Bhāgavata Purāṇa,* IV, 14).
9. *Bhagavad Gītā,* XVIII, 40-48; *Manu,* X, 96-7; *Gautama,*VII,1,1-3; XI, 32-3.
10 *Śatapatha Brāhmaṇa,* IX,1, 6, 24.
11. One of the functions of the State was to uphold *dharma (Arthaśāstra,* III, 1, 150).
12. *Mahābhārata,* Śānti Parvan, 59.
13. *Manu,* IX, 313-22; *Gautama,* VIII, 13; *Mahābhārata,* XII, 56.
14. *Manu,* VII, 337-8; *Arthaśāstra,* IV,10.
15. *Śukra,* 1, 37-47.
16. In the earlier period eight types of marriages were recognized, ranging from arranged marriage to abduction. Later only legal marriage was recognized. Personal choice in marriage was of limited occurrence and largely only among members of the aristocracy, though romantic love and elopement were by no means unknown judging from legends, stories and drama.
17. Obligations which the sons owed to their fathers in the patriarchal system were further underlined in the two inheritance systems current in the mediaeval period, the Dāyabhāga and the Mitākṣara, relating to the property of the joint family.
18. *Mahābhārata,* XII, 57, 21.
19. R.K. Mookerjee, *Education in Ancient India.*
20. *Majjhima Nikāya,* II, 128-30; II, 148-54; II, 88.
21. *Dīgha Nikāya,* III, p. 188.
22. R. Thapar, *Aśoka and the Decline of the Mauryas,* p. 251-66.
23. Heterodox opinions were held in the early period by sects such as the Buddhists, Jainas, Ajīvikas, Cārvākas, etc. Later sects included the Tamil devotional cult, the various facets of the Bhakti movement, and the more esoteric sects such as the Tantrics.
24. The collapse of the republics in the early centuries A.D. and the gradual decline of the mercantile community towards the end of the first millennium A.D. strengthened the forces of orthodoxy and authoritarianism, particularly in the

monarchies which emerged during this time.

25. The history of a silk-weavers guild of the Gupta period, as described in the Mandasor Inscription, is an excellent example of this.
26. This is conceded by the later Law Books and by historical evidence such as inscriptions relating to the functioning of guilds, village councils, caste councils, etc. (*Gautama*, II, 2, 19-21; *Vasiṣṭha*, I). The Uttaramerur inscription gives a detailed account of the functioning of a village council in south India.

Ethics, Religion, and Social Protest in the First Millennium B.C. in Northern India

The first millennium B.C. witnessed a seemingly spontaneous burst of new ideologies in areas that subsequently became nuclear regions for major civilizations. The impression is one of a chain of apparently similar developments linking the then known world. The geographical reach of these civilizations was relatively confined, and allowed the formation of a network of connections resulting from conquest, trade and religious missions. The almost simultaneous and sustained period of speculative thought throughout this area resulted either from the juxtaposition of a number of seminal regions and their interconnections or from internal developments within each society that broke the relative quiescence of the earlier bronze-age cultures.

The sixth to third centuries B.C. in northern India saw the emergence of patterns of thought that were embryonic to the evolution of what was called in later centuries the Indian ethos. This paper is an attempt to observe the historical anatomy of this period and to point up the intellectual processes that gave a legitimacy to these patterns. The focus is narrow and concentrates on Buddhism, seen not merely as the teaching of a single individual but rather as a wider response to a particular doctrine and as a reaction to the changing milieu with which it was associated.

The middle of the first millennium introduces a new ideological perspective, which, although touched upon marginally in Vedic literature, is more fully developed in the teachings of what came to be called 'the heterodox sects'. To the extent that Buddhism subsumes this new perspective, it is convenient to juxtapose the polarity of Vedic thought with that of Buddhism. The primary concern of the new attitude is with the perception of change,

From *Daedalus*, Spring 1975, vol. 104, no. 2, pp. 119-33.

the recognition that the context during this period was different from any that had existed before. The outcome of this recognition was the growth of ideologies that were at the same time innovative and germinal to the social and religious philosophy and ethical thought of subsequent periods. This carried within it the elements both of pessimism at the passing of the old order and of optimism in having discovered a way to deal with the changed situation. The 'way' as perceived by the Buddha was arrived at through an innovation in ideology—the notion of causation. Causation in turn highlighted other aspects of innovative thinking, some entirely new, others resulting from the extension of existing ideas.

To understand the perception of change at this time and the need for a new ideology the authors of these ideas have to be seen in a historical context. The priorities in their questions and the kinds of avenues which they explored in a search for answers were not unconnected with the historical milieu in which they lived. They appeared in response to the essentially urban civilization of the Ganges valley. This is often termed the 'second urbanization' of early India, the first having been that of the third millennium in the Indus valley. The antecedents to this second urbanization point to a shift in geographical location from the nuclear area of the third millennium. The Indus civilization had declined by the middle of the second millennium B.C., and the new culture of the Ganges civilization grew and matured on the other side of the watershed during the first millennium B.C., seemingly unconnected with the earlier copper-age civilization. Technologically the new urbanization was based on iron, the widespread domestication of the horse, the extension of plough agriculture, and a far more sophisticated market economy than that of the earlier period. Until recently it was believed that the new civilization grew under the aegis of nomadic pastoralists speaking an Indo-European language, Sanskrit, who had conquered the existing inhabitants, possibly destroyed the bronze-age cities, and had given rise to the new civilization in the process of settling down in the Ganges valley—thus moving, as it were, from the age of the heroes to that of princes and traders. But fresh evidence has suggested that this discontinuity is more imagined than real: many aspects of the later culture bear the impress of the earlier civilization in spite of the considerable difference in the physical location.[1]

Technological changes were not the only indication of a new historical context, for these changes coincided with various other developments. Tribal identity gradually gave way to territorial identity. The territorial units, or *janapadas*, that emerged were named after the *janas* (tribes) settled thereon, such as Gandhāra, Kuru, Pañcāla, Matsya, Cedi, Kāśi, Kośala, Magadha, etc. Lineage, speech, and customary law were the three criteria of identity and status in the earlier tribal society, with lineage being central to political control and land ownership. The *kṣatriya* tribes were the land-owning tribes, who belonged to either the Candravaṃśi (Lunar) or the Sūryavaṃśi (Solar) lineages that in later centuries were to become the royal lineages. The location of the two was distinct, with the Candravaṃśi lineages centered in the Doāb, and extending southward and westward, and the Sūryavaṃśi centered in the middle Ganges plain. The separate identity of the Doāb and South Bihar is evident at every point. Cultivated land was initially owned in common by members of *kṣatriya* lineage—the *khattiyas* of Buddhist literature—although much of the actual tilling appears to have been done by the *dāsas* (slaves) and *bhritakas* (hired labourers and servants).[2] Lineage rights thus included land ownership, and lineage connections were carefully recorded. This accounts for the predominantly *kṣatriya* oligarchic political organization in many *janapadas*.

The stress on kinship ties was further emphasized by the use of the word *jāti* ('assigned by birth'). It occurs first in a late text and is used in the sense of an extended family.[3] In time, the references to *jana* ('tribe') decreased and those to *jāti* increased, until in Buddhist literature *jāti* is used in the sense of caste, implying an endogamous kinship group, ranked in a list of specialized occupations and service relationships reflecting an increase in social stratification. The bi-polarity of purity and pollution remained an important characteristic of the classification by *varna,* but this classification was of a more theoretical kind involving initially four (*brāhmaṇ, kṣatriya, vaiśya, and śūdra*) and subsequently five (with the addition of the *pañcamma* or 'untouchable') groups in society, and eventually became more closely related to ritual than to social status. *Jāti* slowly became the gauge of a more precise assessment of the socio-economic status of a group, but the criteria of status continued to include ritual status (*varṇa*).

During the time of the Buddha (sixth to fifth centuries B.C.) a major change in the agrarian structure was the emergence of large estates owned by individual *kṣatriya* families; the criterion of wealth came to be associated more with land and money and less with cattle, which had been the measure of riches in earlier Vedic literature. The transfer of land took place largely within the same social group that had earlier maintained joint ownership. As an adjunct to this development of a landed class, there is a noticeable increase in the categories of wage labourer, hired labourer, and slave. The slave had *varṇa* status of a *śūdra,* which was particularly necessary for those who worked as domestic slaves, the more common category met with in the Indian sources. A text of the late first millennium B.C. mentions the price of a slave as being a hundred pieces of money; by comparison, a pair of oxen was twenty-four pieces.[4] Slaves were probably expensive even in earlier centuries and could not therefore be used too extensively in production.

The intensification of agriculture provided the economic base for the growth of towns in the Ganges valley. Many of the cities, apart from being important commercial centres, were also the capitals of the *janapadas* such as Kauśāmbi, Kāśi, Ayodhya and Rajagriha. These were not the temple-cities of bronze-age civilization, but were the nuclei of the affluent and the natural habitat of the *seṭṭhi-gahapatis,* the immensely wealthy traders and financiers. The flexibility of a market economy was facilitated by three innovations—the use of a script, the consequent issuing of promissory notes, letters of credit, and pledges, and the introduction of money in the form of silver and copper punch-marked coins issued initially, it has been suggested, by traders' guilds. These, in turn, resulted in the new profession of trading in money, and the appearance of the banker deriving his wealth from usury. Unlike the Buddhist texts, the *brāhmaṇ* sources disapprove of usury, although the censure is restricted to *brāhmaṇs'* fraternizing with those who live off usury.[5] Apart from the archaeological evidence, another indication, albeit indirect, of the growth of cities is the rapid rise of Jainism when, with the prohibition on agricultural professions and restriction on ownership of land, trade became the predominant occupation of the Jainas. The discovery of new routes and the revival of old routes were further incentives to trade.[6]

The city produced its own social stratification, where the *śreṣṭhin* ('merchant or banker') was the most powerful and where the institutional base was that of the *śreṇi* ('guild'). This explains why various religious sects competed for the patronage of the *śreṣṭhins.*[7] Yet in brahmanical literature the trader is not included among the superior social groups. The *varṇa*-ranking of the *vaiśya* ('trader') in the third position may have been irksome to those who had such access to wealth. Furthermore, power in brahmanical terms was connected with ownership of land; although not forbidden to the *śreṣṭhin,* land was by no means his primary source of wealth. Up to a point there was a distinction between the urban and rural elite—the *seṭṭhi/śreṣṭhin* and the *khattiya/kṣatriya*—because they derived their income from different sources. But some of the *khattiyas* who owned estates were also town-dwellers, and thus formed another group alongside the traders and merchants.

The guild was emerging as an essential institution of urban life, acting as a centre of both professional and kin cohesion. The recognition of *śreṇi-dharma* (the customary law of the guilds) as legitimate law by the end of the millennium is another indication of the powerful status of the *śreṇi.*[8] Ultimately it evolved into an agency of caste organization where the larger and better established guilds took on *jāti* status; no less important was the role of the guilds in later centuries as patrons of the heterodox sects.

The lower orders of the guild were the *karmakāras* ('artisans') and the *antevāsikas* ('apprentices'), who were nevertheless still superior to the *dāsabhritaka* ('slaves and hired labourers'). These, together with the cultivators, were all included in the rank of *śūdras.* In brahmanical texts, their low rank was maintained by the legal fiction that they were of mixed caste origin. The gradation among *śūdras* ran from the *sacchūdra* ('clean *śūdra*') to the edge of untouchability. The untouchables constituted the fifth major group. Their untouchability derived from their being considered polluting either because of their occupation as scavengers, such as Caṇḍālas and Doms and those who maintained the cremation grounds, or because they belonged to primitive tribes such as the Niṣāda and the Bhilla. Their speech was alien and their manner of life was strange. Even the Buddhists despised the Caṇḍālas. The inequities of city life further aggravated the degradation of these groups, already declared impure on account of ritual pollution.

The rise of political authority as symbolized in systems of government and the concept of the state were explained in a variety of ways. Vedic literature had connected the emergence of kingship with the emergence of government and stressed that the qualities of leadership in battle and elements of divinity were essential to kingship.[9] By the middle of the first millennium, tribal egalitarianism had surrendered to the evolution of a system of government that, whether oligarchic or monarchical, was explained as concerning itself with the problems of social disharmony, the need for authority, and the justification for revenue collection. The Buddhist theory emphasized the perfection of society in the pre-government age, thus implying that government had become an unfortunate necessity,[10] through the diffusion of social disharmony resulting from family discord and private property. Seeking a solution, people had gathered together and elected a leader—the *mahāsammata* 'the Great Elect'—in whom they invested the authority to maintain law and order; in payment for this service the *mahāsammata* was paid a share of the revenue. Significantly the Buddhist theory emphasizes contract and seems not to have had any notion of royal divinity. The *Mahābhārata* expresses a similar idea, but with a greater emphasis on the notion that societies without governments result in anarchy, the anarchic society is described as a state of *matsyānyāya* 'the law of fish,' where the big fish devour the smaller ones.[11] In this theory, the king also contracts to maintain law and order, but an element of divinity is introduced in his actual appointment as king.

These theories reflect an increasing sense of alienation where it becomes necessary to enforce harmony, since the pristine natural harmony of society has disappeared. They also reflect the acceptance of the idea of authority based on power and not necessarily on kinship alone. The *janapadas* were coalescing into territorial states. By the fifth century B.C. competition for power had already developed among the stronger of the major *janapadas,* such as Kāśi, Kośala and Magadha, where even close kinship ties were ignored to further political gains. Magadha was to emerge as the most powerful, ultimately becoming the nucleus of the Mauryan empire, which was built on the conquests of Chandragupta Maurya in the fourth century B.C. and comprised, during the reign of his grandson Aśoka, almost the entire Indian sub-continent and eastern Afghanistan

With the growth of political authoritarianism and a complicated state machinery, it is not surprising that the justification for the emergence of government came to be based on the necessity for taxation and the need to maintain law and order.[12]

Two co-existing systems of economic redistribution came into being and sometimes into conflict as well. One, at the level of the state, derived its income from taxes, tributes and fines and redistributed it through awards, salaries, grants, and expenditures on public works and ceremonies. But the redistribution was not equitable, and the prestige economy, particularly in the monarchical states, consumed a large part of the income. The second system, on a lesser scale, was confined to the merchants and bankers of the cities; among them the ethic of redistribution was such that substantial sums were retained as capital for further investment.[13] They were doubtless irritated by the prestige economy of the state. That the second system could function in the cities points to their more diffused political authority; this is also suggested by the absence of citadels in these cities. To some extent money liberated the financier from overarching political control.

Caste structure at this time grew out of a variety of inter-relationships between groups. The purity-pollution dichotomy, which above all demarcated the *brāhmaṇ* from the untouchable and which was absent in the earlier period, is by now well established. The *ārya-dāsa* dichotomy deriving from ethnic, linguistic, and cultural differences in the Ṛg Vedic texts was now replaced by the *ārya-śūdra* dichotomy, where the ethnic differences are minimal and the main criteria are the use of Sanskrit and the observance of the *varṇa* rules. Non-*āryas* are *mleccha* ('the barbarians' or 'the impure') and are generally ranked as *śūdras* except in later centuries, when foreign conquerors such as the Indo-Greeks had to be given the dubious status of 'degenerate *kṣatriyas*'. The formation of new castes, theoretically resulting from the intermixing of the original four, was probably a more open system than has hitherto been recognised. The evidence from subsequent centuries suggests that new *jātis* arose as a result of incorporating tribes and guilds and, still later, religious sects into caste society.

The complexity of the new society is clearly reflected in the need for codifying the laws of the various social groups, which is what is aimed at in the brahmanical *dharmasūtras*. The purpose of the laws is to differentiate between the various social groups generally identified as those of *jana, jāti* and *varṇa*. These, however, are made part of a cohesive view of society. There is an implicit belief that the demarcation of differences would lead to a resolution of tensions, an attitude that could only have been feasible in the absence of a situation of conflict. Also implicit in the *dharmasūtras* is the *brāhmaṇs*' claim to being the arbiters of the law. There was no overt challenge to this claim since the codification did not aim at a uniformity of laws, but, on the contrary, to the recognition of their diversity. The Buddhist social code, on the other hand, stressed broad ethical principles of general application to a variety of social groups into the new patterns. The integration was easier at the theoretical level. At the practical level there was a tendency to separate ritual status (*varṇa*) from actual status (*jāti*). Social roles were not entirely dependent on the one or the other. The older traditions and norms were thus placated, and the new entrants into the social hierarchy were not entirely disappointed. However, the demarcation was in fact by no means facile or simplistic. Many of the later subtleties and intricacies of caste relationships emanate from this early attempt at demarcation.

It was apparent that a condition of permanence was neither feasible nor possible in the world of reality where all was flux. Even the above brief survey of the historical scene shows that the condition of constant change could not be ignored.[14] It affected the assumptions of the philosophers of the time and is still reflected in the prevailing intellectual systems. The consciousness of change is perhaps seen most clearly in the fundamental problem of human salvation or liberation in which three interrelated aspects were emphasized—the ethic of the individual in terms of his own moral consciousness and his search for release from the bonds of human existence, the verification of ultimate knowledge so essential to the working out of a means to salvation, and finally the discovery of a path to salvation. The prime motivation was to find an answer that would subsume changing material conditions and yet remain viable. The Buddhist attempt to analyse these problems makes a point of contrasting the attempts of other groups of thinkers similarly involved.

That these concerns were widespread is apparent from the rise of a variety of 'heterodox sects,' among which Buddhism was included. These sects were not merely a reaction to Vedic religion, as is often suggested, because within the Vedic-*brāhmaṇ* framework there had also been a diversification of views as evidenced by the texts of the *Upaniṣads* and the *Āraṇyakas*. These were the discourses of the renouncers who had isolated themselves from society and lived in forest retreats. They stood apart, disenchanted with the world, seeking ultimate truths. Their discourses show a liberation of the speculative consciousness from the burdens of magical sacrifice and ritual. However, the universalistic basis of their thinking had some limitations. They recognised the need for individual salvation. In isolation and through *saṃnyāsa* ('asceticism'), the individual could find his *mokṣa* ('salvation') which would release his *ātmā* (individual 'soul') and enable it to unite with the *brahma* ('all-soul'). Asceticism was motivated both by a desire to escape from the insecurity of a changing society and by the conviction that meditation was an effective means of acquiring the knowledge that furthers self-realization as well as the power (*tapas*) to become superior even to the gods. Gradually asceticism came to be regarded as a more powerful force than sacrifice, thus admitting the ineffectiveness of a community attempt to reach moments of magic and power. Perhaps more important, asceticism resulted in total freedom, a break with family ties and social regulations, provided sexual needs could be sublimated. Hence the correlation between asceticism and asexuality. This freedom insured the renouncer a moral status far higher than that of even a sacrificing *brāhmaṇ*.

Some sects, such as the Ājīvikas, based their thought on determinism and saw renunciation as the only and ultimate path to *mokṣa*. The Buddhists and the Jainas had both philosophical and social concerns. Access to knowledge did not lie through the authoritative voice of the Vedas, for what is not personally verifiable is unacceptable. Nor is skepticism a path to knowledge; the skeptics for the Buddhists were 'eel-wrigglers'. Even asceticism was not possible as a path to salvation for everyone. Both the Buddha and Mahāvīra, though seeking enlightenment through isolated meditation, nevertheless returned to the world of the cities and villages to preach the path of salvation to the householder who could not become a monk owing to his social obligations. In the case of the Buddha, the emphasis on 'the middle way', the path devoid of excesses, emphasizing moderation and a moral life, was indicative of his concern that the path suggested by him be compatible with the real problems of social existence. Not surprisingly, the early supporters of Buddhism were not only the ascetics but also, and in larger numbers, the *seṭṭhis* and members of the *kṣatriya* clans. At the other extreme were a number of *lokāyata* sects, particularly the Cārvākas, who were based primarily in the towns and who taught a thoroughgoing materialism, such as the teachings of Ajīta Keśakambalin, the result of which was seen by others as an idealization of hedonism.

The thread of social protest winding through these heterodox teachings was indicative of a perception of change: of existing change, the recognition that further changes were imminent, and toward change itself. For the Buddhists, change was symbolized in two strands, which occasionally intertwined, the cosmic and the historical. The universe is transient and in a state of continuous flux. Buddhist cosmic time was cyclical, starting with a pristine utopian society, which had gradually decayed and was slowly reaching its nadir of sorrow and suffering, the direction in which contemporary society was moving. Eventually it would rise upwards again and begin a utopian phase. Brahmanical sources, also positing cyclical time, attempted a mathematical measurement of it, albeit of an infinite magnitude, as did the Buddhists, who indicated infinite eons by spatial descriptions.[15] Time was seen as an unending continuity of which historical time was but a fraction. Within this continuity the individual consciousness also moved unceasingly from one lifetime to the next birth until liberated from the chain of rebirth. It is compared to the flame of a lamp used to light another lamp and so on, *ad infinitum.* In each case the flame of the lamp is both the old and the new flame, and so it is with the perception of change in the continuity of time.

Change, therefore, cannot be seen as a sudden break. But within historical time there is a far sharper awareness of the past and the future. Other 'enlightened ones' have trod the same path in the past as the Buddha. Was this allegorical, or was it a reference to earlier teachers with a similar doctrine? There is also the reference to the Buddha Maitreya, who will reawaken the world to the *Dharma* ('the law') many centuries after the present Buddha.[16] This was to develop in the first centuries after Christ into an almost messianic movement within Buddhism, no doubt further stimulated by contact with the messianic message of Christianity and Manichaeanism.

The decline from utopian beginnings is not accidental. There is a concern with moral decay, which, although partially inherent (the very state of nature having evolved from luminosity to dross), is nevertheless caused by changes in the material content of life. It can be circumvented to some extent by the individual's choice in the manner of adapting to changing social situations.

Central to the awareness of change is the law of causality, and it is around this that much of Buddhist doctrine revolves, claiming to derive from rational arguments and examples. At the individual level, the interconnection between desire, suffering, and rebirth is explained by causality. The elimination of *dukkha* ('suffering') lies in the elimination of *tanha* ('desire'), and this can be achieved by observing the precepts of the *Dhamma/Dharma* ('the Law as taught by the Buddha') and the eight-fold path. Social change is also explained by causality and becomes a part of the underpinning, as it were, of the universal applicability of the *Dharma*, for, once the causal connection is known, change comes under human control.

This led to a new perspective on the significance of the individual. The heterodox teaching, and Buddhism in particular, turned the earlier perspective inside out, and the focus shifted to the individual rather than the social group to which he belonged. Up to a point this encouraged a nihilistic trend, as in the case of the *Ājīvikas*. But nihilism was not characteristic of all sects. On this question the central core of the Buddhist *Dharma* is very clear. Where renunciation or opting out is not feasible, the individual, whatever his social status, had the choice of becoming a lay disciple and observing the rules of 'the middle way'. Furthermore, the moral responsibility of the individual was seen in the choice of action made by him through his chain of rebirth. The *Bṛhadāraṇyaka Upaniṣad* described rebirth as consisting of *saṃsāra*, the transmigration of souls, to which was added the notion of *karma* ('action'), the outcome of the activities of one life affecting the next. The Buddhists modified the notion of *saṃsāra* to exclude the soul and to refer to consciousness as the element that continues, and they appropriated the doctrine of *karma* in its entirety. Thus not only was the individual responsible for the nature and condition of his present and future lives, but the doctrine of *karma* also became a useful means of explaining the origin of social inequality and the creation of caste society.[17] Not only was a man's social condition a reference point in social justice, but disease, physical pain, and even death were seen as aspects of social justice, although the moral responsibility for this condition rested with the individual. Thus the sting of social protest was numbed by insisting that there was no tangible agency responsible for social injustice, or even an abstract deity against whom man could complain, but that responsibility belonged with man himself. This in turn tended to curb non-conformity in behaviour for fear of the consequences in the next life.

It is not altogether fortuitous that Buddhism was popular among the entrepreneurs and the life-affirming groups in Indian society—the merchants and the artisans. Nor should it be forgotten that at the political level Buddhism registered its initial success in the period of the first empire, that of the Mauryas. The life-asserting aspect of *karma* is that, if the rules are observed, the next birth can at least bring a better and more prosperous life, if not freedom from the chain of rebirth. There can be, therefore, considerable motivation for observing the rules. That the onus was on the individual is further emphasized by the necessity of being born a man, rather than any other creature, before salvation can be attained. Moral responsibility was not developed into a philosophy of radical change, which would have meant challenging the existing system. The Buddha made a distinction between caste as the frame of the socio-economic structure, which he accepted, and the notion of the relative purity inherent in the upper castes, which he rejected.[18] The emphasis was on an individual's choice of an ethic, but the end result of this had its social implications.

Fundamental to Buddhist teaching was the notion of the interplay of acts of merit (*puṇya*) and demerit (*pāpa*, literally 'evil, wickedness'), and *puṇya* becomes central to ethical thought from this time onwards. The constituents of merit for the layman are activities motivated by the need to further social good, such as harmonious social relationships and charity, but, above all, sexual control and non-violence. Harmony in social relationships referred not only to those between parents and children, but also between master and slave, and employer and employee in general. This had a clear correlation with the large estates of the *khattiyas* and the new urban culture. Although the Buddha associates the growth of evil in the world with (among other factors) the institutions of the family and private property, both of which, he argues, encouraged sentiments of possessiveness and consequently aggression, he nevertheless projects an undisturbed continuity for both institutions. In spite of its evils, the family did weaken the sense of alienation, and hence there is a stress on respecting kinship ties. Charity was seen not only as a means of alleviating the suffering of the materially poor, but also as the giving of gifts (*dāna*) especially to the *saṅgha* (the order of monks). This had the additional advantage of strengthening the monastic organization and its relations with the lay community.

Both sexual puritanism and non-violence became controversial issues in the debate among the various sects. The Buddha was not loathe to accept the devotion of the more renowned and accomplished courtesans of the towns, such as Ambapalli, but it took considerable persuasion for him to agree to admit women into the *saṅgha*. Family ties were a major obstacle to renunciation, and women were symbolic of these ties. Yet during this time it was only in the Jaina and Buddhist orders that nuns were permitted, and the women were drawn largely from urban society and the royal households.

Non-violence (*ahimsā*), the central focus of Buddhist and Jaina ethics, was less important in other religious sects. Veiled, ambiguous references can be culled from the *Upaniṣads*, but the exposition of the idea as an ethical value was that of Mahāvīra and the Buddha. The Jaina understanding of *ahimsā* appears to be an extreme position involving all created beings and the attempt to preserve them from destruction, whether deliberate or accidental.[19] The Buddhists tend to stress the ethical question of man's actions in furthering or preventing violence.

Ahimsā can be viewed in association with many facets of contemporary life. It has been seen as an objection to the sacrifice of animals during the *yajña*, the sacrificial ceremony essential to the Vedic brahmanical religion. There is repeated mention of the futility of killing animals as a religious ritual.[20] Possibly this coincided with the rapid transformation of pastoral groups into agriculturalists, which resulted in a depletion of animal wealth.[21] The debate on the inviolability of the cow is referred to *en passant* in the *Śatapatha Brāhmaṇa*, but it is again largely due to Buddhist and Jaina disputation that the prohibition is extended from cattle to violence *per se*.[22] *Ahimsā* can also be explained as a reaction among the new urban groups to the prestige economy of non-urban societies, who were wilfully destroying wealth to no purpose. Sacrifice, it was argued, is essentially an offering; consequently it lies not in the destruction of life but in the embodiment of moral values that become the foundation for ethical behaviour—in honouring parents, in honouring all the members of the household from the highest to the lowest, in having patience, meekness, and self-control. The values listed are both conservative and conciliatory. Yet the element of radicalism in this view is the inclusion of slaves and workmen as deserving of honour. At another level *ahimsā* would have suited those who were discouraging inter-tribal warfare and encouraging the expansion of settled agriculture and trade—activities from which both the *khattiyas* and *seṭṭhis* stood to gain.

Ahimsā also included a discouragement of the use of coercion and violence to justify political authoritarianism—very pertinent to the transformation of the *janapadas* into kingdoms laying political claim to large territories. The suspicion of political authoritarianism may have to do with the fact that the heterodox sects often had their genesis in the relatively more egalitarian tradition of the oligarchies and republics, such as that of the Śākyas and Vṛjjis. Those most directly affected by war would be the cultivators, whose fields were the prey of marauding armies, and the traders, who would be unable to transport their goods, or, even worse, whose centres of production would be destroyed in the devastation of a town—so often the symbolic final act of a successful campaign. Possibly *ahimsā* could also undermine the ritualized wars—the campaigns that were fought subsequent to the *aśvamedha* sacrifice, when a king claiming sovereignty over a region would release a sacrificial horse and would then be duty bound to conquer all the lands over which the horse wandered. Implicit in *ahimsā* at the political level is an objection to even the legitimate use of coercion (*daṇḍa*) by the political authority of the state. The king in his role as protector should avoid coercion, modelling himself after the ideal universal monarch, the *cakravartin*, who is *adaṇḍa* 'not having to resort to coercion.'[23]

Ahimsā might have had an ameliorative influence in situations of tension, which were by no means rare. Ultimately there was also the ethical and philosophical level. Conscious non-violence (not to be confused with cowardice) was expressive of the highest ethical stand. The credibility of non-violence can only stem from a belief in man's innate virtue. It has been argued that the Buddha's *ahimsā* represents the negative philosophy of pacifism. To the extent that the Buddha was not preaching rebellion, but rather a conciliatory ethic, as a solution to social ills, the negative aspect of pacifism can be justified. But if *ahimsā* arose from an awareness of varying levels of comprehension and reaction, then pacifism alone cannot be the complete explanation. As a method of social protest, the objection even to ritual sacrifice involving the destruction of life takes on an active and affirmative role, as is evident from the continuing debate on this subject up to recent times. It is perhaps also worth remembering that the brahmanical insistence on vegetarianism dates to the post-Buddhist period.

The significance of renunciation has its own role in the Buddhist moral position and relates to the moral and political authority of the renouncer. There has been a tendency to see renunciation as a purely life-denying process. This it may be if the renouncer moves away from society and lives in isolation, though, even here, the negative aspect to the isolation is rarely foremost. But if the renouncer, after a period of isolation, resumes a function in society, in spite of his having renounced his ties, his influence can become both powerful and positive. Moral and political authority are separated and the former becomes the censor of the latter. This separation can be crucial to the establishing of an independent intellectual tradition, as was the case in the lifetime of the Buddha, provided that the independent relationship between the two is not eroded by the requirements of patronage. If the renouncer is also in sympathy with the aspirations of a community and if he comes from a social background not generally associated with life-denial and renunciation, but rather with political authority and social status (such as the *khattiyas* of the time), his moral authority is almost unlimited. In such situations the renouncer forsakes one life-style to take on another.

Recruitment to the heterodox sects was not limited to any particular group. Those who had an organized body of adherents, enlisted monks, and built monasteries, encouraged people of all castes to join the organization and, in theory at least, did not bar any caste. In the Buddhist *saṅgha* the adoption of a new name by the monk was symbolic not merely of a new birth in the *saṅgha* but also of a removal from his caste and status.[24] The proximity of all castes within the monasteries ran counter to the brahmanical ideal of the segregation of castes in daily living. Commensality among such monks from the lay community broke the food taboos so essential to the *varṇa* system. Outside the monastery and among lay followers the problem of integrating social groups remained.

Each *jāti* had its own religious observances. Religious differentiations were preserved through the mechanism of caste, as were the observance of rituals pertaining to local cults, some of which were assimilated into Buddhist practice.[25] The Buddhist shift of emphasis from deities to the more abstract notion of *Dharma* ('the law') was an attempt in part to undermine these religious differentiations. It may be argued that the absence of a deity in Buddhism inherent in the doctrine strengthened the idea of a universal religion. In some ways, however, *Dharma* almost took on the characteristics of an omniscient presence symbolized in the turning of the wheel of the law. *Dharma* was the eternal Law—ultimate, timeless, temporal, transcendent, immanent. In spite of changing human society the Law remained changeless. It integrated within itself the ethic of the individual, the verification of ultimate knowledge and the path to salvation. Change was perceived, recognized, and understood. But it was not the changed situation that was to be subjected to radical social alteration as much as the law that was to be applicable in all situations. The law was above the particular and was universally viable. Enlightenment lay in the discovery of this law and identification with it. But the law was not to be kept to oneself in isolation. The enlightened ones must return to the cities and the villages and preach the law. There is the repeated parable of the raft, where he who has discovered the law (the raft) must leave the raft for others to cross the waters on it.[26]

The arbiters of the *Dharma* were the Elders of the monastery. The Buddhist monastery was both a retreat for meditation and an institution for action. The early monasteries had to be located close to large concentrations of population, because of the requirement that the monks feed off alms, since they were forbidden to do any manual labour including cultivating their own food. Begging for alms and preaching the doctrine brought them into contact with the lay community. The *saṅgha* was thus a collection of renouncers but not of ascetics. The monks took on a new way of life based on communal sharing and dedication to poverty, evidenced by the prohibition against personal possessions and by the name they adopted, *bhikṣu* (mendicant). Central to the organization of the *saṅgha* was the emphasis on the equal status of every monk, influenced perhaps by the more egalitarian political organization of the oligarchic *janapadas*, familiar to the Buddha. But this insistence on equality did not apply to the world outside. It was almost as if the creation of a radical, egalitarian society within the monastery exhausted the drive toward such a society in the world outside, or at least weakened the urgency of radical change—assuming, however, that this had been intended. Celibacy and the discouraging of manual labour for the monks point up the bi-polarity between the monk and the householder where the latter qualifies himself in part by his ties to family and property.[27] The monk and the householder lived in worlds apart.

The *saṅgha* gradually acquired a strong sense of mission. This is evident from the frequency of the councils determining the true doctrine and the splintering off of sects within the *saṅgha* after the death of the Buddha, each claiming to represent the true doctrine. Even more significant was the system of maintaining records and historical accounts not only of the major events in the history of Buddhism, but also of the more important sects within the *saṅgha* that encouraged the polemics of Buddhist sectarian thought. The community of renouncers was not altogether unaware either of its political role or of its role in the new ethic that they were promulgating.

The sense of mission was encouraged by the literate monks. The monasteries developed into centres of learning. This was again a point of opposition to the Vedic brahmanical approach for which literacy was the preserve of the socially-determined few and which in any case laid greater stress on the oral tradition. As a part of the appeal to the wider audience, the Buddha preached not in Sanskrit but in *ardha-māgadhi*—a *prākṛt* of the middle Ganges plain. At the same time as brahmanical culture was seeking an *ārya* identity and exclusivity, the Buddha was breaking away from it.

The extension of literacy was symbolic of much that the new ideologies stood for, the insufficiency of faith and ritual and the incorporation of reason and moral action in a manner that would have wide applicability to large numbers of people of diverse social origins. The new teachers arose as individuals and not through an institutional base. But the continuance of the new ideologies required the building of their own institutional base. The perception of change and the need to come to terms with it were not seen as synonymous with a radical ideology in favour of a total change. The Buddhists, for example, were more analytical than earlier thinkers in their views on man and society, but they did not feel it necessary to suggest a complete reorganization of the social structure. To that degree, Buddhism in its historical role touched the chords of social protest but went no further. This was perhaps because the groups for which it was projecting a new ideology ceased to be the protesters at a certain historical point and became the heirs. The element of social protest in Buddhism was therefore limited to providing the intellectual encouragement and justification for the formation of a new elite. It can be argued that in the historical context of those times even this was a radical position and it was not necessary to extend causation to its logical limits. The *lokāyatas* who insisted on natural causation and opposed the doctrine of *karma* were either subsumed into the new system or were left on the fringes as anarchists.

The historical mission of Buddhism took it far afield. The monasteries, irrespective of sectarian differences, acted as networks of acculturation and contact within the Indian subcontinent reaching out into the remotest corners, monks travelling either in isolation or accompanying the traders. In the first millennium A.D. the significance of the mission of Buddhism was that it acted as a catalyst in many parts of Asia. Its major orientation was in Central Asia, China, Japan and Southeast Asia. The period when Buddhism took root and prospered in these new areas coincided with its fading in the country of its origin. Can this be regarded as a historical demonstration of the Buddhist notion of change and continuity—the analogy with the flame of one lamp lighting the flame of another before being extinguished?

REFERENCES AND NOTES

1. Archaeological evidence of the post-Harappan period, particularly in Gujarat, Malwa, the Banas valley, and parts of the watershed and upper Doab, points to some continuities of cultural traits from the Harappa culture. Small settlements of primitive agriculturalists in the Doab or the western Ganges plain (the Ochre-Colour Pottery culture) were superseded toward the end of the second millennium

B.C. by larger settlements of more advanced agriculturalists gradually taking to iron technology by the earlier part of the first millennium B.C. (the Painted Gray-Ware Culture). Further east, in the middle Ganges plain and south Bihar, the impetus for using an iron technology is associated with an apparently different group of people (the Black and Red-Ware culture), who appear to have had some links with western India via the northern part of the central Indian plateau. The Doāb was the geographical focus of the later Vedic literature and was identified (in the main) in Brahmanical literature with the *āryā-varta* or the land of the *āryas* (the pure, respectable people), those who spoke Sanskrit and observed the caste laws. South Bihar, which included the territory of Magadha, was to a greater extent the geographical focus of 'the heterodox sects'. In the Buddhist and Jaina texts, south Bihar was the core of the *āryā-varta*, since these texts tended to give a more easterly location to 'pure land'. An area of high precipitation, the Ganges plain was at that time covered with forests. It has been argued that settlement on any appreciable scale would have been virtually impossible before the introduction of iron technology, the monsoon forest being relatively impervious to the tools of copper technology. That the introduction of iron coincided with an increase in population is clear even from fairly impressionistic archaeological data. The iron-age precondition to urbanization is evident from the number of settlements of iron-using cultures that developed into towns. Increase in population not only assisted in the clearing of more land for agriculture in the Ganges plain, but could also have acted as a lever toward encouraging a change to iron technology and more particularly to plough-using agriculture.

2. Patañjali, *Mahābhāṣya* on Pāṇini IV, I, 168.
3. *Kātyāyana Śrauta Sūtra* XV. 4. 14; XV. 2. 11.
4. *Nanda Jātaka* 1.98; *Gāmani Caṇḍa Jātaka* II. 207.
5. *Āpastamba Dharma Sūtra* I.6.18.22; *Baudhāyana Dharma Sūtra* 1.5.93-94.
6. Maritime trade with west Asia was revived in the first millennium B.C. Close contacts were established between Iran and north-western India. Within the sub-continent, overland and maritime routes to the south (Dakṣiṇāpatha) were being explored.
7. Wagle, *Society at the Time of the Buddha* (Bombay, 1966).
8. *Manu Dharmaśāstra* VII. 41.
9. *Ṛg Veda* VIII. 35.17; 86.10-11.
10. *Dīgha Nikāya* III. 93.
11. *Mahābhārata*, Śānti Parvan 67. 3.ff.
12. The words used for the two basic taxes were *bali*, originally meaning a tribute or booty and eventually coming to mean a tax on land, and *bhāga*, meaning 'a share' and applied to the produce of the land, reflecting the more stable distribution of settled times. An early term for the king was *bhāgadugha*, literally, 'he who milks the share'.
13. As suggested by the Buddha in *Dīgha Nikāya* III, p. 188 (P.T.S. ed.).
14. For a correlation of material conditions with the rise of Buddhism, R.S. Sharma, 'Material Milieu of the Birth of Buddhism', paper presented to the Twenty-Ninth International Congress of Orientalists, Paris, 1973.

15. *Samyutta Nikāya*, 15.ii. 178-93.
16. *Dīgha Nikāya* III, 76.
17. *Majjhima Nikāya* I.289; *Aṅguttara Nikāya* V. 288-91. This is made even more explicit in the pre-eminent text of Brahmanism, the *Bhagavad Gītā* IV. 13, composed in the period after the Buddha.
18. *Aṅguttara Nikāya* III. 214; *Samyutta Nikāya* I.167; *Majjhima Nikāya* II. 128-30.
19. *Ācāraṅga Sūtra* II.1.1-4.
20. *Anguttara Nikāya* IV. 42-45.
21. D.D. Kosambi, *The Culture and Civilisation of Ancient India in Historical Outline* (London, [1965]), p. 105. Cattle provided both labour and fertilizer in agricultural societies, and any depletion was a serious loss. That cattle were singled out for protection is clear from the emphasis in some sections of the Buddhist texts, such as *Majjhima Nikāya*, I.220.
22. The debate is perhaps best symbolized by passages in the early text, the *Śatapatha Brāhmaṇa* III. 1-2.21, where the eating of meat (the flesh of the cow is the case in point) is defended by Yājñavalkya, who represents an important point of view, and the later prohibition on it, as for example in the text of Manu dating to the first century B.C.
23. Cakkavati Sinhanādasutta, *Dīgha Nikāya* III, p. 58 (S.B.B. ed.).
24. *Vinaya Piṭaka* II. 239; *Aṅguttara Nikāya* IV. 202
25. Dates for important events such as the *vassa* (the rainy season when the monks had to return to the monastery), the *uposatha* (the days for the hearing of the confession of the monks), etc. were calculated on the basis of the lunar calendar, although the solar calendar was also in use at the time.
26. *Majjhima Nikāya* I.134-5; *Aṅguttara Nikāya* II. 201.
27. S.J. Tambiah, ***Buddhism and the Spirit Cults in North-East Thailand*** (Cambridge, 1970), pp 81 ff.

Renunciation: The Making of a Counter-culture?

One of the paradoxes of the Indian tradition is that the renouncer is a symbol of authority within society. An explanation of this paradox may emerge from an analysis of the social role of the renouncer. Not many decades ago renunciation was described as a life-negating principle; the fact that it involved an opting out of society led to its characterization as a denial of the need to come to terms with society. But in recent years it has been argued that, far from being life-negating, the techniques adopted by ascetics and renouncers and popularized because of them, have, as axiomatic, the belief that life can be the means of discovering immortality and freedom.[1] An attempt will be made in this paper to argue that the organized groups of renouncers of the post-Vedic period were neither negating the society to which they belonged nor trying to radically alter it: but rather that they were seeking to establish a parallel society. Inherent in this attempt was the notion of dissent; but its articulation was often ambiguous. To the extent that the two societies were kept distinct, there was a tacit recognition of the futility of changing the larger society; that the renouncers had links with this society, however, also indicates that there was an equally tacit recognition of osmosis as a process of social change.

Renouncers in any society play a social role. In early India this role is enmeshed with the complexities of caste and with the nature of dissent. The power of the ascetic rubs off onto the renouncer to a far greater degree than, for example, in Christian Europe, and the renouncer becomes a continuing source of both authority and dissent. In the process of osmosis there is also, unlike as in Europe, provision for temporary periods of renunciation

From N. Jagadesan and J. Jeyapragassam (eds.), *Homage to a Historian* (Dr. N. Subramanian Festschrift), Section II, pp. 1-50.

(as among Buddhist Orders) which underlines the central role of the renouncer in society, namely, the relationship between the ascetic, the renouncer and the householder.

The term ascetic refers to a person who has opted out of society, renounced social mores and cast himself away. Ostensibly he has also taken upon himself the goal of discovering the ecstasy (*ānanda*) in the comprehension of the ultimate reality and of characterizing this search by resorting to austerity (*tapas*) and meditation (*dhyāna*) with the final aim of union with the ultimate reality (*yoga*). A further distinction is however required for the purposes of this paper. A differentiation must be made between the individual renouncer who isolates himself totally and is thus lost to his kin and his society and to other ascetic colleagues—in short, the ideal ascetic, and the one who opts out of society but joins a group of renouncers. The distinction can perhaps be maintained by referring to the former as ascetics and the latter as renouncers. The term renouncer approximates more closely to the meaning of *saṃnyāsin*. The first category has always been something of a rarity, more frequently described in literature than encountered in reality.

The renouncer is identified not necessarily with a religious sect but with an order constituting an alternative lifestyle, in many ways contradictory to that of his original social group. Thus he cannot observe caste rules, he must be celibate, he cannot own property, he must carry the distinctive outward symbols of his order and he may be required to break various food tabus. The ascetic on the other hand lived in isolation, observed the food tabus by subsisting on what was naturally available in the forest, stressed the fact of his brahmanhood (where he was, as was often the case, a *brāhmaṇ*) by the austerities which he undertook. A further and fundamental distinction between the two was that whereas the ascetics were figures of loneliness working out their salvation each one for himself, the renouncer was concerned about other people and this concern was expressed in his desire to lead others along the path which he had found. This paper is concerned with the renouncers, who left the society into which they were born and took on the alternative life-style of the sect/order which they joined. At one level the reason for this was that 'the search' required a guide and groups of disciples tended to congregate around individual teachers. At another level there was a conscious attempt to live in a way which would be different from established society.

The focus here is on the social manifestations of these groups and their role in historical change rather than the ideational level and the philosophies which this may have generated. At the ideational level the debate centred on the nature of authority, where the dissenting groups denied the *Vedas* as the source of all knowledge and preferred knowledge acquired through perception and experience.[2] Further, transmigration and notions of salvation were largely acceptable to both the orthodox and the heterodox but the comprehension of these varied. Other matters of controversy related to the nature of the ultimate reality and the juxtaposition of the individual with the universal. The main concern was with the desire for knowledge which in early society was seen as magical power. Initially asceticism arose from groups which questioned the ritual of sacrifice as the means of acquiring magical power. Proponents of asceticism believed that *tapas* and *dhyāna* were more effective. Gradually the idea was extended to more than magical power—to absolute freedom. Primarily this was seen as the freedom of the soul or consciousness to achieve a state of ecstasy. Logically, it also implied freedom from recognizable worldly bonds, of the human body, the mind and of society. By and large there were certain themes which were common to all these groups and which were preconditions to further knowledge: there was a need to comprehend and control the physical body as also the mind, to differentiate between matter and spirit and to derive knowledge from experience and meditation rather than from the claim to revelation.

The initial part of this paper discusses briefly the major groups of renouncers which gained recognition in the early period in the context of the historical background and the social changes which may have encouraged the rise of these groups. The second part is concerned with the bi-polarity of the renouncer and the householder as well as the symbols of difference between the two and among the sects. The last section deals with the element of social protest and concern among these renouncers, and attempts to understand the paradox of their social role.

It has been argued that the term 'sect' is a misnomer for Hindu religious groups since the essential element of a sect—the heretical opposition to orthodox doctrine—is absent among Hindu sects.[3]

The argument is based on the use of the term *saṁpradāya* as the nomenclature for sect, but this refers to the transmission of a tradition which can hardly be called a heretical process. However, *saṁpradāya* is generally used by the established religious groups with reference to their own sects, i.e. of the 'received doctrine'. The more frequently used terms for other sects are *śākhā*, *mata*, *samāya*, suggesting a branching off or a schismatic group (which implies heresy) or a coming together of those with a common perspective. The selection of sects discussed in this paper is governed by an inclusion of those which identify themselves with reference to a specific doctrine, specific symbols and rituals and the acceptance of a relationship between the lay followers and the sacerdotal hierarchy: all of which would justify the group being called a sect in the wider sense of the word. The case of Buddhist and Jaina sects is unambiguous since the basis is heresy and false doctrine is manifestly clear from the history of the splitting off of the *saṅgha* into sects. In the Greek translation of one of the edicts of Aśoka, the original word *pāsaṇḍa* is translated as DIATRIBE.[4] *Pāsaṇḍa* was used both of heretics and imposters and the *Purāṇas* describe the Buddhists and the Jainas as such, whilst the latter used the same term to refer to schismatic groups in their own *saṅghas*. It has been further suggested that the ambiguity in the case of the Hindu sects is due to the absence of a centralized institution to control orthodoxy and although caste sanctions often performed this role it was nevertheless not clearly defined. The flexible nature of the Hindu canon also allowed constant and major interpolations which accommodated heresies as well. The assimilative character of Hinduism weakened the idea of false doctrine. Yet the notion of false doctrine was not absent and is apparent for instance in the dissensions of some of the schools of philosophy. In the post-Śaṅkara period it occurs more frequently in the literature. The heresy was often more apparent on the social plane, hence this attempt to view the question from a social perspective.

Asceticism has a historical continuity from the earliest times, although inevitably the role and nature of the ascetic groups has changed over the centuries. It is believed that the earliest representation of an ascetic practice comes from the supposed Paśupati seal of the Harappa Culture.[5] A known incipient practice is perhaps that of temporary withdrawals from society during periods demanding a condition of ritual purity. Thus the *yajamāna* of the Vedic sacrifice opts out for the period of the sacrifice. This notion may be extended to a life-time in which ritual purity may result in generating extraordinary powers. Ascetic groups are referred to in Vedic literature and some texts such as the *Upaniṣads* and the *Āraṇyakas* are largely concerned with asceticism. However, a distinction should be drawn between the characteristics emphasised in the *Ṛg Veda* and other Vedic texts. The terms used most frequently in the former are *yati*, *muni* and *ṛṣi*.[6] The etymology of these words indicates magic, mystical rites, meditation and the ecstasy which comes with vision and inspiration. In short, the kind of activity which is more often associated with shamanism. The long-haired *muni*, the *keśin*, flying through the air[7] suggests a shamanising technique as also does the reference to magical heat (*tapas*).[8] The shamans would have to be distinguished from the sorcerers and the sorceresses (*yātu-matī*) said to inhabit the ruins of old cities.[9]

Shamanism is often associated with tribal societies surviving on subsistence economies. The attraction of shamanistic practices however continues even when the structure of tribal life undergoes substantial change. In the *Aitereya Brāhmaṇa* Indra is hostile to the *yatis* and on one occasion feeds them to the hyaenas, which possibly led to his being deprived of *soma*.[10] It has been plausibly argued that *soma* was a hallucinogen[11] and this would support the presence of shamanistic activities, incurring the wrath of the tribal deity. Although the shaman was never a renouncer, characteristics of shamanism can nevertheless be seen in the practices of many of the later groups of renouncers. The shaman stood somewhat apart from his tribe, yet was primarily concerned with the well-being (both physical and spiritual) of his tribe. The shaman's norms were a law unto himself, yet at the same time the shaman was dependent on the tribe. His distinctiveness was apparent both from outward symbols of dress and accessories as also by his behaviour. He derived his legitimacy from his claim to superior knowledge acquired through considerable effort involving the claim to magic, meditation and the inducement of visions with the aid of hallucinogens.

In the Later Vedic literature terms such as *tapasvin*, *śramaṇa*, *saṃnyāsin*, *parivrājaka*, *yogi*, occur more commonly. They are suggestive of renunciation, or casting aside one's social obligations, of the taking on of a life of austerity, of controlling the functions of the body (particularly breathing) and above all of wandering from place to place. The *parivrājaka* is sometimes described as a young man who, having finished his education, takes to a life of wandering for a brief period prior to becoming a householder.[12] But more often the *parivrājaka* was a permanent condition. Was this a nostalgia for the nomadic state[13] or was it a flouting of growing authoritarianism which disapproved of wanderers in a society increasingly given to stable agricultural settlements? The mystery surrounding the pre-eminent of wanderers, the *vrātyas*, remains largely unsolved. They appear to have been a group of shamans moving towards ascetic or yogic practices.[14] The *Saṃnyāsa* and *Yoga Upaniṣads* of a later period speak of yogic practices not merely in terms of magical powers (*siddhis*) but also the cultivation of meditation (*dhyāna*) and the control over breathing (*prāṇāyāma*), the ultimate aim of which was in part tied up with the search for immortality—a quest which was to take various forms in later centuries and which ran like a thread through the entire texture of ascetic practices. From visionaries and seers, the ascetic perspective moved to peripatetic teaching and the investigating of man and the universe through a variety of intensive techniques of mental concentration and control over the body.

The mid-first millennium B.C sees a proliferation of sects in the Ganges valley.[15] Many of these were *parivrājakas* wandering in groups under the direction of a teacher or others loosely affiliated to sects, but preferring to wander by themselves, alone.[16] Their main function, apart from acquiring knowledge, was to participate in discussion and debate. They were such an established institution that some of the towns and larger villages provided them with *kutūhala-śālās*, literally places for exciting curiosity or interest, i.e., halls for discussion. Many such wanderers lived on the edges of towns and only those of a markedly ascetic disposition retired to places more isolated.[17] Some *brāhmaṇ* ascetics were sedentary, often living in hermitages, sometimes with their families,[18] although claiming to conform to celibacy all the same. These came to be called the Vaikhānasa and later texts mention names such as Saubhari who lived with his fifty wives in a hermitage.[19] *Brāhmaṇ* orthodoxy was averse to city-dwellers and restrictions were placed on *snātakas* visiting cities.[20] The wanderers were often the dissidents. The questioning of the orthodox tradition had started prior to this period, but what was new was the emergence of various sects such as the Nirgranthas, the Ājīvikas and later the Buddhists, not to mention various Cārvāka sects as well. The dissidence of these groups was however qualitatively different since they were not individual dissenters but had organized their dissent into sects whose identity was based on an opposition to the orthodox doctrines as expressed in the notion of the sanctity of the *Vedas,* the authority of the *brāhmaṇs, varṇāśramadharma* and the worship of the gods.[21] They were seen as a counter-influence on Āryan polytheism, particularly in their recognition of the rule of natural law in the universe. The theory of transmigration, which was the starting point for a number of these sects, may have been developed from older animist theories.

The proliferation of sects has been explained as due to the break-up of tribal society and its consequences.[22] The cushioning effect of kinship ties was declining with the impersonal relations of post-tribal society coming to the fore. The increasingly hierarchical ordering of society would in any case have been hostile to the wanderers. This was further reiterated by the growth of towns and cities during this period with the anonymity and alienation encouraged by urban institutions. Inevitably there was a search for methods of adjustment. It should also be remembered that the introduction of iron technology coupled with urbanization was more traumatic in terms of social change than any experienced earlier. The age of transcendence was not accidental.[23] At the same time it was precisely the economic margin of prosperity made possible by the new situation which allowed for the maintenance of such large groups of renouncers. Supportive evidence for this comes from the literature itself. The new sects of renouncers lived at the edges of towns, drew their recruits mainly from the towns and were dependent for alms on the householders. The Buddha for example spent more years at Rājagriha and Śrāvastī than anywhere else and the early and important monasteries were located at both these towns and at Kauśāmbi.[24] The earlier Jaina *tīrthaṅkara* Pārśvanātha is also associated with towns.[25] It was the towns which provided the renouncers with an audience and later with patronage.

Important towns were capitals of the *janapadas* and were thus either centres of royal patronage or of oligarchic support, depending on whether the state had a monarchical or a *gaṇa* form of government.

The support took the tangible form of offerings and of donations of land for monasteries. Patronage at these social levels was equally effective even when indirect. Thus when Khema, a Madra princess and the queen of Bimbisāra, accepted Buddhism, the fame of the Buddha spread to the distant land of the Madras.[26] When the Mallas were ordered by their assembly, the *santhagāra,* to support the Buddha this greatly enhanced the cause of Buddhism in that *janapada*.[27] Both the Buddhists and the Jainas claim the patronage of the kings of Magadha. Apart from royal patronage there were ministers, bankers and merchants, the *seṭṭhis* and the rich *gahapatis*, who provided *vihāras* for the Buddhist monks.[28] The wealthy *mahāśāla brāhmaṇs* who had received land grants from the king, such as Lohicca and Pokkharasati, were influential persons.[29] In the early years of the Buddhist *saṅgha* the conversions which are singled out for mention were those of the richer *seṭṭhis* and the *brāhmaṇs*. The main body of monks was however drawn from the lower social orders such as artisans, fishermen, hunters, basket-weavers.[30] Similarly, the Mathura inscriptions of the pre-Gupta period indicate support for the Jainas from trading groups, artisans and castes low on the social scale.[31]

The Buddha had greater success among the cities of the monarchical kingdoms. The *kṣatriya* oligarchies were not so forthcoming in their support and some were more partial to the Nirgranthas. The general approval of the Buddhists and Jainas by urban groups was also linked with the ethical views of these sects. Rigorous and extreme ascetic practices although indulged in by some monks were on the whole discouraged. Nor were the earlier shamanistic elements regarded as fundamental. Resorting to the demonstration of *siddhis* was not unknown but in both cases it was permitted only on certain occasions and when persuasive means of conversion through logical argument failed.[32] Some of the symbols of earlier practices such as the sacred tree and the *stūpa* and *caitya* were appropriated into the religious cults. But the emphasis was on knowledge and meditation and the observance of the middle-path (*majjhimā paṭipadā*), eminently suitable for urban householders. Furthermore, both the Buddhists and the Jainas had a distinct role for the lay community vis-a-vis the monks, and in the case of the former the interaction between the *upāsaka* and the *bhikkhu* was an important aspect of monastic functioning. This was partly a reflection of the doctrine of salvation common to a number of heterodox sects where the concern for the lay community is summed up best in the attitude of the Buddha when he uses the parable of the raft, that those who have discovered enlightenment should not keep it to themselves but should leave the raft for the use of others.[33] The social involvement of groups such as the Ājīvikas, Jainas and Buddhists contributed to the manner in which the *saṅgha* developed in each case. Whatever may have been the primary function of the *saṅgha* as a gathering of persons seeking salvation and which continued to dominate the more sectarian angularities within the institution, it very soon also became the main channel through which the sect communicated with the rest of society.

The history of these sects of renouncers moving into new areas follows a similar pattern. It begins with a handful of monks living singly or in small groups in relative isolation in cave sanctuaries (*leṇas*), as for example the hermitages in the vicinity of Rājagṛiha or the habitations dotted in the hills of the Tamil country. The isolation was not total since the caves tended to be on major trade routes or in the vicinity of towns. In more arduous terrain these proto-monasteries often provided welcome staging points as did the later monasteries. This is particularly true of hilly country and mountains such as the routes from the plateau to the coast through the Western Ghats or those across Ladakh and Nepal into Tibet. Monastic establishments thrived near urban centres and in rich agricultural regions where there was a surplus to support the monks. It is not altogether accidental that the initial penetration of the heterodox sects into south India coincides with the Roman trade and the trade with south-east Asia. The expansion of the Mahāsaṅghika sect going from Vaiśāli and Pāṭaliputra south to Andhra carefully avoided the tribal belt south of Magadha. Similarly the Sarvāstivāda spread from Mathura northwards to the Punjab and Kashmir but not into the adjoining areas of Rajasthan where there were well-established tribal areas. Apart from the need for a surplus to support the monks, the ethical teaching of these sects was doubtless more appropriate to richer agriculturalists and urbanites rather than to pastoral and hunting tribal people. The worship of tribal deities and the tribal ethic would hardly be conducive to the acceptance of Buddhism.

Gradually commercial patronage and royal support led to the establishment of a full-fledged *saṅgha* with all its physical edifices and accessories. For the mercantile community the Buddhist and Jaina teaching provided the required ethic.[34] Inscriptional evidence witnesses endowments to the *saṅghas* in every region in the first millennium A.D. The endownments included land, revenue from villages, shops and residences for the monks.[35] There was a noticeable increase in the number of monks and monasteries. So rich and important were some of these centres that the sects came to be named after the place-names of their residence, thus, the Sandeva *gaccha*, and the Kāñci *gaccha* of the Jainas. Royal patrons were well-disposed to the *saṅgha* since they acted as an instrument of acculturation in the new areas, both introducing the Great Tradition as well as assimilating and focusing on the local culture. But royal patronage was also at the root of the destruction of the social involvement of the *saṅgha* as originally perceived. Lavish endowments of land to the monasteries resulted in a greater secularisation of the *saṅgha*. There was a consequent decline in its concern with providing salvation for the lay community and an increase in its concern for acquiring and maintaining authority.

Individual renouncers and those who joined the 'heretical sects' were in the early stages the chief dissenters. Megasthenes' description of the Brachmanes and the Sarmanes living in the forest across the Taprobane is indicative of this.[36] Through a process of historical change many of these dissenting groups in time took on the role of the establishment. The brahmanical theory of the four *āśramas*, first propounded in full in the late *Jabāla Upaniṣad*, brought asceticism into conventional custom by making it the last stage of a man's curriculum and accessible to the upper castes. By implication however the *gṛhastha-āśrama* was a necessary prior requirement. Thus only those who moved directly from *brahmacarya* to *saṃnyāsa* could be called dissenters. An aging *gṛhastha* taking to *saṃnyāsa* was merely conforming to the ideal vita. The heretical *saṅghas* also took on shades of conformism through the acquisition of wealth and power and by association with the ruling elite. At this stage it was necessary for the orthodoxy to consolidate its views on the renouncers and for new groups of renouncers to emerge as the carriers of heresy.

The new groups were to some extent dissidents from among

the renouncers. Both the Buddhist and Jaina sects came under the influence of and incorporated Tantric ideas and practices. Vajrayāna Buddhism with an early nucleus at the Vikramaśīla monastery in Bihar was a reflection of this. It also represented the minor but consistent trend among some Buddhist monks of dabbling in magic and necromancy.[37] The still later Sahajiyā cult among the Buddhists was a protest against the formalities of the life and religion of earlier Buddhism. It questioned the earlier theories of knowledge and emphasized the practice of *yoga*. It was opposed not only to scholarship but also to monasticism,[38] thereby underlining what it regarded as the social irrelevance of monasticism. Up to a point, the Sahajiyā cult can be seen as a return to the twilight area of the shaman.

After the mid-first millennium A.D. when the sects associated with the heterodox religions were on the wane in northern India, there appears to have occurred the spectacular rise of Śaiva monasticism especially in the peninsula. Considering that Śiva is projected as the great ascetic, this is not surprising. Hsüan Tsang refers to various groups associated with 'daiva temples' in the vicinity of towns.[39] These sects and particularly the Kapālikas and Pāśupatas are referred to in earlier literature but are more commonly mentioned in sources from about the seventh century onwards.[40] Clearly there was a gestation period for these monastic orders. From the *Pāśupata Sūtras*, the existence of the Pāśupatas has been dated to at least the second century A.D.[41] The *Purāṇas* regard such groups with contempt.[42] They are mentioned in the inscriptions of the Jainas of the Karnataka with whom there was a sustained relationship of rivalry.[43] The Digambara Jainas were by now concentrated in the Karnataka, well-ensconced in the patronage of traders, merchants and officers of the state.[44] The Kapnālikas had their own patrons who endowed them with land and villages. The sect had a strong likeness to many of the activities and practices of the Tantrics and as such came in for scathing attacks from some of the established social groups. Among the more fierce of its opponents was Śaṅkarācārya who accused the Kapālikas of sexual licence and alcoholism. Another influential Saiva group in the peninsula was that of the Kālāmukhas, sometimes included in the wider category of Pāśupatas. This sect was more sympathetically treated by the orthodox brahmans since it did not question their superiority and, if anything, on occasion subscribed to it. Hsüan Tsang does not refer to distinctively separate monastic organizations associated with these sects although the inscriptions of the subsequent period emphasize this. Possibly this aspect developed after the seventh century A.D. when the survival and effectiveness of dissenting groups once again required the organization of monastic centres, particularly in relation to the competition for patronage and support where some sects with monastic organization were seen to be successful.

By about the ninth century A.D. there had emerged a distinctive group of Śaiva renouncers, the Daśanāmi Samnyāsis. The sect modelled itself on earlier monastic orders with approximately the same broad rules of discipline—permanent residence in monasteries, austerity, celibacy, subsistence on alms and the study and teaching of prescribed texts. The monasteries (*maṭhas*) were attached to temples and these and other properties endowed to the order were administered by the chief of the *maṭha*, the *mahant*.[45] Śaṅkarācārya further organised the Daśanāmi Saṃnyāsis into categories and hierarchies thus simulating the monastic form of earlier sects.[46] The Śaiva *maṭhas* seem to have played the same role as Buddhist and Jaina monasteries, as instruments of acculturation in new areas, since their early distribution was substantially in the peninsula and on the fringes of the heartland in northern India (e.g. Kashmir, Nepal). Śaṅkarācārya's imprint is apparent in as much as the sect took upon itself the defence of the orthodoxy, suggesting perhaps that the earlier heterodoxy had become too influential. The Śaivite tradition appears to have been the indigenous tradition in these areas and Śaiva monasticism grew rapidly. The Daśanāmi sect was organized for deliberate proselytizing, its main competitors being the Buddhists and the Jainas with whom the rivalry was to become acrimonious, and at times violent.[47] Apart from the ideological motives, ambition for power and economic control played its part. It has been plausibly suggested that these monasteries in some ways approximated to feudal authority.[48]

Vaiṣṇavism at this stage did not encourage monasticism. It has been argued that Vaiṣṇavism subsumed *yogà* into the *bhakti* tradition when the *Gītā* speaks of *yoga* as the highest way and the true *yogi* as being one who does not detach himself from society but takes on the suffering of others.[49] Since it is in a sense a salvation religion it did not require the agency of renouncers. The process of *bhakti* in itself offers an alternative to both ritual and asceticism.[50] It may also be suggested that proselytization through monastic groups was not required of Vaiṣṇavism since the theory of *avatāras* acts as an agency of incorporation. Nevertheless, by about the eleventh and twelfth centuries, the Vairāgin or, as it was popularly called, the Bairāgi movement, initiated Vaiṣṇava monastic orders. From the thirteenth century onwards there were violent conflicts between the Saṃnyāsis and the Bairāgis in the competition for status and power.[51]

It was also at about this time that groups of renouncers calling themselves Yogis and propagating the teaching of Gorakhanātha and the Nāthapanthis spread across northern India. The Yogis reflected the growing influence of Tantricism and in their view it was a combination of Haṭhayoga and Tantric practices which were likely to lead to knowledge and fulfilment. The association of Tantricism with Yoga was probably an undercurrent of one strand in the ethos of renouncers since earliest times. Tantricism has to be viewed not as yet another sectarian movement but as a major religious re-orientation, since the fundamentals of Tantricism pervaded the dominant religious forms at many levels. Not only were there Kapālikas among Śaivas and the Rādhā-Kṛṣṇa cult among Vaiṣṇavas, but even the originally more puritanical religious groups, the Buddhists and Jainas, underwent a Tantric phase. Vajrayāna Buddhism acted almost as the harbinger of the arrival of Tantric cults and ideas into the ranks of both established society and the heterodoxy.[52] The Tantric-Yogic combination was predominant in the relatively less Hinduized border regions—the northwest of the subcontinent and Assam, and this may explain it as being a channel by which foreign elements were assimilated into Hinduism coming into importance as it did in the period of such incursions.[53] It may also be said to reflect the rise of the substratum culture coinciding with the social elevation of relatively obscure families and castes in the new areas brought into the political and economic vortex of the Great Tradition via the system of land grants.[54] The *siddhācāryas* of this cult are more frequently of low caste.[55] The substratum culture was opposed to the orthodox tradition, an opposition which came to be symbolically expressed in Tantric ritual, much of which is a reversal of brahman values.[56]

This all too brief survey indicates that the appearance of renouncers as an organized section of society occurs historically at periods of change when there emerge within society not only religious but socio-economic sanctions to maintain such groups, as for example the growth of urban centres and the expansion of the agrarian economy. The religious impetus may come from the need to institutionalize a way of life that is new (the Ājīvika, Jaina and Buddhist *saṅghas*) or as a strategy for proselytizing (the Daśanāmi Saṃnyāsis and the Bairāgis) or as a means of crystallizing a popular religious ethos and providing it with status (the Tantric sects and the Yogis). Not all such sects were opposed to orthodoxy, but the technique of using social heresy was employed to organize a religious identity, and the sects therefore registered various degrees and stages of non-conformity. The Buddhist, Jaina and Ājīvika monks were opposed to brahmanical orthodoxy but the expression of their dissidence took on a puritanical form, in which certain social mores were ultimately strengthened but the manifestations of brahmanical religion were discarded. The groups influenced by Tantricism accepted some of the religious symbols but discarded many of the social mores. The Daśanāmi Saṃnyāsis supported brahmanical orthodoxy but did not conform to the brahmanical view of *saṃnyāsa* in the setting up of monastic centres.

The historical pattern therefore carries within it a range of divergencies. The ideals of brahmanical *saṃnyāsa* are opposed by the renouncers of various persuasions, such as the Ājīvikas, Jainas and Buddhists, who organize themselves into monastic units and who are characterized by an ethic of moderation in action. The notion of monastic organization is then taken up by other groups when it becomes socially necessary for purposes of recognition and support. Some such as the Daśanāmi orders are created to counteract the growth of other religious sects and to propagate orthodoxy. Others such as the Pāśupata and Kapālika sects retain an extreme stance abhorent to orthodoxy. It has been suggested that the Pāśupatas were shamans *manqués* with their vows of beast-imitation and sexual practices,[57] a suggestion which has interesting possibilities vis-a-vis the tradition of later Tantric cults as well. The Vaiṣṇava monastic orders eventually take on the role of competing with the Daśanāmis. The influence of Tantric beliefs and practices extends to all the religious groups and initially it acts as a dissenting line of thought and action. Eventually, groups such as the Sahajiyās produce their own opposition to the Tantrics.

Cutting across the chronological scheme is the lineal descent of certain trends. The *brāhmaṇ saṃnyāsin* remains largely unchanged, playing a role of social conformism but with a potential of protest should he have wished to use it. The renouncer, associated with an ethic of moderation remains primarily within the order of the Buddhists and the Jainas, which however develop their own orthodoxy and become increasingly less linked with dissent. The more shamanistic groups tend to be those opposed to all forms of orthodoxy and consequently carry an immediate potential of protest. Furthermore, the institution of the monastery acts as a curtailment on dissent. There seem to be two phases in the evolution of such groups: the pre-monastic, where the element of protest is stronger, and the monastic, when concessions have been made to conformity.

To the extent that historical change led to the emergence of these sects, the sect itself underwent transformation reflecting historical change. The holding of Councils, characteristic of Buddhism and Jainism, indicates new regional and social demands and schismatic tendencies pointing to a groping towards adjustment in an effort to stabilize. Most of the issues under debate at these councils related to the rules of behaviour and the organization of the monastery—food and the acceptance of money offerings for example. Where the nuances of interpreting the doctrine were at issue the problem could often be traced back to a social cause. The rules of almost every sect underwent change with the gradual accretion of rituals, the introduction of new forms of worship, the deification of the founders and, above all, the encroachment of the lay and monastic communities on each other. It is these 'inner contradictions,' as it were, of orthodoxy and heresy and schism which develop within each sect and which preclude the historian from describing them as either orthodox or heretical in every situation and for all time.

For our purposes, the most important aspect of the social role of the renouncer is the relationship between the renouncer and the lay community. The initial relationship is perhaps best seen in the bi-polarity between the *brāhmaṇ* and the *saṃnyāsin*.[58] Hinduism, it has been said, is a dialogue between these two, where the *brāhmaṇ* represents the religion of the group, assimilative and well-established, whereas the *saṃnyāsin* represents the salvation of the individual, exclusive and separated from society. This bi-polartiy is apparent in much of the symbolism which distinguishes the renouncer from conventional society. The brahmanical ideal of the ascetic was based on a denial of any form of reciprocity between the *saṃnyāsin* and society, thus negating a major focus in Hindu social action, namely reciprocity.[59] But the ideal was rarely observed and more often than not the relationship between the *saṃnyāsin* and *gṛhastha* came to the fore. This was certainly historically the richer and more complex relationship where the bi-polarity of the two takes on a dialectical interconnection. The outward symbols by which the renouncer was recognized were often anathema to brahmanical orthodoxy, but the root of the contradiction of *saṃnyāsa* as a social phenomenon lay in the negation of the social function of *gṛhastha* by the *saṃnyāsin*. The two are polar opposites and yet dependent on each other. The lay community provides material support for the renouncer through *dāna* (gifts and offerings) and alms, and in turn the merit, *puṇya,* accumulated by the renouncer is in part transferred to the lay community. In each case the relationship is initially sharply differentiated and the difference is expressed in the adoption of totally opposite symbols. Gradually the differentiation becomes blurred and, although the symbols may continue, the relationship begins to overlap.

The bi-polarity is made very evident by the totally contradictory rules of discipline as applied to the householder and the renouncer. There is first of all an initiation ceremony at the time of entering *saṃnyāsa*[60] which indicates the renouncing of one's social obligations and ties and opting out of the society into which one was born. Where the entry is according to the ultimate *āśrama*, the *saṁskāra* becomes a life-cycle rite. The concession to *saṃnyāsa* as the ultimate *āśrama* was perhaps to prevent renunciation among young men. To that degree it would also have acted as a check on active dissenters. That *saṃnyāsa* in one's old age, when one's obligations to society had been fulfilled, was gaining the best of both worlds, is reflected in some texts in the debate on the legitimacy of such *saṃnyāsa*, since in old age celibacy and the giving up of property is not too difficult. The true *saṃnyāsin* should avoid the state of *gṛhastha*. The ceremony of the Hindu *saṃnyāsin,* at whatever age he entered *saṃnyāsa,* symbolized his death to society and the acceptance of a life ultimately attached to loneliness and complete self-reliance. He was required therefore to quench the sacrificial fires and perform his own *śrāddha* ceremony. For the *saṃnyāsin* entering an order this was ameliorated as it was in the case of a *bhikkhu* where one life-style, that of the householder, was substituted by that of the community of monks, where the refuge of society was replaced by the refuge of the order and the monastery. The trauma of the change softened by the creation of a new tie, that between the novice and the *ācārya* or *guru*, since in all cases the renouncer had to begin his renunciation under the tutelage of a teacher. The Buddha emphasized that this relationship should be as one between a father and son.

The *gṛhastha* enters his *āśrama* with the reverse values, where he is being introduced to his social obligations and attachment to a family. The procreation of his own family becomes essential to this condition, whereas the renouncer has to remain celibate. Celibacy was a necessary condition to all sects of renouncers although in some of the more extreme Tantric acts ritualized sex was required.[61] The householder concerns himself with the acquisition of material possessions and property for the welfare of the family whereas the renouncer forswears any claims to property or possessions other than a few symbols of his new status.[62] The insistence on the renouncer being a wanderer (a rule which was observed until the sect became prosperous and powerful) was mainly to prevent the development of any attachment, either with the lay community or with fellow monks and *saṃnyāsis*.[63] It also encouraged the notion of individual salvation. The concept of *ahiṃsā* in daily routine was easier in the observance for the renouncer,[64] a case in point being the precautions taken by Jaina monks to clear the ground from living beings before stepping on it and wearing cloth masks to prevent the breathing in of insects. The renouncer was forbidden any kind of profession or occupation and, more particularly, manual labour. This again sharpened the difference between him and the householder. The former was expected to spend his time in study, meditation and the purification of the mind and the body by the practice of *prāṇāyāma* and *yoga*,[65] all of which were, from the material point of view, counter-productive.

Further distinctions were made in the breaking of food tabus. The monks and the *saṃnyāsins* were forbidden from doing their own cooking and could receive only cooked food as alms.[66] This was a contradiction of the *brāhmaṇ* otherwise being permitted to accept only uncooked food from non-*brāhmaṇs* and cooked food only from those of the appropriate caste. The *brāhmaṇ saṃnyāsin,* in one text, is told to avoid food from *śūdra* houses[67] but there was no prohibition on this. Some *brāhmaṇ* ascetic groups however did observe the normal restrictions by living in isolation in forests and surviving on fruit and roots, thus eschewing altogether the acceptance of alms. But this was possible only to those who lived alone or in small groups, such as the ascetics mentioned by Megasthenes.[68] It is interesting that historical references to such groups become more limited in later periods when monastic orders develop. The Jainas had elaborate rules regarding the acceptability of food even within the limitations of living off alms.[69] Further, the fact that food was eaten together in an assembly (irrespective of whether it was collected through alms or cooked for the monastery as in later times), also undermined the rules of caste commensality. Dietary rules differed among the sects. Generally, animal food and alcohol were forbidden. Some groups deliberately contravened this and the *Kanphaṭā Jogis* ate meat, drank alcohol and indulged in narcotics. The *Aghoris* made a fetish of this principle by feeding on human corpses. The eating of meat and fish and the drinking of alcohol were ritualistically prescribed in some of the Tantric sects.

Visual appearance underlined the separation between the householder and the renouncer and was symbolic of the new life-style of the latter. The renouncer was either naked or else wore clothing of a distinctive colour—red, ochre or white—or of a distinctive kind, as for example, unstitched robes. The head was either tonsured or else the hair was unkempt (*jaṭā*). The latter signified a condition of power through danger in as much as hair signified virility and aggression.[70] The Buddhists and the Jainas on the other hand made a ritual out of depilation, perhaps initially to demarcate themselves from *brāhmaṇ jaṭila saṃnyāsins*. Most *saṃnyāsins* carried an alms-bowl and a staff and some identified their sect with a tilak. The *daṇḍa* or staff was so characteristic that the early ascetics were called *maskarin*, i.e. those of the bamboo staff, *maskara*. The later word *daṇḍa* might also have been associated with the secular extension of the meaning of *daṇḍa*, authority. Living in a monastery again demarcated the habitational area of the renouncer from that of the lay community. The final and most symbolic of the oppositions was that the ascetic among Hindu sects was to be buried in a sitting posture and his *samādhī* came to be regarded as a sacred enclosure, an object of veneration. The householder was cremated in a common cremation ground which has always been a place of great impurity, fit only for the *caṇḍālas*. In some cases, the adoption of certain symbols was not merely the breaking of social tabus but also the deliberate cultivation of the horrendous—association with dirt, excreta and corpses—in order to highlight the disassociation with 'normal' society. The courting of dishonour was on occasion deliberately designed to shock the public and attract attention. In the case of the Pāśupatas the justification for this has its own interest.[71] By simulating an anti-social action the Pāśupata was believed to acquire the merit of the observer who unnecessarily reviles him and the bad *karma* of the Pāśupata is transferred to the observer.

The adoption of outward symbols has its own contrapuntal pattern. The *brāhmaṇ* ascetics who kept matted locks, ate uncooked food such as fruit and roots in the forest or accepted alms and ate in the evening, lived beneath trees and emaciated their bodies were directly contradicting the mores of the Buddhist and Jaina *bhikkhus* who demanded depilation, ate only cooked food in the forenoon, and lived in *vihāras,* many among them keeping away from extreme physical austerities. It is only in the acceptance of religious suicide as the ideal manner of dying, and which was abhorrent to the orthodox, that there was agreement, although the particular form in which the suicide was to be achieved differed.

Inherent in the need for this differentiation is not merely the opting out of the existing life-style and substituting it with a distinctively different one but also that the characteristics of the new life-style be seen as a protest against the existing one. To this extent such movements may be regarded as movements of dissent.[72] But the element of protest was muted by the wish, not to change society radically, but to stand aside and create an alternative system. Ideally, salvation lay in joining a sect of renouncers. Some sects such as the Ājīvikas made this conditional to salvation. Others conceded that this was not open to everyone and a via media was suggested, as for example the *upāsaka* or periodic renunciation as among the Buddhists. Ultimately, when the renouncers were themselves viewed as having fallen short of the ideal, they were denounced. This could result in the emergence of schismatic groups. Initially, it was dissent which led to a splitting off from society or an established sect and the renouncers formed elements of a counter-culture. Eventually, many became dependent on society. The splitting off was often led by those who, disgruntled with the order/sect, took a lone path in their search for salvation. Nevertheless the sects of renouncers did create a climate of opinion in which the legitimacy of dissidence was conceded. It is a moot point as to whether such sects can be called protest movements per se or whether they are manifestations of a sustained counter-culture which, from time to time, reacts to social pressures and throws up movements which carry, among other things, traces of social protest. The ultimate in dissidence was still the *parivrājaka* who did not join any order and wandered alone, or for that matter even the isolated *saṃnyāsin*.

One aspect of the dissidence was that, in theory at least, most sects of renouncers disregarded caste observances. There was a debate on whether the two symbols of brahmanhood, the top-knot (*śikhā*) and the sacred thread (*yajñopavīta*), should be retained by *brāhmaṇ saṃnyāsins;*[73] as also the controversy on whether *śūdras* should be recruited as a separate sect, as in some of the later *saṃnyāsin akhārās*.[74] In the main, the *Dharmasūtras,* the Epics and the *Purāṇas* are averse to the idea of *śūdra* ascetics[75] indicating that renunciation was open only to *brāhmaṇs*. Among the Ājīvikas, Buddhists and Jainas, the sect was open to any caste. The physical proximity of all castes in a congregation was also a contradiction of certain caste restrictions. Among some Tantric sects there were no caste identities since all males were considered as forming one caste and all females another.[76] The Sahajiyā cult was unambiguous in its attack on the status of the *brāhmaṇ* and caste society in general.[77] Nor was it only a protest against caste. The preaching of universal values with universal application and the notion of transcendence in the theories of knowledge of such sects was itself a denial of the dominant social values and was implicitly a questioning of the religious beliefs and groups whose identity focused on caste affiliations.

However, religious universalism was also sometimes used for what appears to be a form of social manipulation. The Kālāmukha

Saṃnyāsins, for example, claimed *brāhmaṇ* status and took the name ending of *paṇḍita-deva*, and were often the defenders of *varṇāśramadharma*.[78] One may wonder whether the sect was not used by some non-*brāhmaṇs* to acquire individual *brāhmaṇ* status, since one of the signs of brahmanhood—Vedic and Sanskrit learning—was available to and encouraged among the members of the sect. In this connection it is interesting that the priests of the Yogi caste in Bengal associated with the Nātha cult have been referred to as *rudraja brāhmaṇs*, deriving their origin from Rudra and eventually claiming to belong to a 'Śiva' *gotra*.[79] This would be a case of using the alternative system to acquire status.

The break with society and the anonymity of the new entrant were sought to be established by the taking of a new name. The latter indicated the new identity in terms of the monastery (thus Mahānāma points to a connection with the Mahāvihāra), or the sect (Digvijayanātha indicates a Nāthapanthi), or the desire for the attainment of *mokṣa* (as in the use of *ānanda* as part of the name) or to the degree of attainment (as reflected in the titles such as *avadhūta* or *paramahaṅsa*). Each of the *maṭhas* established by Śaṅkarācārya was said to have been associated with a *gotra*[80] (as for example, the *kāśyapagotra* with the Govardhana *maṭha* at Puri) and the members of the *maṭha* would take on its *gotra*, thus subscribing to a form of Sanskritisation.

The negation of the family as a basic unit of society is evident from the opposition to the *gṛhastha* status and especially the insistence on celibacy. This can also be seen as perhaps an avoidance rather than an infringement of the fundamental rule of caste organization, namely, the prohibition on inter-caste marriage. Women, whether as nuns in the Buddhist and Jaina orders or as *parivrājakās*, were on the whole grudgingly accepted. Nuns were always under the jurisdiction of the monks and in both orders were regarded as an inferior category.[81] This was in spite of the fact that occasionally women of the royal families became nuns, although the majority were from less exalted social groups.

The effectiveness of an alternative life-style could not remain an arbitrary process beyond a certain historical point. The *parivrājakas* and *śramaṇas* of the *Upaniṣads* had, for a variety of reasons, to identify themselves as groups rather than move about as individual wanderers. The authoritarian trends in the states emerging in the mid-first millennium B.C. were not always sympathetic to wanderers.[82] They were often seen as people escaping social responsibility or socio-political demands. Their survival as free thinkers was dependent on their being able to assert the right to an alternative life from a position of institutional security. Only then could they obtain the political rights of passage so essential to their existence. Furthermore, their continuity in an egalitarian parallel system could only be safeguarded if their leaders could confront political authority as powerful heads of sects. The social ineffectiveness of the actions of individuals was demonstrated by the effectiveness of the group. Among the early efforts at assembling groups around specific doctrines were, as we have seen, the sects of the Cārvākas and Ājīvikas.[83] But in order to be effective a name was not enough, a physical habitation was also necessary. This contributed to the evolution of the monastery.

The monastic institution grew out of a need for a permanent residence during the rainy season when mendicancy was difficult. Such seasonal residences (*āvāra)* gradually acquired a longer duration in the *ārāma,* often a park endowed by an individual to the *saṅgha.* such as the Ambavana of Jīvaka at Rājagriha. Ultimately, the settlement of monks expanded into a *vihāra*, a regular monastic complex. In the organization of such a monastery the features of the parallel society are apparent. There is an attempt at imitating the structure of the tribal and oligarchic systems. The hierarchy of units in the Jaina *saṅgha* uses a terminology which is reminiscent of the lineage structure of the earlier tribes—*gaṇa*, *kula, śākhā, anvaya* and *gaccha.* In the Buddhist *saṅgha,* the general assembly of monks was the sovereign authority and even the *saṅghathera* had to abide by its decision.[84] The emphasis on frequent assemblies and unanimous decisions is stressed in the early literature. Every ordained monk was a member of the *saṅgha* and all monks living within the jurisdiction of a particular monastery had to be present at the *uposatha* assembly. Ownership of property vested with the *saṅgha* and never with the individual monk. (In later centuries, however, the shares of the monks in the monastic property led to some of them acquiring a substantial personal wealth.)[85] Grievances against individual monks were discussed at the assembly as also any breach of monastic regulations or the rules of the sect.[86] The ritual of initiation into the *saṅgha* was similar to that of adoption into the tribe, adoption being the only means of entry into both.[87] Underlying the structure of the monastery was the emphasis on conjoint action and discipline and the strict enforcement of monastic regulations. The monastery was not the place for those seeking absolute freedom, for whom asceticism in isolation was preferable. The monastery provided an alternative only to those who opted out of social obligations.

The functioning of the *saṅgha* has been described as an attempt to retrieve the fast vanishing past.[88] It may be argued that the form adopted was also in deliberate opposition to the monarchical system and its centralized power, which system is otherwise seen as ideal for society and to which the lay community is required to give its loyalty.[89] This again serves to underline the distinction between the lay community and the monastic group, where the latter takes on the nuances of a primitive commune, perhaps echoing the utopian egalitarianism of pristine society.[90] Or did the *saṅghas* in newly monarchical societies act as 'safety valves' for the containment of political dissidence, taking on the role of egalitarian sanctuaries?

The relative absence of hierarchy in the monastic structure was however not a permanent feature. The goods and services of monastic living required that some monks be designated the distributors of food (*bhatuddesaka*), accommodation and furniture (*senāsanagāhāpaka*), robes (*cīvarapaṭiggāhaka*)[91] etc.; with donations and endowments, administrative infrastructures became necessary. The revenue from endowed lands had to be collected, the interest from donations to be recorded.[92] Annual dues had to be shared out among the monks who were resident in wealthy monasteries and the profits from endowed lands distributed after meeting the annual expenses. Repairs to old buildings and the construction of new buildings had to be supervised by those monks appointed as *ārāmapesakas*.[93] Administrative responsibilities not only cut into the normal functions of a monk but also required an administrative hierarchy within the monastery. This increased its participation in the local economic life. The monastic calendar increasingly coincided with the agricultural calendar.[94] Ultimately, the monastery was legitimized as a socio-economic institution through the myths explaining its origin, through the establishment of the Vinaya Laws which became the legal code of monastic groups and through the acquiring of an historical identity.[95]

The establishment of the Śaiva monasteries was not a dissimilar process. Śaṅkarācārya is said to have organized *saṃnyāsi* groups on a functional basis by the arrangement of ten orders among the *saṃnyāsins*[96] and by setting up four major monastic nucleii, the four *maṭhas* at Dvārkā, Badrī, Purī and Sṛngerī, with clearly demarcated territorial jurisdiction. Distinctions of sectarian loyalty within the Daśanāmi Saṃnyāsis were evident from the accessories which they carried such as the design of the staff, the type of *rudrākṣa-mālā* and the *tilak*. Contact within the monastic network throughout the country was maintained by *saṃnyāsins* of the same sect going on regular pilgrimages and visiting other *maṭhas* in different parts of the country. The regular assemblies of Śaiva ascetics at the time of festivals in the major pilgrim centres was another means of inter-monastic communication and administration. The proliferation of land grants in the early medieval period accelerated the prosperity of many *maṭhas* as did the donations to the temples attached to these *maṭhas*, converting them into semi-administrative units with a tangible economic viability in agriculture and trade. This prosperity was enhanced by the fact that *saṃnyāsins* and their institutions were free from any taxes,[97] which was a boon in the period after the eighth century A.D., when taxes tended to multiply.

Even more far removed from the ascetic ideal was the organization of the *akhārās*, or military wings of the *maṭhas*. The earliest of these, believed to go back to the ninth or tenth century A.D., were of the Daśanāmi Nāgas. They were maintained by wealthy *maṭhas* almost as a regiment of mercenary soldiers. Some sources maintain that the *akhārās* were manned by *śūdra* recruits.[98] The emphasis was on physical prowess and skilful weaponry, which were used to full effect in later periods in the battles with the Bairāgis.[99] The para-military basis of the *akhārās* is clear from the fact that they were arranged in a hierarchy of importance, the protocol of which was strictly observed at festivals and *melās* when they assembled. Each *akhārā* had its own banner and insignia of identification. The financial maintenance of the *akhārā* came from the lands and buildings owned by the *maṭha*, the offerings and donations made at the temple, a variety of religious levies and participation by the *maṭha* in local banking and commercial activities.

In the eyes of the lay community, the acquisition of an historical identity was crucial to the transformation of the sect and the monastery into a social institution and to the bestowal of a legitimacy reaching into the past. The historical tradition was put together in various ways. A list of succession of the Elders of the monastery was preserved where each dissident monastic sect would mark its break by maintaining a variant list. Thus the Theravāda and Sarvāstivāda lists vary as can be seen in their respective literatures.[100] Similarly there is mention of the succession in the Kālāmukha *maṭha* attached to the Kedāreśvara temple at Belegave.[101] The lists of succession of the nine Nāthas vary from region to region.[102] Founders of sects and important personalities associated with their growth became the subjects of sections of the *Ācārańgasūtra* and *Kalpasūtra* on Mahāvīra, or of Ānandagirī's *Śańkaravijaya*. Sometimes the history of an event was sought to be established by associating a known personality, preferably a king, with the event: thus Ajātaśatru features in Buddhist and Jaina literature and Aśoka in Buddhist literature.[103] Even more effective was the attempt to compile the history of a particular monastery and relate it to the state, such as the Mahāvihāra monastery in the *Mahāvaṃsa*. The history of the sect itself could result in a substantial inclusion of the history of the region such as the *Dīpavaṃsa* in Śri Lanka Tāranātha's *History of Buddhism in India*. At a more local level, the histories of regions or areas, such as the *Śrimāla Mahātmya* of the Jainas, were collections of information, factual and fanciful, on places of sectarian importance, associating the place with the sect. Such records claiming to be historically valid were also necessary to prove the legitimacy of the institution in disputes over property and juridical rights. With the development of missionary activities, these historical antecedents could be used in the balance of power with secular institutions.

The evolution of the monastic institution (irrespective of the religious sect to which it belonged) into a form where it participated to a substantial degree in secular life was in a sense self-annihilating. This participation, especially in economic life, tended to erode the notion of a counter-culture and strengthen that of a parallel society. In the early stages, the reach of the *vihāra* or the *maṭha* into secular economic life was limited and was related at a simple level to redistribution and reciprocity. Redistribution was enforced by the lay community having to maintain the renouncer on alms and by the making of donations and endowments. For the ordinary householder, the feeding of monks was sufficient. For the rich householder, there was the providing of oil and clothing, the repairing and building of monasteries and, for even wealthier patrons, the endowment of land. Reciprocation lay in the tying of *dāna* to *puṇya*, where, in exchange for alms and donations, the householder acquired merit. But when the *dāna* was of a nature that enabled the monastery to lead its own independent existence, the distance from the lay community increased, the reciprocation of *puṇya* became reduced and the character and the role of the monastery underwent a change. This in turn undermined notions of social protest.[104] This was further intensified in situations where the monastery played a major role in the urban or rural economy.[105]

The reciprocal relationship between the lay community and the *saṅgha/maṭha* was pivotal to the making of a parallel society and can be seen at various levels. Royal patronage was the source of reciprocity at the political level. Patronage was of two varieties: there was the direct endowment of caves, monasteries, residences, the revenue from villages and lands to the sects;[106] and there was the indirect support derived from royal investment in commerce and manufacturing guilds, the interest from which was donated to monastic needs.[107] Thus the nexus of royal patronage and the sect was woven into the rural and urban economy. The monasteries in such situations provided a variety of services. Each sectarian group maintained a network of links and control over a large geographical area and thereby helped to build a political base as well. If the sect was politically loyal to the king the monasteries which they controlled would act as focal points in the diffusion of this loyalty, thus providing a further support for the administration. The interplay between the sect and political authority is reflected in those situations where rules of discipline relating to the former may be modified to placate the latter. This it would seem was the main reason for the Buddha prohibiting the recruitment to the monastery of officers in royal service (*rajabhaṭas*), slaves and offenders against the law.[108] The monasteries had access to a large local base in the lay community and could be mobilised to provide a focus for public opinion and possibly even provide political legitimacy to the king. One of the channels for exercising public opinion was through the educational function performed by the *saṅgha* and the *maṭha*. The orientation of the religious institution would inevitably become at least a part of the subconscious of the lay community. This was further strengthened with the emergence of these institutions as the centres of artistic and intellectual life in the community.

For the more powerful richly endowed monasteries, a political role became a necessity.[109] The relative independence of the monastic institution was a threat to political authority. At the individual level, monks and *gurus* were influential and many functioned as advisers through the office of the *rājagurus* to kings and administrators.[110] Not all the incumbents of this office were *brāhmaṇs*. Some of the Kālāmukha monks were preceptors to kings. Theoretically, Jaina monks were supposed to preserve political neutrality by refraining from friendship with kings, royal officers and administrators.[111] However, in the Gaṅga and Hoysaḷa kingdoms they were active participants in political policies and king-making, and in Rajasthan and Gujarat were closely associated with royalty. They had the advantages both of a high degree of literacy and of close links with the banking and financial groups, both of which the royal family could not ignore. With the patronage of royalty and wealthy citizens providing such an expansive area of social intrusion, it is not surprising that the competition for this patronage among the sects sometimes took a violent turn.

A less quantifiable reciprocity between the monasteries and the lay community related to the former providing an ethic and discipline for the latter. This emerged from and complemented the activities of a particular social group which supported the sect. The Buddhist attitude to the laity illustrates the point most clearly. A distinction was made between the general run of lay followers and those who were especially devoted to and closely associated with the *saṅgha*, namely the *upāsakas*. This rippling out of the degrees of support strengthened the position of the *saṅgha*, vis-a-vis the lay community. The majority of the *upāsakas* were *gahapatis* and in the *gahapativagga* sections of some of the *Nikāyas*, their problems in accepting the teaching and discipline of the *saṅgha* are discussed. Central to these was the inability of the *gahapati* to detach himself from worldly possessions particularly the accumulation of gold, property, servants, etc.[112] The category of *upāsaka* seems to have been created to circumvent this problem so that the *gahapati* could be associated with the *saṅgha* as more than just a lay follower without renouncing his attachment to all possessions. Thus the duties of the *upāsakas* were not only to maintain the *saṅgha* but also to look after the welfare of their own families. The moral precepts required of the *upāsaka* focused on the puritan ethic of austerity, saving and investment, as much as on being generous in making donations to the *saṅgha*[113] —the two not being entirely unrelated. Some of the abstinences prescribed for *uposatha* days were required of the *upāsaka* but none of these were especially arduous and the promise of wealth and prosperity (among other things such as attaining heaven) was the reward. The directions given to women lay followers in particular, underline the requirements of a well-to-do housewife attending to the well-being of her husband and his material comfort.[114]

Overt concern with the lay community is not so clearly ascertainable from the literature and practices of sects other than the Buddhists and the Jainas. But, by and large, the providing of an ethic remains an essential part of the relationship. The Daśanāmi sects provide a base for Hindu orthodoxy to the same extent as the Tantric sects reversed the ideals of this orthodoxy. The social groups from which they sought their support were of course not the same and, upto a point, the sects were embodying the ethical systems which these social groups found most conducive. The advantage to the lay community, quite apart from the acquisition of merit and other non-material rewards, was that their ethical systems were validated and imbued with moral authority when they were seen to emanate from a body of renouncers.

The moral authority of the renouncers was derived from two sources. One was the non-tangible psychological relationship with the lay community based on the charisma of the renouncer. The other lay in the apparent contradiction of a social nexus based on the repudiation of society which we have been attempting to discuss in this paper.

The charisma of the renouncer has been a continuing feature of Indian society. The great men of the tradition include those who are seen as successful ascetics. There is no limit to their power for even the gods fear them.[115] The authority of the ascetic is not only of parallel stature but often exceeds that of kings, for the ascetic is associated with powers beyond the ordinary, symbolised as magical powers. It is this which attracts the respect and awe of the lay community. Here the achievements of the individual isolated ascetic imbued with mystical powers rub off onto the renouncer in the monastery and add to the prestige of the latter. The charisma is seen at the simplest level in the fact that the renouncer is able to detach himself from material possessions. Furthermore, he is celibate and yet, at the same time, the most virile of men.[116] The ascetic's demonstration of sexual prowess is not a contradiction in terms: it is in fact a demonstration of his complete control over body functions, since ideally the emission of semen is prohibited to him.[117] Sexual practices were associated with this and with magic and both of these became a prerequisite for claims to mystical powers. They were insisted upon even in the ritualized sexual practices of Tantric sects, which practices were essential to detachment from the normal rules of morality.[118] The mystical element was enhanced by the association of fecundity and sanctity with sexual union performed on ritual occasions. This had antecedents in the *aśvamedha* and *mahāvrata* ceremonies.[119]

Celibacy or, alternatively, ritualised sexual practices were not however the main component of the charisma. It lay as much in the magical powers derived from the comprehension of bodily functions and from knowledge ensuing out of prolonged meditation. The search for knowledge often led to non-conformist directions. This involved experimenting with the human body at a physical level, either by using external aids such as hallucinogens or by manipulating the functions of the organs of the body such as breathing, pulse- and heart-beat and either extending or atrophying the muscles. Experimenting with states of mind took the form of exercises in meditation. Some of these practices went back to the shamanistic practices of at least the Vedic period if not earlier. Others evolved with the coming of new knowledge, both genuine and spurious, which tended to gravitate in non-conformist circles.

Theories of knowledge was yet another area in which the renouncers sometimes functioned as dissenters. These ranged from the development of logic and analytical concepts to secret cults antagonistic to orthodoxy. The early groups, as we have seen, objected to Vedic orthodoxy and the tradition of received knowledge. They sought experiential knowledge or tried to understand it as a function of the intellect. Yogic powers achieved through *tapas* were seen as a manifestation of control over the human body extending into the mind. Levitation, flight and invisibility were possible through yogic power.[120] The generally non-conformist trend among such sects was in part a search for a non-orthodox comprehension of knowledge and in part a means of asserting power through claiming to know the incomprehensible. Emanating from this was, on the one hand, the development of philosophical schools and, on the other, the exercise of what was generally regarded as non-conformist knowledge. Among the latter, medicine attracted attention as also did alchemy (*dhātuvidyā, rasāyanavidyā*). In neither case was the knowledge tabu in orthodox circles but the investigation was hedged round with social restrictions. The ascetic tradition emphasized experimentation and demonstration which was antithetical to the scholastic tradition.

The interest in medicine can be related to yogic exercises where the aim is to control breathing (*prāṇāyāma*), to understand the structure and inter-connection of various parts of the body, to prolong life by these processes and by the use of certain vegetable and mineral matter, and, in the understanding of the mind, the use of hypnosis, hallucination and meditation. Nāgārjuna in a sense sums it up when he refers to the transformation of *prakṛti* (substance) by the use of *oṣadhi* and *samādhi*.[121] Patañjali in the Kaivalyapada of the *Yogasūtra* states that *siddhi* can be attained by the application of a herb, and the commentators explain this as a reference to *rasāyana*.[122] It is not surprising that the earliest of the major compendia on medicine, that of Suśruta is associated with Nāgārjuna.[123] Nor is it strange that Taxila, apart from being a culturally cosmopolitan town with important Buddhist monasteries, was equally renowned as a centre of medical knowledge. That some form of approximate medicine was practised by ascetic sects is mentioned specifically by Megasthenes in his description of the *sarmanes*.[124] In the Buddhist and Jaina tradition, attending to the medical well-being of the lay community is incumbent upon the monk.[125]

The interest in alchemy developed in the early centuries A.D., presumably when both mercury and sulphur were available and their properties familiar.[126] Nāgārjuna, the Buddhist philosopher, is described as being conversant with alchemy.[127] A Chinese source refers to an Indian taken to China by Wan Hsuan Tse in the seventh century A.D. who claimed that he knew the substance for prolonging life.[128] The early medieval period saw a considerable interest in alchemy among certain Jaina groups and later among Yogi sects associated with Tantricism.[129] The fascination lay in two processes fundamental to alchemy—sublimation and transmutation.[130] Through sublimation the structure of the metal was decoded and could be changed. Transmutation was the actual changing of one metal into another, the most common attempt being to change bronze or copper into gold. Both these processes had an analogy with yoga—the changing of bodily structures to enable the body to be transmuted into one capable of performing feats beyond the normal and gaining new perceptions. The connection with Tantric practice can be subtle but apparent, as for example in the statement that Hara and Gauri (mercury and mica) must combine in order to produce a new substance[131]—a clearly sexual symbolism for the transformation of substances. The close connection of alchemy with medical knowledge was through the use of various metals in medication.

Much of this knowledge remained secret, passed on orally from the *guru* to the novice. Eventually the secrecy became a cult and developed its own language, as for example the *sandhā-bhāṣa*,[132] which helped not only to perpetuate the cult and permit free communication among its practitioners, but also protected the *yogi* from the non-initiate and separated him from the profane universe.[133] Some Tantric sects do generally stand out as being different and it has been plausibly argued that their materialism contributed to concepts of the physical sciences. The *dehavāda* tradition led to their taking an interest in human anatomy and these sects argued that the brain was the seat of consciousness and not the heart.[134] In their alchemical ideas, emphasis was placed on experiment and observation, as is evident from the eighth century text, the *Rasaratnākara*. (Whether the enhanced interest in the conversion of base metal into gold was motivated entirely by the wish to control the magical alchemical process or whether it was due to a shortfall in the availability of gold still requires to be investigated. The interest seems to coincide with the decline of supplies of gold from Central Asia and the hoarding of golden objects in temples. However, other sources of supply such as west Asia were also becoming available.)

Experimentation in the use of hallucinogens was primarily to achieve heightened perception and these are described in detail in the *Yogasūtra*, the *Abhidharmakoṣa* and certain Buddhist texts. This was also part of the tradition of non-conformist knowledge since hallucinogens change perception even if they do not transmute bodily substances. That these experiments were only for the initiates was clearly stated. The ritual of the use of hallucinogens had moved from the *soma* rites of the Vedic sacrifices, where it was part of the mainstream of orthodox ritual, to the twilight areas of secret, heretical practices, indicating thereby the change which the orthodoxy itself had undergone, particularly in its attitude towards experimentation and perception.

The charisma of the renouncer therefore derived from the practice and pursuit of non-orthodox knowledge, which provided one aspect of the ultimate moral authority of the renouncer. Equally important was the fact of their creating an alternate or parallel society. The renouncers demonstrated their power by maintaining a recognized style of life without resort to any profession. The prohibition on manual labour highlighted their ability to live off society: yet they were not *of* society. The renouncers were above and beyond the conventional laws, for they conformed to their own laws and these were often in contradiction to the accepted social laws. This gave them added prestige as it also gave them the freedom to protest against the laws of normal society. The form which their protest took was the flouting of social convention. The accommodation of this protest, and the investing of it with charisma and moral authority, has been in a sense characteristic of Indian society. But it has also been subject to the fact that, ultimately, the society of the renouncers had to be supported by the lay community. The opposition inherent in the status of *gṛhastha* and *saṃnyāsa* remains, but the relationship is essentially dialectical, for the one cannot exist without the other. Changes within the lay community affected the community of renouncers and the lay community was, in turn, influenced by them. The acceptance of the renouncer as a necessary counter-weight to conventional society may account for the continuing authority of the renouncer.

REFERENCES AND NOTES

I am grateful to my colleagues, Drs. Suvira Jaiswal, B.D. Chattopadhyaya and R. Champakalakshmi for their comments on this paper.

1. M. Eliade, *Yoga* (Princeton. 1971).
2. K.N. Jayatilleke, *Early Buddhist Theory of Knowledge* (London, 1963); A.L. Basham, *The History and Doctrine of the Ājīvikas* (London, 1951).
3. A. Eschmann, 'Religion, Reaction and Change: The Role of Sects in Hinduism: from *Religion and Development in Asian Societies*. The Greek root HAIRESIS indicates the choice of a doctrine, again by implication referring to a range to choose from. The Latin root *secta* refers to a body of followers, the heretical element being a contribution from Christian ecclesiastical history.
4. D. Schlumberger and E. Benveniste, 'A New Greek Inscription of Aśoka at Kandahar,' *Ep. Ind.* XXXVII, part V. no. 35. pp. 193-200.
5. J. Marshall, *Mohenjo-daro and the Indus Civilisation* (London, 1931)p. 52 ff.
6. *Ṛg Veda*,-VII.22.9; VII.56.3: 370.4; X.109; 136; 130.5; VIII.3.9; 6.18; Z.72.7.
7. *Ibid.*, X.136.
8. M. Eliade, *Shamanism* (Princeton, 1974).
9. T. Burrow, *'Arma* and *Armaka'*, *Journal of Indian History*, XLI. 1963.I. p. 159 ff.
10. *Aitereya Brāhmaṇa*, VII.28.
11. G. Wasson, *Soma: Divine Mushroom of Immortality* (New York, 1968).
12. *Bṛhadāraṇyaka Upaniṣad*, IV.4.22; IV.5.1.
13. F. Staal, *Exploring Mysticism*, p. 204 (Berkeley, 1975).
14. J. W. Hauer, *Der Vratya* (Stuttgart, 1927); M. Eliade, *Yoga* (Princeton, 1971), pp. 103-5.
15. Buddhist sources mention fifty-eight major sects whereas Jaina sources take the number up to three hundred and sixty-three. *Dīgha Nikāya*, Brahmajālasuta I.12.30; *Sūtrakṛtāṅga* (S.B.E. XIV, pp. 315-19).
16. *Dīgha Nikāya*, Udumbarika-Sihanādasutta, III; N. Dutt, *Early Monastic Buddhism* (Calcutta, 1973), I. p. 31 ff.
17. Strabo XV.1.60; Curtius, VIII.12.
18. Strabo, XV.1.59.
19. *Viṣṇu Purāṇa*, IV.3.1.ff.
20. *Manu*, IV.107; *Gautama*, XVI.45; *Baudhāyana*, II.46.33.
21. N. Dutt, op. cit., I. p. 104 ff; S.B. Deo, *The History of Jaina Monachism*, (Poona, 1956), p. 60 ff.
22. A.L. Basham, op. cit., p. 4 ff.
23. Romila Thapar, 'Ethics, Religion and Social Protest in the First Millennium B.C. in Northern India,' *Daedalus*, Spring 1975, vol. 104, no. 2, pp. 119-33. Also p. 36 in this volume.
24. N. Dutt, op. cit., p. 147 ff and 167 ff.
25. S.B. Deo, op. cit., p. 60 ff.
26. N. Dutt, op. cit., p. I, p. 197.
27. *Ibid.*, p. 183.
28. Such as Anāthapiṇḍaka and Viśkahā (the daughter of a *seṭṭhi* of *Sāketa*). *Mahāvastu*, I. 2; *Cullavagga*, VI.4.10; VIII. 7.4.

29. *Dīgha Nikāya*, I. Lohiccasutta; Ambatthasutta.
30. D. Chattopadhyaya, *Lokāyata* (New Delhi, 1968), p. 468 ff.
31. S.B. Deo, op. cit., p. 101 ff.
32. *Ibid.*, p. 420 ff; *Ep. Carnatica*, VII.64, 66, 117, 127, 140, 351; *Dīgha Nikāya*, Samannaphalasutta.
33. *Majjhima Nikāya*, I.134-5. The idea was developed further in the notion of the Bodhisattva as the saviour and the compassionate one who defers his own *nirvāṇa* to help others attain it, and also in the concept of the Buddha Maitreya as a chiliastic principle.
34. D.D. Kosambi, *Introduction to the Study of Indian History* (Bombay, 1956); Romila Thapar, *The Past and Prejudice* (New Delhi, 1975), p. 28 ff.
35. S.B. Deo, op. cit., p. 105.
36. Strabo, XV.1.59.
37. A. L. Basham, *The Wonder that was India* (London, 1954), p. 280.
38. S. Dasgupta, *Obscure Religious Cults* (Calcutta, 1946), p. 35 ff.
39. T. Watters, *On Yuan Chwang's Travels in India* (New Delhi, 1973 reprint), I. p. 221.
40. D. Lorenzen, *The Kapalikas and the Kalamukhas*, (New Delhi, 1972) p.13 ff; V.S. Pathak, *History of Śaiva Cults in Northern India from Inscriptions*, (Varanasi, 1960).
41. *A Comprehensive History of India*, vol. II, p. 393 ff.
42. *Vāyu*, LVIII. 64-5; *Brahmāṇḍa*, II.31. 64-66.
43. Lorenzen, op. cit., p. 24 ff.
44. S.B. Deo, op. cit, p. 114 ff and p. 568 ff.
45. R.N. Nandi, *Religious Institutions and Cults in the Deccan* (Varanasi, 1975), p. 96 ff.
46. G.S. Ghurye, *Indian Sadhus* (Bombay, 1964), p. 70 ff; H. Chakraborty, *Asceticism in Ancient India in Brahmanical, Buddhist, Jaina and Ajivika Societies* (Calcutta, 1973), p. 178 ff.
47. The later rivalry of the Jainas and the Lingāyatas in Karnataka took in its sweep, idol breaking and temple destruction as well. The Buddhist disapproval of Śaṅkarācārya was expressed in a number of Buddhist works. One among these refers to his losing a debate with Buddhist monks and, as a result, being ducked thrice in the Ganges, Tāranātha's *History of Buddhism in India.*
48. R.N. Nandi, op. cit., p. 65 ff.
49. M. Eliade, *Yoga*, p. 153.
50. F. Staal, op. cit., p. 171.
51. G.S. Ghurye, op. cit., p. 177.
52. S. Dasgupta, op. cit., p. 14 ff.
53. M. Eliade, *Yoga* (Calcutta, 1965), p. 200 ff.
54. R.S. Sharma, *Indian Feudalism*, (Calcutta, 1965), p. 263 ff; B.N.S. Yadava, *Society and Culture in Northern India*, p. 375 ff (Allahabad, 1973); R.S. Sharma, 'Material Roots of Tantricism', International Orientalists Conference, Canberra, 1971.
55. N.N. Bhattacharya, *Ancient Indian Rituals*, (Calcutta, 1975), p. 139.
56. L. Dumont, 'World Renunciation in Indian Religions', *Contributions to Indian Sociology*, 1960, IV. pp. 33-62.

57. D.H. Ingalls, 'Cynics and Pāśupatas: The Seeking of Dishonor', *Harvard Theological Review*, LV, 1962. pp. 281-98.
58. L. Dumont, *Homo Hierarchicus*, (London, 1972).
59. J.C. Heesterman, 'Vrātya and Sacrifice', *Indo-Iranian Journal*, 1962, VI, pp. 1-37.
60. *Vinaya Piṭaka Patimokkha Anguttara Nikāya IV.202; Baudhāyana Dh. S.* II.10. 11-30; *Manu* VI.38; *Yājñavalkya* III.56; *Viṣṇu Dh. S.* 96.1.
61. D Lorenzen, op. cit., p. 97; G. Briggs, *Gorakhanātha and the Kānphāṭā Jogis*, (Calcutta, 1930).
62. *Bṛhadāraṇyaka Upaniṣad* II.4.1; III.5.1.
63. *Manu* VI.41-44; *Vasiṣṭha Dh. S.* X.12-15.
64. *Manu* VI.40, 92-94; *Yājñavalkya* III.61-66; *Gautama* III.23.
65. *Manu* VI.70-75.
66. *Manu* IV.207ff; V.129; VI.43; *Apastambha Dh. S.* I.5.16.21-22
67. *Vasiṣṭha Dh. S.* X.31.
68. Strabo XV.i.59.
69. *Ācārāṅgasūtra* II.1.1.10.
70. J.P.S. Uberoi, 'On Being Unshorn,' in *Sikhism and Indian Society*, Transactions of the Indian Institute of Advanced Study, Simla, no. IV, 1967.
71. D.H. Ingalls, op. cit.
72. It is perhaps worth keeping in mind that the word 'dissent' has only relatively recently been secularised in English. Dissent is embedded in the ecclesiastical history of European Christianity and refers to groups in opposition to the doctrine of (particularly) the Church of England. Until the eighteenth century it referred to Christian non-conformists. It is only when political sectarianism became significant in the nineteenth century that it took on the secular connotation of differences of opinion on politics and society and the articulation of seemingly radical action for change. Etymologically the word is based on the negative prefix and is the reverse of consent. 'Protest' derives from an act of protestation or a formal declaration in legal terms. Its etymological root relates it to being a witness in a court of law or parliament. Again, it is not until the eighteenth century that it comes to be accepted as a formal expression of dissent or disapproval in matters other than the law (O.E.D.).
73. *Jābālopaniṣad* 5; Śaṅkara on *Bṛhadāraṇyaka Upaniṣad* III.5.1.
74. *Ibid.*, IV.5.15.
75. *Rāmāyaṇa*, Uttarakāṇḍ 67.1-6; Kālidāsa, *Raghuvaṁśa*, XV.53; *Viṣṇu Purāṇa*, VI.1.37.
76. Ānandagiri, *Śaṅkaravijaya* XVII, quoted in D. Chattopadhyaya, *Lokāyata*, p. 274 ff.
77. S. Dasgupta, op. cit., p. 35 ff.
78. D Lorenzen, op. cit., p. 149
79. S Dasgupta, op. cit., p. 198.
80. H Chakraborty, op. cit., pp. 171-2.
81. S.B. Deo, op. cit., p. 465 ff. : A curious feature in Jaina literature is that in listing the number of followers of various *tīrthāṅkaras*, the figures for the number of nuns and women lay-followers is always substantially larger than for the men, *Kalpasūtra*, SBE XXII, p. 267-68.

82. A.K. Warder, 'Early Buddhism and Other Contemporary Systems', *Bulletin of the School of Oriental and African Studies*, 1956, XVIII.1, p. 43 ff.
83. A.L. Basham, op. cit., argues that perhaps *Ājīvikas* were the earliest to evlove a *saṅgha*.
84. *Dīgha Nikāya*, XVI, Mahāparinibbanasutta.
85. cf. R.A.L.H. Gunawardana, 'Some Economic Aspects of Monastic Life in the later Anuradhapura Period: Two New Inscriptions from Madirigiriya'. *The Ceylon Journal of Historical and Social Studies,* January-June 1972, vol. II, no.1, p. 60 ff.
86. N. Dutt, op. cit., p. 290 ff and 313 ff.
87. D. Chattopadhyaya, op. cit., p. 483.
88. *Ibid.*
89. *Dīgha Nikāya* III, Cakkavatisihanādasutta.
90. *Mahāvaṁsa* II.1, ff.
91. *Vinaya* II.160-75.
92. Fa Hsien in S. Beal, *Chinese Accounts of India*, (Calcutta, 1958), I, p. 22; I Tsing in J. Takakusu, *A Record of the Buddhist Religion*, (Delhi, 1966), p. 193.
93. *Vinaya* II.160-75.
94. R.N. Nandi, op. cit., p. 59; S.J. Tambiah, *Buddhism and the Spirit Cults in North-eastern Thailand*, (Cambridge, 1970), p. 81 ff.
95. S. Dutt, *Buddhist Monks and Monasteries of India*, (London, 1962), p. 76.
96. G.S. Ghurye, op. cit., p. 82 ff; H. Chakraborty, op. cit., p. 178 ff.
97. *Viṣṇu Dh. S.* V.132; *Āpastambha Dh.S.* II.10.26, 14-17.
98. G.S. Ghurye, op. cit., p. 103 ff. In this connection it might be mentioned in passing that there is a curious institution of the *caṭṭas* and *bhaṭṭas* referred to in various sources but whose exact function is not very clear. They occur in the post-Gupta period, are associated with *maṭhas*, were trained in Sanskrit and Vedic studies and in the handling of weapons and arms. They are generally accorded *brāhmaṇ* status but are nevertheless differentiated from the other *brāhmaṇs*. M.G.S. Narayanan, 'Kantalur Salai—New Light on the Nature of Aryan Expansion into South India', *PIHC*, Jabalpur 1970, pp. 125-36. The epigraphs recording land grants prohibit the entry into the area by these persons in the phrase, '*a-cāṭa-baṭṭa-praveśya*.' They have been described as a para-military vanguard of brahman settlements or else as a category of semi-officials. Might they have been the precursors of the later *akhārās*, who were not to be encouraged in *agrahāras* and other land granted by the king, since, living off alms as they were (and possibly enforcing the *dāna*) they would be a financial liability?
99. G.S. Ghurye, op. cit., p. 98, 177; G. Briggs, op. cit, p. 35.
100. As, for example, the variation as recorded in the *Mahāvaṁsa* and the *Aśokāvadāna*.
101. B.L. Rice, *Ep. Carnatica* VII. J.F. Fleet, 'Inscription at Albur', *Ep. Ind.* V. 1890-99, pp. 213-65.
102. S. Dasgupta, op. cit., pp. 208-9
103. Hemcandra, *Triśaṣṭiśalākapuruṣacarita*, pp. 160-64; *Divyāvadāna; Aśokāvadāna*.
104. The installation of a *mahant* described by J.C. Oman in *The Mystics, Ascetics and Saints of India*, (London, 1903), p. 253 ff, takes on the character of a

gigantic potlatch in which the redistribution is limited to the *saṃnyāsis* alone. Such an occurrence indicates a departure from the notion of reciprocity or at any rate the return flow is obscured.

105. R.A.L.H. Gunawardana, 'Irrigation and Hydraulic Society in Early Mediaeval Ceylon', *Past and Present*, November 1971, no. 53.
106. Such as the Baniyan Cave in the Barabar Hills given to the Ājīvikas by Aśoka Maurya and those in the Nāgārjuna Hills given by Daśaratha. Romila Thapar, *Aśoka and the Decline of the Mauryas*, (London, 1961), pp. 260, 186; Donations of this nature to the Jainas are listed in S.B. Deo, op. cit., pp. 101-35; similarly for Kapālikas and Kālāmukhas in D. Lorenzen, op. cit., pp. 24-28 and 111-14. The monastery at Nālandā was financed through an endowment of the revenue of two hundred villages according to I. Tsing and J. Takakusu, *A Record of the Buddhist Religion*, p. 65.
107. R.N. Nandi, op. cit., p. 88 ff and p. 96 ff.
108. *Mahāvagga* I.61.1. to I.72.1.
109. This is perhaps best described with reference to the Mahāvihāra monastery in the *Mahāvaṁśa*, particularly in the period subsequent to Devānampiya Tissa.
110. R.N. Nandi, op. cit., pp. 88, 90.
111. S.B. Deo, op. cit., p. 239.
112. N. Dutt, op. cit., II, p. 210 ff.
113. *Dīgha Nikāya* III, Sigalovādasutta.
114. N. Dutt, op. cit., II, p. 217 ff.
115. As is evident from the general contempt with which Indra is treated by the great ascetics in the *Mahābhārata*.
116. As for example, Kṛṣṇa Dvaipāyana in the *Mahābhārata*.
117. W.D. O'Flaherty in *Asceticism and Eroticism in the Mythology of Śiva*, (Oxford, 1973), tends to treat it as a contradiction.
118. F. Staal, op. cit., p. 104.
119. M. Eliade, *Yoga*, p. 254.
120. *Ibid.*
121. Quoted in M. Eliade, *The Forge and the Crucible*, (New York, 1971), p. 127 ff.
122. S. Dasgupta, op. cit., p. 193.
123. There is a controversy as to whether this is the same Nāgārjuna as the Mādhyamika philosopher. J. Filliozat in *The Classical Doctrine of Indian Medicine*, (Delhi, 1964), p. 11 ff, argues for this identification. It is significant that Hsüan Tsang (T. Watters, op. cit., II. pp. 200-06) refers to the philosopher as being an expert in medicine and alchemy.
124. Strabo. XV.1.59.
125. *Mahāvagga* I.39.1. Even a monastery as late in date as Nālandā is described as a centre for the study of medicine, astronomy and mathematics, (S. Beal, *The Life of Hsüan Tsang* . . . pp. 112, 153).
126. For a discussion of the pre-Arab date for the use of mercury in India, see P.C. Ray, *A History of Hindu Chemistry*, (Calcutta, 1907-25), II. p. 8 ff.
127. T. Watters, op. cit., II. pp. 200-06.
128. J. Needham, *Science and Civilisation in China*, (Cambridge, 1954), I. p. 212.
129. The twelfth century text, *Rasārṇava*, is associated with Tantric groups. The

highly respectable Merutuṅga wrote a commentary on the alchemical text *Rasādhyāya*, in the fourteenth century.

130. *Encyclopaedia Brittanica*, 1972, qv. ALCHEM
131. D. Chattopadhyaya, op. cit., p. 329.
132. The word is probably a mis-reading for *sandhya-bhāṣā*, but it has gained currency as *sandhā-bhāṣā*. qv. Monier-Williams, *Sanskrit-English Dictionary*, although most scholars would accept its meaning as "intentional language."
133. M. Eliade, *Yoga*, p. 251 ff.
134. D. Chattopadhyaya, op. cit., p. 335 ff.

Dāna and *Dakṣiṇā* as forms of Exchange

In the study of the society and economy of ancient India information has often to be ferreted out from seemingly unlikely sources. What is often associated with apparently non-economic activity such as religious rituals, can sometimes provide insights into social and economic concerns. It is intended in this paper to examine the custom of *dāna*, the act of giving, in its major forms, from this point of view. The earliest literary sources refer to the giving of *dāna, dakṣiṇā*, etc. to priests and *brāhmaṇs*. The occasions for making these gifts are mentioned and there is generally an itemization of the objects considered appropriate for each occasion. Gradually gift-giving ceased to be something arbitrary and became systemised. This is evident from the discussion in some of the *smṛti* literature on the elements and aspects involved in the concept of *dāna*. Reference is made to six distinct elements and these include the *dātā* (donor), the *pratigrahītā* (recipient), *śraddhā*, the appropriateness of the gift, and the place and the time, for making the gift.[1] Gift-giving gradually evolved its own rules and requirements and can therefore be examined as an important aspect of the social and economic life of the early period.

Gift-giving has been seen largely in the context of its association with religious ritual and symbolism. There are however at least two other aspects which will be explored in this paper. Firstly, there is the obvious one of the changing items included in the listing of *dāna* and the correlation of these items with economic change. Secondly, the degree to which the nature of gift-giving reflects the socio-economic structure of the society: this hinges on the question of whether *dāna* and *dakṣiṇā* can be regarded as forms of gift-exchange and, if so, at what point do they cease to perform this function. Needless to say, gift-giving in this connection refers to major gifts given on particular and special occasions and not to the daily or routine ritual of small-scale *dāna*.

From *Indica*, vol 13 (1976), nos. 1 and 2, pp. 37-48.

In the Vedic texts the two more commonly used words for gift-giving are *dāna* and *dakṣiṇā*. The two words are by no means synonymous. The first is the generic word for gift with its etymological root in ✓*dā*, to give. *Dāna* therefore refers to the act of giving, bestowing, granting, yielding and prestation, irrespective of what is being given and when. *Dakṣiṇā* has a more specific connotation although its meaning remains a little ambiguous. It is a gift by extension of its meaning. The etymon refers to the right side, the side of purity and of respect. It also carries the meaning of invigorating or strengthening the sacrifice for which purpose the gift is made to the performer of the sacrifice.[2] By extension therefore it came to mean either a gift or a donation made to a priest or a sacrificial fee.[3] The *dakṣiṇā* to the gods can be symbolic but that to the priests must consist of actual objects. It has been agrued that the *dakṣiṇā* was never a salary or a sacrificial fee, but has to be seen as part of the economic system of Vedic times, that of gift-exchange.[4] It is possible to argue that it was not a sacrificial fee to begin with but came to be regarded as such by the time of the *Manu Dharmaśāstra* when gift-exchange was no longer an important aspect of the economic system.[5]

The concept of gift-exchange (particularly with reference to early Indian texts) was first formulated at length by Marcel Mauss in his now well-known work, *The Gift.* Mauss argued that the earliest forms of exchange were those of total prestation between clan and clan and family and family. Subsequent to this stage comes that of gift-exchange in which certain categories of people are involved in almost ritualised exchanges which are embedded in the larger continuum of social and economic relations.[6] This stage precedes the change to individual contract and the money-market with fixed price and weighed and coined money. Gift-exchange would therefore tend to become less embedded in those primarily agricultural societies which experienced the gradual impinging of changing attitudes to land and the ownership of land and where land slowly emerges as the major economic unit. Literary sources which relate both to tribal societies with a base in primitive agriculture and to societies with more complex social stratification based on advanced plough agriculture would reflect this change.

Mauss maintains that gift-exchange is not arbitrary but is based on the notion of value. What is exchanged is a token of wealth and this is different from money as it is imbued with a magical power. It is not an impersonal gift as it is linked to an individual or a particular group. Thus utility alone is not the motivating force in this exchange. The accepted token of wealth is significant since wealth is a demonstration of status; it is a means of controlling others by winning followers and by placing those who accept the gift under obligation. The exchange is essentially of consumable items and luxuries—food and clothing for example. The gift is not one-sided and implies a return gift, although the return of the actual gift presented was forbidden. The symbolic motivation in making the gift was the belief that it is reproductive and that the donor would receive the same in larger quantity. More recent studies of the system of gift-exchange in tribal societies have pointed to the functional aspect as well. The system of gift-exchange kept goods and people in circulation in a particular pattern and also acted as a means of maintaining political relationships and ranking.[7]

The earliest references to *dāna* as a distinct function in society come from the *dāna-stuti* hymns of the *Ṛg Veda*, hymns in praise of those who make generous and handsome gifts.[8] The subject of these particular hymns is either the donor or the event which occasioned the gift. Thus in one of the hymns Kaśu, the Cedi king is honoured and in another the victory at Hariyūpīyā.[9] The *dātā* (donor) can be a deity—primarily Indra and occasionally Soma, with Aśvins, Viśvadevas and Sarasvatī also included—but is frequently a king/tribal chief or hero. The *pratigrahītā* (recipients) are the hymnodists, the priests or the bards who have composed the verses in praise of the person or the event. The gift comes from human hands but sometimes via the mediation of a god.[10] Thus the god is requested for favours and if these are granted then the kings bestow gifts on the priests who immortalize them in verse.[11] The event is generally a successful battle or cattle raid or victory over the enemy or the destruction of the enemy. In these the role of Indra is pre-eminent: he destroys the forts of the enemy, he attacks the Dāsas jointly and individually.[12] The gift is made therefore not so much in the spirit of charity but as symbolic of success and as an investment towards further success on future occasions. The appropriateness of the gift is exalted but the time and place are rarely mentioned. The association with Soma may imply that it was made on the occasion of the soma-pressing ceremony. Evidently the purpose of *dāna* in the Ṛgvedic age was different from what it was to become in later times.

The *dāna-stutis* have a fairly uniform format. The composer's *gotra* is usually mentioned early on so that his social bona fides are established and this also provides the evidence for the hymns being priestly compositions. The deity is invoked, the exploits of the deity are lauded and an appeal is made to the deity for aid. Frequently, parallel situations are described which in the past had a successful outcome and were followed by generous gift-giving. Reference is made to the giving of gifts by human heroes. The gifts are unambiguously objects of wealth and are recorded in what can only be, on many occasions, exaggerated figures. The most prized gift and object of wealth is cattle with figures ranging from a hundred cows to sixty thousand head of cattle.[13] Horses come next in priority and although smaller numbers are listed they are often described in greater detail than the cows. Ten horses is a common figure although thousands of steed are also mentioned and, in one case, sixty thousand.[14] There is a preference for stallions over mares, whereas in bovine wealth the preference is for cows. Other gifts include wagons, chariots, slave-girls/maidens, camels, treasure-chests, garments and robes, measures of gold and, infrequently, cauldrons of metal.[15] Perhaps the epitome of the *dāna-stutis* is the paean to *dakṣiṇā* itself where the liberal bestowers of *dakṣiṇā*, the *yajamānas* are described as immortals inhabiting the highest heaven, secure from harm, victorious in battle and living with their brides in eternal bliss—the vision of a hero's paradise.[16]

The *dāna-stuti* hymns are expressions of heroic poetry. The givers of *dāna* are the heroes of the tribe, sometimes equated with the tribe, often carrying the tribal name in place of the individual name. The listing of the wealth was an indication of status, for those who gave large gifts such as Kaśu and Cedi king, Divodāsa, Pṛthuśravas or the Yādavas were acknowledged as being more powerful and wealthy than those who made lesser gifts such as Asaṅga or Saṇḍa. The gifts were functional items of wealth and not tokens of wealth. In this case, what was probably the implicit token was not the actual item but the exaggerated quantities in some of the figures.

Among the gifts there is a noticeable absence of the mention of land and, quite evidently, as has been pointed out, it was cattle that was synonymous with wealth.[17] This is also evident from the frequency of words and phrases incorporating cattle as synonyms for other aspects of material life, as for example in the extended meaning of words such as *gaviṣṭi, gopati* or *gomat.* Even grain is rarely listed as an item of *dāna*. This is indicative of the relative unimportance of land as an economic unit.

It has been argued that the Ṛgvedic evidence suggests that the king was essentially a protector of cattle and not of land; consequently it is cattle which is a source of inter-tribal conflict and not land.[18] This may well indicate that land was owned jointly by the clan and, furthermore, despite the references to agricultural activities scattered throughout the *Ṛg Veda*, land was still seen in essence as territory encompassing both fields and grazing ground. The lifting of cattle was a more serious economic problem than trespassing into fields. The Paṇis are feared for they are both rich in cattle as well as being stealers of cattle. Wealth (*rayi*) was computed primarily in cattle.[19] It is also of some interest that male slaves are rarely mentioned as constituting *dāna*, whereas female slaves were a recognized item of *dāna*. This would suggest that perhaps domestic slavery as a source of luxury among the wealthy was evident but the use of slavery in economic production was not the prevalent system.[20] That the possible clan ownership of land continued awhile is reflected in the story of the king Viśvakarman Bhauvana who is rebuked by the earth when he tries to gift the earth he has conquered through his *aśvamedha* to Kaśyapa.[21] But this is almost anachronistic since other sections of the same Later Vedic literature include land as part of the recognised *dāna*.

The purpose of extensive gift-making in early societies is three-fold. Ostensibly it serves a magico-religious function where the gift is symbolic of communion with the supernatural. In effect it also has two other less evident functions: one is that the donor and the recipient confer status on each other, although the source of the respective status may be different in each case, and secondly, gift-giving acts as a means of exchanging and redistributing economic wealth.

In the *dāna-stutis* of the *Ṛg Veda* the two groups involved in conferring status on each other are the *brāhmaṇs* and *rājanyas/ kṣatriyas*. The former mediate with the gods on behalf of the latter and ensure success in battle and cattle-raids, which success invests the latter with power and political status. The latter bestow wealth on the priests, thus providing them with their major source of income as well as conceding to them charismatic powers inherent in the process of ensuring success. By the time of the composition of these hymns a limited social group was involved in the exchange. However, the existence of a more extensive exchange can be postulated for an earlier phase.[22] A successful battle or cattle-raid resulted in an enforced acquisition of wealth on the part of the victorious tribe.

The process of gift-exchange was however more equitable if it occurred through the performance of the *yajña*, which in turn may be seen as a variant on the potlatch. As far as the redistribution of wealth was concerned, even at the *yajña* it seems by now to have been limited to the same two social groups, the *kṣatriya* and the *brāhmaṇ*. Thus, tribal wealth acquired through the labour of the *viś*, whether in war or in peace, was channelled via the king to the priests either through *dāna* or through the *dakṣiṇā* at the *yajña*. In earlier periods, when it is presumed that the tribe participated in the *yajña*, some of the wealth may have been redistributed among a wider group. But, by the time of the composition of the *Ṛg Veda*, both the redistribution as well as the participation of the tribe in the *yajña* was more limited.

In such a situation there must have been a distinction between those who were the possessors of wealth and the rest of the tribe. Was this distinction expressed in the term *ārya* which Bailey has analyzed in considerable detail and which analysis leads him to state that *ārya* referred to the owner or possessor of wealth?[23] This is also suggested in the *Nighaṇṭu* which equates *ārya* with *īśvara* (owner/master) and in Pāṇini, who explains it by the phrase *āryaḥ-svāmi-vaiśyayoḥ*.[24] The *āryas* as possessors of wealth were distinguished from the *viś*, the rest of the tribe, who by now were not longer equal partners in tribal wealth. As Bailey states, the association of wealth and ownership suggests nobility of class and not an ethnic group. The significance of birth into the *ārya-varṇa* relates an *ārya* to social status and wealth and not to race.

The literature of the Later Vedic period gradually introduces a change in the concept of *dāna*. It is no longer the arbitrary liberality of a generous patron celebrating his success. It is now less a channel of redistribution of wealth and much more pointedly a channel of deliberate exchange. The changing concept is expressed in the more frequent use of the word *dakṣiṇā*. The strengthening of the notion of exchange is perhaps best summed up in the statement, *dehi me dadāmi te ni me dehi ni te dadhe.*[25] The donor and the recipient remain the same. The appropriateness of the gift and the faith with which it is given are emphasized and the place and time are made much more precise. This is done by a closer linking of gift-giving with the sacrificial ritual via the *dakṣiṇā*. The justification for *dāna* is also spelled out. We are told that there are two kinds of *devas*, the gods and the *brāhmaṇs* learned in the Vedas: both have to be propitiated, the former through *yajñas* and the latter through *dāna*.[26] It is also at this point that there is mention of fields and villages as appropriate items of *dāna*, although these references are as yet infrequent.[27] Although *paśu* or animal wealth is still very significant there are some texts which disapprove of the acceptance of animals as *dāna* and presumably preferred gold and land.[28] This is not surprising since by the mid-first millennium B.C. animal wealth as an economic asset was gradually giving way to land. An interesting indication of the shift in the items gifted is evident from the study of the Rājasūya sacrifice. The concept of *iṣṭipūrta* becomes more central to the procedure with a distinction being made not only between *iṣṭi* and *pūrta* but between *iṣṭi* and *dakṣiṇā*. This is a ritual distinction but not altogether unrelated to the relative decline of livestock breeding and increase of agriculture. The *iṣṭi* which is the offering made to the gods during the performance of the sacrifice is almost invariably a mixture or a cake of some form of cereal, the most frequently used cereals being varieties of rice. The *dakṣiṇā* on the other hand is in most cases an ox, cow or bull, generally a single animal with specified markings, or else a unit of gold.[29] The number of animals is considerably less than the numbers listed in the Ṛgvedic *dāna-stutis*. Sometimes for the seasonal sacrifices the *dakṣiṇā* may include a chariot and mares or stallions.[30] The more spectacular *dakṣiṇā*, which, for instance, is given during the soma rituals of the Rajasuya, continues however to be in the form of livestock. The list ranges from one thousand to four thousand cows adding up to a total of ten thousand in some texts—a reasonable figure for a wealthy king, to five thousand to thirty thousand cows with a total of a hundred thousand in other texts—an evidently exaggerated figure.[31] Nevertheless the number of cows listed continues to be less than the figures given in the *Ṛg Veda.* Since many of the higher figures in both the earlier and later texts were in any case exaggerated, their significance symbolizes the use of animals rather than the actual numbers involved.

Dakṣiṇās associated with particular royal rituals as part of the major sacrifices often consisted of gifting to the priest the most valuable objects used in the ritual. Thus in one text we are told that the *adhvaryu* receives the chariot of the *yajamāna* and the golden dice used in the symbolic game. The carts are distributed among other priests as are also the one thousand cows used in the mock cattle-raid.[32] The *adhvaryu* and the *hotṛ* who recite the legend of Śunaḥ-śepa at the Rājasūya are given the golden seats on which they sit for the recitation in addition to a certain number of cows.[33] It is also in connection with this sacrifice that one of the forms of *dakṣiṇā* listed is that of *catuṣpat kṣetra* (field with four parts) which is given to a priest.[34] It has been suggested that this was the land used in a royal ploughing rite as part of the Rājasūya, being the survival of a rudimentary agrarian fertility rite.

In all these cases the *dakṣiṇā* is specifically linked to a particular ritual or a ceremony. Heesterman has argued at length that the *dakṣiṇā* is not a sacrificial fee or salary; it forms a part of the bigger sphere of gift-exchange.[35] His main point is that the *dakṣiṇā* is given to both the *ṛtvij* or officiating priests and to others such as the *brāhmaṇs* of the *prasarpaka* category whose role is essentially that of observers sitting in the *sadas.* In one of the texts it is specificially stated that the *dakṣiṇā* to the *sadasyas* is to buy them off from drinking the *soma*.[36] Another text maintains that the *yajamāna* by giving *dakṣiṇā* buys himself loose from obligations to the priest.[37] The ritual link is broken or is at least replaced by a status link. Not all texts however accept that the link is broken. The *dakṣiṇā* is seen as a bond between the donor and the recipient, if not as an act by which the recipient is placed under an obligation to the donor. This implies a danger and the danger can only be averted by careful consideration of the propriety of the gift, the place and the time.[38] It is a moot question as to whether the notion of the implicit danger arose from the ritual connection or whether it was a means of diverting attention from regarding the *dakṣiṇā* as a 'fee'.

Heesterman suggests that the *dakṣiṇā* may reflect an earlier stage when the entire clan took part in the ritual and the wealth was shared. This would be more characteristic of the potlatch. In course of time the ritual may have moved into the hands of the sacrificial priests and the others may have become observers. The symbolic nature of the *dakṣiṇā* is evident from the continued gifting of cattle in a society where land was becoming increasingly more lucrative. Clearly, golden seats and golden dice would have to be converted into more mundane objects for the priests to derive a livelihood from these gifts. The question is whether the *dakṣiṇā* was over and above the normal livelihood of the priest or was it his main source of income. Given the nature of later Vedic society where there are not too many references to *brāhmaṇs* owning land or large herds of cattle it is likely that the *dakṣiṇā* from the king would often be the basic source of livelihood for those performing the rituals

The collection of *dakṣiṇā* was not restricted to the large-scale *yajñas*, for the life of the *ārya* was now beset by *saṃskāras*—the rituals of the individual biography, the prescription and practice of which ensured well-being. The definition of donor gradually began to include more than just the king or the tribal chief, for others were also required to perform *saṃskāras*. This widening definition of the donor in terms of social categories reaches a qualitative change in Manu, where logic takes it to the point of stating that it is the duty of the *gṛhastha* (the householder) to be concerned with *dāna*.[39] The relevance of gift-exchange in a tribal context of potlatch activities seemed to be receding.

Marcel Mauss in his discussion of gift-exchange maintains that the *Mahābhārata* is the story of a tremendous potlatch.[40] He has particularly pointed to the *Anuśāsana-parvan* as the section par excellence devoted to gift-giving. Here we find a further elaboration of the categories of *dāna*. The distinction for example between *iṣṭa* and *pūrta* is emphasized. The *iṣṭa* is that which is offered into the *gṛhya* and *śrauta* ritual fires. *Pūrta* is a larger enterprise and consists of the donation of wells, tanks, temples, gardens and lands.[41] The donation of immovable property as a special category is a relatively new concept. Hitherto donations were of animals, gold, slaves, food, clothing, chariots and so on. The listing of what is included in *pūrta* has its own significance since it points clearly to the establishment of an agricultural economy where wells, tanks, gardens and land have a utility which they would not have had in a pre-eminently pastoral economy. Another interesting aspect to this distinction which develops in the legal literature is that the *iṣṭa* can only be handled by the ritually pure but the *pūrta-dāna*, which in economic terms was the more effective, can also be made by *śūdras*.[42]

Not only in the items listed but in spirit too the notion of *dāna* had by now undergone further changes. It was no longer given merely in celebration of an event or a heroic personality or in connection with a ceremony. It was now associated with a new idea which in part derived from the concept of *dakṣiṇā*, namely, the ethical aspect of performing an action such as giving a gift. The notion of exchange remains central, but in return for tangible wealth the donor acquires merit. Not that all exchange discussed in the *Anuśāsana-parvan* is motivated by the acquisition of merit. We are told that *dāna* increases one's material wealth; nevertheless, in every act of giving, whether it be the *pañcadakṣiṇā* service of host to guest or offerings at a ritual, there is merit to be acquired as the ultimate aim.[43] Gift-giving almost develops its own ritual in which the six-fold definition of *dāna* as stated in *smṛti* literature is given due emphasis. The definition of the *pratigrahītā* is further refined and it is stated that the recipient must be deserving of the *dāna*.[44] This has relevance not only to the fact that the acquisition of merit can only accrue if the *dāna* is given to a deserving person but also carries a hint of competition among potential recipients for the acquisition of economic status in a system where, perhaps, more attention was being paid to economic status than in earlier times. *Dāna*, therefore, is not to be given to those *brāhmaṇs* who are physicians, image-worshippers, dancers, musicians; who perform ceremonies for the *śūdras* and who practise usury. The deserving *brāhmaṇs* are those who perform the required ceremonies as indicated in the texts, who are of noble birth and who live off alms. Even if any among this category have had to take to professions such as agriculture and soldiery, they still qualify for *dāna*. The emphasis on the time and place for gift-giving is accompanied by threats that untimely gifts are appropriated by the *rākṣasas*. The emphasis on the recipient being a deserving person may also be a reflection of competition for *dāna*-bestowing patrons, a competition extending not only to brahmanical sects but including Buddhist, Jaina and other heterodox sects as well, many of the latter claiming to have wealthy patrons.

The exchange of *dāna* for merit echoes the Buddhist notion of charity or *dāna*. The idea may therefore have come from Buddhist sources or may have grown independently as a result of changing social forms. For Buddhism the stress on *dāna* was essential; for, even at the mundane level, the Buddhist religious order—the *saṅgha*—was required to subsist on the alms and the charity of the lay followers. All that the *bhikṣu* or the *saṅgha* could provide to the donor in exchange for *dāna* was *puṇya* or merit, since exchange was between economically unequal sections of society. In the early stages, when Buddhism was not a powerful religious movement, it could neither provide social status to its lay supporters nor did its doctrinal teaching promise immortality or heavenly abodes. At most it could maintain that a material gift would be reciprocated with preaching the Buddhist ethic which in turn might provide the gift of vision or enlightenment to the donors. Puranic texts are unequivocal in making promises: thus we are told that the acquisition of merit through *dāna* can release one from the chain of rebirth.[45]

The reciprocity of *dāna* with *puṇya* may also have been conditioned by the fact that in the larger towns, where there was a Buddhist following, the gift-exchange economy was on the decline and was being gradually replaced by an approximation to the impersonal market economy of commerce, where the unit of money was the currency of exchange. In such an ethos gift-exchange made little sense and the *dāna-puṇya* reciprocity held out some compensation for the donor. It is significant that among the non-deserving *brāhmaṇs* listed in the *Anuśāsana-parvan* are those who practise usury and those whose occupation is trade, both activities closely related to a market system. In contrast to the market system, *dāna* is not an impersonal exchange. It involves two parties in a clearly defined relationship, which relationship is affected by the giving of *dāna*. It is also accompanied by an elaborate etiquette, much more elaborate than the frank appeal for *dāna* in the *Ṛg Veda* or the partially disguised *dakṣiṇā* of the *yajñas* and the *saṃskāras*.[46] It would almost appear that by insisting on the institution of *dāna* and the ensuing nexus there was an attempt to invert the values of the market system and to reincarnate those of the gift-exchange.

It is also at this time that attention is given to the acceptance of food as *dāna*. Manu lists the categories of food, chiefly uncooked, which are regarded as legitimate *dāna* for the *brāhmaṇ*.[47] If a *brāhmaṇ* unwittingly accepts forbidden food he has to fast for three days as expiation. Among the types of uncooked food, it is the produce of agriculture, grain, which is the most acceptable. Manu repeats the dictum that the giver will be rewarded many-fold but also adds that he who gives and he who receives, both, go to heaven. The eulogizing of the *dāna* of food, especially to *brāhmaṇs*, continues in the later literature of the *Purāṇas* where *annadāna* is sometimes referred to as the highest form of *dāna*.[48] The relative purity of uncooked food is in contrast to the practice of sects of Buddhists and Jainas among whom cooked food is regarded as the most acceptable.[49] In terms of conferring status via exchange, the *dāna* of food has a direct relation to caste status, where the acceptability of particular types of food is dependent on social ranking. The discussion therefore of food as *dāna* is also an indication of the extension of caste society.

The gifting of land and the precedence which this began to take over other items reflects the increased interest in agriculture and the fact that land was more lucrative than heads of cattle. This would certainly conform to the known extension of the agrarian economy during the Mauryan and the post-Mauryan period. The general decline of pastoralism is evident from the fact that cows were still gifted but not as major items of *dāna*. Their gifting was to become almost a symbolic gesture of the process of making a gift. The gifting of land brought its own problems since land was both immovable and indestructible. It could not be transported as could a herd of cattle or other objects, nor did it get consumed or die during the lifetime of the recipient. Land was inheritable and alienable and this brought it under the purview of the legal system relating to the inheritance and the sale of land. A land-gift had therefore to be recorded so that it would remain with the recipient or his family even if he changed his domicile or after his death. A gift of land was even further removed from gift-exchange since it could help establish the family of the recipient for many generations and, to that extent, it was not a momentary episode but an investment for the future.

A discussion on the necessity to record a gift of land suggests that the record should act as the legal claim of the grantee and his family before future kings.[50] Hence the record should be a permanent, signed, sealed edict referring to the lineage of the king, the identity of the recipient, the extent and characteristics of the land gifted, the nature of the gift, the seals of the officials concerned with the grant and, according to some texts, a declaration to the effect that it was not to be resumed at a later date. That these instructions were meticulously observed is evident from the copper-plate and other charters recording such gifts of land from the Gupta period onwards.[51] The granting of land and villages to *brāhmaṇs* became so institutionalized that it was referred to by the special term of *agrahāra* and later an officer was appointed to look after grants, the *agrahārika*.

With the granting of land other gifts assumed lesser importance with the exception, of course, of gold which retained its economic value. A special category of gifts was evolved based on gold and referred to as the *mahādānas*.[52] These were made on very special occasions such as can hardly be listed in the normal course of gift-giving. Among the more commonly referred to *mahādānas* were the Tulapuruṣa (weighing a man against gold) and the Hiranyagarbha (the symbolic rebirth through a golden womb often performed during coronations). It is significant that this latter ceremony is particularly associated with those who were claiming *kṣatriya* status. Usually sixteen objects are listed among the *mahādānas* including trees, cows, horses, chariots, vessels, all made of gold, and such objects were gifted to the priests on the conclusion of the ceremony. A golden cow studded with precious stones was a long way away from the ten thousand head of cattle which the Ṛgvedic priests acclaimed as a gift. The *mahādānas* are clearly of another category and another time.

Land grants constituted the germ of what was later to develop into a new agrarian structure with its own implications for social and economic formations.[53] For our purposes, suffice it to say that the extensive granting of land as *dāna* changed the comprehension of *dāna* as part of gift-exchange. A new institutionalizing of *dāna* took place, reflecting both a departure from the earlier socio-economic system as well as the evolving of a changed metaphor for both the donor and the recipient.

REFERENCES AND NOTES

1. P.V. Kane, *History of Dharmaśāstra* (Poona 1941), vol. II. part 2, p. 843 ff.
2. *Śatapatha Brāhmaṇa* II.2.2.1-2; IV.3.4. 1-2.
3. *Manu* III. 128-37.
4. J.C. Heesterman, *The Ancient Indian Royal Consecration*, p. 164.
5. *Manu* XI. 38-40.
6. *The Gift* (London, 1954), pp. 45 ff, 53 ff, 71 ff.
7. J.P.S. Uberoi, *Politics of the Kula Ring* (Manchester, 1962).
8. *Ṛg Veda* VI.63.9; V.27; V.30. 12-14; VI.47; VIII.1.33; VIII.5.37; VIII.6.47;
9. *Ṛg Veda* VIII.5; VI.27.
10. *Ṛg Veda* VIII.46; X.93.
11. *Ṛg Veda* VI.47.
12. *Ṛg Veda* VI.47; VIII.1.
13. *Ṛg Veda* VI.47; I.126.
14. *Ṛg Veda* VI.33. 1; VI.63.9; VIII.46. 21-24
15. *Ṛg Veda* V.30.15; VI.47.
16. *Ṛg Veda* X.107.
17. R.S. Sharma, 'Forms of Property in the Early Portions of the Ṛg Veda', *Proceedings of the Indian History Congress,* 1973.
18. *Ibid.*
19. *Ṛg Veda* I.33.3; IV.28.5; V.34.5; VI.13.3; VIII.64.2—4
20. R.S. Sharma, op. cit.
21. *Aitareya Brāhmaṇa* VIII.21. *Śatapatha Brāhmaṇa* XIII.7.1 13-15.
22. As has been suggested by K.P. Jayaswal, *Hindu Polity*, in arguing that perhaps the *vidatha* was a tribal assembly, pp. 69-70.
    This has been further discussed by R.S. Sharma, *Political Ideas and Institutions in Ancient India*, (Delhi 1959), pp. 63-80, and J.P. Sharma, *Republics in Ancient India* (Leiden 1968), p. 70 ff. See also *Ṛg Veda,* I.24.3; I.27; I.31.6; IX.81.5; I.1024.4; I.141.1; II.2.12; VII.76.4-5.
23. H.W. Bailey, 'Iranian Arya and Daha', *Transactions of the Philological Society* 1959, p. 71 ff.
24. *Nighaṇṭu* 2.6; *Pāṇini* 3.1.103.
25. *Taittirīya Saṃhitā* I.8.4.1.
26. *Śatapatha Brāhmaṇa* IV.6.6.1.ff
27. *Aitareya Brāhmaṇa* VIII.20; *Chāndogya Upaniṣad* IV.2.4-5.
28. Kane, op. cit., p. 837 ff.
29. *Taittirīya Saṃhitā* I.8.9; I.7.3. Heesterman, op. cit., pp. 49, 174.
30. *Āpastamba Śrauta Sūtra* 5.23.5; 6.30.7.
31. Heesterman, op. cit., p. 162.
32. *Baudhāyana Śrauta Sūtra* 12.7. 95.15 ff.
33. *Aitareya Brāhmaṇa* VII.18.
34. Heesterman, op. cit., p. 166.
35. Heesterman, 'Reflections on the Significance of the Dakṣiṇā', *Indo-Iranian Journal*, 1959. no. 3. pp. 241-58.
36. *Kātyāyana Śrauta Sūtra* 28.5.

37. *Āpastamba Śrauta Sūtra* 13.6.4.
38. *Śatapatha Brāhmaṇa* IX.5.2.16; *Āpastamba Śrauta Sūtra* 13.6.4-6; *Kātyāyana Śrauta Sūtra* 28. 158.4; 159.16.
39. *Manu* III.78.
40. M. Mauss, *The Gift* (London, 1954), p. 53 ff.
41. Kane, op. cit., p. 844.
42. *Ibid.*, p. 845.
43. *Anuśāsana-parvan* II, VII, VIII, IX.
44. *Ibid.*, XXIII.
45. *Agni Purāṇa* 209. 1-2.
46. *Anuśāsana-parvan* LXXII.
47. *Manu* IV. 205-25; 235-50.
48. *Agni Purāṇa* 211.44-46; *Padma Purāṇa* V.19.289-307; *Brahmāṇḍa Purāṇa* 218.10.32.
49. As for example in the *Ācārāṅgasūtra* II.1.1-10. Manu does however insist that the *saṃnyāsin* must only accept cooked food (VI.38) and the reason for this may well have been that he was outside the norms of social regulations.
50. *Yājñavalkya* I. 318-20.
51. Inscription of Śivaskandavarman, *Ep. Ind.* I. p. 7; Maitraka Vyāghrasena, *Ep. Ind.* XI. p. 221; p. 107.111.
52. *Agni Purāṇa* 209, 210; *Matsya Purāṇa* 274-89; *Liṅga Purāṇa* II.28.
53. D. D. Kosambi, *Introduction to the Study of Indian History* (Bombay, 1956), p. 275 ff; R.S. Sharma, *Indian Feudalism* (Calcutta, 1965).

Social Mobility in Ancient India with Special Reference to Elite Groups

D. D. Kosambi made a major contribution to our understanding of the ancient Indian social structure.[1] Its study involves an examination of at least two major aspects of a society—the functioning of its social groups and their mobility inasmuch as it can be measured. In the case of ancient India the problem is clouded by the lack of precise evidence which can be used to formulate exact and verifiable hypotheses. It is partly for this reason that this article is confined to elite groups. Much of our ancient source material refers comparatively more fully to the upper sections of society; the study of the lower sections has to be far more deductive. Nevertheless an intensive study of the social structure of ancient India is an urgent necessity because only on its basis can meaningful generalizations be made about the nature of Indian society and consequently of the pattern of Indian history. My intention here is to draw attention to some of the more relevant aspects of a study of elites in early India. I have tried to draw on non-*Dharmaśāstra* sources as often as possible, largely because in the historical context such sources point to some interesting deviations from the norm as obtained from the *Dharmaśāstras*. The study generally relates to northern India, since it is impossible to generalize about the entire sub-continent as a single unit in any period.

The attempt to discuss social mobility for a period for which there is little or no demographic evidence and for which the precise nature of economic institutions is not definitely known is perhaps merely an exercise in a series of hypotheses. An important element in the study of elite groups is their size

From R.S. Sharma (ed.), *Indian Society: Historical Probings* (New Delhi, 1974), pp. 95-123.

in relation to the society to which they belong. This cannot be properly calculated for early India since no statistics are available. At best, inferences can be drawn from the sources. A detailed study of technology, particularly agricultural, would be useful. Here archaeological evidence may provide some clues. Technology as the basis of the economy could suggest approximate sizes for human habitations. A detailed study of urban sites, excavated to date, may also suggest population sizes in various forms and changes in population sizes through the centuries. Associated with the study of agricultural technology would be the question of the availability of waste land. References to uncultivated areas may be collected and comparative charts made of the encroachment into waste lands because of population pressure.[2] As long as waste land was available for settlement, one avenue of social mobility would be available. Literary references to population figures cannot be totally ignored. The *Skanda Purāṇa*, for example, gives us the figure of 96 crores of *grāmas* in the whole of Bhāratavarṣa.[3] Even if we take the *grāmas* to mean inhabitants rather than a regular village, the figure is clearly exaggerated. What is interesting however is the distribution of population in various parts of Bhāratavarṣa. A study of the figures suggests areas of heavier population such as Kānyakubja and Gauḍa (36 lakhs and 18 lakhs) and areas of sparse population such as Saurāṣṭra (55,000). Allowing for ecological factors creating such discrepancies, it would all the same be worthwhile to inquire whether there is evidence of greater mobility in the more sparsely populated areas. Similarly epigraphic evidence relating to land grants also occasionally mentions figures of *grāmas*.[4] Figures from these sources can also be collected and compared with those from literary sources.

Certain broad phases of economic change in northern India during the period from 1000 B.C. to A.D. 1000 can be recognized. The earliest Vedic literature comes from a background of pastoralism giving way gradually to agricultural settlements. Early Buddhist literature suggests a more settled agrarian economy and an emergent commercial-urban economy. The Mauryan period (fourth and third centuries B.C.) saw the development of an imperial system based on an agrarian economy. The subsequent five centuries saw a series of small kingdoms ruling in various parts of the sub-continent and at the same time a tremendous expansion in both internal and foreign trade. The Gupta period (fourth and fifth centuries A.D.) marked the beginning of a major change in the agrarian system with the assignment of land grants and revenue grants to both religious and secular assignees resulting in a new politico-economic structure in many parts of the sub-continent.[5] The changing character of economic relationships inhibits any attempt at uniform generalizations about society for the entire period of early India.

Changes at the level of elite groups were most obviously brought about by foreign invasions and migrations. The migration of the Āryan-speaking peoples starting in c. 1500 B.C. brought in the new Āryan elite. The campaign of Alexander may have been too brief to seriously disturb the centres of power in the Punjab and Sind. But the invasions of the Indo-Greeks, Śakas and Kuṣāṇas in the first century B.C. and the first century A.D. clearly did affect Indian society in the northern and western parts of the sub-continent. The impact of the Hūṇa invasions in the fifth century A.D. was felt as far as the heart-land of the Ganga. The migrations of peoples from Central Asia to northern and western India in the post-Gupta period produced even greater impact. The gradual penetration of the Āryan culture south of the Vindhyas created its problems for the local elite. The migrations affected status relationships inasmuch as the rules of endogamy had to be adjusted to allow for hypergamy.

The causes which arise from within a society and which provide a more meaningful picture of social change are less obvious. Analytical studies of society in early India have in the past been hampered by two assumptions which were accepted unquestioningly by most historians. First of all, it was assumed that society in early India remained in a more or less frozen condition throughout the period under consideration, registering only a marginal social change. Secondly, this argument sought support from the *varṇa* concept which was believed to be an actual description of the social functioning and which had as one of its essentials a rigidly structured society based on a hierarchy of status. Both these assumptions have now been questioned. A re-examination of the evidence suggests periods of change which influenced social institutions as well as other aspects of life. The *varṇa* concept, it has been suggested may always have been largely a theoretical model and never an actual description of society. Our information on the *varṇa* concept comes largely from the *Dharmaśāstras*, and the description of it in these sources is not always corroborated and occasionally even contradicted by other sources. For our purposes however it may be worthwhile to use the *varṇa* model as the starting-point and see how the evidence conforms to it or contradicts it.

The concept of *varṇa* was closely tied up with the concept of *dharma* in the sense of a universal law. Thus the *varṇadharma* was the attempt to establish a social law or a systematic functioning of society which would ensure its well-being. It was stated that society was made up of four orders, and later a fifth order was added. The first four were the *brāhmaṇ*, *kṣatriya, vaiśya* and *śūdra*, of which the first three were regarded as *dvija* or twice-born. The fifth order was later identified with the untouchables. According to the *puruṣasūkta* the four groups were divinely created and arose out of the great god Prajāpati.[6] This imbued the scheme with sanctity. The concept of *varṇa* assumes the following characteristics: status by birth, a hierarchical ordering of social units and rules of endogamy and ritual purity. Clearly it depicts a rigid social system. Theoretically there were only two obvious means of improving status. One was by opting out of society and becoming an ascetic. The other was by ensuring rebirth in a higher social status in one's next life, and here the social implications of the idea of *karma* are significant. However, mobility was not totally excluded from this scheme. Downward mobility was easy enough. Upward mobility was far more difficult and not open to the individual. It could be rendered possible nevertheless via the group, through a period of time (over several generations), and was further facilitated by a change in habitation or geographical location. The concept of *varṇa* was based on a variety of factors, such as, the idea of pollution extending to social hierarchies, clearly defined and recognized specialization of labour and differentiation between occupations, and the maintaining of distinctions between ethnic and regional populations. So much for the *varṇa* model. Here the elite would be a closed group with perhaps a limited horizontal mobility but no upward mobility.

Recruitment to each group would be strictly through birth.

The definition of elite as functional groups with high status raises a problem in the early Indian context since status has to be evaluated from two points of view—ritual status and actual status in terms of economic and political power. These two levels of status frequently confuse the picture of social stratification as the separation between the two is not always clearly maintained. Brahmanical literature is more concerned with the order of ritual status and this is what it describes. It is not concerned with how a group arrived at a particular status. We are concerned here not with ritual status alone but also with actual status and its relationship with ritual status. Ideas of ritual status owe their origin to concepts of pollution which may have been current in the pre-Āryan period. Pollution was controlled through the functioning of two taboos—the taboo regarding kinship in the context of marriage and the concern for eating with or taking food from only those ritually permitted. The taboo on not touching the ritually impure gained in importance gradually. As long as endogamous and exogamous rules of marriage and rules of commensality were observed and maintained, the social identity of these groups in a caste structure would continue, and the acquiring of ritual status be necessary. It was the concern with ritual status which led to the theory of mixed castes—*varṇa—saṃkara*—which castes are looked down upon as ritually impure. In a standard *Dharmaśāstra* such as that of Manu the mixed castes were occasionally occupational groups but generally those tribes which obviously were not easily assimilated into Āryan society.[7] What is interesting is that these tribal names continue to occur with separate identities right up to the medieval period.[8] Thus we are told that a *brāhmaṇ* marrying a *vaiśya* woman produces children who are categorized as the Ambaṣṭha; the later *Purāṇas* refer to the Ambaṣṭha tribe as deriving its origin from the Ānava *kṣatriyas* and the tribal identity remains.[9] A *brāhmaṇ* marrying a *śūdra* woman resulted in a Niṣāda.[10] This appears to have been an aboriginal tribe. It is curious that the Niṣāda and Śūdra tribes are described as neighbours, which would perhaps explain why it was necessary for a *śūdra* to be one of the parents. Clearly the tribes which were not assimilated had to be given a ritual status in the system and thus the theory of mixed castes was worked out.

On the basis of *varṇa* the elite would be a closed group with little or no upward mobility. Recruitment to each group would be strictly through birth. The elite would be drawn from the first three orders—*brāhmaṇ, kṣatriya* and *vaiśya*—the orders which constituted the *dvija* or twice-born castes. But since the *varṇa* stratification cuts across economic lines, a further selection may be necessary. Members of the *brāhmaṇ* group because of their ritual status would automatically be a part of the elite irrespective of their economic status. This would apply to some extent to the *kṣatriyas* as well. But the case of the *vaiśyas* would be more complex since this category could well include members of a low economic group, who, although included in the elite by virtue of being *vaiśyas*, would nevertheless not actually be a part of the elite. Non-brahmanical literature does however refer to impoverished *brāhmaṇs* in the early part of our period. It would seem therefore that ritual status was not sufficient for membership of the elite.

The theoretical origin of the *varṇa* system is usually traced to the *puruṣasūkta*. Yet it seems very obvious that this was a later addition to the *Ṛg Veda*. Not only is the tenth *maṇḍala* believed to be a late addition, but the evidence of the hymn itself suggests that it is an interpolation. Of the four *varṇas* mentioned, only the *brāhmaṇs* are referred to in other parts of the *Ṛg Veda*. The other three, listed as *rājanya, vaiśya* and *śūdra*, are mentioned for the one and only time in the *Ṛg Veda* in this hymn. Even the term *brāhmaṇ*, although it referred to a priest, did not necessarily mean one who guides the sacrifice.[11] A *kṣatriya* was permitted to officiate at his own sacrifice. Evidently, even if a proto-caste society existed during the Ṛgvedic period, the theoretical model had not been fully formed as yet. A pristine stage of casteless society is projected in the tradition of the *kṛta* age, the first of the four *yugas*.[12] The terminology used for the castes has its own interest. The terms *brāhmaṇ* and *vaiśya* are used more in the sense of people with particular vocations—the special priesthood in the one case, the commoners of the tribe given to agriculture and trade in the other. But the terms *rājanya* (and later *kṣatriya*) and *śūdra* are either tribal names or words qualifying a category of tribes. The existence of the Rājanya tribe is attested by both literary and numismatic sources well into the historical period.[13] Perhaps the occupational term *rājanya*, meaning a member of the royal family or a noble, may be an extended meaning of the original term derived from the tribe with an oligarchic system. The identification of the *śūdras* with a tribe is far more conclusively stated in a variety of literary sources.[14] The *varṇa* category may have originated from the low status of this tribe vis-a-vis Āryan society. The fact that the status of the *śūdras* was low is clearly indicated by their association with the Niṣāda, the Ābhīra and the Malla, the first two being regarded as mixed castes and the third as *vrātya*. The *vrātyas* remain something of a puzzle.[15] But whether Āryan or non-Āryan, they were looked down upon and held as inferior. The indication that the *vrātyastoma* is at first an initiation ritual and finally takes on the form of an expiation ritual would support the fact of a less exalted position of the *vrātya*.

It may therefore be suggested that the key to the understanding of the *varṇa* system lies in not seeing it as a framework of hierarchical layers of social orders each fitting neatly below the other. It may be more meaningful to see it as a series of vertical parallels, each *varṇa* (pure or mixed) as an independent entity with its own hierarchy based either on a tribal identity or an occupational identity. Furthermore, the *jāti* identity would be subsumed within this hierarchy. When the concept of the social structure was first formulated as a theory it may have been felt that the four categories were adequate. Gradually, when they were seen to be inadequate, the idea of *varṇasaṃkara* was added and enlarged upon. Thus the original references to the *rājanyas* and the *kṣatriyas* may not have been to such groups within each tribe, but to an entire tribe which was referred to by either of these names. The names seem to have been applied to those tribes in particular which had a distinctly oligarchic, republican system, with a representative of each family participating in the government.[16] The increasing familiarity with the *kṣatriya* tribes led to the adoption of the term *kṣatriya* in lieu of *rājanya*. Once the four-fold category had been accepted, there was no attempt to alter the basic structure, which had in any case been given divine sanction by the later Vedic period. New castes arising either out of tribal associations, such as the Gonds, or out of occupational associations, such as the *kāyasthas*, were treated as mixed castes deriving their origin from a combination of partners from the original four. Insistence on ritual status was necessary because each new caste had to be fitted into the ritual hierarchy. Ritual status was firm and fixed, irrespective of what the actual status of a caste might be. Social mobility therefore in Indian society did not necessarily mean a change in the actual status of a caste, but perhaps more often the attempt to improve the ritual status or else to deny its importance. That the listing of *varṇa*-occupations in the *Dharmaśāstra*[17] was largely theoretical (although in origin it appears to have been descriptive of actual functioning) is suggested by the large number of instances provided by non-*Dharmaśāstra*, sources of occupations directly conflicting with those legitimized by the *varṇa* theory. It is precisely this contradiction which enables one to suggest that in terms of actual status there was mobility. The survival of caste is partly because of the continuance of marriage and kinship rules and partly because the economic relationships are also an integral part of this structure. The opposition to caste therefore would be primarily aimed at the abolition of the ritual status aspect of its structure.

Had the *varṇa* system functioned as a superimposed hierarchical layer of social groups, the distinctions between the four main groups and the other permutations and combinations would have remained very clear and distinct. What is curious however is that, while the identity of the *brāhmaṇ* and the untouchable is generally clear, references to the intermediate groups often appear to be of a rather confused, if not contradictory kind.

A clearer definition of these categories can perhaps be obtained from the Buddhist sources, particularly the texts in Pāli. Here the four-fold division of *brāhmañña, khattiya*, *vessa* and *sudda* is recognized in terms of social categories, but not always as actual social units. The first two groups can be identified with actual social units, but the second two are left vague. The references to *varṇa* in general are not always precise or necessarily identified with Indian society. We are told for example that in the region of Yona and Kāmboja (north-west India) there are two *varṇas*, the master and the slave and these are interchangeable.[18] For purposes of actual social functioning kinship relationships appear to be more relevant.

Judging from the Pāli literature the two-fold division of society into upper and lower categories (*ukkaṭthajāti, hīnajāti*) constituting the *varṇa* seems to have been more commonly in use. The upper category is frequently described as consisting of the *brāhmañña, khattiya* and *gahapati*.[19] The identification of the *brāhmaṇ* is quite clear. The term *khattiya* (Sanskrit *kṣatriya*) is generally used for the ruling families of the oligarchies or what a recent writer has called the extended kin-groups,[20] such as those of the Śākyas, Mallas, Licchavis, etc., many of which constituted themselves into the oligarchies or republics of northern India in the sixth century B.C. Thus according to this literature, the use of the term *kṣatriya* would be limited to those who traditionally held political power, particularly in a non-monarchical system, and who belonged to an extended kin-group.

The term *gahapati* can also be identified in precise social terms as the affluent householder. The wealth of the *gahapati* derived either from his owning land or from his being a wealthy merchant, in which case he was called a *seṭṭhi-gahapati*. It is significant that although there is an occasional reference to the *brāhmaṇ gahapati* as the *brāhmaṇ* who had received a donation of land, there is never a reference to a *khattiya gahapati*. Possibly the political status of the *khattiya* subsumed extensive land ownership, and his inherent political status was superior to the wealth of the *gahapati*. Since this was a period when commercial activity was nascent, political status in itself had a value. There is rarely any marked tension between the *khattiya* and the *gahapati*, even though the more wealthy *gahapatis* being the chief donors are often the centres of attention. The tension is more frequent between the *brāhmaṇ* and the *khattiya*.

The same tension is reflected in some sections of Vedic literature, and it seems to have gradually increased in time. The *Purāṇas*, presumably harking back to an earlier period, mention *kṣatriyas* who carry out brahmanical functions. The tension revolved around the competition for ritual status and the distribution of spiritual and temporal power, and was easier to define in a monarchical system. Not surprisingly it was in a monarchical structure that a working arrangement was gradually fashioned. The ritual status of the *brāhmaṇ* and the *kṣatriya* was kept distinct. It was clear that aspiration to political power could not be strictly limited to the *kṣatriya* caste, and therefore a concession had to be made. The concession appears to have been that a king of non-*kṣatriya* origin had to seek validation and be proclaimed of *kṣatriya* origin and be given an appropriate genealogy. Thus although in theory kingship was the prerogative of the *kṣatriyas* alone, in fact the office was frequently held by non-*kṣatriyas*. By seeking validation the ritual status in the *brāhmaṇ-kṣatriya* relationship was preserved. It also illustrates more clearly the distinction between ritual status and actual status by the fact that a person of non-*kṣatriya* origin could be given *kṣatriya* status when he became a king. The superior ritual status of the *brāhmaṇ* lay in the fact that he provided the validation. But this working arrangement took many centuries to evolve and did not come into practice in any extensive way until about the Gupta period.

The ritual superiority of the *brāhmaṇ* over the *kṣatriya* was originally established in part by associating the king with the gods. It is possible to trace the gradual evolution of the idea of kingship from a secular function of leadership and protection to being divinely appointed and finally to being constituted of divine elements.[21] However, the idea of divinity was a limited one since the king was never a god-king or worshipped as a deity. The channels of divinity were the royal sacrifices—*rājasūya, vajapeya, aśvamedha*, etc.—for the performance of which the presence of the priest was essential. The idea of divinity was never exploited to any significant degree by Indian rulers. The kings who did claim descent from the gods were the Kuṣāṇas who took the title of *devaputra*.[22] It has been suggested that this was an imitation of the Chinese title Son-of-Heaven. In the post-Gupta period royal titles rarely refer to divine descent, and even the *Dharmaśāstra* literature in effect pays little attention to the question of the king's direct relation with the gods. The idea of divinity seems to have been influential during the earlier phases of the establishment of monarchies and appears to have been more closely associated with the magical belief in the king as the insurance against evil. For the kingdoms of the post-Gupta period the validation of *kṣatriya* status assumed greater importance.

The validation of *kṣatriya* status was essentially an attempt to prove status by birth and to acquire the appropriate and legitimate lineage. The first major example of validation occurs in the *Purāṇas*. The *Viṣṇu Purāṇa*, composed in the Gupta period, lists in its section on dynastic chronicles the various dynasties and kings who were believed to have ruled in northern India from a period of mythological beginning to the coming of the Hūṇas.[23] The earlier dynasties are all neatly classified into two categories—the *Sūryavaṃśī* (Sun-Family) and the *Candravaṃśī* (Moon-Family), both having as their common ancestor the hermaphrodite son of Manu, the primeval man. Apart from the symbolic significance of this myth, the system itself became the prototype of all rulers seeking *kṣatriya* genealogies, since the *Sūryavaṃśa* and the *Candravaṃśa* became the two major royal traditions.

It is clear from the *Purāṇas* that in the earlier period not every dynasty had sought validation. Some were not only of non-*kṣatriya* origin but also did not bother to acquire the right genealogies, and the period from about the fourth century B.C. to the fourth century A.D. saw considerable neglect in this matter. Thus the *Purāṇas* refer to the Nandas who had a *śūdra* association, to the Mauryas who were of low origin, to the Yavanas and the Śakas who were foreign and grudgingly conceded the status of degenerate *kṣatriyas* or *śūdras,* and worse still to the Hūṇas who had openly to be called *mleccha* (the impure).[24] In the case of the Yavanas and the Śakas it was a question of reconciling political status with ritual status. Manu does not seem to be too clear as to exactly what status they were to be given. At one point we are told that they are *vrātya-kṣatriyas* and are to be given the status of *śūdras*, but in the very next verse we are told that all those whose origin is other than that described in the *puruṣasūkta* are to be regarded as *dasyus* irrespective of whether they speak the language of the Āryans or that of the *mleccha*.[25] Patañjali refers to a special category of *śūdras*, the *aniravasita*, who, presumably because of their actual status, were regarded as clean and therefore not polluting.[26] The contradictions seem to have been resolved by the Śakas themselves, who in their inscriptions of the early centuries A.D. claim *kṣatriya* status.[27] It is perhaps ironical that precisely the kings who were given *vrātya-kṣatriya* and *śūdra* status took exalted imperial titles such as *Basileus Besileon* and set the fashion for later-day Indian royal titles such as *mahārājādhirāja*.

In the post-Gupta period the position begins to change, and particularly after the eighth and ninth centuries A.D. there is a rush for fabrication of genealogies proving the *Sūryavaṃśī* or *Candravaṃśī* origin of local dynasties. This is evident from the genealogies of the Rajput kings; even more interesting is the case of the Gonds of central India associated with the Candella kings who claimed *Candravaṃśī* status.[28] It would seem from this that the stabilization of the ritual status vis-a-vis the actual status with reference to *brāhmaṇs* and kings was achieved in the post-Gupta period. Some of the historical dynasties ruling in the earlier part of our period, as we have seen, ruled without acquiring ritual status. This may have been owing at least to two reasons: one, that the actual status of the *brāhmans* was not as yet sufficiently powerful to demand the validation of dynasties; and two, that many of the north Indian dynasties were those of foreign conquerors (the Indo-Greeks, the Śakas, the Kuṣāṇas, etc. and would therefore not require validation. Possibly the rise to political power was faster in the post-Gupta period, and recent memories of low caste origins had to be more rapidly expunged. A further reason for giving the genealogy in the inscription was to prove that the grant was legally valid as well. Provision of genealogies was accompanied by an attempt to emulate the *kṣatriya* kings of the past and appropriate the functions (at least in theory) of the *kṣatriya* model as described in the *Dharmaśāstra* texts. The increasing importance of validation through genealogies was perhaps one of the reasons for the declining interest in association with divinity. Again, it was only the *brāhmaṇs* who could provide the genealogies of the new kings. The rise and multiplication of small, regional kingdoms during this period provided both work and status for the genealogists. The traditional castes of chroniclers and bards—the *sūta* and *māgadha*—had been reduced to a low position in the hierarchy of status,[29] and royal genealogies were firmly in the hands of the *brāhmaṇs*.

Medhātithi, writing his commentary on Manu in the ninth century A.D., concedes that the office of kingship could be extended to anyone who had acquired a throne.[30] Hsüan Tsang mentions kings of all the four castes who were ruling in various parts of India when he visited the country.[31]

Ritual status gave the *brāhmaṇs* a unique position. The insistence on recruitment by birth had to be more carefully observed owing to the ritual purity of their religious function. Instances of non-*brāhmaṇs* being recruited to the ranks of *brāhmaṇs* are mentioned, but these are rare and are always referred to as something distinctly unusual. Yet some form of recruitment must have existed to account for the growth of *brāhmaṇ* numbers with the spread of 'Aryanization' in the sub-continent. This was presumably done either through hypergamy or through the recruitment of local cult priests, the latter process being the equivalent in social terms to the absorbing of the local cult into the 'Great Tradition' of Hinduism. But the process is nowhere clearly indicated, perhaps for obvious reasons. However, hints of status-gradation amongst the *brāhmaṇs* do occur. Thus we are told in Buddhist sources that the *udicca brāhmaṇs* from the Kuru-Pañcāla area looked down upon the *satakalakkhana brāhmaṇs* who were from further east, from Magadha.[32] The latter are said to indulge in magical and other practices which were not approved of by the former. In the early part of our period the *brāhmaṇs* of Magadha were looked down upon even in brahmanical sources, and are referred to as the 'so-called' *brāhmaṇs*. The phrase *magadha-deśīya brahmabandhu* carries obvious contempt.[33] This probably arose at a time when Magadha had not come within the direct orbit of Āryan brahmanism and its *brāhmaṇs* therefore continued various non-Āryan practices. In the post-Gupta period the eastern *brāhmaṇs* became the more established group and began to migrate to the new kingdoms where they were very much in demand, as is evident from the frequent mention of Gauḍa *brāhmaṇs* and those of Mithilā in inscriptions. This was the period when western Indian *brāhmaṇs*, the Maga, the Bhojaka and the Śakadvīpī, who had been regarded with some suspicion from the point of view of ritual status, were beginning to establish their bona fides.[34] The process of the assimilation of the Maga *brāhmaṇs* who practised cults deeply influenced by sun-worship, is characteristic of the acquiring of *brāhmaṇ* status by rather similar groups. So low was their position within the *brāhmaṇ* hierarchy that the *brāhmaṇs* are contemptuously described as associated with the *mlecchavaṃśa,*[35] although in the *Bhaviṣya Purāṇa* they acquired respectability. It could be argued that every tribe or occupational group has its own priests to minister to its religious needs, and as the tribe or the group moved up in the social scale and improved its ritual status, the priests likewise moved into and up in the *brāhmaṇ* hierarchy. This could account for the curious phenomenon of the Ābhīra *brāhmaṇs* or the obvious implications of the myth concerning the origin of the Chitpāvan *brāhmaṇs* in more recent times. This would also suggest fresh orientations to the history of religious movements, which would need to be studied to a far greater extent in the context of social orders. A religious movement could also become a mechanism for social mobility.

Ritual status did not however prevent the *brāhmaṇs* from participating in other activities open to other members of the elite. *Brāhmaṇ* dynasties did not have to seek validation. Thus the Śuṅgas and the Kaṇvas and many other *brāhmaṇ* families ruled in various parts of India. Even the more obviously *kṣatriya* position of being a military commander was on occasion held by a *brāhmaṇ*.[36] A close association with political power was maintained through the office of the *purohita* or the *rāja-guru*. In the early texts the work of the *purohita* appears to have been largely of a religious if not of a magical nature.[37] By the medieval period the office of the *purohita* is not only frequently hereditary but has also been politicalized.[38] The gradual politicalization of the office of the *purohita* can also be seen in the *purohita* becoming a check on the monarch.[39] The fact that the right to legitimate political opposition is also limited to the *brāhmaṇ* is pertinent.[40] In eleventh-century Kashmir we notice a conflict between the *brāhmaṇs* and the king in which the former resort to their legitimate right.[41] Further association with political power and administration was through the channel of ministers to the king and the bureaucracy.[42] The *mantripāriṣad* (ministerial council) and the *amātyas* (ministers) may often have been *brāhmaṇs* or members of the royal family. The qualifications demanded of a minister, such as familiarity with the *Dharmaśāstra* and the *Arthaśāstra* works, would often have precluded all but the *brāhmaṇs*. The king and the *brāhmaṇs* were theoretically the upholders of law—*dharma* in its various manifestations.[43] The power relationship between the king and his ministers was essentially based on the personality of each, and therefore varied considerably.

The caste composition of the bureaucracy is almost impossible to determine, since references are generally to the office and not to the name of the officer. Some inferences can be drawn from the descriptions of the functions of the officers. Viceroys and governors are often referred to as being either related to or associated with the royal family. If the royal family had been of low caste origin and had sought validation then presumably the validation would be extended to more than just the immediate members of the king's family. The more senior officials, such as the revenue collectors, the treasurers and those concerned with legal matters, might well have been of *brāhmaṇ* origin as they would require a background of formal education. The same was probably true of the important but less exalted rank of scribes, recorders and accountants. This stratum of the administrative hierarchy was not however restricted to the *brāhmaṇs* alone. From the Gupta period onwards there is occasional mention of the *kāyasthas* who served as scribes.[44] They wrote documents, maintained revenue records and assisted the judges. By the ninth century the *kāyasthas* had evolved into a caste and were given a low ritual status, described as originating from the inter-mixing of *brāhmaṇ* and *śūdra*. By the eleventh century they were such a widespread caste that they had to take local descriptive names, such as the Gauḍa *kāyasthas* from eastern India or the Vālabhya *kāyastha-vaṃśa*. Some rose to high office, received land grants, held feudatory status under the Gahaḍavālas, Candellas and others, and patronized religion. They were scorned by the *brāhmaṇs* because of their low ritual status and yet at the same time feared since the *kāyasthas* had access to wealth and political power in some parts of the country by the eleventh century.[45] The rise of the *kāyasthas* is a good example of the upward mobility of an occupational group, caused by the administrative and economic need for scribes and administrators, which situation was fully exploited by the *kāyasthas* to establish their actual status. At the lower levels of administration, it is likely that the officials were locally appointed and became hereditary, as in the medieval and later periods. At the village level, officers may not have been brought in from elsewhere. The majority of the administrative functionaries would probably have been local non-*brāhmaṇs* since in this case the qualifications for holding office would not have required considerable formal education.

There is little evidence to suggest an institutionalized means of recruitment to the bureaucracy. There was no examination system and no clearly formulated minimum qualifications. It would seem logical therefore to assume that, but for senior officials, appointments were made from amongst local persons. Such a system would not necessitate a complete change of officials at the local level each time there was a change of dynasty or an invasion. This would also partly account for the importance of the village councils, *pañca-kula,* etc., particularly in the post-Gupta period. The recruitment of senior officials may have been carried out in a more organized fashion. Evidence from the Mauryan period clearly indicates that such officers were liable to be transferred from one area to another and were in any case expected to tour frequently their own areas of administration.[46] The sheer physical necessity of transferring officers would have made it difficult to appoint local persons in their local capacity.

In contrast to this, the evidence from the Gupta period suggests a different situation. The range of the bureaucracy in terms of functionaries appears to have increased. More important, there is a marked tendency towards senior positions becoming hereditary. This becomes a regular feature in inscriptions relating to such families from the ninth century onwards in some of the central Indian kingdoms. It is possible to trace the descent of the office of minister from father to son in the Candella kingdom and to relate each minister with the contemporary king. The tendency for administrative office to become hereditary was doubtless associated with the fact that many senior officers were paid by the grant of revenue from a particular area or a grant of land. Revenue rights soon came to be regarded as land rights and in order to ensure continuity the office became hereditary. *Brāhmaṇ* names are not infrequent in such grants. Thus *brāhmaṇ* officials could become powerful through acquiring land rights.

Brāhmaṇ land holdings further increased during the Gupta and post-Gupta period through the institution of *brahmadeya* and *agrahāra* grants—the granting of tax-free land to a learned *brāhmaṇ* in perpetuity as a recognition of his learning or religious achievement. The idea of making such grants as donations to the *brāhmaṇs* is an early feature.[47] But charters referring to such grants do not occur in any significant number until about the fourth century A.D. In the Gupta period was created the office of the *agrahārika,* who presumably kept a record of such grants.[48] The post-Gupta period saw an increase in the number of inscriptions referring to *agrahāra* and *brahmadeya* grants. The acquisition of tax-free land, whether as an *agrahāra* or for services rendered to the king, brought with it the problems of property and ownership, if not those resulting from a closer and more real access to political power and that too in a period of low political stability. It is hardly surprising that laws of inheritance and ownership became far more complex during this period. A comparison of the relevant chapters in the *Manu Smṛti* with those of Kātyāyana or the Mitākṣara and Dāyabhāga systems provides abundant evidence of the complexities of changing concepts of property. It is likely that the increase in the number of *brāhmaṇ* families which had to attend to matters relating to their own property and sources of revenue sometimes extending over considerable areas and including one or more villages, or of those which had to administer the property of richly endowed temples, created vacancies at certain fairly senior levels in the bureaucracy which were occupied by the enterprising *kāyasthas*. The increase in the number of kingdoms, each requiring to be fully serviced with administrators in an age of conspicuous consumption and fierce competition, may also have led to the recruitment of the *kāyasthas*. The latter may have begun as routine scribes, having picked up the bare essentials of a formal education and efficient administration, and entrenched themselves in the bureaucracy by working primarily in the sphere of revenue collection.

In determining the role of education as a means of social change a distinction must be made in the early period between oral education and formal education. In the early Vedic period, before the use of a script, brahmanical education was an oral tradition. The contents of this tradition were religious or magical formulae and the rituals appropriate to various occasions. The memorizing of chronicles, dynastic histories or epic tales was the work of a different group of people, the *sūtas* and *māgadhas*. Even after much of the brahmanical literature had been recorded in writing, the actual recitation of certain sacrosanct sections was kept secret and remained a part of oral learning. The element of magic was never totally eliminated from early religious literature; hence the injunction that a *śūdra* who dares to listen to the recitation of the Vedas must be severely punished.[49] The secret knowledge of the recitation of the Vedas gave magical powers to those *brāhmaṇs* who had acquired this knowledge, even in an area of literate civilization.

Formal education was theoretically available to members of the *dvija* caste. For a *brāhmaṇ* a knowledge of the Vedas was essential and this required many years of training and study. In addition, formal education would entail a familiarity with the śāstric tradition which included a study of grammar, rhetoric poetry, logic, philosophy, astrology and the various *śāstras,* particularly the *Dharmaśāstra*. Not every *brāhmaṇ* however was conversant with the full range of these subjects. Some picked up a minimum knowledge of religious texts and rituals and earned their living as village priests. With the spread of Buddhism formal education was also imparted in Buddhist monasteries, but was often restricted to Buddhist monks. The brahmanical centres, though technically open to all *dvija* castes, appear to have attracted mainly *brāhmaṇ* students. Those of *kṣatriya* status being largely members of royal families often had their own preceptor at court who would be a learned *brāhmaṇ*. It is hard to determine how many members of the *vaiśya* caste would have been interested in formal education, since most professional people would acquire professional skills through apprenticeship or working in the guilds. Buddhist monasteries technically had no caste restrictions. Members of the non-*brāhmaṇ* castes who were lay Buddhists may have acquired at least the rudiments of formal education in the monasteries which gradually became affluent from donations and endowments and could afford to maintain a large number of students. Hsüan Tsang's statement that the monastery at Nalanda fed and accommodated thousands of students may not be exaggerated in view of the lavish endowments made to the monastery.[50] But the majority of these students were monks; therefore the educational feedback into society was limited.

The brahmanical system of learning in the early period was not based on large institutions. More often than not students were attached to individual teachers, who, we are told, were supported by donations from the pupils. Although impoverished students were accepted and are referred to, it seems likely that well-to-do students would naturally have been preferred. This would coincide with the fact that only in sufficiently wealthy families would it be possible for the sons to have enough leisure to do justice to a brahmanical formal education. The very nature of this education was such as to provide qualifications for those intending to become priests, rulers, bureaucrats and men of letters. For those going into less exalted professions, such an education would have been largely a luxury. The post-Gupta period shows a change in the process of brahmanical education in that it is based on an institution and acquires a precise physical location—the temple and the *agrahāra*. In the Gupta period temples began to be built and quite soon became the physical nuclei of brahmanical culture. The teaching of young pupils was frequently carried out in the temple precincts. The more richly endowed temples acquired centres of higher learning such as the *ghatikā*. In the process of institutionalizing education, as it were, it is possible that formal education was extended to more than just the *brāhmaṇ* pupils. This would have been more possible at the lower levels where affluent non-*brāhmaṇs* (provided they were not *śūdras* or worse) were accommodated. In the centres of higher learning the students appear to have been entirely *brāhmaṇs*.

The institutions of education served the needs of bureaucracy inasmuch as one can speak of bureaucracy as an organization in itself. In early India the definition of bureaucracy was by no means clear. Its social composition was varied, and it did not share an identity of culture amongst its upper and lower ranks. The identity of culture was much more with the social origins of each individual functionary. Mobility within the ranks of bureaucratic office was related to mobility within the wider context of society itself. Bureaucratic status became a means of obtaining social status for the kin-group; therefore upward mobility even when possible was probably slow. Acceleration of this process would occur during periods of political crisis and instability.

The organization of the army was of a similar order. Theoretically the high ranking officials should all have been of the *kṣatriya* caste, but this was by no means uniform in practice. The political importance of the army varied from period to period. Medieval Kashmir provides an example of mercenary officers of the royal bodyguard—the Tantrins and the Ekaṅgas—being the effective king-makers for a period of almost two hundred years.[51] Such a situation is not described as being in any way strange or peculiar. It may therefore have been more common during this period. How the royal bodyguard acquired such power is not clearly indicated, although it is hinted that the bodyguard was symbolic of a bigger political faction based on the *ḍāmaras* or land-owners. The ritual status of the Tantrins and the Ekaṅgas is not quite clear. They are not referred to as *kṣatriyas*, as one might expect them to be.

It would seem evident from what has been said so far that, of the three *dvija* castes, the *brāhmaṇ* is the most easily identifiable as a concrete social group. The *kṣatriyas* as the *khattiyas* of Buddhist literature had a distinct identity at the time of the Buddha, but later their actual identity becomes vague. The same is true of the last of the *dvija* castes, the *vaiśyas*. Although theoretically widely known, it is difficult to find groups which actually recognize themselves as *vaiśyas*. Nevertheless, there is a large range of castes and occupations which could be included within the theoretical functions of the *vaiśya* caste. According to the *śastric* sources, the *vaiśyas* are those who tend cattle and cultivate land, are handicraftsmen, and also include merchants and traders.[52] Presumably the reference to cultivation is to fairly wealthy cultivators, since the association of *vaiśyas* with wealth is a consistent association.[53] The *vaiśyas* are also described as being the group in society which provides the essential taxes.[54]

In considering the *vaiśyas* as part of the elite, the discussion will be confined to the more wealthy among the *vaiśyas*. In Buddhist sources, the nearest identification of the affluent *vaiśya* would be with the *gahapati* (*gṛhapati*) or the householder whose wealth was derived from land or trade, in which case he was referred to as the *seṭṭhi-gahapati*. The affluent *vaiśya* group would also include the *jyeṣṭha* (head) of the *śreṇī* (guild). The latter category of the elite was essentially urban. Both their potential and actual power and status derived from the economy of the urban centres. With the growth and establishment of the towns, the *gahapati* also became the focus of urban life in the second half of the first millennium B.C. Both the Buddhists and the *brāhmaṇs* competed for the patronage of the *gahapati*. Buddhist literature implies that much of the early support for Buddhism came from the *khattiyas* and the *gahapatis*.

The urban elite, therefore, although technically it could include *brāhmaṇs*, was composed in the early period at least of a large number of non-*brāhmaṇs*. Its chief concern appears to have been an attempt to maintain its own identity, status and power. This was done largely through the organization of guilds, which were fundamental to the economic well-being of this group. Members of the guilds do not seem to have competed in any significant way for political power. Recruitment to the guild was through family association, and there appears to have been little or no cross-recruitment from the guilds to the higher ranks of the bureaucracy; this was so in spite of the fact that during the Gupta period senior members of guilds were frequently associated with urban administration, and it would seem that these town councils had considerable autonomy. The transformation of guilds into castes with elaborate rules of endogamy must have tightened the intra-guild identity. Members of royal families are known to have invested their money in guilds.[55] Often the interest on such investments was endowed to religious institutions. The Buddhist Saṅgha also invested money in guilds and on occasions acted as a bank. It is possible that in the early history of certain guilds, such as those of western India, a sizeable investment came from royal sources, in which case the guild would tend to remain subordinate to royal authority. Financiers would obviously benefit from royal backing. From the purely practical point of view, the risks involved in the transportation of goods even within the sub-continent were such that it lay in the interests of the guilds to remain on the right side of authority. In the latter half of our period it was gradually and implicitly recognized that access to political power had to be based on property in land and could not be achieved through commercial wealth alone; furthermore, that the amount of land necessary for the purpose could not be purchased. Grants of lands, as we have seen, were generally made to learned *brāhmaṇs* and able administrators; the category of the prosperous trader is rarely mentioned. It is hard to believe however that kings in times of economic pressure would not have willingly granted land to a wealthy financier in return for a large sum of ready money—unless of course the supply of available currency was inadequate to cover the cost of granting land, as may have been the case in the post-Gupta period when there appears to have been a decline in the use of coins.

In most periods of early India and in most areas a clear distinction was maintained between land and trade as sources of income, and land was regarded as superior. Revenue from land was invested in trade by the *gahapatis*, various royal families and the Buddhist *saṅgha*. The recipients of land grants in the later period tended to be more cautious. There was however a striking exception to this. During the Coḷa period the more wealthy *brāhmaṇs*, many of whom were the beneficiaries of substantial *brahmadeya* grants, began investing their own money in trade or else became partners in financial guilds. The identity of landed wealth with commerce must have considerably strengthened the position of the *brāhmaṇs*. Generally, investment in land as a source of capital on the part of affluent merchants was not unknown, although infrequent. However, those who built their wealth through commerce rarely seemed to have acquired land in order to use it as a base for political power. Perhaps the socio-economic organization of the commercial structure did not encourage this.

The hierarchy and ranking of various social groups included within the wider bracket of *vaiśya* appears to have been somewhat fluid. One of the more important inscriptions of the Gupta period records the building of a *Sūrya* (Sun) temple the finances for which came from a guild of silk-weavers of western India.[56] The inscription records that when the guild could no longer maintain itself through silk-weaving, its members moved to another part of western India and took up a variety of other professions and some became archers, soldiers, bards and scholars. This is a clear case of mobility occurring through change of habitation, geographical location and occupation of the entire group. What is puzzling however is: how did an erstwhile weaver—low in caste ranking—become a scholar? This can only be explained by suggesting that if the actual status was sufficiently high (and the silk-weavers in this case were obviously wealthy enough to build a temple to the Sun) then it could provide access to professions which theoretically were barred. Not surprisingly, when Alberuni refers to the *varṇa* theory of social structure in India, he says that he finds it very difficult to distinguish in fact between *vaiśyas* and *śūdras*.[57]

From the broad group of the *vaiśyas,* some of the religious movements which had an element of social protest tended to draw their biggest support. The association of Buddhism with the *gahapatis* was not entirely accidental. The close association of Buddhism and Jainism with the period of an increase in population and trade has been commented upon,[58] as indeed also the fact that the literature of these traditions has primarily an urban setting and emanates from the republican sources. An equally obvious case is that of certain sections of the *bhakti* teachers such as the Ālvārs and Nāyanārs of Tamil Nadu. They frequently belonged to urban and artisan groups who objected to both brahmanical rituals and the iniquities of caste ranking. The creation of new religious groups disowning identification with any caste or adherence to caste rules produced a temporary sense of mobility. Over a period of time, the new religious group either grew extensively in numbers, as was the case with the Buddhists, and had to accept the socio-economic functioning of the caste society; or else the subscribers to the new religious movement became a separate caste and had to be located in the order of ranking. During the latter process, by imitating some of the norms of the higher castes, these could acquire a higher status than was their due on considerations of birth alone. The process of improving status by as it were 'jumping the line' and working through a non-caste religious movement appears to have been an avenue of mobility. Judging by their literature, those religious movements which had a stronger element of social awareness initially drew a larger support from urban areas. Thus the possibilities of mobility in the early phases of such movements would be largely among urban groups. If the new cult acquired the right kind of patronage as well, it was soon incorporated into the 'Great Tradition' of Hinduism, as happened with the Tamil devotional cult during the Pallava period and with certain aspects of the tantric cult. But the incorporation of a cult was not merely because of royal or influential patronage or the desire on the part of the brahmanical tradition to assimilate popular movements. Cults essentially associated with particular social groups would have to be incorporated into the 'Great Tradition' when those groups had moved into the higher ritual status categories of the *varṇa* system. The validation of *kṣatriya* status in the post-Gupta period also meant the validation of a variety of religious cults. The cult of a particular deity could either be incorporated in toto or an attempt could be made to associate the cult deity with the existing range of the Sanskritic pantheon, which was also the more common method.

Another crucial factor contributing to the continuance of the caste structure was the nature of the organization of economic activities, and the service relationships involved in these activities. Unfortunately, information on the working of these relationships at the village level is meagre. But what seems obvious from the references is that relations similar to that of *jajmānī* were in vogue. Artisans in the village such as the potter, blacksmith, carpenter, barber and weaver[59] were paid a share of the grain. This system is also suggested as payment for more formal service relationship.[60] In the urban areas also, where monetary economy was the usual norm, the system of service relationships was quite extensive. A careful distinction is maintained in the *Arthaśāstra* between revenue from the rural areas and that from urban sources, and keeping a careful record of the latter in the form of required services is suggested.[61] As regards the relationship between artisans and the state, it is indicated that they were required to put in a specified amount of free labour even at a later period.[62] This is corroborated by Megasthenes. Artisans provided free services for a specified time, usually one day a month.[63] Such a system would not only reduce mobility but also ensure the preservation of service relationships. That the *śreṇī* in the town tended to become a caste emerging out of a professional group is not surprising.

The organization of service relationships in the towns is fairly clear. The distribution of work was not only organized in terms of the professions living in the town but also in terms of the physical occupation by different professions of different parts of the town.[64] Each *śreṇī* had its own professional code, working arrangements, duties and obligations and even religious observances.[65] Matters relating to wider areas of dispute were sometimes settled by *śreṇīs* among themselves.[66] Social mobility among such groups, where an entire group would seek to change its ritual status on the basis of an improvement of actual status, would be more frequent, since the economic opportunities for improving actual status would be more easily available, particularly in periods of expanding trade. It is not coincidental that the greatest activity of heterodox sects and of religious movements associated with social protest was in periods of expanding trade.

The study of the social structure in early India involves primarily a consideration of the factors which led to the evolution of a caste society—the idea of ritual pollution, the preservation of kinship systems involving rules of endogamy and exogamy, the conflict between tribal systems and village economies and the nature of service relationships. Ritual pollution expressed itself most readily in food tabus and the laws of commensality, and was extended to include the concept of physical contact. It was partly because of this that laws of endogamy and exogamy had to be strictly maintained in the unfolding of kinship relationships. The conflict between tribal systems and village economies is expressed not only in the concept of the *varnas* themselves, where some derive from tribal origins and some from professional groups, but also in the preservation of regional names and identities in various castes. The nature of service relationships was the socio-economic matrix which ensured the continuity of the system. The triumph of the village economy over the tribal system ensured the success of the caste structure. The grant of land to the *brāhmaṇs* was not for the acquisition of religious merit alone, for the establishment of brahmanical nuclei, particularly in the new areas, meant the acculturation of such areas to the Sanskritic mould. The theoretical model of the *varṇa* system could not be rigidly enforced in practice since it would require a static society for proper functioning. The distinction between ritual status—the fixed status, and actual status—the mobile status, may have been the ingenious solution to an otherwise insurmountable problem.

REFERENCES AND NOTES

1. I have in mind his articles in the *Journal of the American Oriental Society*, lxxv (1955), p. 35 ff, p. 226 ff and *Journal of the Bombay Branch of the Royal Asiatic Society*, xxvi (1950-51) and xxvii (1951-52).
2. The *Purāṇas*, for example, refer to such areas. See S. M. Ali, *The Geography of the Purāṇas* (New Delhi, 1966), p. 134.
3. *Maheśvara Khaṇḍa* 39. v. 127 ff.
4. e.g. Aihole Inscription of Pulekeśin II, *EI*, vi. p. 1 ff; Malkapur Inscription of the Kalacuri dynasty, *JAHRS*, iv (1929), p. 156.
5. Cf. R. S. Sharma, 'Stages in Ancient Indian Economy', *Light on Early Indian Society and Economy* (Bombay, 1966), pp. 52-89
6. *Rg Veda*, x, 90.
7. *Manu*, x. 98; *Nirukta*, ii. 10.
8. This is evident if one compares the lists in *Manu* with those of the ethnic groups mentioned in the later *Purāṇas*.
9. *Manu*, x. 8; Pargiter, *Ancient Indian Historical Tradition* (London, 1922), p. 109.
10. *Manu*, x. 18.
11. *Ṛg Veda*, x. 98; *Nirukta*, ii. 10.
12. *Viṣṇu Purāṇa*, i. 3.
13. *Pāṇini*, iv. 2. 53; Rapson (ed.), *The Cambridge History of India*, (Cambridge, 1921), p. 528.
14. Mahābhārata, vi; ii, 27. 10; *Mahābhāsya*, i. 2, 3; 10.65 ff, *Indika*, IV; *Visṇu Puraṇa*, ii. 3. 16; *Kūrma Purāṇa*, i. 47.
15. Cf. A. C. Banerjee, *Studies in the Brāhmaṇas* (Delhi, 1963), p. 81 f.
16. This may also be a comprehensible explanation of the reference to persons such as Paraśurāma destroying the *kṣatriya*.
17. *Manu*, x. 47-49.
18. *Majjhima Nikāya* (referred to hereafter as *Maj. N.*), ii. 149.

19. *Vinaya Piṭaka* (mentioned hereafter as *Vin. P.*), iv.
20. N. Wagle, *Society at the Time of the Buddha* (Bombay, 1963), p. 35.
21. *Ṛg Veda*, x. 173; *Śatapathā Brahmana* (mentioned hereafter as *Śat. Br.*), 8.4.23.ff; *Aitareya Brahmaṇa* (referred to hereafter as *ait. Br.*) vii.22; *Bṛhadāraṇyaka Upanisad*, i. 4. 11; *Śanti Parva* (hereafter *Śānti P.*), 59; *Manu* vii. 8.
22. *EI*, ix. p. 239.
23. *Viṣṇu Purāṇa*, iv.1.
24. *Ibid.*, iv. 21-24.
25. *Manu*, x. 43-45.
26. *Mahābhāṣya*, i. 4. 10.
27. *EI*, viii. pp. 86-95.
28. Kauthem Plates, *IA*, xvi (1887), p. 21; Kalyan Inscription, *Bombay Gazetteer*, i, ii, p. 339; Khajuraho Stone Inscription of Dhaṅga, *EI*, i, p. 124.
29. *Manu*, x. 26.
30. On *Manu*, iv. 84.
31. T. Watters, *On Yuan Chwang's Travels in India*, ii (London, 1905), pp. 186, 250, 252.
32. *Jātakas*, i. 324; ii. 83; iii. 232;
33. *Ait. Br.*, vii. 27.
34. *Bhāgavata Purāṇa*, xii. 1. 38-39; *Harṣacarita*, iv; E. C. Sachau (ed. & tr.), *Alberuni's India*, i. (London, 1910), p. 21.
35. *Rājataraṅgiṇī*, i. 306-14.
36. An obvious example is Puṣyamitra, the founder of the Śuṅga dynasty.
37. *Ait. Br.*, vii. 24-26; *Śat. Br.*, iv. 1-5-6 4. *Manu*, vii. 78.
38. *Rājataraṅgiṇī*, v. 465; viii. 900.
39. *Yājñavalkya*, i. 312; *Vasiṣtha*. xix.
40. *Anuśāsana Parva*, 60.18.ff
41. *Rājataraṅgiṇī*, iv. 122-25; vi. 336; vii. 400.
42. *Śānti P.*, 80-84; *Arthaśāstra*, I & II
43. *Gautama*, viii; *Vasiṣṭha*, XIX.
44. *Yājñavalkya*, i. 336; Damodarpur Copper Plate Inscription of Budhagupta, *EI*, xv, p. 138; Kanaswa Inscription, *IA*, xix (1899), p. 55.
45. *Rājataraṅgiṇī*, v. 439; viii. 258.
46. Edict I. of Aśoka Maurya, Block, *Les Inscriptions d' Asoka* (Paris, 1950), p. 139.
47. *Anuśāsana Parva*, ascribable to the first century A.D., has a whole chapter called *bhūmidāna-praśaṃsā*.
48. *Corpus Inscriptionum Indicarum* (hereafter *CII*), iii, nos. 12 and 60.
49. *Vedānta Sūtra*, i. 3. 34-38; *Manu*, iii. 156; iv. 99.
50. Watters, op. cit., 165; cf. Takakusu, *A Record of Buddhist Religion* (Oxford, 1896), p. 154, for I-tsing's account in which he gives an estimate of over 3000 students.
51. *Rājataraṅgiṇī*, v. 248; vi. 121.
52. *Manu*, ix. 326-33.
53. *Taittirīya Saṃhitā*, v.
54. *Ait. Br.*, iii. where the assumption is that the offerings are coming from the ms/ vais'ya

55. Sircar, *Select Inscriptions Bearing on Indian History and Civilization* (University of Calcutta, 1965), nos. 85, 86.
56. *Mandasor Inscription*, *CII*, iii, no. 18.
57. Sachau, op. cit., p. 101.
58. D.D. Kosambi, 'Ancient Kosala and Magadha,' *JBBRAS*, xxvii, (1952), pp. 180-213.
59. *Pāṇini*, i. 1.48; *Mahābhāṣya*, i. 118.
60. *Arthaśāstra*, v. 2.
61. *Ibid*. ii. 6.15, 35.
62. *Manu*, vii. 138; *Viṣṇu*, iii. 32; *Gautama*, x. 31-32.
63. *Gautama*, x. 31.
64. *Jātakas*, i. 320; iv. 81; v. 13; vi. 276; *Arthaśāstra*, ii. 4.
65. *Nārada*, x. 2-3; *Gautama*, xi. 21.
66. *Bṛhaspati*, i. 28; *Yājñavalkya*, ii. 30;

The Image of the Barbarian in Early India

The concept of the barbarian in early India arises out of the curious situation of the arrival of Indo-Aryan-speaking nomadic pastoralists in northern India who came into contact with the indigenous population (possibly the remnants of the urban civilization of the Indus) and regarded them as barbarians. The earliest distinction made by the Āryan speakers was a linguistic distinction and, to a smaller extent, a physical distinction. The Indo-Aryan speakers spoke Sanskrit whereas the indigenous peoples probably spoke Dravidian and Munda. However, the distinction was not one of binary opposition—in fact it admitted to many nuances and degrees of variation, hence the complication of trying to trace the history of the concept. The distinction was rarely clearly manifest and based either on language, ethnic origins or culture. Political status, ritual status and economic power, all tended to blur the contours of the distinction. Added to this has been the confusion introduced by those who tend to identify language with race and who thereby see all speakers of Sanskrit as members of that nineteenth-century myth, the Āryan race.[1]

The Āryans,[2] although unfamiliar with city civilization, did bring with them the central Asian horse and the light, spoke-wheeled chariot which gave them a military advantage over the local people still using ox-drawn carts. Furthermore it is also believed that the Āryans either brought with them, or else were instrumental in the dispersion of, iron technology, which again was superior to the existing copper technology. It is likely that the cities of the Harappa culture had already declined or at least were in the final stages of decline when the Āryans arrived. They were virtually faced therefore with a series of chalcolithic cultures extending

From *Comparative Studies in Society and History,* vol.13, no. 4, October 1971, pp. 408-36.

from the Indus valley to Rajasthan and across the Ganges valley. Their association with iron technology would probably explain why they were so successful in spreading the Indo-Aryan language system through a major part of northern India.[3] The anomaly of a less civilized people referring to the inheritors of a higher civilization as barbarians can thus be explained.

The word most frequently used in Sanskrit to describe the barbarian is *mleccha.* Attempts have been made to derive the etymology of the word from the root *vāc* speech, hence one who is not familiar with the known speech or is of alien speech.[4] This also provides a clue to the early distinction being based on speech which fact is stressed in late works as well.[5] The etymology however is false as *mleccha* represents a cultural event rather than a linguistic fact. It has been suggested that *mleccha* may have been derived from Me-luh-ha, the Sumerian name for an eastern land with which the Sumerians had trading relations, possibly the people of the Indus civilization.[6] The Pāli word for *mleccha* is *milakkha,* which relates even more closely in phonetics to the Sumerian version.[7] Buddhist sources explain *milakkha* as referring to the non-Āryan people, the Āndhra, Tamil, etc.[8] This is further substantiated by the *Dharmaśāstra* of Jaimini in which he mentions certain *mleccha* words which are Sanskritized versions of words occurring in the Dravidian languages. Thus the etymology of *mleccha* would relate it to the indigenous inhabitants of northern India at the time of the arrival of the Āryan-speaking peoples, a far more plausible derivation than the earlier one. Another attempt derives *mleccha* from the proto-Tibetan **mltse* meaning 'tongue' and the Kukish *mlei.* This would associate the early use of the word with the non-Āryan speaking peoples living close to the Tibeto-Burman area.[9]

The verb *mlech* means 'to speak indistinctly'. It may have been an onomatopoeic sound imitating the harshness of an alien tongue. Retroflex consonants are believed to have been assimilated into Indo-Aryan from Dravidian. The earliest of the better-known grammarians, Pāṇini, gives a form of the word *mliṣṭa* as 'that which is spoken indistinctly or barbarously' and treats it in its noun form as indistinct speech or a foreign language.[10] Used as a noun, the word also has the rather significant association with copper and copper-coloured.

This may have had some connection with the Āryan speakers introducing iron to Indian cultures erstwhile based on a copper technology.[11] From the early centuries A.D. onwards the adjectival use of *mleccha* becomes quite frequent.[12]

The gradual emphasis on speech differentiation is apparent in the use of another range of words for barbarians which are clearly onomatopoeic and indicate an incomprehension of the language concerned; words such as *barbara, marmara* and *sarsara*. The first may well be borrowed from the Greek *barabaros*, since it occurs in late works in Sanskrit and refers to people of the north who are said to be sinful, low and barbarous.[13] The word also occurs in Pāli as *babbhara* and means 'people of an unknown tongue.'[14] Further variants in Sanskrit are *bhara-bhara* and *balbalakaroti*, 'to stammer or stutter'. *Marmara* and *sarsara* carry the same meaning and are intended to convey the sounds of a halting and alien speech.

In the *Ṛg Veda*, the earliest of the Vedic texts, there is no mention of the *mleccha* as such but there are references to the Dāsa or the Dasyu, the local tribes who were subordinated to the Āryan speakers and who were then regarded as alien and barbaric. They are compared with demons, being black-skinned (*kṛṣṇa-tvach*) and snub-nosed, speaking a strange language *(mṛdra-vāc);* they practise black-magic and do not perform the required sacrifices; they are treacherous and they live in fortified habitations.[15] The distinction of language and physical appearance is recorded. Society is divided into two main groups, the *Ārya-varṇa* and the *Dāsa-varṇa*[16] suggesting a rather simple division into 'us' and 'them' where political success justifies the superiority of the former over the latter.

That speech was the chief component in distinguishing the Āryan from the others is clearly indicated in a text from the later Vedic literature. An example of barbarian speech, that of the Asuras, is quoted in the *Śatapatha Brāhmaṇa*[17] and is later quoted and discussed by a grammarian of the fourth century B.C., Patañjali.[18] It is evident from the example that the barbarian speech in this case was a Prākrit dialect of eastern India.[19] This would also suggest that when the Āryans settled in the middle Ganges velley the difference in speech was not only noticed but recorded and examined. The emphasis on language was important as the knowledge of correct Sanskrit was crucial to the notion of being an Āryan, and to the efficacy of the ritual hymns.

Having established a distinction in language, a demarcation was also made with regard to territory. Those areas where a *mleccha bhāṣā* (language) was spoken came to be regarded as the *mleccha-deśa* or country of the *mleccha*, and this in theory at any rate, was clearly cordoned off.[20] The *mleccha* areas were impure lands not only because those who lived there spoke an alien language but what was more important they did not perform the correct rituals. These were lands where the *śrāddha* ceremony (offerings to ancestors on stipulated occasions) was not carried out, and where people did not observe the laws of the *varṇa*. The pure land was *Āryāvarta,*[21] traditionally the region inhabited by the Āryas, all else was *mleccha-deśa*. Since the *mleccha* is ritually impure, Āryas visiting the lands of the *mleccha* must perform *prāyaścitta* or expiatory rites before they can be regarded as cleansed and fit for normal association again.[22] The concept of ritual impurity relates to the functioning of caste and this particular aspect of the image of the barbarian appears to be unique to early Indian culture. It was this dichotomy of purity-impurity which gave added significance to the role and status of the ritually pure—the Ārya and pre-eminent amongst the Āryas, the *brāhmaṇ*. If *mleccha* epitomizes the barbarian, then Ārya includes all that is noble and civilized. It is doubtful that the term *ārya* was ever used in an ethnic sense. In Sanskrit and Pāli literature it is used primarily as a descriptive term or an honorific referring to a respectable and honourable man.[23] Ritual purity or the absence of it was used not to justify aggression against the barbarian, but to justify the laws of exclusion on the part of the *ārya*.

The perspective from the south was rather different. The barbarian was defined as one whose language was incomprehensible. The *ārya* was more often merely the northerner and the word was sometimes used synonymously for Vaḍavar, also a person from the north.[24] Later *ārya* was used in the sense of a noble, respected person. Curiously enough, one of the synonyms given for *ārya* in certain Tamil lexicons is *mleccha*, and it is used for those who cannot speak Tamil, separating them from the northerners—tribes such as the Vaḍukar and the Malavar who live in the forests as hunters and who rob travellers and also steal cattle from the neighbouring settlements. Their language is alien and they use long and unlearned words. Beyond them lies Danḍakāranya (in the north-eastern Deccan) which is part of *ārya-deśa*. This attitude compares favourably with modern tribes of the Chota Nagpur region who refer to the neighbouring aryanized Hindus (non-tribals) as *diku*, meaning foreigners, a word which was used to great effect in recent years in the building up of a tribal political movement, which sought to exclude the neighbours.

The relationship between the *mleccha* and the *ārya* was conditioned by all the different facets which went into the making of a caste society. There was, first, a network of exogamous and endogamous kinship relations (*jāti*); second, a hierarchical ordering of occupations and a division of labour which functioned on the basis of service relationships. The third essential was the notion that every social group has a ritual status determined by the degree to which its occupation is clean or polluting. The ritual status need not coincide with the actual socio-economic status. It can be maintained that ritual status is expressed in the notion of *varṇa* with its four categories of *brāhmaṇ* (priest), *kṣatriya* (warrior), *vaiśya* (trader), and *śūdra* (cultivator). But for the purposes of the actual functioning of society, *jāti* (literally meaning 'birth') was the more significant unit. Fourth, each group was associated with a geographical location. The *mleccha* had to respond to each of these facets. Kinship relations were excluded and the *mleccha* therefore formed their own *mleccha jātis*. No self-respecting *ārya* would marry into a *mleccha* family. Where the *mlecchas* in question were technologically inferior, their occupation was low and this affected their ritual status which was heavily weighted on the side of impurity and therefore low. Consistency with regard to geographical location is evident from the long periods of designating particular regions as *mleccha-deśa*.

Theoretically this seems to be a fairly clear situation. But in fact there were not only lapses from the theory but rarely did society function in strict accordance with these rules although the facade of the rules was maintained. This has to be kept in mind when seeking information from the sources. Whereas the *Dharmaśāstras*, being legal treatises and social codes, maintain the theory and much of religious brahmanical literature tries to conform to the theory, the non-brahmanical literature, particularly secular literature, and epigraphic evidence provide pointers to the actual situation.

By the latter half of the first millennium B.C. the picture had become far more complex. The amalgamation of existing local cultures, which was inevitable in the evolution of Āryan culture, created problems for the theorists of caste society. Not all social groups could be given a precise *varṇa* status. The process of *anuloma* (hypergamy) and *pratiloma* (where the mother is of a higher caste than the father) had to be conceded and a number of new and, inevitably, mixed castes (*saṃkīrṇa jāti*) were admitted to the theory of social order.[25] They were given the rank of *śūdras*. Of these many came to be described as *mleccha* such as the Āmbaṣṭha, Ugra and Niṣādha among the *anuloma*[26] and the Sūta, Māgadha, Caṇḍāla, Ayogava and Pulkasa among the *pratiloma*.[27] Even within the *saṃkīrṇā jātis* there is a hierarchy of ranking as recorded in the *Dharmaśāstras*.[28] Professionally they followed occupations which were regarded by the theorists as activities associated with unclean tasks such as washermen, fishermen, potters, leather-workers, iron-smiths, basket-makers, hunters and scavengers.

That the members of the *saṃkīrṇa jātis* did not necessarily in fact have a low social status is indicated by the sources. The *Aitāreya Brāhmaṇa* mentions an Āmbaṣṭha king.[29] The *Taittirīya Brāhmaṇa* refers to the material well-being of the Ugras, one of whom is mentioned as a king's officer.[30] Similarly the Sūta and the Māgadha were traditionally the bards and the chroniclers, in fact the preservers of the early Indian historical tradition. They were close to the king not only because of their profession, but we are told that the presence of the Sūta was essential to one of the rites in a royal sacrifice.[31] In contrast the case of the Caṇḍālas is exceptional, the emphasis being on impurity and not on a difference in culture. They were regarded as so polluting that they had to live outside the village or town.[32]

One of the most interesting and yet at the same time ambiguous cases of the classification of a people as near-*mleccha* is that of the *vrātyas*. Vedic sources on the *vrātyas* appear confused as to their exact status.[33] Later legal literature uses the word *vrātya* in the sense of 'degenerate'.[34] According to Vedic literature the *vrātyas* were not brahmanical in culture and had a different language; but they did speak the language of the initiated although with difficulty. Yet the *vrātyas* were not dismissed as *mleccha* and considerable efforts were made to try to circumvent this problem, one of them being the famous ritual of the *vrātya-stoma,* the rite by which the *vrātya* was purified and accepted into Āryan society.[35] Clearly the *vrātyas* were a powerful group whose power seems to have emanated from a religious sanction and who were therefore treated with a barely disguised veneration by the authors of the *Atharvaveda,* but with some condescension by the authors of the *Dharmaśāstras.*

The second half of the first millennium B.C. was also the period which saw the gradual but extensive urbanization of the Ganges valley. The river itself became the main channel of communication and trade with cities rising on its banks. The agrarian settlements had also tended to lie closer to the river. There were still large areas of uncleared forest, especially nearer the hills where the Āryan agrarian economy had not reached. It was now possible for the Āryan speakers to assume the role of the advanced urban civilization based on technological and economic sophistication. They could therefore regard with contempt the tribes living in the forests who had remained at the food-gathering and hunting stage. Such technologically inferior tribes as for example the Śabara, Pulinda, Mutība and Kirāta constituted yet another category which came to be included in the term *mleccha.*[36] The distinction which is made in the epic *Rāmāyaṇa* between the urban culture of the kingdom of Ayodhyā based on a fairly extensive agricultural economy can be contrasted with the hunting and food-gathering culture of the enemies of Rāma, the *rākṣasa* peoples.[37] Very often these tribes inhabited the fringes of Āryan culture and had to move up into the hills with the gradual expansion of the agrarian economy. By extension therefore the tribes on the frontiers also came to be called *mleccha*, even in cases such as those of the Yavanas and the Kāmbojas who were as civilized as the Āryans.[38] Thus the use of the word *mleccha* had now been extended to include speakers of an alien language, social groups ranked as mixed castes, technologically backward tribes and the peoples along the frontiers.

The stabilizing of what were to be the *Ārya* lands and the *mleccha*-lands took some time. In the *Ṛg Veda* the geographical focus was the *sapta-sindhu* (the Indus valley and the Punjab) with Sarasvatī as the sacred river, but within a few centuries *āryāvarta* is located in the Gaṅga-Yamūnā Doāb with the Ganges becoming the sacred river. Together with the shift eastwards of 'the pure land' the northern Punjab and the trans-Indus region came to be regarded as *mleccha-deśa*. Later Vedic literature speaks of the western Ānava tribes as *mlecchas* and occupying northern Punjab, Sind and eastern Rajasthan, as also the eastern Ānava tribes occupying parts of Bihar, Bengal and Orissa.[39] The tribes of the north were *mleccha* either because they were located on the frontier such as the Gandhāra and Kāmboja and therefore both their speech and culture had become contaminated and differed from that of *āryāvarta*, or else, as in the case of the Madras, they were once *āryas* but having forsaken the rituals were relegated to *mleccha* status. The latter was obviously an attempt to explain the contradiction of the earlier texts mentioning the tribe as *āryas* and the later texts, written when the *āryāvarta* had shifted eastwards, referring to them as *mleccha*.

That the northern region was once the land of 'the pure speech' is stated with reference to the Udicya (northern region) where peoples such as the Uttarakurus and the Kuru-Pañcālas are held up as the model in speech and it is recommended that *brāhmaṇs* be sent there to learn the language.[40] Buddhist literature describes Uttarakuru as a mythical paradise, a land reminiscent of the utopian past when there were no institutions such as private property and the family and when there was no need to work because food was available from the trees and all man's desires were satisfied.[41] The later Puranic tradition echoes this description for we are told that the land is covered with milk trees which eliminate the need for cultivating food, that the women are beautiful like the *apsarās* (celestial nymphs) and that people are born as couples, presumably thereby intensifying sexual pleasure.[42] Possibly the brahmanical conception of Uttarakuru as the land of the purest speech may have symbolized the brahmanical utopia, a land of non-polluting peoples, observing all the required rituals and speaking the purest language. Not surprisingly, of the tribes of *āryāvarta* by far the most significant are the Kuru-Pañcāla.[43] They emerge as a confederation of a number of existing tribes earlier associated through war and matrimonial alliances.

The Himalayan region was largely *mleccha-deśa* since it was not only a border region but was mainly inhabited by Tibeto-Mongoloid people and the dissimilarity of language and culture would be indicative of difference. The other mountainous region, that of the Vindhyas and their extensions, is probably the most interesting from the point of view of geo-politics. The Aravalli hills formed the natural watershed between the Indus and Ganges valleys and this would be the natural frontier region between the two valleys. For a long period up to the early centuries A.D. it was occupied by non-Āryan tribal republics, which survived the general decline of republics in the valley areas, and which were consequently the frontier for the Ganges valley. The central Indian complex of the Vindhya and Satpura ranges with the rivers Narmada, Tapti and Wainganga cutting through them and the plateau areas of Chota Nagpur and Chhatisgarh to the east has formed throughout Indian history an ideal setting for the tribal peoples. It lent itself easily to a pastoral and food-gathering economy with the possibilities of agriculture in some parts of the river valley and the proximity of rich agricultural areas in the plains. With the expansion of Āryan culture and the clearing of the forest in the Ganges valley the existing population of the valley would have sought refuge in the central Indian highlands. Up to about the middle of the first millennium A.D. the Vindhyan tribes lived in comparative isolation totally unconcerned with the *mleccha* status conferred upon them by the Āryans. The Chambal and Narmada valleys being the main route from the urban centres of the Ganges valley to the western ports (e.g. Bhrighukaccha, modern Broach) and the Deccan, the plundering of trading caravans and travellers may well have provided the tribes with extra comforts. Plundering was always a means of livelihood which they could resort to, especially during periods of political disturbance. It is not until the post A.D. 500 period that they begin to participate in the politics of both northern and southern India.

The pre-Aryan settlement of eastern India is attested to by advanced Neolithic cultures and the Chalcolithic copper hoards in Bihar and Bengal.[44] Literary evidence dating to about the middle of the first millennium B.C. indicates that the people of these areas spoke a non-Aryan language. The boundary of Āryan control in the Ganges valley is perhaps referred to in a striking story related about king Videga Māthava, the king of the Videhas, who is said to have travelled with the god of fire, Agni, across the Ganges valley as far as river Sadānīra. Here he paused as the land to the east of the river had not been sanctified by Agni. Once this was done the king established the Videha people on the other bank and the lands to the east of the Videhas were the *mleccha-deśa.*[45]

Yet it was the *mleccha-deśa* close to Videha, Magadha, which was to play a leading role in Indian history during the subsequent millennium. Magadha is described as the accursed land with a people of mixed caste status. An expiatory rite is required from those who visit it and this injunction is continuously repeated in the *Dharmaśāstras* for many centuries, right through the period when the state of Magadha was the centre of empires and powerful kingdoms, viz., the Maurya and Gupta.[46] The other eastern peoples, those of Aṅga, Vaṅga and Kaliṅga were even more polluting and required more elaborate expiatory rites.[47]

This was not the attitude however among the Jainas and Buddhists since it was in these areas that the heterodox religions first gained ground, as for example, Aṅga, which was an early centre of Jainism. The Jaina texts clearly define the *milakkhu* as the Varvara, Sarvara, and Pulinda tribes and discourage monks and nuns from keeping their company.[48] Buddhist sources make no distinction between *ārya* lands and *mleccha* lands when describing the sixteen major states of northern India. Since the Buddha himself preached in Māgadhan Prākrit he would hardly have accepted the term *mleccha* for the people of the region. A late Buddhist work mentions the Magadha *bhāṣā* as the speech of the Āryans indicating that Sanskrit did finally come to be accepted in Magadha.[49] The word *milakkha* is used in Buddhist writing, and as we have seen, one very reliable definition of it reads *Andha Damil, ādi,* 'Āndhras, Tamils, etc;' i.e. the people of the peninsula.[50] *Milakkha* is also used to describe those *āryas* who had lost their status and the Kāmboja are quoted as an example;[51] also, foreigners such as the Yavanas or Yonas whose status was high but who spoke an alien language,[52] and finally the tribes of the jungle, such as the Pulinda and Kirāta, where they are not only less civilized but again their language is incomprehensible.[53] It would seem from the Buddhist sources that language was the most important criterion of differentiation. Ritual impurity was not a major item in Buddhist thought, thus discrimination was not as severe as in brahmanical writing.[54] The Buddhists tended to underplay the *mleccha* consciousness probably because of the Buddhist association with the *mleccha* regions, these being the areas where it gained most ground. Nevertheless even powerful rulers motivated by the Buddhist ethic such as the Mauryan emperor Aśoka (third century B.C.) could not disregard the differentiation. His list of the tribal peoples in his empire recorded in one of his inscriptions agrees closely with the lists of *mleccha* peoples mentioned in other sources, although he does not actually call them *mleccha*.[55]

Aśoka makes a distinction between the tribal peoples and the forest tribes, the latter having to be wooed by his officers in the context of a paternalistic policy where he regards himself in the image of the father and his subjects as his children. It would seem that the forest tribes did not easily reconcile themselves to law and order.[56] The same problem is reflected in the *Arthaśāstra,* the treatise on political economy ascribed to Kauṭalya the minister of Aśoka's grandfather (fourth century B.C.). Kauṭalya also distinguishes between the *mleccha* and the forest tribes (*aranyacārah, atvikah*). He recognizes the political advantages to be gained from keeping the forest tribes happy since they had their own strongholds and could be used effectively in campaigns. Furthermore it was necessary to pay them off from time to time to prevent their resorting to plundering and pillaging.[57] Another source of the same period, the *Indika* of Megasthenes, the Seleucid ambassador to the Mauryan court, refers to the Indians as surrounded by barbarian tribes, possibly a reference to *āryāvarta* surrounded by the *mleccha-deśa*. Megasthenes adds that all these tribes were indigenous but that they differed in mind and disposition from the Indians.[58]

Although Megasthenes does not describe the Indians as barbarians, the Indians undoubtedly regarded him as a *mleccha*. For the Indians, the Greeks on every count were *mlecchas*. They were referred to by the term Yavana, a back-formation from the Prākrit *yona*, which is said to derive from Ionia, suggesting that the Ionian Greeks were the earliest to have come into contact with India. Indian tradition however maintains that the Yavanas originated from Turvaśu the son of Yayāti, associated with one of the very early and important tribes of northern India.[59] But this may well be a late attempt to find the Greeks a respectable ancestry when their role in the history of northern India became more than marginal. For the Bactrian Greeks (or the Indo-Greeks as they are called in Indian history), the Śakas (Scythians) and Kuṣāṇas aggravated the problem of having to concede the existence of *mleccha* rulers. In spite of the dismal prophecies of the ancient seers that the Kaliyuga (the period under discussion) would initiate the rule of the low-caste, nevertheless the *mleccha* origin of these rulers had to be faced.[60] The problem was further complicated by the fact that these rulers patronized and used Sanskrit as is evident from their inscriptions and coins and they inter-married into the local ruling families. The description of these areas as *mleccha-deśa* was technically also problematical. The inscriptions of the Śaka satraps (rulers and governors of western India from *c.* 100 B.C. to A.D. 300) are not only composed in good literary Sanskrit, but also assert with much vehemence that the kings are doing their utmost to prevent the mixing of the castes and are protecting the law of *varṇa*.[61] Thus the two main criteria of barbarism could not theoretically be said to prevail.

The *mleccha* both indigenous and foreign had acquired political power and a new concept was necessary. It was probably largely to circumvent this problem that the term *vrātyakṣatriya* (degenerate *kṣatriya*) became current in describing the origin and status of such peoples. It was maintained that in origin they were of the *kṣatriya varṇa* and that their degeneration was due to the non-performance of sacred rites, or because of the wrath of the *brāhmaṇs* when they ceased to perform the sacred rites.[62] Among the foreign rulers included as *vrātya kṣatriyas* were the Yavanas and the Śakas (Scythians).

The term Yavana was gradually extended to include not only the local Greeks but any group of people coming from west Asia or the eastern Mediterranean. Much the same was to happen to the term Śaka with reference to central Asia, but Yavana remained the more commonly used one. Even in South India, traders from Rome and later the Arabs were called Yavanas. Early Tamil literature has descriptions of the Yavana settlements in the trading ports of the peninsula. The Yavanas here referred to were also described as *mleccha*, since they spoke an alien language which was so incomprehensible that it sounded as if their tongues were cut off.[63]

Among the tribes of indigenous origin also referred to as *vrātya kṣatriyas* in some sources are listed the Drāviḍa, Ābhīra, Śabara, Kirāta, Mālava, Śibi, Trigarta and Yaudheya. The majority of such tribes tended to be the inhabitants of the Himalayan and Vindhyan region, traditionally called the *mleccha-deśa*. There is evidence from numismatic sources of the increasing political importance of some of these tribes which would explain their elevation to the status of *vrātya kṣatriyas* from being plain *mlecchas*. The period from the first century B.C. to about the fourth century A.D. saw the rise of a number of tribal republics in the Punjab and eastern Rajasthan, in fact in and around the watershed between the Indus and Ganges valleys. The Mālava tribe, mentioned by the Greeks as the Malloi, established themselves in the Jaipur area having migrated from the Rāvi.[64] The Śibi, the Siboi of the Greeks, migrated to north-eastern Rajasthan.[65] The Trigarta referred to by Pāṇini, were settled in the Rāvi-Sutlej Doāb. The Yaudheyas also referred to by Pāṇini moved from Haryana northwards.[66] The fact that these tribes were politically powerful after they had settled in an area is clear from the use of the term *janapada* in the coin legends indicating their assertion over the territory on which they had settled. The Gupta conqueror Samudragupta, campaigning in the fourth century A.D., takes great pride in having destroyed the power of these tribal republics.[67] The coin legends also clearly demonstrate that these tribal peoples were now using Sanskrit.

In the middle of the first millennium A.D. when it was evident that *mleccha* dynasties were dominating politics, the Puranic tradition (as it was then recorded) had much to say on the problem of the *mleccha*.[68] There is a general bewailing of the increase in *mleccha* influence which is associated with the prophecy that the *kaliyuga* will see *mleccha* dominance.[69] This will result in the establishment of the *mleccha dharma*, a barbarous ordering of the universe when vice will be rampant, the authority of the sacred texts neglected, the *śūdras* respected—in short, a complete reversal of the world order as seen by the *āryas*.[70] Passages such as these seem to express the sentiments of a small group fighting to preserve itself and prevent the change which is engulfing its world and its very existence. Not surprisingly the idea of the Saviour Deity is introduced in some of the *Purāṇas* where it is stated that the god Viṣṇu in his tenth incarnation as Kalkin will ride through the world in an attempt to turn men back to the path of virtue. Some of the *mleccha* peoples such as the Drāviḍa, Śabara and Vṛṣala will be destroyed by Kalkin.[71] But this was a temporary measure as Purāṇic cosmology did not really envisage the coming of the millennium since ultimately the entire universe was to be destroyed at the finale of the *kaliyuga*.

It is curious that in spite of considerably increased communication between the Ganges valley and the peninsula and the spread of Sanskrit and of Āryan culture to the south, there is a persistence in regarding the southern regions as *mleccha-deśa*. The Āndhras, for example, who had ruled the northern Deccan for four centuries, are described as *mleccha* kings and their lands unfit for the *śrāddha* ceremony. At the same time the Āndhra kings were claiming to be the protectors of the *varṇa dharma,* and the destroyers of the Śakas and Yavanas.[72] That less concession was made to the southern kings as compared to the northern kings was partly due to distance and partly perhaps due to the belt of tribes inhabiting the Vindhyas who doubtless acted as a barrier.

However, the attitude towards even these tribes was beginning to change and this is reflected partially in the genesis myths associated with their origin. The most frequently referred to are the Niṣāda. References to the four *varṇas* in Vedic literature includes mention of the Niṣāda who appear to have been a non-Āryan tribe who succeeded in remaining outside Āryan control[73] but had a low status in ritual ranking.[74] They are generally located in the region of the Narmada river or among the Vindhya and Satpura mountains.[75] They are described as being dark-skinned, flat-featured with blood-shot eyes and of short stature.[76] A series of myths is related regarding their origin.[77] The variations apart, the main narrative states that they were born from the thigh of king Veṇa. The king Veṇa was extremely wicked and flouted the sacred laws and the holy rites. The infuriated sages pierced him with the sharp ears of the *kuśa* grass and, according to some versions, killed him. In order to avoid anarchy, since the land was now without a king, they churned his left thigh and from it came a dark, ugly, short man, the ancestor of the Niṣāda, and in some versions, the ancestor of the *mleccha*.[78] Being unsatisfied with this result they then churned the right arm of Veṇa and from it emerged Pṛthu who was crowned king and was so righteous that the earth was named after him, Pṛthivi. Whatever the deeper meaning of these myths may be, it seems obvious that the original Niṣāda and Pṛthu represent two factions which may have fought for power. There also seems to be an association of guilt with the killing of Veṇa and the manner of the birth of Niṣāda suggests that he may have been the rightful heir but was replaced by Pṛthu. The tribes with whom the Niṣāda are associated in these texts such as the Bhīla, Kol, etc., are often the tribes connected with the rise of new dynasties in central India in the period after the eighth century A.D.

The Vindhyan region was the locale for the three tribes which came to be mentioned almost as the synonyms for *mleccha*, the Kirāta, Pulinda and Śabara.[79] The Kirāta are described as a non-Āryan tribe living in the hills and jungles of Magadha.[80] The *Mahābhārata* describes them as being dressed in skins, eating fruit and roots and inflicting cruel wounds with their weapons. Yet they were not as wild as the text would have us believe because they also brought as gifts to one of the heroes, sandalwood, aloes wood, expensive skins, gold, perfume, rare animals and birds and ten thousand serving girls. They arrived riding on elephants.[81] If the gifts amounted to even a portion of what is described then the Kirātas cannot be said to have had a primitive economy. Early texts speak of them as living in the east but later texts give the Vindhyas as their place of residence.[82] Their migration may have been due to the expansion of the agrarian settlements in the Ganges valley. The most interesting reference to them however is the famous literary work, the *Kirātārjunīya* where significantly the Kirāta is identified with the god Śiva and gives battle to Arjuna, one of the heroes of the *Mahābhārata*.[83] South Indian sources as late as the seventeenth century continue to refer to them as living in the Vindhyas in a semi-barbarous condition.[84]

The names Pulinda and Śabara in particular seem to have become generic for barbarian tribes.[85] Ptolemy uses the curious expression 'agriophagoi', the eaters of wild things,[86] in describing the Pulinda, and locates them to the east of Malava. The Pulinda may have migrated from the Mathura region to the Vindhyas for the same reasons as did the Kirātas.[87] They too are described as being dwarf-sized, black in complexion like burnt tree-trunks and living in forest caves.[88] The Śabaras were also located in the Vindhyan region.[89] A ninth-century inscription mentions the *mleccha* along the Chambal river and a fifteenth-century inscription refers to the quelling of a revolt by the Śabaras inhabiting the Chambal valley.[90] (This valley has remained throughout Indian history the main route from the Ganges valley to the north-western Deccan and a major centre of dacoity to this day. Perhaps the plundering of caravans was too lucrative for the area to develop any other substantial economy.) An early medieval adaptation of the *Rāmāyaṇa* from the south speaks of the Śabara chief as a powerful ruler of *mleccha-deśa*.[91] It is not clear whether this is poetic imagination or whether it reflects a real impression of the Śabaras as seen from a south Indian perspective. As late as the sixteenth century the king Kṛṣṇa Deva Raya of Vijayanagara writes in his manual on government that the Vindhyan tribes must be brought round to accepting the administration by gaining their trust,[92] a sentiment reminiscent of the emperor Aśoka. A Śabara tribe exists to the present day in western Orissa. The Kol tribes preserve a traditional memory of the name Śabara and the Śabari river in Chhatisgarh reflects an association with these tribes.

The authors of the *Dharmaśāstras* continued to prescribe dire punishments for those who travelled in *mleccha* lands, yet this did not deter people. Needless to say Indian traders (*brāhmaṇs* included) did travel extensively and profitably in *mleccha* lands, the performance of the expiatory *prāyaścitta* on returning home providing a convenient solution to the problem.[93] However, with the incursions of *mleccha* rulers into *āryāvarta* itself, a new problem arose: the pure land was being turned into a *mleccha* land. This had happened in the case of the Yavanas who had come a fair way into the Gaṅgā-Yamunā Doāb. It was to happen again with the coming of the Central Asian Huns or Hūṇas as they were called in India. The solution to this problem in the words of the medieval commentator Medātithi was that if the *varṇa* laws were introduced into the region (or continued to be maintained) then it would be fit for the performance of sacrifices.[94]

The coming of the Huns was not a traumatic event in the history of India. Its impact has perhaps exaggerated owing to its continual comparison with the arrival of the Huns in Europe. Even the parallel which is frequently drawn between the Huns dealing a death blow to the Roman empire and the Hūṇas doing the same to the Gupta empire (fourth-fifth centuries A.D.) is not strictly comparable since the nature of the two empires was different as also the cause of their decline. Northern India was by now familiar with foreign invasions and government under *mleccha* dynasties. The Hūṇas were known to inhabit the northern regions and are sometimes mentioned together with the Cīna (Chinese).[95] The close of the fifth century A.D. saw the Hūṇa invasions of India under their chief Toramāṇa. The location of his inscription at Eran (Madhya Pradesh) and the discovery of his seals at Kauśāmbī (Uttar Pradesh) point to his having controlled a substantial part of *āryāvarta*.[96] Hence the problem of living in a region overrun by the *mleccha* referred to earlier. Toramāna's son Mihīrakula lived up to the conventional image of the Hun. He is particularly remembered for his cruelty which has become a part of northern Indian folklore.[97] His violence however was directed mainly against the Buddhists and the Jainas, whose literature is replete with complaints about him.[98] He was however forced back from the Ganges valley and the Hūṇa kingdom after him was reduced to a small area of northern India. The Hūṇa invasion itself did not produce any major changes in the life of northern India, except at the topmost political level. Epigraphical evidence suggests that the feudatories of the Gupta kings continued as the local governors under Hūṇa rule.[99] Hūṇas used Sanskrit as their official language and patronized Hindu cults and sects.

The impact of the Huns was greater in other spheres. Hun activities in Central Asia affected north Indian trade which had close links with central Asia. Furthermore in the wake of the Huns came a number of other tribes and peoples from central Asia jostling for land and occupation in northern India. This led to a migration of peoples in these parts which in turn upset one of the stabilizing factors of caste structure, the inter-relationship between caste and locality. Some of these movements of peoples from the north southwards can be traced in the place names and the caste names, as in the case of the Gurjaras and Ābhiras.[100]

Politically too the period from the sixth to the ninth century tended to be unstable in northern India, barring perhaps the reign of Harṣa. The kingdoms of the northern Deccan were also beginning to take a political interest in the areas adjoining the Vindhyas, which culminated in the attempts of the Rāṣṭrakūṭa kings to capture and hold the city of Kanauj. In addition to this the system of making land grants to *brāhmaṇs* and to secular officials (to the latter in lieu of salary) was becoming more widespread.[101] In cases where the land was virgin the system resulted in the expansion of the agrarian economy. The tribes of central India were forced to adjust to both the population movements from the north as also to the encroaching agrarian economy often in the form of enforced settlements of *brāhmaṇs* and agriculturalists. That this is also the period in which the areas on the fringes of the Vindhyan uplands give rise to a number of principalities some of which play a major role in the politics of central India is not surprising. Some provided armies to neighbouring states, others became the nuclei of new states which arose on the debris of dynastic changes. The area continued to be a major artery of trade which made it a prey to many ambitious dynasties and the scene of constant battles. This uncertainty benefited the tribal peoples who exploited it to secure power for themselves.[102] However, many parts of central India remained comparatively untouched by either the agrarian economy or Āryan culture since pockets in this part of the sub-continent still harbour Dravidian and Muṇḍā-speaking tribes existing at a food-gathering stage, or at most, using primitive agriculture.

From the ninth century A.D. political power moved more recognizably into the hands of the erstwhile feudatories, the recipients of land grants. The new feudatories in turn became independent kings, granted land and revenue in lieu of salaries to their officers, and to learned *brāhmaṇs* for the acquisition of religious merit. The legal sanction of the grant was generally recorded in an inscription in stone or on plates of copper, and the preamble to the grant contained the genealogy of the kings. The remarkable fact of these genealogies is that most kings claim full *kṣatriya* status on the basis of a genealogical connection with the ancient royal families, the *Sūryavaṃśa* (Solar lineage) and the *Candravaṃśa* (Lunar lineage); or else there is the myth among some Rajput dynasties of the ancestor having emerged from the sacrificial fire, the Agnikula lineage. Such genealogical connections were claimed by the majority of the dynasties of this time though not all.[103] What is even more significant is that most of these families are found on examination to be at least partially if not wholly of non-Āryan origin.[104] Thus instead of being described as *mleccha* kings, they claim *kṣatriya* status and have had genealogies fabricated to prove the claim. Whereas the Śakas and Yavanas were denounced as *vrātya kṣatriyas* and the Āndhras were described as *mleccha* kings, the kings of this period, some of whom caming from *mleccha* stock such as the Gonds and Gurjaras, are willingly accorded *kṣatriya* status. Why did the *brāhmaṇs* agree to this validation? It is possible that the distinction between *ārya* and *mleccha* had become blurred in actual practice although the *dharmaśāstras* continued to maintain it. The system of land grants appears to have played a significant part. *Brāhmaṇ* grantees were often given land in virgin areas: thus they became the nuclei of Āryan culture in non-Āryan regions.[105] This process having started in the early centuries A.D. not only resulted in more land coming under cultivation but also Aryanized fresh regions. The return on the part of the *brāhman* may have been the fabrication of a genealogy for the new ruler.

The advantage of the fabricated genealogy was that *mleccha* antecedents were soon overlooked or forgotten, particularly in those areas where the *mleccha* had become powerful. In a ninth-century inscription of a Cālukya feudatory of the Pratihāra king great pride is taken in 'freeing the earth from the Hūṇa peoples'.[106] At almost the same time a Guhilla king of the Udaipur region proudly married the daughter of a Hūṇa king.[107] Yet the founder of the Guhilla dynasty claimed to be a *brāhmaṇ*. Marriage alliances broke the kinship barrier and *mleccha* rulers became patrons of Sanskrit learning and culture, so that they were as good as *āryas* for all practical purposes. Ultimately the Hūṇas came to be regarded as on par with the Rajput clans and today the name survives merely as a caste name in the Punjab.[108] The degree of assimilation can be seen in the fact that the accepted lexicon, the Amarkoṣa, in its definition of *mleccha* merely lists the three tribes—the Kirāta, Pulinda and Śabara.[109] The names of erstwhile *mleccha* tribes are defined according to occupations. Thus the Ābhīras are herdsmen, the Āmbaṣṭhas physicians and scribes and the Dārada dealers in antidotes. The erstwhile *mleccha-deśa* are described with reference to their produce: thus Vaṅga produces tin and Yavana-deśa horses fit for the *aśvamedha* sacrifice.

The process of Sanskritization (the acquisition of Sanskritic culture and higher ritual status) was usually spread over some centuries. The Bedars, a *mleccha* tribe of the Deccan, are recorded in seventh-century A.D. sources as molesting *brāhmaṇs* who had received land grants and settled in the new areas.[110] It is stated that these plundering raids had to be warded off by the villagers themselves as the king could not enforce law and order in those areas.[111] The situation continued until about the thirteenth century. Gradually the Bedar chiefs themselves were bought off with land grants and other concessions.[112] In periods of political confusion the chiefs began to found independent principalities. Trouble between the Bahmani kings and Vijayanagara was fully exploited and the Bedars not only plundered the city of Vijayanagara in 1565 but strengthened their principalities. Sanskritization continued apace and can be seen in the claim of the Bedar kings to a high ritual status in the use of Sanskrit names such as *mahānāyakācarya*, and also in the endowment made to the temple of Gopāla-Kṛṣṇa by the Bedar chief in 1568 and ultimately in the fact that the famous Śaivite Kannappa was of Bedar origin.[113]

From about the ninth century onwards references to large numbers of indigenous peoples as *mleccha* begin to decrease. Where they are mentioned and are other than the Vindhyan tribes, it is generally for a particular reason. The tenth-century Ābhīra king is called a *mleccha* because he indulges in beef eating and plundering the pilgrims who visit the famous temple at Somanātha.[114] In eastern India there is the interesting inscriptional reference to the kingdom of Kāmarūpā (Assam) being occupied by a *mleccha* ruler, Śālastambha, who starts a new dynasty.[115] We are not told why he is a *mleccha*. Was he of tribal origin or did he have Tibetan connections?

Among the foreigners with whom there was a fair amount of contact, especially through trade, were the Chinese, the Arabs and the Turks, all of whom were of course considered *mlecchas*. Contact with the Chinese goes back to the third century B.C. through trade in silk. Although silk was greatly appreciated in India, the Chinese were firmly relegated to the ranks of the barbarians and their land declared unfit for *śrāddha* rites.[116] They are often associated with the Kāmboja and the Yavana (presumably because of the central Asian connection) and with the Kirāta and eastern India—the two regions from which trade with China was conducted in the early period.[117] But the interest in China waned with the arrival of the Turks on the northwestern borders of India and the Arabs in the west.

The Arabs are most frequently referred to as Yavanas and are regarded as *mleccha*.[118] The former relates to the fact that they came from west Asia and were in a sense the inheritors of the earlier Yavana role in India. The Turks are described correctly as Turuṣkas in some cases but more often they too came under the general term *mleccha* or are called Śakas and Yavanas.[119] The latter was probably the result of their coming from the same geographical direction as the earlier invaders. It would suggest that to the Indian mind the Turks represented a historical continuity of the Śakas and Yavanas. It does however point to a comparative lack of interest in events across the frontiers of the sub-continent that the new invaders should not have been clearly demarcated from the old. It is also possible, however, that in using the old terms there was a sub-conscious attempt on the part of the Indian rulers to compare themselves with earlier kings who had tried to stem the tide of the Śaka and Yavana invasions. Perhaps this degree of romanticism was essential to the medieval ethos.

It was after all the same romanticism which led comparatively minor kings to claim suzerainty over vast areas of the continent. There is a recurring list of places which occurs in many of the inscriptions of this period and becomes almost a convention and which reads '. . . had suzerainty over the *mleccha,* Aṅga, Kaliṅga, Vaṅga, Odra Pāṇḍya, Karnāṭa, Lāṭa, Suhma, Gurjara, Krita and Cīn a . . .' [120] It is not clear in this case who the *mleccha* were, whether they were the Arabs or indigenous people, although it could well be that the word was used in an adjectival sense to cover these places which were in the earlier tradition regarded as *mleccha-deśa*. A similar convention relates to the conquest of the tribal peoples and the capture of their hill forts such as Ānarta, Mālava, Kirāta, Turuṣka, Vatsa, Matsya, etc.[121] The 'eulogy' style of inscriptions in which these conventions are observed continued to be used even for the Turkish Sultans after they had established their rule.

Mleccha as a term of exclusion also carried within it the possibility of assimilation, in this case the process by which the norms of the sub-culture find their way in varying degrees into the cultural mainstream. Assimilation can be achieved at various levels. The obvious forms are noticeable in external habits such as names, dress, eating-habits and amusements. The more subtle forms are those which can be seen in the framework of law and of religious beliefs. The Sanskritizing of names was a common feature among both indigenous and foreign *mlecchas* who slowly tried to move away from their status of *mleccha*.[122] Very often in the case of ruling families it took one or two generations to make the transition. In other situations it took a longer time. The importation of foreign fashions is evident from the terracotta and stone sculpture of various periods. The tendency was to follow the dictates of the court circles. The coûture of the deities however was more rigidly bound by conventional forms. Assimilation can also be seen in the appropriation of melodies and musical forms associated with *mleccha* peoples into the mainstream of music.[123] One of the most direct forms of the expression of brahmanical ritual purity was on the form and type of food which the *brāhmaṇ* could eat. He was forbidden to accept cooked food from any non-*brāhmaṇ*.[124] Eatables were ranked in a carefully determined order of priority. Thus when the Punjab became a *mleccha* area, its staple food was given a lower place in the hierarchy of food-ranking. Whereas the Ṛg-Vedic Āryan had a staple diet of wheat and barley, by the twelfth century A.D. wheat was described in one lexicon as 'the food of the *mlecchas' (Mleccha-bhojana*) and rice became the 'pure' cereal.[125] Onions and garlic were also regarded as the food of the *mleccha* and therefore prohibited to the *brāhmaṇ*. One of the habits of the *mlecchas* which seriously defiled them was the fact that they drank alcohol and ate the flesh of the cow, and this in later periods was strictly forbidden to the Āryan twice-born.[126]

We have seen that an essential difference between the *ārya* and the *mleccha* was that the latter did not conform to the law of *varṇa*. On one occasion the god Indra is asked how the Yavanas, Śakas, Cīnas, Kāmbojas, Pulindas, etc., can be brought within the social pale, and he replies that if they follow the *dharma* of the *śāstras* (essentially the law of the *varṇa*), they can be admitted.[127] For the laws of the *mleccha* and the laws of the *āryas* were distinct. As was the case with other *jātis,* the *mleccha* appear to have had their own customary laws and functioned within the framework of these. Within the law of the *śāstras* a sharp differentiation was maintained between the status and rights of the *ārya* and the *mleccha*. A significant and relevant example of this is that the *mleccha* is permitted to sell or mortgage his own life and that of his offspring.[128] But an *ārya* can never be subjected to slavery, except for very short periods when he is in adverse circumstances.

An even more subtle form of assimilation was through the incorporation of cults and cult-priests into the religious beliefs and rituals of the established religions of the *āryas*. In the case of the Buddhists the problem was easier since there was not the same stress on ritual ranking as among the *brāhmaṇs*. The Śaka and Yavana rulers and particularly their queens who were patrons of Buddhism were accepted as fully as other Indian ruling families.[129] For the indigenous *mleccha* the acceptance of Buddhism did not necessitate the disavowal of earlier cults, since Buddhism has commonly assimilated local cults in its process of expansion. Buddhism itself arose in *mleccha* areas and it is significant that the main strongholds of Buddhism were in these areas. However, it tended to by-pass the tribes of the Vindhyas probably because the nature of their cults, stressing violence and the shedding of blood at sacrifices, precluded easy acceptance into Buddhism.

The brahmanical religion did not remain rigid either. The Bhāgavata tradition in Vaiṣṇavism and Śaivism which emerged in the early centuries A.D. stressing the personal devotion, *bhakti*, of the worshipper for an individual deity, made the religion more flexible and more easily exportable. It was this tradition of brahmanism that could and did attract foreign *mlecchas*. The Greek Heliodorus records his devotion to Viṣṇu and speaks of himself as a member of the Bhāgavata sect[130] The Hūṇas appear to have been quite acceptable to both the major sects of Hinduism. Toramāna was a Vaiṣṇavite and was a patron of those who worshipped the *varāha* (boar) incarnation of Viṣṇu. As a royal patron he was the direct successor to one of the Gupta emperors who had earlier donated a cave to this worship at a place not too far from the site of Toramāna's inscription.[131] Mihīrakula was such an ardent Śaivite that he was led to an extreme intolerance of the Buddhists and Jainas, again a tradition which is recorded of earlier rulers of Kashmir.[132] Perhaps the Sun and Fire cults of the Hūṇas acted as a bridge towards their acceptance of and by Hinduism. With the strengthening of the Bhāgavata tradition there was a proliferation of new sects, some of which in their social attitudes were recognizably anti-brahmanical, such as the Śaiva Siddhāntas and others which maintained a flexible attitude to caste such as the Liṅgāyatas. As in the case of the Buddhists and Jainas, such sects did not discriminate between *ārya* and *mleccha* peoples, and for the latter this became an avenue of entry into Āryan society, since ultimately many of these sects became independent castes within the *varṇa* system.

In the case of the indigenous *mleccha* many of the cults were slowly absorbed into the main cultural tradition. Of these perhaps the most obvious were the fertility cults, especially those devoted to the worship of the mother goddess, and the phallus (*liṅgam*) and snake cults.[133] These cults were not totally foreign to brāhmaṇism, but in the period after the fifth century A.D. they began to play a more dominant role in the evolution of Hinduism.[134] The mother goddess, Devi, in various manifestations appears to have been the most popular deity among the *mleccha*. Vindhyavāsinī, one of the names for the consort of Śiva, was worshipped by the Śabaras, Barbaras and Pulindas.[135] The name itself means 'she who inhabits the Vindhyas', and clearly she was in origin a mountain goddess. She is said to be commonly worshipped by brigands, and the rites involved the eating of meat and the drinking of wine.[136] In another form she is described as the goddess of the outcastes who bring her oblations of sacrificed animals.[137] Elsewhere she is identified with Nārāyaṇī and Durgā, both well-known manifestations of Śiva's wife and both repeatedly associated with the *mleccha* tribes in early literature.[138] The name Śavari, meaning a Śabara woman, occurs as the name of a goddess in a medieval work.[139] The Śavarotsava or Festival of the Śabaras was a bacchanalian gathering of the tribe, as well it might have been with a fertility cult as its focus. The Kirāta worshipped the goddess Caṇḍikā, yet another manifestation of Śiva's wife Durgā, a more fearsome form of the goddess being responsible for the destruction of the buffalo-demon Mahiṣāsura. The Devi *Mahātmya*, one of the more important sources on the mother-goddess cult, suggests an eastern if not Tibetan origin for the birth of the goddess Caṇḍi.[140] By the medieval period the cults of Durgā and Candi had been absorbed into classical Hinduism. In fact, a substantial part of Hinduism itself had undergone transformation with the popularity of the Śakti-Śakta cults and Tantricism.

Nor were the cult priests left behind. Depending on the status of the cult they would enter the hierarchy of brāhmaṇism. As the cult became refined and found a niche in classical Hinduism the cult priest would also become Sanskritized and be given ritual status in the *brāhmaṇ varṇa*. This would account for the existence of contradictory categories such as the Āmbaṣṭha *brāhmaṇ* and the Ābhīra *brāhmaṇ*. It would also explain the gradual evolution in status of the Maga *brāhmaṇs* who are said to have come from Śakadvīpa in the west.[141] They are at first looked down upon and not admitted to all the *śrāddha* ceremonies. This may have been because they were soothsayers and astrologers rather than genuine *brāhmaṇs* or else because of their association with the sun cult, which, being a more powerful religious force in western Asia, may have been regarded as somewhat foreign.[142] But gradually their position improved when they were patronized by the royal courts, especially at Thānesar and Kāmarūpa, and they were regarded as the proper people to install and consecrate images of Sūrya and the sun-god.[143] Their association with the sun cult remained constant. However, they still married into non-*brāhmaṇ* castes such as the Bhojas and the Yādavas. By the medieval period however they were treated with considerable respect. The curious legends which are told about the origin of certain *brāhmaṇ* families such as those of the Chitpavans who virtually walked in from the sea,[144] would also suggest that these were families of cult priests who were gradually assimilated into the Hindu social structure.

There was however one facet in the concept of barbarian which was absent—the notion of the pagan. This did finally arrive in India but never became an intrinsic part of the Indian notion since the form of the indigenous Indian religions had no use for this concept. It was applied by the Muslims who came to India to the non-Muslim inhabitants of India. They were regarded as pagans and by extension less civilized. From about the fifteenth century onwards, when Turkish and Afghan rule had been established in virtually all parts of the sub-continent, the Muslims at all levels of society came to be described more extensively as *mleccha*. They were *mleccha* partly because some were foreign in origin, but what was more important they spoke an alien language (either Arabic, Turki or Persian) and they could not conform to the laws of *varna* since Islamic laws demand an egalitarian society. Certainly they did not observe the rules of ritual purity. Gradually however the social organization of the Muslims began to approximate that of the Hindus in that various castes evolved and became similar to Hindu castes in many matters. A focus of separation was then provided by the distinctively theological quality of Islam which took on a forceful shape alien to Indian notions of religion. It is also possible that since a sizeable proportion of conversions to Islam in India were from the lower castes (conversion to a non-caste religion being one of the traditional methods of trying to by-pass caste), this also encouraged the use of the description *mleccha*.

The most significant clue to assimilation lies not so much in the loss of ethnic identity as in participation in the sense of the past. There is a mutual appropriation of the past on the part of two groups where the group with the weaker historical tradition accepts the stronger tradition. This was certainly the case with foreign peoples who settled in India and with the indigenous tribes. Sanskritization implied the acceptance of the historical tradition to the same degree as the orgnization of the tribe according to the laws of *varṇa* and *jāti*. Hence the importance of genealogies in the process of both historical and social validation. Yet this sense of the past was in itself the result of assimilation at various points in time and was given direction by the elements which went into the making of the social fabric. Islamic historiography however brought with it its own highly developed philosophy of the past which had little in common with traditional Indian historiography except that they were both powerful traditions within the culture.

It is perhaps the very contradiction in the Indian concept of the barbarian which makes it distinctively different from that of Europe. The perception of differences—linguistic, cultural and physical—set the barbarian apart. The separateness was seen not so much in terms of what the barbarians did as in the fact that they did not observe the norms of ritual purity and were to that extent polluted. The lack of description of the *mleccha*, comparatively speaking, was based on the assumption that no self-respecting man would associate with them as long as they were designated as *mleccha*. In a sense, this was the ultimate in segregation. Theoretically this position was maintained throughout. Yet in practice not only were concessions made, as for example, in the notion of the *vrātya-kṣatriya*, but large numbers of *mleccha* peoples were incorporated into the social, political and religious system and were in fact the progenitors of many of the essentials of Indian culture. It would be a moot point as to whether this could be called a culture which excludes the barbarian.

REFERENCES AND NOTES

1. E.g. Caldwell, *A Comparative Grammar of the Dravidian or South Indian Family of Languages* (London, 1875). Thus, all south Indian *brāhmaṇs* who use Sanskrit were seen as originally Āryan.
2. The use of the word 'Āryan' in this article refers to those peoples who spoke an Indo-Aryan language. It has no ethnic connotation and is merely used as a more manageable form than the phrase 'Aryan-speaking' with which it is synonymous.
3. For a discussion of the nature and impact of Āryan culture on existing cultures in northern India, see Romila Thapar, Presidential Address, Ancient History Section, Proceedings of the Indian History Congress, December 1969; pp. 189-213 of this volume.
4. Categories of speech are demarcated in Vedic literature, reflecting a considerable concern for the correctness of speech. *Śatapatha Brāhmaṇa,* IV, 1, 3, 16; *Kāṭhaka Samhita,* I, 11, 5; *Taittirīya Samhitā,* VI, 4, 7, 3; *Maitrāyaṇī Samhita,* III, 6, 8.
5. The *Nyāyamalavistāra. Manu,* X, 45, distinguishes between *mleccha-vāc* and *ārya-vāc.*
6. Recent exponents of this view are the Finnish scholars, Parpola *et. al.*, who have made this identification basic to their reading of the Harappa script as proto-Dravidian, *Decipherment of the Proto-Dravidian Inscriptions of the Indus Civilisation*, Copenhagen, 1969. An even more recent reading is that of I. Mahadevan who reads two Harappan pictograms as **mil-ey* which becomes **mil-ec* which turn becomes *mleccha* in Sanskrit, all of which mean 'the resplendent ones'—the assumption being that this was the name by which the Harappan people called themselves. *Journal of Tamil Studies,* II, no.1, 1970.
7. *Vinaya Piṭaka,* III, 28.
8. Buddhaghoṣa's commentary explains it as *'Andha Damil, ādi'*. The *Jaimini Dharmaśāstra* gives a short list of *mleccha* words, 1, 3, 10. There are all words used in the Dravidian languages, but are given in this text in a slightly Sanskritized form-*pika, nema, śata, tamaras,* meaning respectively, a bird, a half, a vessel, a red lotus. Pāṇini mentions that the affix *an* denoting descent occurs in the name of persons of the Andhaka, Vṛṣṇi or Kuru tribes, IV, 1, 115. The affix *an* in this context is characteristic of Dravidian languages.
9. R. Shafer, *Ethnography of Ancient India,* (Weisbaden, 1954), p. 23.
10. *Aṣṭādhyāyi,* VII, 2, 18.
11. N. R. Bannerjee, *The Iron Age in India,* (Delhi, 1965).
12. Such as *mleccha-deśa* (country), *mleccha-bhāṣā* (language), *Mleccha-nivāha* (horde), *mleccha-bhojana* (food—used by rice-eaters for non-rice eaters, particularly those eating wheat), *mleccha-vāc* (speech).

13. *Mahābhārata,* XII, 200, 40.
14. *Majjhima Nikāya,* I, 128.
15. *Ṛg Veda,* III, 12, 6; II, 12, 4; III, 34, 9; V; 29; 10; IV, 16, 9; I, 33, 4; X, 22, 8; II, 20, 8;
16. *Ṛg Veda,* III, 34, 9; II, 24, 4; I, 104, 2. The word *'varṇa'* literally means 'colour' and came to be used for *varṇa* society or caste society. The word *varṇa* does not refer to the actual caste of a person but to a more broadly differentiated group which some writers mistook for caste. With the exception of the *brāhmaṇs* and the *kṣatriyas* the precise caste status of the other two groups was never uniform.
17. *Śatapatha Brāhmaṇa,* III, 2, 1, 23; which reads *te'surā ātta-vacaso he'lavo he'lava iti vadantaḥ pārābabhūbuh.* The Kanva recension has a variant reading (Sacred Books of the East, XXVI; p. 31, n. 3) but the end result is similar.
18. *Vyākaraṇa Mahābhāṣya,* I, 1, 1, which reads, *te'surā helayo helaya iti kurvantaḥ parābabhūbuḥ.* In both cases the word for enemy, *ari,* uses 'l' instead of the pure Indo-Aryan 'r'. The Asuras here referred to are a puzzle. They are described as demons, but also as a maritime people whom the Āryans of the *Ṛg Veda* had to contend with. Were they the people of the Harappa Culture or were they a branch of the Āryans who came from the southern coast of Iran? Archaeological remains in Chota Nagpur are associated by the local tribes with the Asuras. Banerji Sastri, *Journal of the Bihar Oriental Research Society,* XII, pt. ii, 246 ff.
19. A characteristic of the Prakrit of eastern India attested by the inscriptions of Aśoka is that the 'r' sound changes into 'l', J. Bloch, *Les Inscriptions d' Asoka,* (Paris, 1950), p. 112.
20 *Manu,* II, 23; X, 45.
21. *Āryāvarta* was traditionally the region inhabited by the *āryas.* Its precise geographical area is difficult to define as the concept was not static in history. Broadly speaking, however, the Ganges-Yamuna Doāb and the plain of Kurukshetra to the north of Delhi would roughly correspond to *āryāvarta,* in the strict sense. Some texts extend the definition to include almost the entire Indo-Gangetic plain, e.g., *Manu,* II, 17-74.
22. *Viṣṇu,* LXXXIV, 1-4.
23. *Manu,* X, 45, 57; speaks of *ārya-vāc* and *ārya-rūpa* (noble speech and noble visage) where *ārya* is used in an adjectival form. The Pali *ayya* or *ajja* carries the same sense. The antonym of *anārya, dāsa* or *dasyu* again carries the meaning of lacking in worthiness and respect and cannot be taken in an ethnic sense alone.
24. S.K. Aiyangar, *Some Contributions of South India to Indian Culture,* (Calcutta, 1923), pp.1-42.
25. *Manu,* X, 10-12; 16-17.
26. Others included the Āndhras, Ābhīra, Pulinda, Khāsa, Magadha, Kirāta, Malla. *Gautama Dharmaśāstra,* IV, 4; *Baudhāyana,* I, 9, 3; *Vasiṣṭha,* XVIII, 9.
27. *Gautama,* IV, *15ff; Baudhāyana,* I, 8, 8; *Vasiṣṭha,* XVIII, 1-6.
28. *Manu,* X, 39.
29. *Aitereya Brāhmaṇa,* VIII, 21; The Āmbaṣṭha tribe is frequently identified by modern scholars with Ambastanoi of Arrian and the Sambastoi of Ḍiodorus.

H.C. Raichaudhury, *Political History of Ancient India,* (Calcutta, 1952), p. 255.

30. *Taittirīya Brāhmaṇa,* III, 8, 5.
31. *Taittirīya Samhitā,* I, 8, 9, 1-2; The *sūta* was one of the *ratnins* at the rites of the *vājapeya* sacrifice.
32. Pāṇini, II, 4, 10. R.S. Sharma, *Śūdras in Ancient India,* (Delhi, 1958), p. 125, suggests that originally they may have been an aboriginal tribe using their own dialect, the *cāṇḍāla-bhāṣā.*
33. *Pañcavimśataka Brāhmaṇa,* XVII, 1, 9; 53, 2. *Āpastambha Dharmasūtra,* XXII, 5, 4.
34. As for example the use *Manu* makes of the term *vrātya-kṣatriya* or 'degenerate *kṣatriyas'* when describing the Greeks, or *vrātya* for those who have failed to fulfil their sacred duties, X, 20; II, 39.
35. *Atharvaveda,* XV.
36. Also included were the Bedar, Daśārṇa, Mātaṅga, Pundra, Lambakarṇa, Ekpāda, Yakṣa, Kinnara,. Kīkata, Niṣāda. Some of these are fanciful names—Long-ears, Single-footed; some were celestial beings; but in the main both literature and epigraphs record the names of many of these tribal peoples.
37. D.R. Chanana, *Agriculture in the Rāmāyaṇa,* (New Delhi, 1964).
38. Yāska in *Nirukta,* II, 2. *Atharvaveda,* V, 22, 14; *Chāndogya Upaniṣad.* VI, 14, 1, 2.
39. The western Ānavas were the Yaudheyas, Āmbaṣṭha, Śibi, Sindhu, Sauvira, Kaikeya, Madra; Vṛṣadarbha. The eastern Ānavas were the people of Aṅga, Vaṅga, Kaliṅga, Pundra and Suhma. It has been suggested that the names ending in *aṅga* are of Muṇḍā origin and these tribes would therefore be pre-Aryan. P.C. Bagchi, ed., *Pre-Aryan and Pre-Dravidian in India,* (Calcutta, 1929).
40. *Aitereya Brāhmaṇa,* VIII, 14, 23: *Śatapatha Brāhmaṇa,* III, 2, a
41. Atanatīya Sutta, *Dīgha Nikāya,* III, p. 199 ff.
42. Brāhmāṇḍa Purāṇa II, 19, 24; III, 59, 46, *Vāyu,* 91, 7; *Matsya,* 83, 34; 105, 20.
43. The Kuru tribe had a well-known status and antiquity. They acquired fame through the epic *Mahābhārata* which concerns a family feud between the Kauravas and the Pāṇḍavas, both members of the Kuru lineage. The Pañcālas were a confederation of five tribes. According to bardic tradition the royal family of the Pañcālas was an off-shoot of the Bharata family.
44. B.B. Lal, 'Further Copper Hoards from the Gangetic Basin . . .', *Ancient India,* no. 7, 1951, pp. 20 ff. S.P. Gupta, 'Indian Copper Hoards', *Journal of the Bihar Research Society,* XLIX, 1963, pp. 147 ff.
45. *Śatapatha Brāhmaṇa,* I, 4, 1, 10.
46. *Atharvaveda,* V.22.14. *Baudhāyana Dharmasūtra,* I, 1, 32-3; *Manu,* X, 11.
47. Texts as late as the *Mārkaṇḍeya Purāṇa* and the *Yajñvalkya Smṛti,* III, 292, repeat the need for the *prāyaścitta.*
48. *Prajñapaṇa Upaṅga,* p. 397; *Ācaraṅga Sūtra,* II, 3, 1; II, 11, 17.
49. *Anguttara Nikāya,* I, 213. The sixteen *mahājanapadas* or major states are listed as Gandhāra, Kāmboja, Kuru, Pañcāla, Śūrasena, Matsya, Kośala, Kāśi,

Malla, Vṛjji, Magadha, Aṅga, Vatsa, Cedi, Āvanti, Asmaka.

50. *Sammoha-vinodini,* Vibhaṅga commentary, 388; *Manoratha-purāṇi,* Anguttara Commentary, I, 409; *Apādāna,* II, 359; *Sutta Nipāta,* 977.

51. *Jātaka,* VI, 208, 210. Cf. *Manu,* X, 44.

52. *Summaṅgala Vilāsinī,* I, 276; *Sammoha-vinodini,* 388.

53. *Ibid.* the ancestry of the Pulinda located in Ceylon alone, according to the Buddhist sources, derives from the marriage of prince Vijaya with the demoness Kuveni.

54. The *Cāṇḍāla* is known and mentioned in Buddhist sources but usually in the context of his overcoming his low status although this is often done through the acquisition of some spiritual power.

55. Major Rock Edict, XII. J. Bloch, *Les Inscriptions d' Aśoka,* pp. 130 ff. Aśoka lists the Yona, Kāmboja Nābhaka, Bhoja, Pitinika, Āndhra and Pālida.

56. The Second Separate Edict. J. Bloch, *Les Inscriptions d' Aśoka,* pp. 140 ff.

57. *Arthaśāstra,* II, 1; III, 16; VII, 8; VIII, 4; IX, 1; IX, 3; X, 2.

58. McCrindle, *India as Described by Megasthenes and Arrian,* pp. 20-1; McCrindle, *India as Described by Ktesias,* pp. 23-4, 86. Earlier Greek writers such as Ktesias, the Greek physician at the Persian court in the sixth century B.C., referred to the Indian king trading cotton and weapons for fruit, dyes and gum with the Kynokephaloi or Kynomolgoi, a barbarian tribe. The identity of this tribe has not been conclusively established as yet.

59. *Matsya Purāṇa,* 34, 30; 50, 76.

60. Utpala's commentary on the *Bṛhatsamhitā,* XIII, 3, describes the Śakas as *mleccha-jātayo-rājanas* and adds that the period of their destruction by Vikramāditya would be known as *Śaka-kāla.*

61. A large number of early Sanskrit inscriptions come from the *mleccha* areas of northern and western India. *Corpus Inscriptionum Indicarum,* vol. II. The Greeks had used Greek and Prākrit or Sanskrit bilingually as on their coins: Obverse—*Basileus Suthos Menandros,* Reverse—*Mahārājas Trādarasa Menamdrasa.* Smith, *Catalogue of Coins in the Indian Museum, Calcutta,* vol. I, pp. 22 ff. Kuṣāṇa coins show a slow but increasing adoption of Indian deities particularly of the Śaivite family. The Śaka kings not only affirm their protection of the law of *varṇa* but even record large donations of cows and villages and wealth to the *brāhmaṇs.* Rudradāman's Junāgadh Inscription, *Epigraphia Indica,* VIII, no. 6, pp. 44 ff.

62. *Manu,* X, 43-4; *Mahābhārata,* Anuśāsana Parva, 35.17ff Vana Parva 48.20ff Sa Parva 65.13ff LII, p. 145.

63. Kanakasabhai, *The Tamils Eighteen Hundred Years Ago,* (Madras, 1904), pp. 37 ff. M. Subramaniam, *Pre-Pallava Tamil Index,* (Madras 1966), p. 618.

64. McCrindle, *Invasion of India by Alexander,* p. 234; *Mahābhārata,* Sabha Parva, 29.5ff *British Museum Catalogue of Indian Coins,* p. cv. The legend reads, *mālava-gaṇasya-jaya.*

65. McCrindle, *The Invasion of India by Alexander,* p. 232; *Mahābhārata,* Sabhā Parva, 29.5ff *Journal of the Numismatic Society of India,* IX, p. 82; *British Museum Catalogue,* p. cxxiv; the legend reads *sibi janapadasa.*

66. *Aṣṭādhyāyi,* V, 3, 116; *Mahābhārata.* Sabhā Parva, 29.5.ff; the legends reads *trakaṭaka janapadasa. Aṣṭādhyāyi,* IV, 1, 178; *British Museum Catalogue,*

pp. cxlix-cl. The legend reads, *yaudheya-bahū-dhānyake*, and a fourth-century coin-mould reads, *yaudheya-gaṇsya-jaya.*

67. The Allahabad *praśasti* of Samudragupta. *Corpus Inscriptionum Indicarum*, III, pp. 66 ff.

68. The eighteen major *Purāṇas* were recorded from about the third century A.D. onwards. They claim to be compendia of information orally transmitted over a period going back to *c.* 3000 B.C. The texts deal with the mythologies of the creation of the universe, genealogies of kings and sages, social custom and religious practices generally pertaining to a particular sect of which each *Purāṇa* claims to be the sacred book. In fact much of the material reflects contemporary attitudes at the time of the composition of the *Purāṇa.* The genealogical sections are in the form of a prophecy, an obvious attempt to claim antiquity.

69. Puranic cosmology envisages a cyclical movement of time and the world goes through a period of four ages with the golden age at the start and an increase in evil through the duration of the cycle. The last of the four is the Kaliyuga at the end of which evil will be prevalent and the *mleccha* all-powerful. Ultimately the entire universe will be totally destroyed after which a new universe will be created and the cycle will start again.

70. *Vāyu Purāṇa,* 99; *Bhāgvata,* XII, 2, 11-16; II, 38; XII, 3, 44-51 ; 25; 3, 35-6. Deprived of sacrificial activities the world will be reduced to *mleccha*-hood.

71. *Matsya Purāṇa,* 47, 252, *Vāyu,* 98 114; *Brahmāṇḍa,* III, 14, 80; 22, 22; 73, 108; 35, 10; IV, 29, 131.

72. *Viṣṇu Purāṇa,* IV, 24, 51; *Brahamāṇḍa,* II, 16, 59; III, 14, 80; IV, 29, 131; *Manu,* X., 8-38; *Yājñavalkya smṛti,* III, 292; *Smṛticandrikā,* I, 22-24. This is particularly contradictory in the case of the *Purāṇas* where a number of *mleccha* cults and rites had become incorporated into the recognized religion, particularly rites associated with the mother-goddess. For the reference to the Śakas and Yavanas, see, e.g. Nasik Cave Inscription, *Epigraphia Indica,* VIII, no. 8, pp. 60 ff.

73. In the Rudrādhyāya of the *Yajurveda.* Other degraded professions are the nomads, carpenters, chariot-makers, potters, smiths, fowlers, dog-keepers and hunters. In this text as also the *Nirukta* of Yāska they are mentioned as the fifth group after the four *varṇas,* III, 8; X, 3, 5-7.

74. *Manu,* X, 8, 18, 48. They were descended from the marriage between a *brāhmaṇ* and a *sūdra* woman.

75. *Garuḍa Purāṇa,* VI, 6; LV, 15; *Padma,* II, 27, 42-3; *Harivaṁśa,* XV, 27, 33.

76. *Viṣṇu Purāṇa,* I, 13.

77. *Matsya Purāṇa,* 10, 4-10; *Bhāgvata,* IV, 13, 42, 47; *Mahābhārata,* Śānti Parva, 59. 99.ff.

78. *Matsya Purāṇa,* 10, 7.

79. *The Amarakoṣa,* VII, 21; a lexicon of the post-Gupta period, in its definition of *mleccha* mentions these three tribes and describes them as hunters and deer killers, living in mountainous country, armed with bows and arrows and speaking an unintelligible language—the conventional description of the *mleccha*

by the time of the medieval period. Yet the location of *mleccha-deśa* in this text is not in central India but in northern India.

80. *Rg Veda*, III, 53, 14; ***Mahābhārata***, II:13.19ff *Bhāgvata Purāṇa* 11, 21, 8; *Manu*, X, 44.

81. *Mahābhārata* 7.87.27ff.

82. ***Mārkaṇḍeya Purāṇa***, p. 284; ***Matsya Purāṇa***, **114, 307; a seventh-century author identifies them with the Bhila and Lubhdhaka tribes of the Vindhyas** and also connects them with the Mātaṅga, the lawless hunters of the region, Daṇḍin, *Daśakumārcarita*, III, 104; VIII, 203. The name Mātaṅga is very curious and suggests a Muṇḍā-Dravidian combination. The twelfth-century *Pampa Rāmāyaṇa* of Abhināva Pampa VII, 105-55, also refers to them.

83. Bhāravi's long poem, the *Kirātārjunīya*, is based on an episode from the *Mahābhārata* when Arjuna goes into the Himalayas and does penance. He finally meets the god Śiva in the form of a Kirāta with whom he has a protracted fight, but eventually acquires the divine weapons which he is seeking. It is interesting that the Kirāta should be identified with Śiva—perhaps suggesting their worship of Śiva, and also that it is through a Kirāta that the great hero Arjuna acquires the divine weapons.

84. *Pampa Rāmāyaṇa*, Nijagunayogi's Vivekcintāmaṇi, pp. 423-4. Chikka Deva inscription of the seventeenth century in Rice, *Mysore and Coorg from its Inscriptions*, p. 129.

85. Buddhist sources refer to the children of the demoness whom prince Vijaya married on his arrival in Ceylon as the Pulinda and state that they lived in the interior of the island at a place called Sabaragamuva (=Śabaragrāma, the village of the Śabaras?), *Mahāvaṃśa*, VII, 68; *Vinaya Piṭaka*, I, 168. These have come to be associated with the primitive Veddah tribes of Ceylon. **In early brahmanical sources they are mentioned as a wild mountain** tribe of the Deccan, *Aitereya Brāhmana*, VII, 18; *Mahābhārata*. Adi Parva 165.3ff. Later sources connect them with the Bhilas, *Mathasāritasagāra*, II, 12; *Amarakoṣa*, II, 20-1.

86. **Ptolemy, VII, 1, 64; Ptolemy's phrase brings to mind the use of the *Piśāca*** in Indian literature which also carries the meaning of those who eat raw flesh. Its most obvious connection is with the famous *Bṛhatkathā* of Guṇāḍhya which was written in a *Piśāca* or goblin language, and the location was the Vindhyas. Possibly the *Piśāca* language was that of these *mleccha* tribes. Interestingly, it is often associated by some scholars with the north western areas which may suggest a migration of some at least of these peoples from the northwest to the Vindhyas. Keith, *A History of Sanskrit Literature*, (Oxford, 1928), pp. 266 ff.

87. *Rāmāyaṇa I.54.1-3 Kathāsaritasāgara*, IV, 22.

88. ***Nātyasāstra***, XXI, 89; ***Brhatkathāślokasangraha***, **VIII**, 31.

89. ***Rāmāyaṇa***, Adi Kaṇda, 47ff; Aranya Kaṇda, LXXVII, 6-32. Bana, *Kadambari*, p. 12.

90. **Dholpur Inscription, *Indian Antiquary*, XIX, p.** 35; **Khadavada Inscription** of the time of Gyas Sahi of Mandu, *Journal of the Bombay Branch of the Royal Asiatic Society*, XXIII, p. 12.

91. *Rāmāyaṇa*, IV, 37-8.

92. *Amuktamālyada,* IV, 206.
93. *Viṣṇu Dharmasūtra,* 71, 59, 84, 2-4; *Vasiṣṭha,* 6, 41; *Gautama,* IX, 17; *Atri,* VII. 2. The *śrāddha* ceremony was an essential rite for the *ārya* since it concerned the offering of food to the spirits of the ancestors and thereby strengthened and re-affirmed kin-ties. It is clearly stated in the above texts that the *ārya* is prohibited from speaking with the *mleccha,* from learning their language or from making journeys to a *mleccha-deśa* since contact with the *mleccha* was polluting. The journeys were regarded with particular disapproval since the *śrāddha* ceremony could not be performed in such areas.
94. *Medātithi,* a tenth-century commentator, on *Manu,* II, 23.
95. *Mahāvastu,* I, 135, *Raghuvaṁśa,* IV, 67-68.
6
96. Eran Stone Boar Inscription, *Corpus Inscriptionum Indicarum,* vol. III, p. 158; G.R. Sharma, *Excavations at Kauśāmbi,* pp. 15-16.
97. *Rājataraṅgiṇī,* I, 306-7; Kalhaṇa calls him the 'god of destruction'. I. 289.
98. E.g. Hsüan Tsang's descriptions: S. Beal, *Buddhist Records of the Western World,* I, (London, 1883), pp. 177 ff.
99. Dhānyaviṣṇu the brother of Matṛviṣṇu (*vśayapati* of the Gupta king Budhagupta) became the feudatory of Toramāna. Cf. The Eran Inscription of Budhagupta, *Corpus Inscriptionum Indicarum,* III, p. 89, with the Eran Stone Boar Inscription of Toramāna, op. cit., p. 158. Budhagupta in his inscription is referred to merely as *bhupati* (king), whereas Toramāna takes the full imperial title of *Mahārājādhirāja* and is described as 'the glorious', 'of great fame and lustre' and 'ruling the earth.'
100. It is believed that the Gurjaras came from central India after the sixth century A.D. and were of Tocharian extraction, D.R. Bhandarkar, *Indian Antiquary,* January 1911, p. 21-2; A. C. Bannerjee, *Lectures in Rajput History,* p. 7; P.C. Bagchi, *India and Central Asia,* (Calcutta, 1955), p. 17. Place names in the Punjab—Gujrat, Gujeranwala, etc.,—suggest a settlement there as do the presence of the Gujjar herdsmen in Kashmir. The Gurjara Pratihāras ruled in western India, and there is the more recent Gujrat as a name of western India. The existence of the Gujjar caste in Maharashtra points to a further movement towards the south; I. Karve, *Hindu Society,* (Poona, 1961), The Bad-Gujar clan survives among the Rajputs as also the *brāhmaṇ* caste, Gujar-Gauḍa.

The Ābhīra are nomadic herdsmen who are believed to have migrated into India with the Scythians. Some of them very soon rose to importance, such as the general Rudrabhūti, Gunda Inscription of A.D. 181 in *Epigraphia Indica,* VIII, p. 188. They are located in the lower Indus and Kathiawar region, *Bhāgvata Purāṇa,* 1, 10, 35; *Periplus,* 41; Ptolemy, VII, 1, 55. The Ābhīras are described as *mlecchas* and *śūdras* in status, *Manu,* X, 15; *Mahābhāṣya,* I, 2, 72. They gradually took over political power from the Śakas and the Sātavāhanas and spread down the west coast of India where there is mention of the Konkànābhīra, *Bṛhatsamhitā,* 14, 12; 5, 42; 14, 18. Samudragupta in the Allahabad *praśasti* refers to the conquest of the Ābhīras, *Corpus Inscriptionum Indicarum,* III, 6 ff. A tenth-century Pratihāra inscription speaks of removing the menace of the Ābhīras in western India, Ghatiyala Pillar Inscription,

Epigraphia Indica, IX, p. 280.

101. This situation is discussed by R.S. Sharma in the book, *Indian Feudalism,* (Calcutta, 1965).

102 Ghatiyala Pillar Inscription, *Epigraphia Indica,* IX, p. 280.

103. The Gaṅga and Caṇḍella dynasty claim Candravaṁśi descent, the Gurjara-Pratihāras Sūryavaṁśī descent and the Parmāras regard their ancestor as having emerged from the Agnikula. The Guhilas, the Cālukyas of Veṅgi, the Cālukyas of Bādāmi and the Cālukyas of Kalyāni all claim solar descent, D.C. Sircar, 'The Guhila Claim of Solar Origin', *The Journal of Indian History,* 1964, no. 42.

104. An example of this, which was a common condition, is discussed in D.C. Sircar, *The Guhilas of Kishkinda,* (Calcutta, 1965). Even the Khaśa chiefs claim *kṣatriya* status in the Bodh Gaya inscription, *Epigraphia Indica,* XII, p. 30. The Pratihāra claim to descent from Lakṣmaṇa the younger brother of Rāma who acted as a door-keeper (pratihāra) is very suspicious, *Indian Antiquary.* January 1911, p. 23.

105. R.S. Sharma, 'Early Indian Feudalism', in S. Gopal and R. Thapar, ed., *Problems of Historical Writing in India,* (New Delhi, 1963), p. 74. These ideas are further worked out in his *Social Changes in Early Medieval India.*

The same policy was adopted by the Mughals who located colonists in these areas partly to encourage them in the ways of Islam and of 'civilization' and partly to keep a check on them, particularly at the time of the Maratha-Mughal conflict when the Vindhyan tribes occupied a strategic geographical position. It is not surprising that, during the period of British rule in India, Christian missionaries were extremely active in these regions.

106. Una Pillar Inscription of Avantivarman II dated A.D. 899, *Epigraphia Indica,* IX, p. 6 ff.

107. Atpur Inscription of Śaktikumār, *Indian Antiquary,* XXXIX, p. 191 ff.

108. *Kanhadeprabandha* of Padmanābha, a fifteenth-century work, mentions a Hūṇa among the list of Rajput *jagīrdārs, The Journal of Indian History,* XXXVIII, p. 106.

109. *Amarkoṣa,* II, 10, 2;

110. Rice, *Mysore and Coorg from the Inscriptions,* (London, 1913), p. 5.

111. *Epigraphia Carnatica,* VII, p. 188; VI, p. 113-14.

112. The Gaṅga king Koṅgunivarman gave a grant in A.D. 887.

113. B.N. Saletore, *Wild Tribes in Indian History,* (Delhi, 1936), p. 81 ff.

114. Ray, *Dynastic History of Northern India,* II, (Calcutta, 1936), p. 941.

115. Bargaon Copper-plate of Ratnapāla, *Journal of the Asiatic Society of Bengal,* p. 99; Pārbatiya plates of Vanmālaverrāmadeva, *Epigraphia Indica,* XXIX, pp. 145 ff. It has been suggested that the name Śālastambha approximates a Sanskritized version of the name of the Tibetan king, Sron-bstam-sgam-po.

116. *Manu,* X. 43-4; *Matsva Purāṇa,* 16, 16.

117. *Bṛhatsamhita,* V, 80; *Mārkaṇḍeya Purāṇa,* 57, 39. Chinese interest in eastern India during the seventh century A.D. is attested to in the reign of Harṣa and by his contemporaries in Assam. The pedestal inscription on the tomb of Tai Tsung mentions a diplomatic connection with eastern India.

118. Gwalior Inscription of Nagabhatta I; Sagar Tal Inscription, *Epigraphia Indica,* XVIII, p. 107 ff. An Arab attack on Kashmir in the eighth century is mentioned in the *Rājataraṅginī,* VIII, 2764.
119. Māhamadi Sāhi Inscription, *Epigraphia Indica,* I, p. 93; Jaitrasiṃhadeva grant, *Epigraphia Indica,* XXXII, pp. 220 ff.; Chitorgarh *praśasti, Journal of the Bombay Branch of the Royal Asiatic Society,* XXIII, p. 49; Madras Museum Plates, *Epigraphia Indica* VIII, p. 9; Bhilsa Inscription of Jayasiṃha, *Epigraphia Indica* XXXV, p. 187; Dantewara Inscription of A.D. 1703, *Epigraphia Indica.* IX, p. 164.
120. Bhatūrya Inscription of Rajyapāla, *Epigraphia Indica,* XXXIII, p. 150; Chitorgarh *praśasti* of Rana Kumbhakarṇa, *Journal of the Bombay Branch of the Royal Asiatic Society,* XXIII, p. 49; Bālaghāta Plate of Prithviśena II, *Epigraphia Indica,* IX, p. 270.
121. Sāgar Tal Inscription of Mihīra Bhoja, *Epigraphia Indica,* XVIII, p.107.ff
122. Śaka inscriptions reveal this very clearly as also the names of the Indo-Greeks. *Epigraphia Indica,* VII, p. 53, 55; *Epigraphia Indica,* VIII, 90; *Archaeological Survey of Western India,* IV, pp. 92 ff.
123. Mention is made of the Gandhāra and Kāmbhoja melodies as also of Śaka and Ābhīra melodies, *Pañcatantra,* Apanikṣetakanakam, 55.
124. From this point of view at least Indian eating habits and rituals would form an ideal subject for structuralist analysis, along the lines of the theories developed by Lévi-Strauss. See *Maṇu,* IV, 205-25; 247-53; for laws regarding the acceptance of various kinds of food.
125. Trikāṇdaśesa in *Nāmalinganuśāsana* of Amarkoṣa.
126. For the prohibition on onions and garlic, *Maṇu,* V, 19; for references to eating the flesh of the cow, *Jaiminī,* I, 3, 10 and *Rājataraṅginī,* VII, 1232.
127. *Mahābhārata,* Śānti Parva, LXV, 13-15.
128. *Viṣṇu Dharmaśāstra,* 84. 4; *Arthaśāstra,* III, 13-15.
129. Mathura Lion Capital Inscription, *Epigraphia Indica,* IX, p. 141; Mandasor Inscription, Viṣṇudatta Inscription, *Epigraphia Indica,* VIII, p. 88. Śaka kings often refer to themselves as *dhārmika* on coin legends with the symbol of the *Dharmacakra on the coin.*
130. *Journal of the Royal Asiatic Society,* 1909, pp. 1053 ff.
131. Eran Stone Boar Inscription. The *varāha* cave is at Udayagiri.
132. As for example the reference to Jalauka in the *Rājataraṅginī,* I, 108-52.
133. The snake cult or worship of the Nāga is attested to in literature as well as in the archaeological remains of a multitude of *nāga* shrines. It is frequently seen as the symbol of the chthonic goddess, of the ancestors and of lunar and fertility cults, and is commonly found even to this day in the Himalayan and Vindhyan regions. In the historical period it gained considerable respectability particularly in the peninsula.
134. There is mention in the *Ṛg Veda* of the pre-Āryan cults such as the worship of the phallus, *śiṣṇadevaḥ,* and the existence of sorceresses, *yatumati,* practising magic. The Harappan evidence clearly indicates the worship of the mother goddess which was new to the Āryan religion.
135. *Harivaṃśa,* II, 22, 59.

136. *Ibid.*, II, 22, 53-4.
137. *Ibid.*, II, 3, 12. She is sometimes described as *kṛṣṇācahvisama, kṛṣṇa* (as black as can be), adorned with peacock feathers and with dishevelled hair. Bāṇa, writing in the seventh century A.D. when speaking of the ***mleccha*** tribe of the Vindhyas, describes a Durgā temple, *Kadambari*. Of the Pulindas said to be living in the Vindhyan region, an eleventh-century text states that their king adores the cruel Devi, offers her human victims and pillages the caravans, *Kathāsaritasāgara*, IV, 22.
138. ***Harivaṃśa***, II, 58; ***Daśakumāracarita***, I, 14; VI, 149; VIII, 206.
139. Vākpati, *Gauḍavāho*, V, 305.
140. *Mārkaṇḍeya Purāṇa*, LXXXII, 10-18.
141. *Bhaviṣya Purāṇa*, II, 26; I, 39. *Samba Purāṇa*, 27, 28.
142. *Mahābhārata*, Aṇu Parva, XC, 11. *Manu*, III, 162.
143. *Bṛhatsaṃhitā*, LX, 19.
144. Maureen Patterson, 'Chitpavan Brahman Family Histories', in *Structure and Change in Indian Society*, (ed.) Milton Singer and B. Cohn (Chicago, 1968).

The Historian and Archaeological Data

It is now a truism to say that significant new evidence on early periods of history is more likely to come from archaeological data than from literary sources. This makes the close collaboration between the historian and the archaeologist imperative. The collaboration inevitably becomes a two-way process, where the historian has to familiarize himself with archaeological data and methodology and the archaeologist has to be aware of the kind of evidence which the historian is seeking. Whereas the method of data-collection may differ between the two, the final process, that is, the interpretation of the data is similar to both disciplines. At this latter stage, the existence of common models would jointly benefit the historian and the archaeologist.

It is not my intention to cover all aspects of mutual interest to historians and archaeologists, but rather to draw attention to the less obvious aspects. Architecture and iconography, for example, have already profited by the dual approach of history and archaeology as also have various studies on chronology. The corroboration of literary sources through cross-checking with archaeological evidence is now also in practice. There are, however, some fields where either the archaeological data are not sufficient or else the archaeological interpretation has not been incorporated by historians, and it is these fields which require attention. The study of social history, economic history and the role of technology in Indian history, being comparatively new to the concern of both archaeologists and historians, require appropriate emphasis. Furthermore, in these fields, the evidence from archaeology can be used more directly. The historian has data on these aspects from literary sources but the data tends to be impressionistic and confined by the context. Archaeology can provide the historian with more precise data on the fundamentals of these aspects of history, resulting thereby in

From D.P. Agarwal and A. Ghosh (eds.), *Radiocarbon and Indian Archaeology* (Bombay, 1973), pp. 378-90.

a better comprehension of the early forms of socio-economic institutions. This, however, would require the working out of a common model for historians and archaeologists working on the early period, so that the questions asked by both relate to a common set of problems.

It might be premature at this stage to agree on a model for archaeological reconstruction, since archaeological and historical studies in India have so far been largely of a descriptive nature and the kind of questions which need to be posed for the construction of a model have, with rare exceptions, been neglected. (This word 'model' is perhaps preferable to 'hypothesis', since it implies a precisely stated, overall view, which can be verified either segmentally or as an entity.) Where an evolution of cultures is attempted in the protohistoric period it tends to rely on the preconceptions of literary evidence. The hunt for the Āryans is a particular case in point. We have all, at various occasions, spent time and energy in trying to identify the Āryans. If the identification of social groups referred to in literature is believed to be necessary, then it would be more purposeful to use the evidence of the early literature itself rather than the theories on race evolved in recent decades. Early literary traditions in India—Vedic, Epic and Puranic—claim to preserve the lineages of tribal groups. In some cases, such as that of the Yādavas, there is not only the initial lineage but also references to what may be called 'segmented' lineages, which branched off from the main lineage. The memory of geographical movements and migrations are often preserved in such lineages, and this may be a more worthwhile unit to identify than the Āryan or Dravidian race. Perhaps it would be more profitable to ignore the Āryans for the moment and concentrate on an evolution of cultures using the archaeological evidence alone. Alternatively, if on the basis of a common model the evolution of early Indian society from literary sources can be postulated, it can then be seen on comparison whether the two types of parallel evidence cohere. The social evolution derived from Vedic sources may be compared with that derived from the Painted Grey Ware (PGW) and the Northern Black Polished Ware (NBPW) in the Ganga valley or a similar procedure as seen in Sangam literature may be compared with Megalithic cultures of the same region. This is a very different procedure from trying to identify archaeological cultures as Āryan or Dravidian.

A Possible Model

The initial model may be most profitable if it merely presents a broad framework which nevertheless permits of a variety of precise questions. One could postulate a model with which some historians of socio-economic history are currently working. The model is sufficiently broad-based and requires a greater degree of refinement which will emerge through the joint efforts of historians and archaeologists. The model presupposes that the basic units of society consist of tribal groups, peasant groups and urban groups; that some groups remain constant at the primary stage, others evolve from among a variety of tribal organizations to peasant societies; that among the latter there is a wide variety of forms where some support urban cultures and others are involved in a diversification of agrarian cultures. The model derives substantially from archaeological evidence and is being used by historians and anthropologists as well, as an underpinning to explaining the evolution of societies. A precise definition of each unit would require detailed data on the ecological, technological, economic, social and cultural context. The ensuing generalization would be the result of a double-pronged approach, that of the excavator, the palaeobotanist, the hydrologist, etc., at the empirical level, as also the theoretical analysis of the historian, anthropologist and archaeologist.

The model does not necessarily propose a linear progression. Not all cultural groups evolve from one to the other to the third. The fundamental question is that of the relationship between the three units and their interaction on each other; and the nature of change when it occurs. Furthermore, it requires not merely a listing of causes and reasons but an evaluation among these of the priorities, pertinent to each particular problem; as also an understanding of the variations among each of the units and the factors which encourage evolution from one unit to another. Such an evaluation of priorities makes the analysis more precise. Certain problems relating to early Indian history could be seen more clearly if there was more discussion on the nature of the transition to agrarian village societies, these forming the basis of many of the kingdoms of the historical period. This relates initially to the transition and evolution of Neolithic and Chalcolithic cultures. Was there one centre of diffusion or were there a number of centres of independent origination? If it was the former, then how was the change diffused? If it was the latter, then what were the reasons for independent origination in each centre and how did one differ from the other? The question of the origin of the Neolithic is not altogether divorced from that of the areas of the progenitor of the staple crop and the spread of the latter. Similarly, the change to iron technology can only be properly studied by examining the ore producing areas and the communication between these and consumption points. Diffusion can only take place when populations are in close contact. Diffusion as a major factor in change necessitates a demographic analysis of the distribution of a culture. This in turn would relate to the pace of urbanization, where it seemingly occurs more rapidly in one area than in another, given similarity of preconditions. Ultimately any understanding of cultural change—change in the total pattern of living—must rely on a multidisciplinary approach, for no single discipline in isolation can adequately explain all aspects of change. Change takes place at different times and for different reasons. The basic question why some cultures changed and others did not remains unanswered as yet in any real sense. Irrespective of whether one is an evolutionist or a structuralist there is a need to answer this question with as precise a degree of evidence as possible. The question itself reveals various dimensions, each of which has to be considered in the general concept of change and evolution.

Ecology

Ecological studies, at one level, provide evidence on the environmental background of a culture, which may help to explain many facets of its development as also its peculiarities. But in areas of human habitation an eco-system is rarely static. A study of the eco-system in every major phase of cultural change may help answer the primary question of the role of natural agencies and of human action in the change. The ensuing change should then be applied to all the three units where they exist. The recent debate on the hydrology of Sind and Baluchistan in the Harappa period is a case in point (Raikes, 1964). It has been used to explain the decline of Mohenjo-daro. But little has been said on its effect on the peasant communities which were economically linked with the city; for still water causing a flood over a vast area must have seriously affected the agrarian centres in the environs of the city. Where human action has been the main agency of change—such as deforestation, soil exhaustion, over-grazing and over-population—the studies would provide clues to a major economic activity of a culture. The degree of change would also help to explain whether or not it resulted in migrations. There have been major hydrological changes in the Indo-Gangetic watershed. By mapping the geographical extent and chronology of these changes and comparing this evidence with that from archaeology, it may be possible to determine the impact of the change on human society in that region and, furthermore, may point to new areas for research—as for example: did these changes cause population movements? If so, where did people migrate to? Vedic and Puranic literature mentions a number of migrations of various peoples such as the Ābhīra, Andhaka-Vṛṣṇi, Yaudheyas, Mālavas and Śibis. The movement in many cases appears to have been from the Punjab and the eastern bank of the Sutlej to the western bank of the Yamuna or from the latter to Malwa and western India. Were these migrations the result of invasions, population pressures, search for new agricultural lands, pursuit of trade or changing ecology, or a combination of two or more of these? The areas and routes involved appear to be those known from earlier cultures.

The Geographical Unit or the Region

Basic to such studies is the dimension of the geographical unit, the region. Regional factors such as topography, geography and ecology, are often the bedrock of early cultures using a pre-industrial technology. The definition of a region should relate to what geographers have called the perennial nuclear region (Spate, 1967; Subba Rao, 1958). It would be worthwhile to do an intensive archaeological survey and investigation of such a region using the entire gamut of archaeological methodology, primarily to understand the nature of the cultures which it has produced and the characteristics of change in these cultures (which may in some cases have a regional genesis). The study could co-ordinate ecological evidence, changing topography and the material remains of cultures. In this instance historical data could also be used in defining a region. For many centuries in the early period, the territorial unit was the *janapada* and the very fact of its survival suggests that there must have been characteristics of a geographical-ecological nature which gave the *janapada* its identity. In many cases it also represents the change from a tribal identity to a territorial identity and to that degree registers a socio-economic change. In such cases the original tribal entity evolved into a closely-knit peasant society, sometimes with its nuclei in towns. The association of linguistic, occupational or religious-sectarian identities, as in the case of the Yaudheyas, Auḍumbaras and Arjunāyanas, indicated in literary and numismatic sources, suggest that not only did these units survive the change of dynasties, but, in certain areas, were probably little affected by them. (There is a curious continuity of tribal organization in areas associated with post-Harappan cultures carrying traces of late Harappan survivals—northern Rajasthan, the Indo-Gangetic watershed and Malwa.) As such, they would be more authentic units of initial study than kingdoms defined by political boundaries. Where the historical *janapada* coincides with a geographical nuclear region, such as the Kuru, Matsya, Kāśi and Kośala *janapadas*, surveys and investigations should prove to be rewarding. Even major historical nuclear areas, such as Magadha, have not as yet been subjected to such a scrutiny. (Apart from anything else, it would be interesting to see if the archaeological evidence confirms, at least proportionately, the figures for population and habitation in the major *janapadas* as given in the literary sources, such as the *Skandapurāṇa* and Vinayacandra's *Kāvyaśikṣā*.)

Settlement Patterns

The study of settlement patterns remains neglected. The plotting of settlements belonging to a particular culture on a topographical map is a comparatively uncomplicated way of indicating settlement preferences. This could be attempted in the first instance on the basis of intensive survey evidence and limited to a region. It may provide some pointers as to whether the settlements conform to nucleated or linear habitations if the approximate sizes of the sites are also included. Horizontal excavations of selected sites could corroborate (or not) the earlier indications. Are the early settlement lines in the Ganga-Yamuna Doāb consistently on river buffs? Is there a preference for elevated areas in the Ganga valley? And would this indicate that tribal movements in the early historical period followed areas of elevation? Within the category of nucleated villages, are some of these fortified and do they tend to be on elevated ground? Is there any substantial difference in material culture between fortified and unfortified villages? (Gimbutas, 1970) Continuous settlement on a particular site, with or without lacunae, would raise the question of the geographical and/or economic importance of the site. Why was Hastināpur reoccupied in spite of the long break and the flood? Is it merely a conservative outlook which leads to reoccupation of sites or are there other factors which are more central? Why do some towns survive centuries of change and continue, whereas others die out?

Settlement patterns also provide clues to communication lines, since routes and habitations tend to co-exist. The Indo-Gangetic watershed would be an obvious area to examine for continuity of routes, since it was the highway from the Ganga valley to the north-west. Other routes were those connecting western India with the Ganga valley either via the Aravallis, or via Malwa and the Chambal river, or along the Narmada and Son valleys. The ascertaining of communication lines would assist in understanding the spread of technologies and, in later periods, the spread of ideas. A systematic study of strategically located sites needs to be carried out to ascertain the importance of routes. Geographical and topographical features would be central to such a study. Thus habitations at the base of mountain passes and sites at river crossings and fordable points need investigation. It is interesting that urban sites along the Yamuna in the Doāb follow the south bank whereas those on the Ganga, in the mid-Ganga valley, follow the north bank.

Demographic Studies

The study of settlement patterns presupposes an interest in demographic data and this is a crucial factor in the understanding of cultural change. The change from the Upper Palaeolithic to the Mesolithic, it is believed, results in a decrease in mortality rates (Genovese, 1969), and the change from tribal to peasant societies results in an increase in population (Ratzel, 1891). Are these generalizations true of the Indian evidence? The greater frequency of infant burials in the pre-Neolithic phases would suggest the validity of a decrease in infant mortality rates as compared to the Neolithic and later phases. The numerical increase of the Neolithic settlements over the earlier cultures would point to an increase in population. But this needs to be verified. Other variables, the most obvious being a paucity of sites for the earlier period, have also to be considered.

Methods for extracting demographic data are well-known and include, in the main, the evidence from burials and skeletal remains, the calculation of the number of persons required for a conjoint effort and the extent and nature of the habitation (Ascadi and Nemeskeri, 1957). The evidence may not always be forthcoming and the results may be imprecise, but the attempt can nevertheless be made. The extent of habitation can be ascertained, albeit impressionistically, by a judicious use of the horizontal excavation—not necessarily by exposing the entire area of habitation put by selecting particular points for exposure. In cases of clear-cut cultural occupations there is a need to know the demographic contours, since these would provide information on the pace of change and the nature of change. The ratio of population to land provides further insights into the nature of the settlement. It can also indicate the degree to which initiative towards further development was present or absent. The clearing of the monsoon forests of the Ganga valley required not only iron technology but also larger populations than did the clearing of forests in drier areas. If the vegetation is of a variety which grows rapidly then this again would require the availability of manpower. Are larger populations a prerequisite to urbanization? Does the demographic factor in itself influence change?

Technology

The specialist study of technologies has emerged as a major area of interest in archaeology. The typology of various artifacts has been worked out to an impressive degree by Indian archaeologists. The point has now been reached where the correlation of artifacts with patterns of living should form the next stage of study. The historian may wish to ask a wide range of questions in this connection. Some relate to the identification of technologies. Swidden agriculture is an essential feature of early tribal economy. Can the archaeologist indicate the groups which were dependent on swidden agriculture? Presumably the absence of any agricultural implement other than the weight attached to the digging stick would be a pointer to this. Plough agriculture raises another series of questions. Did the ard precede the plough? In the case of the former, the yield would not be sufficient to produce the required surplus for transition to urban centres. It would be useful to know what kind of plough was used in the field excavated at Kalibangan and this can perhaps be determined by an examination of the furrows and the soil colouring, as has been done elsewhere (Gimbutas, 1970). Definite evidence of the use of metal-tipped plough shares would mark a distinct advance in agricultural technology. Does the metal-tipped ploughshare associated with a heavier plough coincide with an increase in the domestication of draught animals? Are there certain implements which occur more frequently in the cultivation of particular crops? For example, is the hoe found more frequently in areas of rice cultivation? The functional capacity of technology requires to be measured. If the carrying capacity of a bullock-cart or a boat can be ascertained as well as the distance it can cover in a given time, then some idea of the volume of trade can be calculated from literary sources which occasionally mention the number of carts or boats involved. There is now enough evidence on the size and shape of carts and the changing form of the yoke in various periods of the Indian past. A functional study of the cart therefore would not prove to be impossible.

Equally important is the question of whether a change in a single technology results in a new cultural pattern. This is particularly relevant in the study of ceramic industries, where there is a tendency to assume that a change of colour or of form indicates a new people. For example, does the change from PGW to NBPW reflect a new people or is it an evolution within the same ceramic technology? If the forms are similar then the functions must have been similar. Yet PGW occurs in larger quantities in wheat using areas and NBP ware in rice using areas. Was this fundamental dietary difference (and incidentally culinary difference too) reflected in the pottery types? The criterion of design in indicating diffusion or change is extremely tricky as it has to be examined on the basis of a combination of factors: naturalistic design associated with indigenous products, abstract design which may be symbolic or could have evolved functionally, and design as a result of technology and the process of manufacture. Crucial artifacts such as pottery should be viewed in the perspective of all the possible indices of a culture.

Food Production

Food production is partially dependent on the nature of the soil. Increased fertility in early periods would either be due to the use of manure or better irrigation facilities. Evidence of manuring would suggest more advanced agriculture and a larger domestication of animals. Crop patterns have their role in history, if it can be proved that certain crops give a higher yield for the same input. This may result in a faster rate of development thus affecting both the demographic structure and the production of surplus food (and, in later periods, revenue). In this context, would there be a difference between wheat and rice or between different varieties of the same crop?

Irrigation and hydraulic systems would also relate to the material conditions of a culture. Wells, tanks, terracing, dams, cisterns and ancient river channels not only need to be mapped but their capacity ascertained. Irrigation relates to a highly controversial debate hinging on the model of 'oriental despotism' (Wittfogel, 1957). The controversy over who owned the hydraulic machinery can be effectively dealt with once the type of irrigation system in an area is known with relevance to its environmental context. Was it possible for the village of the megalithic culture to construct through cooperative effort the tanks with which the culture is associated, or would the construction have required the enforcement of an overall state system? The answer would involve a co-ordination of demographic, technological and ecological data.

Urbanization

The process of urbanization (i.e., the evolution of towns) involves certain relationships between the unit of the town and the unit of the peasant society supporting it. A primary requisite is surplus food production. This involves an analysis in each case of how the surplus was transported to the urban centre—here again demography becomes crucial, apart from transport technology; and what was the mechanism by which the urban centre could extract the surplus—was it a tribute to a conqueror, or a political authority deriving sanction from either secular or religious demands or an economic exchange? Once again, the relationship between the town and the peasant community can be better grasped by a comprehension of the function of towns and villages rather than by a description of cultural assemblages alone. A further prerequisite for urbanization is trade. This involves more than a listing of the items produced in a particular town and presumably traded. It involves the placing of a town within an entire trading network, the latter being constituted of areas of production, areas of distribution and the means of contact and transportation. Each item of trade would have to be discussed in these terms. Ceramic industries, metals, beads and precious stones are useful criteria for this kind of analysis. Is it true, as it has been maintained by some, that trade develops in areas which are the meeting point of contrasting ecologies and contrasting cultures? (Mandel, 1968) This would relate not only to the choice of sites for towns, but would also explain the rationale for the production and exchange of goods. Is there a deliberate production of particular items solely for trading purposes? The latter would suggest a more sophisticated trading network. In assessing the source and distribution of artifacts, methods of quantification can be used, provided the variables are accounted for.

An understanding of the processes of urbanization affords a better explanation for the decline of cities as well. The pre-industrial city is dependent on the coming together of various factors—a favourable ecological base, cross-cultural contacts in goods and ideas, advanced technology relating particularly to food-production and metallurgy, social organization involving specialized skills, a power structure with the control of the city in the hands of an elite and communication with the environs (Sjoberg, 1960). The decline of cities is due to the malfunctioning of these factors either jointly or individually on an appreciably massive scale. Invasions alone rarely lead to the decline of cities although they generally result in temporary dislocation. Only the systematic destruction of a city by invaders can lead to its decline through invasion.

The settlement pattern of towns can indicate social organization. Much of the history of a town is contained in its pattern of growth. Population estimates would help explain the agrarian environment and the trading network. The existence and organization of markets, either as arbitrary centres of exchange or as control points, would provide evidence on the role of the elite. Concern for the nature of the market again means, essentially, a detailed study of the area surrounding the urban centre and its relationship with this area. Material and cultural differences occurring consistently in distinctive sections of the town may suggest a variation of social groups, though the central factor here would be the precise nature of the differences. Skeletal remains at Mohenjo-daro have led to the idea that it was inhabited by four ethnic types (Wheeler, 1968). Are these types represented in socio-cultural differences in the settlement of the town itself?

The Historian's Use of the Evidence: Economic History

For the historian the answer to these questions can make a substantial difference to the understanding of the material foundations of the Indian past. The expansion of the agrarian economy together with certain technologies provided the incentive for urbanization in the Ganga valley and further expansion along these lines provided the material base for the Mauryan empire. The systematic cultivation of waste land, whether through state initiative as suggested by Kauṭalya or through land grants as in the post-Gupta period, was one of the avenues through which the formation of states was accelerated. The new settlements became the nuclei of the Sanskritic tradition, which thus spread into new areas and which in turn was modified by the local or non-Sanskritic tradition: a process which continues to this day in various parts of the country. The degree of modification depended on the circumstances under which the new settlement grew. The two economic channels through which Indian civilization advanced and evolved were the spread of the agrarian village economy and the expansion of trade. Political forms have a relationship with the economic background. The evolution of the notion of the state—a qualitative departure from earlier political systems—seems to have coincided, in ancient India, with the expansion of the agrarian village economy. This is clearly suggested in some literary sources (*Dīgha Nikāya, Mahābhārata*) and is borne out by the evidence of later transitions from tribal to peasant societies and the emergence of the state in the latter. The state had to be maintained through revenue and taxes and these were regular, easier to collect and more substantial in agrarian village economies. In this connection, what may be termed 'medieval archaeology' would be of great help to the historian. From the eighth century A.D. onwards, land-grant inscriptions relating to waste land, indirectly record the spread of the agrarian economy. This evidence could be collated with surveys of the habitation sites of the period—deserted villages appear to be the most obvious type of site for this kind of work. Similarly the innumerable references to villages in Cola inscriptions could be mapped and attempts made to find their archaeological counterparts.

Trade played a similar role. As a channel of culture its significance depended on the degree to which it dominated the trade network. In the case of some states, where the major revenue was from trade, it played the same role as did agrarian revenue in other states, in sustaining the state machinery. The role of Roman trade as an economic backing to state-formation among the early south Indian kingdoms—the Colas, Ceras and Pāṇḍyas—could be investigated. West Asian trade generally may have been a consistent factor in the political forms of the west coast kingdoms, heavily dependent on this trade. A more specialized study of ports, harbours and maritime technology would assist in assessing the volume of trade and its economic role. The possibilities of underwater archaeology as sources of data for this enquiry have not as yet been seriously tapped in India. Admittedly, conditions for exploration and underwater excavation would by no means be so ideal as in the Mediterranean, but in certain areas the techniques may be used. Tanks, lakes, *baolis*, wells, pilgrimage centres on rivers, may well prove fruitful.

Given the comparatively slow change in technology in the early periods, patterns of settlement would not change radically from century to century. Settlement patterns may indicate how waste land was utilized in historical periods. Demographic studies are in any case useful to the historian who has to consider population pressures on the economy and eventually on political events. Did the Mauryan empire decline because among many other factors, the economy was unable to sustain the imperial system? Was the expansion of agriculture inadequate for the required revenue? These are legitimate questions which the economic historian can ask. Can archaeology supplement the data, perhaps through a study of agricultural technology (in its widest sense) of the approximate Mauryan period and by an assessment of the degree of material advance in the village sites of this period? Literary evidence on such questions would tend to be inferential.

The Historian's Use of the Evidence: Social History

In social history the basic process was that of the transition from a non-caste group to a caste (*jāti*). In some cases, tribes were converted into castes, generally in the transition from tribal to peasant society. The religious-sectarian groups which eventually became castes drew their support from either or both the village and the town. Change to caste status also meant being accommodated into the hierarchy of society. The process can best be studied if there is evidence on the material basis of these groups which might explain why they voluntarily or otherwise were incorporated into the caste hierarchy, apart from the fact that the comparative analysis of the literary and material data would provide a better understanding of the process.

The motivation for caste formation and constraints on mobility often relate to ecological, demographic or technological factors, which are then clothed in the garb of social and religious custom. These factors could perhaps be better elucidated through archaeological data. The hierarchical ranking in the social organization of skilled groups practising certain technologies—weavers, blacksmiths, potters—could be made more clear if a picture of the actual context could be given. Why were hunting and fishing groups or bamboo-workers often regarded as untouchables? What was the level of material culture of professional groups? Did they control the technology or was their role that of subservient artisans? Regional variation in the ranking of cast groups, and the difference between the actual status and the 'ritual' status, could also be clarified by the conjoint use of archaeological and literary evidence.

If archaeological data can provide us with more precise answers to some of the questions posed, it will also encourage historians to look more analytically at the literary evidence. For example, the identification of technological implements can become more exact. The relationship of a town to its rural environments can be studied. The characteristics of tribal and peasant societies can be more easily observed, as also the migrations of groups. Evidence on the rate of change may explain why change occurs at a faster pace in some areas and less so in others or why some areas tend to be historically isolated. The degree of change also needs to be examined. Does a new ceramic industry indicate a new culture, or can it be called a new culture only when there is evidence of change in all the major technologies or component elements of that culture? In short, the process of change and transition from one type of society to another can be better culled from literary sources if there is a general framework from archaeology with which it can be correlated or at least compared; a framework which will be based on the tangibles of archaeological data in addition to the all-too-frequent abstractions of literary sources. Archaeology can thus assist in answering the question relating to the 'how' and 'why' of cultural change, of which the total image is reflected in literary sources. If precise evidence on material culture is available it enables a historian to discuss institutions with greater clarity. Human institutions emerge as a result of many factors and material culture together with ideology join in varying proportions to evolve an institution. Archaeology can at least provide the data for the former.

If the basic units of tribal, peasant and urban are used, then a number of orientations emerge. The indigenous evolution of cultures will have to be looked at more carefully. It may be necessary, for example, to work out an indigenous evolutionary pattern for the Ganga valley with another civilizational thrust possibly in southern Bihar, which was not entirely unconnected with Harappa survivals but whose momentum would be local and linked primarily to iron technology. Again, if the basic units become central to the interpretation of the data, archaeological evidence would become increasingly relevant for later periods of history as well, including the medieval period. The nature of change within peasant societies and their variations as well as the nature of urbanization would continue to be basic to these periods. The periodization of historical archaeology which, today, conventionally follows the dynastic periodization, which is neither relevant nor precise in many areas, could be made more functional.

I am well aware that a number of the questions raised here have already been asked by some archaeologists working on Indian material. In reiterating these questions I am making a plea for their inclusion in the training of archaeologists. The archaeologist's concern should not be limited to the typology of artifacts and the sequence of cultures. Among recent publications, one at least does show the effectiveness of asking new questions and seeking data from what might appear to be, at first, impossible sources (Brothwell and Higgs, 1969). I am also aware that it is equally necessary for many of us as historians to ask these questions and there is a need to change the orientation towards data and analysis of those historians who are concerned with social and economic history. The crisis in history also relates to the needs for models and a departure from arbitrary data collection. It is only when such questions are jointly asked by historians and archaeologists that there can be a termination to the present divorce between the two disciplines. Even if the evidence for these questions is at the moment lacking there is nevertheless a need to pose the questions. For if the questions loom large then new techniques of investigation may also be discovered, as has happened not only in other disciplines, but also in archaeology itself in other parts of the world.

BIBLIOGRAPHY

Ascadi, G. and Nemeskeri, J. 1957. 'Palaeodemographische Problem', *Homo*, 8, B.

Brothwell, D. and E.S. Higgs. (eds.) 1969. *Science in Archaeology* (London).

Genovese, S. 1969.'Estimation of Age and Mortality' in (eds.) D Brothwell and E. Higgs, *Science in Archaeology*, p. 440.

Gimbutas, M. 1970. 'Proto Indo-European Culture' in (ed.) G. Cardoma, *Indo-European and Indo-Europeans*, p. 164, (Philadelphia).

Mandel, E. 1968. *Marxist Economic Theory* (London).

Raikes, R. 1964. 'End of the Ancient Cities of the Indus', *American Anthropologist*, vol. 66, no. 2.

Ratzel, F. 1891, *Anthropogeographie*, II (Stuttgart).

Sjoberg, G. 1960. *The Pre-Industrial City* (Glencoe).

Spate, O. 1967. *India and Pakistan—A Regional and General Geography* (London).

Subba Rao, B. 1958. *The Personality of India* (Baroda).

Wheeler, R.E.M. 1968. *The Indus Civilisation* (Cambridge).

Wittfogel, K. 1957. *Oriental Despotism* (New Haven).

The Study of Society in Ancient India

Mr. President, Ladies and Gentlemen,

I would like to thank the Executive Committee of the Indian History Congress for the honour which they have done me in electing me President of the Ancient Indian History Section of this session. My work in this field still being of a limited kind I have taken the honour essentially as a gesture of encouragement: a gesture which, coming from such an august body, is especially welcome to those of us who are sometimes regarded almost as heretics in the profession. The fact that this is linked with the session being held at Varanasi strikes me, for various well-known reasons, as being a particularly happy augury for the future.

I am standing here in the place of a distinguished elder in the profession—Dr. Moreshwar Dikshit. It is indeed a great loss to us that he passed away suddenly this year. Dr. Dikshit's work in Indian archaeology requires little introduction. Apart from his work in the field at sites such as Rangpur, Sirpur, Karad and Tripuri which is available to us in his excavation reports, he will be particularly remembered for his studies of beads and of glass in India.[1]

It would be a fitting tribute to Dr. Dikshit for me to emphasize the need to integrate archaeological and literary evidence in the historical study of those periods where the two types of evidence are available. Such an integration, however, demands a rather different approach to ancient Indian history, and more especially social history, from the one which predominates. It demands a search for a more realistic picture of the past and the need to ask a series of precise and pertinent questions (even if we cannot give as yet precise answers), on the 'why' and 'how' of the functioning of a society and its culture.

I would like therefore to take as my theme, the study of society in ancient India and to deal with the period from *circa* 2500 B.C

Presidential Address, Ancient Indian History Section, XXXI Indian History Congress, 28-30 December, 1969, Varanasi.

to 500 B.C. in northern India, treating it principally as a case study to demonstrate what I mean by a reorientation of perspectives.*

Let me say at the outset that I am not concerned with 'the Āryan problem' per se. It is perhaps the biggest red herring that was dragged across the path of historians of India.[2] What I am concerned with is the need to understand the evolution of society at this time. This is a crucial period not only because it saw the initial pattern of Indian culture take shape, but also because it can provide clues to a more analytical understanding of subsequent periods of Indian history. As it happens, the more important and controversial announcements pertaining to ancient Indian studies made during the year also relate to this period. The most serious of the many claims to have deciphered the Harappa script, in terms of the methodology used and the discussion it has provoked, is that of the Finnish scholars, who read the script as proto-Dravidian.[3] An interesting facet of the controversy has been the vehemence of the loyalty to the Indo-Aryan and Dravidian language groups, with undertones almost of an Āryan and a Dravidian nationalism. This, in spite of the fact that specialists in both languages have for many years been suggesting that at the cultural level at least this dichotomy is false.[4]

Our starting point in the study of the period 2500-500 B.C. could be the fact that we have two types of evidence, archaeological and literary. The literary sources are well-known and comprise the corpus of Vedic literature. The archaeological evidence consists of a number of cultures, most of them seemingly disparate. The earliest are the pre-Harappan cultures; the Sothi culture[5] of the Sarasvati valley and the Chalcolithic village sites of Baluchistan and Sind. These were the precursors of the Harappa culture (*c.* 2300-1750) which extended from southern Punjab and Sind to the Narmada delta largely following the coastal region, and eastwards as far as the upper Ganga-Yamuna Doāb.[6] Of the post-Harappan cultures there is evidence from both the Indus and Ganges valleys. In northern Punjab the Gandhara Grave culture[7] (*c.* 1500-500 B.C.), using a red ware and a plain grey ware, shows evidence of copper in the early stages and later an iron technology, and close contacts

* Owing to the shortage of time I have confined myself to general remarks and observations in the text of this Address. Further discussion and references are included in the notes at the end of the Address.

with Iran and central Asia. The Banas culture of southern Rajasthan (*c*. 2000-1200 B.C., with possible extensions in the Ganges valley coming down to 800 B.C.) with its characteristic white-painted black-and-red pottery and its probable internalizing of certain Harappan forms, possibly acted as a bridge between the Harappan and post-Harappan cultures.[8] The chalcolithic cultures of the Narmada and central India also show some contact with west Asia. In the upper Ganges valley the earliest remains belong to the culture represented by the Ochre Colour Pottery which is post-Harappan in time range (*c*. 1400-1200). This has been associated sometimes with the Copper Hoard Culture[9] found both in the Doāb and in southern Bihar and west Bengal, and whose authors were perhaps the Muṇḍā speaking peoples. At some sites in Bihar there is evidence of the black-and-red ware (occasionally white-painted and similar to that of the Banas culture) forming the earliest level. In parts of the Doāb it succeeds the Ochre Colour Pottery and precedes the pre-dominant culture of the region. The latter is the Painted Grey Ware[10] (*c*.1100-400) an initially agrarian culture familiar with iron technology and the horse. Finally, the Northern Black Polished Ware culture (*c*. 500-100) is associated with urbanization in the Ganges valley.

The archaeological picture therefore shows a large variety of cultures, none of which can be identified as specifically Āryan.[11] Nor does the evidence suggest that there was a single dominating culture which slowly spread throughout northern India bringing the various diverse cultures into its fold, which is what one would expect if the popular notion of the spread of Āryan culture be accepted. In comparing the Indian and west Asian material there is again little consistent evidence of a dominant culture recognisably coming from west Asia to India, or for that matter going from India to west Asia, though, there are certain similarities of techniques, such as the socketed axe and, in pottery, coming from west Asia. This would suggest migrants carrying aspects of technology and probably the language.

In comparing literary and archaeological evidence it is important to determine the nature of the society concerned. In the case of the *Ṛg Veda* the geographical focus is that of the *sapta sindhava* roughly from the Kabul river to the Sarasvati river.[12] Ṛgvedic society is essentially a pre-urban society with a copper and possibly iron technology.[13] It is evolving from nomadic pastoralism dependent on cattle to an agrarian form with more settled communities. Barley (*yava*) appears to have been the staple food. There is a strong sense of tribal identity and the basic social unit is the patriarchal family. Close linguistic connections with Iran are evident. The important deities are Indra, Mitra, Varuṇa, Savitṛ, Soma and Agni. There is a distinct feeling of cultural exclusiveness and separation from the local people who are both feared and disliked and with whom relations are frequently hostile (e.g. the Dasyus and the Paṇis).

The Later Vedic literature depicts a recognizable change in material culture. The geographical focus includes the Punjab and the middle Ganges valley in the main, with a more marginal familiarity with the Indus area, western and eastern India and the Vindhyas. The society is essentially agrarian culminating in a series of urban centres. There is a considerable acquaintance with iron technology. Frequent mention is made of rice (*vrīhi*) which is not mentioned in the *Ṛg Veda*. The tribal identity continues and in many cases is extended to territorial identity. The Ṛgvedic deities do not have the pre-eminent position which they had earlier since equal importance is now given to more recently incorporated deities. The four-fold caste structure mentioned only once in the *Ṛg Veda* is now a recognized feature. The geographical and philosophical connections with west Asia have weakened. There is evidence of a much greater assimilation of local cultures. In comparing the early and late Vedic literature it would seem that the major characteristic of continuity remains the language, Sanskrit.

Whatever our cherished notions about the Āryans may be, the archaeological evidence does not suggest a massive invasion or a massive migration.[14] Even if it be conceded that the presence of Indo-Aryan in the *sapta sindhava* region can be attributed to invasion, which is at times suggested in the *Ṛg Veda,* the same reason cannot be given for its presence in other parts of northern India. At most it can be said that the Indo-Aryan speakers were small groups of migrants with a strong adherence to a linguistic equipment deriving from Indo-European. Both linguistic evidence and the literature point to the Indo-Aryan speakers living in the vicinity of those who spoke an alien language (*mṛdhra vāc*) and those later called the *mlecchas*.[15] Were these the Muṇḍā or Dravidian speakers? Were they also the authors of pre-iron Chalcolithic cultures? In the Ganges valley archaeological evidence does not suggest that the earlier inhabitants fled or migrated. Therefore their continued presence must have necessitated a process of acculturation. What then was the nature of the impact of these Indo-Aryan speakers? Perhaps it would make greater historical sense if we see it not as the imposition of Āryan culture on the existing Indian cultures, but rather, as the diffusion of Indo-Aryan. The new language could have been accepted for various reasons without necessitating the imposition of a totally new culture.[16]

In the study of the inter-action of cultures there are many facets which require investigation. Let me start with the most primary, the question of the numbers of people involved. This would imply demographic studies of various sites and settlements. Comparative assessments of population figures from the sites of varying cultures could be helpful, as also the detailed charting of the location of sites—whether they are superimposed or adjacent. Would there be a greater possibility of cross-cultural assimilation if the numbers are consistently small and equally matched?[17] A demographic analysis, even if impressionistic, studied together with the nature of the terrain and technology and facilities for transportation would provide indications of the pace and flow of migration. The Painted Grey Ware settlements being generally small, the nature of the terrain being thick jungle, the pace of migration would be slow even if the river was used as the main channel of communication. It should not be forgotten that in spite of a time-span of about six hundred years the geographical distribution of the Painted Grey Ware remains broadly the Ganga-Yamuna Doāb and the Sarasvati valley. However, acceleration in the pace of communication seems to accompany the development of an urban culture as it would appear from the distribution of the Northern Black Polished Ware.

Even a rough demographic picture will introduce an element of reality into the study. If the settlements of a particular culture are small then production is also likely to be small. A comparison between such data and literary descriptions of extravagant wealth may lead to a correcting of the poetic licence implicit in great works of literature. Estimates of production are relevant to the study of towns owing to the interdependence of towns and villages.[18] More mundane factors such as food habits have their own significance. The Ṛgvedic people had a diet substantially of barley, and the Later Vedic literature introduces rice. From the archaeological evidence we know that the Harappans were mainly barley and wheat eating, whereas the Ganges valley, the Banas valley and probably western India was predominantly rice eating.[19] This points to a major difference of staple diet between the Ṛgvedic and Later Vedic people. If they were the same ethnically then they must have rapidly adjusted to a change of diet. However, the Painted Grey Ware levels in the Doāb suggest a people long accustomed to rice. It is interesting that in later Sanskrit literature wheat is sometimes referred to as *mleccha-bhojana*.[20]

Another aspect in the process of acculturation is the role of technology. A language which is associated with an advanced technology can often make a very effective impact. The use of the horse and of iron would point to an advanced technology. The acceptance of the Indo-Aryan language would therefore not require the physical conquest of the areas where it came to be spoken but rather the control of the advanced technology by the speakers of Indo-Aryan.[21] The horse-drawn chariot seems to have swung the balance militarily in favour of the Indo-Aryan speakers, judging from the hymns of the *Ṛg Veda*. The horse as compared to the ox was a swifter means of transportation as also was the chariot as compared with the cart.[22] The introduction of iron did not mean totally new technological implements. It was more a qualitative improvement of existing forms particularly in relation to the ecological conditions of the region. The hafted copper axe gave way to the socketed iron axe, the wooden plough had an iron tip added to it and the stone hoe was replaced by the iron hoe (or it was introduced where the hoe was not known before), not to mention adzes, arrow-heads, spear-heads, knives, daggers, nails, etc.[23] The technology of Painted Grey Ware culture seems to support this assessment. The question of who introduced iron technology to India has its own importance, but for our purposes it is more relevant to enquire as to whether the speakers of Indo-Aryan exploited the knowledge of iron technology to their advantage. That the new technology was essentially the improvement of existing forms is supported by the use of certain significant words in Vedic literature which appear to have a non-Indo-Aryan origin. Thus the most frequently used word for plough is *lāṅgala* which is of Muṇḍā origin and the word for rice *vrīhi* is believed to be of Dravidian origin.[24] Could there have been a correlation between the degree of technological change and the utilization of Indo-Aryan? That the caste status of iron smiths ultimately became low would accord with the probability that as long as the control of the technology lay with the higher status groups, the actual working of the technology could remain with low status groups.[25]

In ancient agricultural societies, apart from agricultural technology, another factor of some consequence would be the knowledge of the calendar. It is thought that the earliest calendar used in India was the lunar calendar. Yet the solar calendar was more efficient in its application to agriculture and astronomy (and thereby to astrology). The discovery and use of the solar calendar would require more advanced knowledge in mathematics and astronomy. A basis of mathematical knowledge must be assumed in order to explain the construction of the Harappan cities. Was this knowledge continued in some tradition? If the Harappans had used a binary system (by and large) then the decimal system referred to in the Vedic literature would have been an improvement.[26] The essential geometrical knowledge necessary for evolving a solar calendar may have been inherent in the geometry required for the construction of complex sacrificial altars.[27] There appears to be a groping towards understanding the principles of the solar calendar in the Vedic literature. The year of 360 days (30 x 12 months) was known to be defective and attempts were made at intercalation in which the 366-day year was not excluded.[28] It is true that the widespread knowledge of the solar calendar is associated with Greek contacts at a later period. It is not to be ruled out however that a secret knowledge or a restricted knowledge of it may have existed earlier. The appropriation of such knowledge by certain groups may well have given them access to power and influence. A scientific study of the application of astronomy and mathematics to activities such as agriculture and astrology within the context of contemporary society might be revealing: as also the transmission of mathematical ideas between Babylon and India.

In the post-Harappa period the centre of historical activity moved away from the Indus valley towards other directions: to the Ganges valley with Magadha eventually emerging as a nuclear region, to western India, and later, to the coastal regions of the peninsula. Part of the reason for the movement away from the Indus valley was the break-down in the Harappan economic system.[29] The post-

Harappan sites in western India appear to have re-introduced the ealier maritime contacts with Mesopotamia, from at least the first millennium B.C. As such, western India would have acted as a point of communication for goods and ideas between India and west Asia. A further archaeological investigation of the west coast and routes from here to the Ganges valley may prove worthwhile.[30]

Another aspect worth considering in assessing the reasons for the spread of Indo-Aryan is the interrelationship between language and society. The fact that the earliest Sanskrit grammars were written in the north points to a greater use or longer tradition of the language in this region. By contrast the lower Ganges valley retains a Prākṛt tradition for a longer period.[31] Was this distinction due to the linguistic differences in Indo-Aryan itself or was it due to a greater influence of non-Indo-Aryan languages in eastern India? Magadha is described as an impure land and the people of Aṅga, Vaṅga and Kaliṅga are referred to as *mleccha*.[32] It is also worth examining why certain important words relating to technology were introduced from non-Indo-Aryan sources and retained in Indo-Aryan. We have already noticed the case of *lāṅgala* and *vrīhi*. The Indo-Aryan for horse is *aśva*, yet *aśva* was never as commonly used in the Late Indo-Aryan languages as *ghoṭa* and its derivatives.[33] That this could happen with items as important as the plough, rice and the horse, makes one wonder whether the question of loan words from Muṇḍā and Dravidian does not call for a co-ordinated study by the specialist in linguistics and the historian, which would not merely trace the loan or the etymology of words, but would also throw light on the cultural context of their incorporation. The etymology of technical and professional words in their historical context would alone be worth a study.

It is historically well-known that in the spread of a language associated with an advanced technology it is often the dominant groups in the existing society which take up the new language first. This would be easier to understand in our peiod if we had some concrete evidence on the origin of the caste structure. It is curious that although the origin of the caste structure is frequently associated with the Āryan speakers it occurs only in India and not in other societies which were also recipients of Āryan culture. It may therefore have been a pre-Āryan system which was reconstituted somewhat, and described in Later Vedic literature. To see caste as the distinction between fair Āryans and dark non-Āryans is to over-simplify a very complex system. In the study of social structure the historian of ancient India must of necessity now take the help of social anthropology. The essentials of a caste society are, firstly, marriage and lineage functioning through exogamous and endogamous kinship relations (*jāti*); secondly, the integration of the division of labour into a hierarchical system which eventually takes the form of service relationships; thirdly, the idea of pollution where some groups are seen as ritually pure, others less so and yet others totally impure or polluting; and finally the association of castes with particular geographical locations. All these factors could have been present in the Harappa culture where social stratification can at least be surmised.[34] If a similar system prevailed in the Banas culture and those of the Ganges valley, then the spread of a new language could be achieved through influencing the groups which held high status and by re-arrangement of endogamous groups.[35]

Ascribing caste status did not merely depend on the occupation of a group. In some cases an entire tribe was ascribed a particular rank. Those speaking a non-Indo-Aryan language were frequently given a low rank and described as *mleccha*. In the case of the *cāṇḍālas* there is reference to a *cāṇḍāla-bhāṣā*.[36] Some of these tribes remained consistently of low status over many centuries, such as the Kirāta and the Pulinda[37]; others acquired political power and thereby higher status. Even today there are pockets of Muṇḍā and Dravidian-speaking people in areas of Indo-Aryan languages. This is not due to any historical oversight. The Muṇḍā-speaking groups until recently were hunters and pastoralists with, at most, digging-stick agriculture. In contrast to this the Indo-Aryan speaking people are, by and large, plough and hoe-using agriculturalists. Were the *śūdra* tribes those who in the initial stages either did not accept the new agricultural technology or did not apply it? Did the Aryanization of language accompany the expansion of the iron-using agrarian village?

This village was not the neolithic village growing essentially in isolation, nor the Chalcolithic village with restricted trade interrelationships. It was the prosperous iron-using village whose prosperity increased with easier access to both iron ore and more land for cultivation. This prosperity could not only give these villages a political edge over the others but also provide a larger surplus for those in control. At one level this became the stable base for the growth of towns[38]; at another level it strengthened the language, Indo-Aryan.

With the change from nomadic pastoralism to settled agrarian villages, tribal identity was extended to territorial identity, as is reflected in tribal names being given to geographical areas. This in turn gave rise to the concept of the state with both monarchical and non-monarchical forms of government. Woven into this concept were the institutions of caste and private property.[39]

Even among those tribes who had accepted the new technology and language, the priests—the ritually pure groups—would have resisted the new culture unless their own status was safeguarded. Was this done by allowing them to preserve their ritual purity through the caste structure and by their continuing to hold a priestly status, and also by incorporating much of their religion into the new culture? The assimilation of a tribe into the caste structure would also require some assimilation of its religion. The religious aspects of Later Vedic literature, inasmuch as they differ from the *Ṛg Veda*, include a large amount of non-Āryan practice and belief—both at the level of ritual and of deities.[40] It is indeed a moot point whether this literature can be called the religious literature of the Āryans alone.

Every society has a method of remembering what it regards as the important aspects of its past and this is woven into its historical tradition. For our period it is the *itihāsa-purāṇa* tradition which sets out to record the past. The most significant section of this tradition is the preservation of the royal genealogies and the myths associated with them. The royal genealogies (*vamśāvalī*) may not be historically correct but when studied carefully they indicate the pattern of the migration and spread of various peoples. Such an analysis can be more useful than the repeated but so far unsuccessful attempts to identify the tribes as either Āryan or non-Āryan. Genealogies have played a noticeably important part in the Indian historical tradition, even when they are known to be fabricated. This is surely the clue to understanding the role of the genealogy, not necessarily as an authentic dynastic chronicle but rather as a social document. Similarly, what is important about the myths is not whether they are historically authentic, but the cultural assumptions of the society which are implicit in the myth.[41]

The questions which arise in the study of the proto-historic period have a relevance to later history. It would seem that in northern India the expansion of the village economy based on iron technology accompanied the diffusion of Indo-Aryan, judging by the archaeological evidence for the distribution of iron in association with literary evidence for Indo-Aryan. Indo-Aryan therefore would not be widely accepted in those areas where iron technology was already known. In the peninsula the area covered by the iron-using Megalithic culture roughly coincides with the area of the widespread use of Dravidian languages.

If we can explain the reasons for the shift in focus from the Indus valley to the Ganges valley in proto-historic times, then we can also throw some light on one of the more interesting facets of ancient Indian history, namely, the geographical shift in the nuclear regions which were the matrices of large states and empires. At least three regions come immediately to mind: Magadha, the Raichur-Bijapur districts, and the area between Kanchipuram and Tanjore. Why did these regions give rise to a series of politically dominant states and then go into quiescence?[42] Was it due to the fertility of the region yielding large revenues, or the abundant availability of iron, or access to trade routes, or the exploitation of a new technology or the rise of ideologies motivating political action? Or was it merely the strange but happy coincidence of a series of strong rulers, which is the explanation generally offered?

In the analysis of social structure there is a need for re-defining social relationships. To see caste only in terms of the four-fold *varṇa* does not take us very far. One would like to know how tribes and social groups were adjusted into the caste hierarchy and assigned a caste status. The theory that the cast-structure was initially flexible but gradually became rigid and allowed of little mobility, is now open to question. There is enough evidence to suggest that there have been in all periods deviations from the theoretical concept of caste.[43] We also know that there was a continual emergence of new castes for a variety of reasons. Furthermore social change presupposes social tension and at times even conflicts between groups, and these are referred to in the sources. The origin, nature and consequences of these tensions constitutes another significant area of study.

The history of religion, apart from its theological, philosophical and iconographical aspects, also has a social aspect, since religion has to be practised by people in order to be viable. The interrelation therefore of religious cults and movements with social groups is very close. What were the social roots of Buddhism and Jainism? Why were certain cults assimilated and others left out in what later came to be called Hinduism? What accounts for the remarkable popularity of the mother-goddess cults in various forms in the post-Gupta period? More precise answers to such questions would help us ascertain with greater accuracy the nature of the 'brahmanical renaissance' as it is called in the Gupta and post-Gupta periods.

It will be evident that I am making a plea for more intensive studies of the nature of society in ancient India: and by this I mean an integrated understanding of the many facets which go into the functioning of a society. Such a study involves not merely additional dimensions in terms of methods and sources, it also means, if need be, altering the perspective from which we view the past. New perspectives, although they may initially appear whimsical, often provide new insights. The immense labour and scholarship of our predecessors has provided us with a firm foundation on which to base our studies of ancient Indian history. We can with confidence, therefore, explore new perspectives. Ultimately as historians we are concerned not merely with attempting to discover the past, but with trying to understand it.

REFERENCES AND FURTHER DISCUSSION

1. *Explorations at Karad,* Bharat Itihasa Samshodhaka Mandala, no. 74, 1949.
   Etched Beads in India, Deccan College Monograph Series, no. 4, 1949.
   'Excavations at Rangpur, 1947', *Bulletin of the Deccan College Post-Graduate Research Inst.*, XI, no. 1, December 1950.
   'Beads from Ahichhatra, U.P.', *Ancient India,* no. 8, 1952, p. 33ff.
   Tripuri 1952, University of Saugar, 1955.
   History of Indian Glass, University of Bombay, 1969.
   Dr. Dikshit's interest in Indian glass extended to maintaining a personal collection of rare pieces. I am also told by his friends that his philatelic interests were equally impressive.
2. The Āryan problem arose out of a series of philological studies in the eighteenth and nineteenth century which recorded the similarities between a number of languages of Asia and Europe and postulated a common ancestry in Indo-European. Max Müller's statement about the Āryan nation as the physical manifestation of Āryan culture lent support to the search for the Āryan race. His later repeated

attempts to deny the existence of an Āryan race were often ignored (*Biographies of Words and the Home of the Vedas*, p. 90, 1887). Incidentally, it is conceivable that Max-Müller's Aryan-Semitic dichotomy may well have influenced the Āryan-Dravidian dichotomy. The real damage was caused by his assertion of the superiority of Āryan culture over all other cultures, which has been made axiomatic to the study of the Indian past (*Chips from a German Workshop*, 1867, I, p. 63. '. . . In continual struggle with each other and with Semitic and Turanian races, these Āryan nations have become the rulers of history, and it seems to be their mission to link all parts of the world together by chains of civilisation, commerce and religion. . . .') Āryan culture is often taken as the starting point of Indian culture and is projected both backwards (in attempts to prove the Āryan basis of the Harappa culture) and forwards in time. It is also sought to be associated with every worthwhile achievement in early India.

In his enthusiasm for the Āryan way of life (as he saw it), Max Müller further depicted Āryan society as an idyllic society of village communities where people were concerned not with the mundane things of everyday living but with other wordly thoughts and values (*India, What can it teach us?* p. 101ff.) This has also acted as a check on the more realistic study of the actual conditions of life in the Vedic period. That the motives of Max Müller and other Indologists of his views in acclaiming Āryan culture derived from a genuine admiration for Āryan society as they saw it, has to be conceded, but this does not exonerate them from gilding the lily. Max Müller's attempt to link India and Europe via the Āryans was in part to connect the origins of Indian culture with the Greeks who were regarded as the founders of European culture. Thus Indian culture could acquire status in the eyes of Europe and, at the same time, early Indian nationalism could exploit this connection to combat the cultural inferiority complex generated among Indians as a result of British rule. In fact early Indian nationalism gave greater attention to extolling the Āryans in India rather than to the connection with Europe. Historical scholarship has now moved beyond the needs and confines of nineteenth century nationalism and a re-evaluation of Max Müller's theories is necessary.

Even some modern sociological theorists have made sweeping generalisations on contemporary India and Indian society on the basis of the nineteenth century understanding of Indian history. Max Weber in his study, *The Religion of India,* (New York 1967 reprint) used fairly uncritically much of the writing of Orientalists such as Max Müller. A more recent example of the acceptance of this tradition, without a sufficient investigation of the alternatives, is Louis Dumont's *Homo Hierarchicus* (1967). That the influence of such thinking, stressing the other worldly character of Indian society, is apparent even on economic historians is evident from Gunnar Myrdal, *Asian Drama* (1969), where the Weberian thesis is given considerable emphasis to explain the failure of the development of capitalism in India.

3. Asko Parpola et al, *Decipherment of the Proto-Dravidian Inscriptions of the Indus Civilisation,* The Scandinavian Institute of Asian Studies, Copenhagen, 1969.

   Asko Parpola, *Progress in the Decipherment of the Proto-Dravidian Indus*

Script, 1969.

Asko Parpola, *Further Progress in the Decipherment of the Proto-Indus Script*, 1969.

A less publicised attempt was made by a number of Russian scholars and published last year. Y. Knorozov, *Proto-Indica*, 1968. Two other recent attempts, those of Dr. Fateh Singh and Mr. Krishna Rao, are generally not acceptable to scholars.

Owing to a lack of a bi-lingual inscription most attempts so far have used a system of intelligent (and in some cases not so intelligent) guesswork. Using the iconographic representation as the starting point attempts have been made to try and read the script as that of an Indo-Aryan language (Wadell, S. K. Ray, Krishna Rao). Those who have used the script as their starting point have more often arrived at Proto-Dravidian (Hunter, Heras, the Russians and the Finns). The Finns read it as a largely logographic script based on the principles of homophony. The advance made by the Finnish scholars and to some extent the earlier Russian studies is that they have placed greater reliance on linguistic and mathematical techniques rather than on historical guesswork. Any claims to decipherment must satisfy certain preconditions. The decipherment must conform to a grammatical and linguistic system and cannot be arbitrary (this being the major objection to the attempt by Krishna Rao); it must conform to the archaeological evidence of the culture and to the chronological span of the Harappa culture; the reading of the inscriptions must make sense in terms of the context of the culture. Of the recent attempts, the Russian and the Finnish conform most to these preconditions. However, even their readings present problems which they have not satisfactorily overcome. As to whether the Finnish claim is justified will depend on the publication of their readings of complete texts, which are still awaited.

As for example in the essays of Sylvain Levi, Jean Przyluski and Jules Bloch, translated and published by P.C. Bagchi in *Pre-Aryan and Pre-Dravidian in India*, 1929, and more recently in the writings of S.K. Chatterjee, T. Burrow and M.B. Emeneau.

A. Ghosh, "The Indus Civilisation—Its Origins, Authors, Extent and Chronology" in V.N. Misra and N.S. Mate (ed.), *Indian Pre-history*, 1964. An attempt has been made to try and identify the Sothi Culture with the Ṛgvedic people by A.D. 'Pusalkar, 'Pre-Harappan, Harappan and post-Harappan culture and the Āryan problem', *The Quarterly Review of Historical Studies*, VII, no. 4, 1967-68, p. 233 ff. Apart from the problem that the geographical extent does not coincide since the Ṛgvedic culture included northern Punjab and excluded Sind and western India, there is also the problem of chronology. Attempts to date the *Ṛg Veda* to the fourth and fifth millennia B.C. are based mainly on references to astronomical positions mentioned in the texts, viz., Tilak, *The Orion* . . . ; Jacobi, 'On the date of the *Ṛg Veda', Indian Antiquary*, June 1894; and Bühler, *Indian Antiquary*, Sept. 1894. Such evidence is not conclusive, since references to astronomy could have been incorporated from the traditions of an earlier people. The parallels with Gāthic Avestan and with Kassite and Mitanni inscriptions which are very close, would date the *Ṛg Veda* to the middle of the second millennium B.C.

6. The attempted identification of the Harappa culture with the later Vedic society on the basis of both being agro-urban societies is again controverted by the differences not only in the total culture but also in the geographical nuclei. The Harappa culture is located in the Indus valley and western India and its urbanization is based on a chalcolithic system with an absence of iron. Later Vedic society centering on the Ganges valley from which the Harappa culture is largely absent (except for a few minor sites in the upper Doāb) owes its gradual urbanization to iron technology. The technology of the two cultures is different. The pre-eminent role of the fertility cult among the Harappans is absent in Vedic society. The Harappans buried their dead, the Vedic people largely cremated their dead. (It is interesting that so far no graves have been found in association with the Painted Grey Ware cultures, which may suggest that they cremated their dead.) The horse so characteristic of Vedic society is not associated with the Harappans. The Harappa culture from the very beginning used a script whereas references to writing in Vedic society come at a later stage. If, finally, the Harappan script is read as Proto-Dravidian then there will be hardly any possibility of identifying the Harappa culture with Indo-Aryan speakers.
7. A.H. Dani, 'Gandhara Grave Culture', *Ancient Pakistan,* III, 1967.
8. B.B. Lal, *Indian Archaeology—A Review*, 1959-60 (for the site of Gilund); D.P. Agarwal, 'C-14 Dates, Banas Culture and the Aryans', *Current Science*, 5 March 1966, p. 114 ff.; H.D. Sankalia, 'New Light on the Indo-Iranian or Western Asiatic Relations between 1700-1200 B.C.'. *Artibus Asiae, XXVI*, 1963; H.D. Sankalia, S.B. Deo, Z.D. Ansari, *Excavations at Ahar,* 1969.
9. B.B. Lal, 'Further Copper Hoards from the Gangetic Basin and a Review of the Problem', *Ancient India,* no. 7, 1951, p. 20 ff; S.P. Gupta, 'Indian Copper Hoards', *Journal of the Bihar Research Society,* 49, 1963, p. 147 ff.
10. B.B. Lal, 'Excavations at Hastinapur', *Ancient India,* nos. 10 and 11, 1954-55, p. 5 ff.; T.N. Roy, 'Stratigraphical Position of the Painted Grey Ware in the Gangetic Valley', *Bharati,* no. 8, II, 1964-65, p. 64 ff.
11. A recent summary of attempts to identify the Āryans with archaeological evidence is that of Dilip K. Chakrabarti, 'The Āryan Hypothesis in Indian Archaeology', *Indian Studies*, IX, no. 4, July-Sept. 1968, p. 343 ff. The more recent evidence of the Gandhara Grave Culture has been interpreted by Dani as representing perhaps, the early Indo-Aryan migration identified with the Ṛg Vedic literature. This may in turn have developed into the Painted Grey Ware culture which is often equated with the later Vedic literature, although the link in southern Punjab is as yet missing. This identification does fit the geographical focii and conforms broadly to the technological evidence of the Vedic literature. The linguistic theories of Hoernle and Grierson, suggesting that there were two bands of migration and therefore of language, have been used in the argument that the first band settled in the *sapta sindhava* region, and the second, skirting round the Indus, perhaps settled in the Banas valley. From here there was a movement both along the northern slopes of the Vindhyas to Bihar and also into the Doāb. Incidentally, in the latter case it followed a route which was frequently used in historical times to connect the Doāb with the west coast.

12. There are incidental references to migration in the *Rg Veda*, in verses such as I.30.9.; I.36.18; and they read clearly as for example, VI.45.1, '. . . *ya ānayat parāvataḥ sūnītī turvaśam yaduṁ indroḥ sa yuva sakhā.* .'. Furthermore it must be remembered that the *nadī stuti* hymn which is often quoted to contradict the theory of migration is in fact from the tenth *maṇḍala* of the *Ṛg Veda* which is generally regarded as being later than the other sections.
13. The element of doubt arises because of the meaning of the word *ayas*. It is possible that it originally meant copper, as it seems to in some contexts, but later with the introduction of iron it was qualified by the terms *kṛṣṇa ayas* and *śyāma ayas*. When the association of *tāmra* with copper became common, then *ayas* may have been reserved for iron. It has however been argued that *ayas* originally meant iron and that the earliest knowledge of iron in India has therefore to be associated with the Ṛgvedic people. L. Gopal, *Uttar Bharati*, IV, no. 3, p. 71 ff. and N.R. Banerjee, *The Iron Age in India*, p. 158 ff. The Indo-European root of *ayas* and its consistent use as iron in other Indo-European languages (*aes, ais, aisa, eisarn*) is a strong argument in favour of this view.
14. The migration theory would seem more acceptable than the invasion theory. The association or the Cemetry H evidence with the Āryans and the supposed massacre at Mohenjo-daro has been doubted. B.B. Lal, 'Protohistoric Investigations', *Ancient India*, no. 9, 1953, p. 88; G.F. Dales, 'The Mythical Massacre at Mohenjo-daro', *Expedition*, VI, no. 3, 1964, p. 36 ff.; A. Ghosh, 'The archaeological background,' *M.A.S.I.* no. 9, 1962, p. 1: G.F. Dales, 'The Decline of the Harappans', *Scientific American*, vol. 214, no. 5, 1966. There is no evidence of Kalibangan having been attacked and it is unlikely that it would have been spared, being so close, if Harappa had been attacked. Post-Harappan cultures rarely build directly on the debris of Harappan sites except at Rupar and Alamgirpur. The extremely interesting discussion by Burrow on the significance of the terms *arma* and *armaka* in the Vedic literature and Pāṇini (*Journal of Indian History*, XLI, 1963, Part 1, p. 159 ff) suggests that the references to ruins were to the Indus Civilization cities. What is curious however is that in some cases it would appear that Indra and Agni were responsible for the destruction of these cities, whereas in other cases they appear already to have been in ruins. It would seem that most of these cities were in the Sarasvati and Punjab region. It is stated that the dark coloured inhabitants fled and migrated. This would agree with the archaeological evidence that the cities were deserted and not occupied by the new arrivals. They were regarded as places of evil and the haunt of sorceresses (*yātumatī*) and therefore to be avoided. This would hardly be the attitude of a conquering people who had actually destroyed the cities. Could the cities have been deserted owing to a natural calamity before the arrival of the Indo-Aryan speakers, who associated the ruins of cities with evil, perhaps set fire to the remaining ruins and ultimately attributed the destruction of the cities to Indra and Agni? This would also explain the chronological gap, i.e., the Harappa culture having declined by 1750 B.C. and the Ṛgvedic Āryans being dated to *circa* 1500 B.C.

The Allchins still adhere to the invasion theory in *The Birth of Indian Civilisation*, p. 144 ff. Even if the theory is conceded, the archaeological evidence in support of invasion is limited to Harappa and Mohenjo-daro and literary references which can be read as an invasion occur mainly in the *Ṛg Veda* which mentions attacks on fortified settlements inhabited by the hostile locals. The actual area involved in the invasion was therefore limited.

Recent skeleton analysis of the Harappa culture sites are tending to puncture the theory of the Indo-Aryan speakers representing a large and separate racial group. S.S. Sarkar, *Ancient Races of Baluchistan, Punjab and Sind,* maintains that the Harappans were the same as the present-day predominant ethnic types living in these areas, which would contradict the theory of a large scale Āryan invasion or migration. Dr. K. Sen, 'Ancient Races of India and Pakistan, a study of methods', *Ancient India*, nos. 20 and 21, 1964-65, p. 178 ff, has suggested that the ethnic stock of Cemetry R 37 and Cemetry H appears to have been the same although there are cultural differences.

15. In describing the *dāsa* the references to their being conquered in battle are only a few among a large number of other references to the differences between the Ārya and the *dāsa*. These differences emphasise the fact of the latter having an alien culture. Thus the *dāsa* are described in the *Ṛg Veda* as *hatvā dasyūn pura āyasīr ni tārit* (II, 20.8); *yo dāsam varṇam* (II.12.4); *hatvī dasyūn prāryan varṇam āvat* (III, 34.9); *ayajvānah* (I.33.4) *māyāvān abrahmā dasyurarta* (IV.16.9); *anāsa* (V.29.10); *akarma dasyūr abhi no amantur anyavrato amānuṣah tvam tasyamitrāhan vadhar dāsasya dambhaya* (X.22.8.); *mrdhra-vāc* (V.29.10). etc.

The word *mleccha* occurs in Later Vedic literature, e.g. in the *Śatapatha Brāhmaṇa* III.2.1.23-24, and is essentially a term of contempt for those who cannot speak the Āryan language and only gradually comes to acquire the meaning of a barbarian in a cultural sense. The etymology of the word is uncertain and does not appear to be Indo-Aryan, although it is said to derive from *vac.* It is also said to be onomatopoeic, based on the strange sounds of an alien tongue. A reference to *milakhuka* (from Pali *milakkhu,* Sanskrit *mleccha*) in the *Vinaya Piṭaka* III.28 is explained by Buddhaghosa as, *Andha-Damil ādi.*

16. It is not surprising that elsewhere too where Indo-European speakers have migrated and settled, the evidence for their presence is largely the Indo-European base of some of the languages of those areas. Greek contains elements of pre-Greek languages and the culture of classical Greece is rooted more in the pre-existing cultures of the region than in Indo-European culture (Luigi Pareti, *The Ancient World,* Part I; Moses Finlay, *The Ancient Greeks*; George Thompson, *Studies in Ancient Greek Society*). The culture of the Hittites is derived from the Hattians and only the language is Indo-European. The Mitannis worshipped 'Āryan' gods and used technical terms for chariotry which are Indo-European, but their language Hurrian is not included in the Indo-European group. Similarly the Kassites had Aryan-sounding names but only their ruling class seems to have been familiar with the Indo-European language. The idea of a common culture of the Indo-European speakers grew out of philological evidence. Archaeological evidence does not support such an idea. It might be worthwhile for philologists to reconsider the question of how common in fact was the culture of the Indo-European speakers. Clearly there was an early stage when certain ideas and perhaps some institutions were common to the Indo-European speakers. This stage is reflected in, for example, parts of the *Ṛg Veda*, the Avestan Gāthas, the inscriptions of the Mitanni

and passages of Homer. This forms the starting point of the ideas on comparative mythology developed for instance in the Kuhn-Müller theory and more recently in the writings of George Dumezil and Paul Thieme, which theories were applied to other areas on the basis of philological evidence. Had the spread of the language also resulted in the spread of similar ideas and institutions then there would have been a far greater identity in the subsequent development of the cultures of the regions where Indo-European languages were spoken. S.C. Malik in *Indian Civilisation, The Formative Period* (1969), p. 144, refers to the Āryan superstructure of ideology being imposed upon the earlier socio-economic organization. 'Hence, it was contrary to the general opinion, not the Aryanisation of India, but rather the Indianisation of the Āryan nomadic pastoralist hordes.'

17. The large concentration of people in the Harappan towns immediately indicates a different type of organization from the smaller settlements of the Painted Grey Ware. Even when describing the Harappan cities it is sobering to remember that Kalibangan for instance could hardly have had a population larger than 5,000. In cases where a series of trenches have been cut across a mound it is possible to assess the increase or decrease of population in an area of habitation at particular periods by comparing the stratigraphy. For example, a comparative study on these lines of P.G. Ware levels and N.B.P. levels could provide considerable information. Population estimates are, of course, best carried out from the evidence of burials and of habitation sites uncovered in a horizontal excavation. Where the latter is not possible, a controlled series of soundings may help. Palaeo-demography has already attracted the attention of scholars after the pioneering work of Matiga half a century ago. Attempts have been made to compute population by studying the relative density of remains, by estimating the mean number of individuals in a village site through the habitations and the burials, the land-man ratio in the context of the technology of the period, the estimated number of persons required for a co-operative effort, the setting-up of menhirs, and by a variety of statistical methods.

18. Attempts can be made to estimate the nature of food production by calculating the area of land required to feed a given number of people on the basis of the agricultural technology and possible soil conditions of the time. The inter-relation of town and village raises the question of the precise use of the term 'urban'. Does it refer to a fortified village, a town or a city? The Indo-European root of *pura* means a wall or a rampart, therefore, although in later periods the word *pura* referred to a town, in the early period it could have been a fortified village. A distinction has also to be maintained between the village which becomes an important market and thus the focus of the region, and the town. These distinctions in the degrees of urbanization are relevant not only to the study of pre-history but also in historical periods.

19. The words *dhānya* meaning corn or grain, and *yava* barley, occur in the *Ṛg Veda* and in Later Vedic literature. Specific words for rice, of which the most frequent is *vrīhi* and others are *taṇḍula* and *śāli* occur only in the Later Vedic literature, e.g., *Atharvaveda* VI. 140.2 etc; S.K. Chatterjee suggests a possible Dravidian origin for *vrīhi* in *arichi* (History and Culture of the Indian People, vol. I, *The Vedic Age*, p. 1449). Wheat is referred to as, *godhuma*, in Later

Vedic literature. It is still not certain whether the rice remains at Lothal indicate rice cultivation or merely a wild variety growing in the marshes (Visnu Mittre, unpublished paper read at Patna, 1969, 'Environmental Background to the Neolithic-Chalcolithic complex in North-Western India'). Archaeological evidence suggests that rice was the staple food in a major part of the sub-continent during this period. The use of the word *dhānya* for paddy is late.

20. As for example in the *Trikāṇḍaśeṣa,* a supplement to the *Nāmaliṅgānuśāsana* of Amarsiṁha, by Puruṣottamadeva, who is said to have flourished in the court of Lakṣmaṇasena in the twelfth century A.D.
21. It is not entirely coincidental that the spread of Indo-European elsewhere is frequently associated with the arrival of the horse-drawn chariot and on occasion with iron technology.
22. It is curious that there should be no substantial remains of at least the metal parts of the chariot in various excavations, and particularly at Harappa and Mohenjo-daro if we are to accept the theory that these cities were invaded by the Ṛgvedic people. This is in striking contrast to the evidence from Egypt where the new arrivals in their horse-drawn chariots are depicted clearly in reliefs and engravings on stone. The Āryan chariot was lighter, had spoked wheels, could accommodate three persons and was horse-drawn. It was therefore speedier, had greater manoeuvrability and consequently the two combatants had a vantage position (O.R. Gurney, *The Hittites*, p. 104 ff and S. Piggott, *Prehistoric India*, p. 273 ff).
23. The significance of these improvements is that the socketed iron axe is more efficient in a heavily forested region, the iron hoe makes a substantial difference in rice cultivation where more continual weeding is necessary than in other crops. This is also suggested in one of the frequently used words for 'hoe' in Vedic literature, *stambhaghna,* literally that which destroys clumps. The importance of the iron hoe has not received sufficient attention in the evaluation of technological change during this period.
24. The Muṇḍā derivation of *lāṅgala* is discussed by J. Przyluski in Bagchi (ed.). *Pre-Aryan and Pre-Dravidian in India,* p. 8 ff.; also in T. Burrow, *The Sanskrit Language*, p. 379. It occurs as *nāngal* in Dravidian (Dravidian Etymological Dictionary, no. 2368). An attempt to associate it with the Indo-European *leg/leng* as in J. Pokorny, *Vergleichens des Worterbuch der Indo-Germanischen Sprachen* and thereby to link it with *Nirukta* VI. 26 of Yāska has not been accepted for linguistic reasons (S.K. Chatterjee, 'Non-Aryan Elements in Indo-Aryan', *JGIS*, III. 42). It could be added that even from the point of view of the technology of the plough, the ploughshare is the central object and not an attachment.

    The early occurrence of the word for 'plough' in non-Indo-Aryan languages would invalidate the suggestion that the Āryan speakers introduced the plough. The possibility that the plough may have been known to the Harappans on the basis of a particular sign in the script resembling the Sumerian sign for plough has now been confirmed by the last season's excavations at Kalibangan which uncovered the furrow marks in a field outside the city's fortification which date to the pre-Harappan period. On a purely impressionistic view it seems unlikely that a sufficient food surplus could have been produced to maintain the cities without plough agriculture.

25 In the *Saṁhitā* literature the *karmāra* is respected, but gradually his status becomes low. *Ṛg Veda* X. 72.2; IX. 112.2, *Atharvaveda* III.5.6. Ultimately the *karmāra* is ranked with the *Niṣāda* and the *kulāla. Manu* IV.215; Kane, *History of the Dharmashastras*, II, p. 73. The lowering of the status may have had to do with the fact that the smiths were possibly non-tribal artisans, (it has been suggested that the copper-smiths were itinerant smiths) who would be allowed commensality and participation in the ritual, but not marriage relationships with the tribe. The social rights and obligations of such professional groups would be worth examining.

26. The Harappan system of weights has been described as binary in the lower weights—1, 2, 8/3, 16, 32, 64 . . . and decimal in the higher weights. The decimal basis of counting is referred to in the *Taittirīya Saṁhitā* IV. 40. 11. 4; *Maitrāyāṇīya Sam*. II.8.14: *Kāthaka Sam*. XVII.10 and XXXIX.6; *Vājasaneyi Sam*. XVII.2. There are references to ten raised to the power of twelve. The existence of the earlier binary system suggests that calculations may have been on the basis of the square. The commonly used cosmoloy of the Babylonians and Sumerians is believed to have had the mathematical base of the square. The use of both the square and circular cosmology in Indian sources at this time does suggest that new ideas on astronomy may have been in the air. There is a great likelihood that the circular theory was first developed among navigators, perhaps the Phoenicians, and would have then travelled to those in contact with the Phoenicians. C.P.S. Menon, *Early Astronomy and Cosmology*, p. 36 ff., makes an interesting correlation between the prevalence of the square cosmology and the circular cosmology in early India.

27. The need for exact geometrical knowledge arose in part because, although there were a variety of shapes permitted for altars such as the falcon, the chariot-wheel, the tortoise, the triangle, etc., their area had to be identical. The number of bricks was also prescribed. The geometrical principles involved in both creating precisely measured forms and converting one form into another are described in detail in the *Śulva Sūtras*. Admittedly most of these texts belong to the end of the Vedic period or even to the immediately post-Vedic period. Nevertheless they contain the developed and classified knowledge of geometry which must certainly have had earlier beginnings. This geometrical knowledge would be of use in other spheres of life as well, as for example in measuring land.

28. One year of twelve months comprising 360 days is frequently referred to in the *Ṛg Veda*, I.164.11; I.164.48. A year of 366 days has been suggested on the basis of the Ribhus in *Ṛg Veda* IV.33.7. An intercalary month in a five-year circle finds mention in a late section of the *Ṛg Veda*, X.85.13. An intercalary thirteenth month of 30 days in a five-year circle occurs in the *atharvaveda*, IX.9.19.

A primaeval element in Vedic society is indicated by the fact that magic is a substantial feature in both religious and technological concepts. It would be expected therefore that mathematical and astronomical knowledge would tend to be hidden in a mesh of symbolism and magic. That this element persists is apparent from the consultations with the village pandit which are still a part of the rural scene for determining the 'right day' for important agricultural activities such as sowing and harvesting. This has implications relating to the calendar as well as the notion of the auspicious day. The latter almost certainly derives its sanctity from the former.

It may be mentioned in passing that the Egyptians were by now regularly using the solar calendar. Knowledge of this calendar could well have travelled to India around the first millennium B.C. via traders. Of course, if the Land of Punt mentioned in Egyptian sources can be identified with India then the connection may have been reasonably close (M. Murray, *The Splendour that was Egypt*, pp. xxi, 20, 49, 98). Details of expeditions to Punt are recorded as early as the Fifth Dynasty, but Queen Hathshepsut of the Eighteenth Dynasty appears to have been the great patron of this trade. (*c.* 1400 B.C.).

29. In the Indus valley this would be caused by any or all of the following factors: the geological uplift at Sehwan resulting in the excessive flooding of the Indus near Mohenjo-daro, the salination of the soil, deforestation causing soil erosion and decrease in natural irrigation and thereby rendering agriculture difficult, and finally, the termination specifically of the Harappan trade with Sumer in the eighteenth century B.C.; apart from a possible attack on the cities of Harappa and Mohenjo-daro. Some of these factors are discussed by R.L. Raikes 'The end of the ancient cities of the Indus'. *American Anthropology*, 1964 and 'The Mohenjo-daro Floods' *Antiquity*, 40; G.F. Dales, 'New Investigations at Mohenjo-daro' *Archaeology*, 18, 1965; H.T. Lambrick, 'The Indus Flood Plain and the Indus Civilisation', *Geographical Journal* 133, 1967. Detailed discussion of the Sumerian trade is available in L. Oppenheim, *Ancient Mesopotamia* and W.F. Leemans, *Foreign Trade in the Old Babylonian Period*. The breakdown in trade is supported by the fact that the dockyard at Lothal had fallen into disuse by *circa* 1800 B.C. (*Ancient India*, nos. 18 and 19, 1962-63, p. 213).

30. The trade with Ophira during the reign of Solomon, the obelisk of Shalmanesar III depicting Indian elephants, the evidence of Indian teak at Mugheir and in the palace of Nebuchandnezzar and a variety of linguistic evidence (some of which is discussed in Rawlinson, *Intercourse between India and the Western World*) would attest to trading contacts between India and the Near East. The *brāhmī* script may have originated in western India as a kind of merchant's code partially associated with the Semitic script and in course of time and use in commerce travelled to the Ganges valley and to north India where it was perfected for use with Sanskrit and Prākrit. The *aramaic* adaptations in *kharoṣṭhī* clearly arose from commercial and administrative needs.

31. In the *Śatapatha Brāhmaṇa* III.2.3.15 and the *Kauṣītaki Brāh.* VII.6., the speech of the Kurü Pañcālas and the north generally is extolled and made a model for study. This ties in with the fact that Pāṇini is associated with the north. Yet the Punjab had been relegated to the status of a *mleccha-deśa* in the *Atharvaveda* V.22.14.

The linguistic differences between the Punjab and the middle Ganges valley were earlier sought to be explained on the basis of the theory that there were two bands of Aryan speakers and this theory was developed by Hoernle, *A Grammar of the Eastern Hindi compared with the other Gaudian Languages*.

1880, and by G. Grierson, *Languages*, I.G.I. vol. I, 1907. More recently, S.K. Chatterjee and S.M. Katre in *Languages*, G.I. 1965, have preferred the argument that the differences are due to many more groups mutually interacting. What is perhaps called for at this stage is a comparative study of the linguistic structure of the various Prākrits and the pre-Aryan languages.

32. *Atharvaveda*, V.22.14; *Gopatha Brāhmaṇa* II.9; *Vājasaneyi Sam*. XXX.5.22; *Taittirīya Brāh*. III.4.1.1; *Baudhāyana Dharma Sūtra*, I.1.14.

33. Jules Bloch, 'Sanskrit and Dravidian,' in Bagchi (ed.) *Pre-Aryan and Pre-Dravidian in India*, p. 46 ff. The use of the word *ghoṭa* in Sanskrit is late occurring in such texts as the *Āpastamba Śrauta Sūtra* XV.3.12; *ghoṭaka* in *Pañcatantra* V.10.4., *Vikramādityacarita*, etc. An early use of *ghoṭaka* in Pāli occurs in *Jātaka* VI.452.

A micro-study of the etymology of place-names, even contemporary place-names, would be revealing particularly in the context of early Muṇḍā and Dravidian settlement in northern India. Names such as Gaṇga, Kaliṅga, Aṅga, Vaṅga, etc., have already been discussed as probable Muṇḍā names, Bagchi, *Pre-Aryan and Pre-Dravidian in India*, p. 72 ff.

34. The pattern of settlement at Harappa, Mohenjo-daro, Kalibangan suggests an elite in residence on the citadel mound; the large and separate residential area to the east of the citadel occupied by lesser status groups; and the single or double-roomed 'workmen's quarters' indicating a third level of stratification. The question has often been asked as to who was in authority in the Harappa culture and how was authority maintained? The answer could lie in the existence of a caste structure, where a small group preserving itself through strict endogamous marriage and organizing its authority through a hierarchy of service relationships in which it was assigned a high status, and stressing its ritual purity, could have held power. The great Bath at Mohenjo-daro is now almost universally recognized as being indicative of an ablution ritual which was probably central to the notion of ritual purity.

35. All tribal societies have a social organization based on kinship relations deriving from rules of exogamy and endogamy. Family structure, whether matrilineal or patriarchal, lineage and tribal lidentity are some of the features which might be ferreted out of the references to the earlier populations. Chalcolithic cultures invariably indicate a division of labour, and where there is trading activity as well, the division of labour is intensified. Nor would identity with a particular geographical location be precluded. The evidence of the notion of pollution in non-Aryanized societies has been noticed by anthropologists and some would regard it as essential to the development of religion and society in India (e. g. M.N. Srinivas, *Religion and Society among the Coorgs*). Thus the pre-requisites for a caste structure were available. It could be suggested that a rudimentary form of the caste structure existed in the pre-Aryan Ganges cultures and perhaps a better defined form in the Harappa culture. The Ṛgvedic people show an unfamiliarity with this structure which is not surprising if they regarded the non-Aryan culture as alien. The division of society into four groups has a single reference in the Puruṣasūkta hymn in the late tenth *maṇḍala* of the *Ṛg Veda* (X.90.12). The logic implicit in this particular myth regarding the origin of the

castes would in itself suggest the re-arranging of endogamous groups into a carefully worked-out pattern. The word *varṇa* with the connotation of caste is used in the *Ṛg Veda* to differentiate between two groups, the *ārya* and the *dasyu*. The later literature clearly refers to the *catvāro varṇāḥ* (*Śatapatha Brah.* V.5.4.9.; VI.4.4.13.) and reflects the introduction of the caste system. The expansion to four categories would be necessary once society became more complex and endogamous groups were incorporated and had to be arranged in a pattern. The *jāti* structure may well reflect the pre-Aryan aspect of the caste structure.

36. e.g. *Chāndogya Upaniṣad* V.10.7; Manu (X.45) makes a distinction between the Dasyus who speak the Āryan language and those who do not.

37. The Kirāta are referred to as low status tribes in the *Vājasaneyi Sam.* XXX.16; *Taittirīya Brah.* III.4.12.1; *Atharvaveda* X.4.14; *Manu* X.44; *Raghuvaṁśa* XVI.57. The Pulinda are similarly referred to in the *Aitareya Brāhmana,* 7.18 XV.20; Aśoka's Thirteenth Major Rock Edict.

38. The urbanization of the Ganges valley in the first millennium B.C. is often referred to as the second urbanization. The crucial factor in this urbanization was iron technology as is evident when one compares the N.B.P. levels with P.G.W. levels or black-and-red ware levels. Surplus produce and the specialization of crafts both utilizing the *dāsa-bhṛtaka,* increase in trade based on production as well as improved communication (both by land and through the use of river navigation) all combined to make urbanization possible. This in turn produced the characteristics associated with urban culture—the building of fortified cities, the introduction of a script (*brāhmī*), the use of coinage (punch-marked coins for example), a wide range of intellectual and metaphysical speculation (from the Cārvākas to the Ājīvikas), some of which reflected the requirements and aspirations of the new urban groups—the artisans and the merchants and traders.

    Unlike the first urbanization in the Indus valley, we have for the Ganges valley enough evidence to be able to trace its gradual evolution. The quality of the early urbanization of the Ganges valley as compared to that of the Indus valley was less impressive in terms of material culture. But there seems to have been a more even distribution of the characteristics of urbanization, suggesting perhaps that the perquisites of urban living were concentrated and centralized to a lesser degree than in the Indus civilization.

39. The origin of the state is ascribed to a number of interesting factors in early literary sources. We are told, for example, that the surplus production of rice led to the emergence of the institution of family and private property (initially connoting fields). The state arose because both of these had to be protected as also because of the need to prevent conflict between castes (*Vāyu Purāṇa*, VIII, 128-161; *Mahāvastu*, I, 342; *Mārkaṇḍeya Purāṇa*, 74ff). The literature of the mid-first millennium B.C. indicates the beginning of political concepts. This is in contrast to the Ṛgvedic period where loyalty is primarily tribal and where, therefore, government is seen in more simplistic terms, namely, authority invested in the tribal chief or leader whose main function is to protect the tribe. This concept is assumed in the various stories regarding the appointment of Indra as the king, which stories are elaborated upon with the growth of the contractual element in the notion of the state in Later Vedic literature (*Ṛg Veda*

VIII, 35, 86; *Aitareya Brāh.* I. 14; *Śatapatha Brāh.* III.4 2.1-3). The purpose of the contract gradually changes from the king protecting the tribe militarily, to the king maintaining the order of the castes and also protecting private property (*Arthaśāstra* III.1; *Manu* VII. 17—.35; *Śānti Parva*, 75.10; *Manu* X.115). The contract is complete when the king is paid one-sixth in tax as his wage for services to the people (*sadbhāgbhṛto rājā rakṣet prajām, Baudhāyana Dharma Sūtra* I.10.6). The king is associated with divinity which permits of adifferent perspective in the notion of contract.

Buddhist texts however indicate the contractual basis of the concept of the state, more clearly as the association with divinity is absent (*Dīgha Nikāya*, III 84-96; *Mahāvastu*, I. 338-48). It was more suited to the context of the non-monarchical systems of government.

40. At the level of ritual there was the incorporation of prayers, spells and magic, as for example in the *Atharvaveda* and the *Yajurveda*. At the level of deities the acceptance of the erstwhile distant Rudra and the growth of the Rudra-Śiva concept for instance. The recruitment of local priests into the *brāhmaṇ* fold can be seen not only in the various purification rites for those of degenerate castes, such as the *Vrātyastoma*, but is also perhaps reflected in the mysterious origin of many *brāhmaṇ gotras*. The concession to the worship of the mother goddess, to any appreciable extent, is a later phenomenon as also the acceptance of phallic worship.

41. Pargiter's attempt to sort out the genealogies on the basis of Āryan and non-Āryan has been criticized. It is possible that, eventually, the Puranic genealogies will be found to be more true to the essence of the history of this period since they are not concerned with the Āryan problem as such but with the activities of a large number of tribes and kings in northern India. It is interesting that the two royal lineages, the Ailas and Ikṣvākus are both based in the Ganges valley, from where various lineages move in various directions.

The *vaṁṣāvalī* tradition has as its genesis the myth of the Flood and this agrees in many particulars with the Sumerian Flood legend. Indeed it is the agreement in details which is so striking. What is even more interesting is that the traditional date of the *kaliyuga* according to the astronomical tradition of Āryabhaṭa works out to about 3102 B.C., which agrees with the archaeological date ascribed to the flooding of Shuruppak in Sumer which is probably the genesis of the Sumerian Flood legend (C. Leonard Woolley, *The Early Periods—Ur, Excavations*, vol. IV, 1956; M. Mallowan, 'Noah's Flood Reconsidered', *Iraq*, XXVI, 1964). The reference to this legend in Vedic literature is late, in the *Śatapatha Brāh.* I.8.1.1. and the *Kāthaka Sam.* XI.2. Had the legend been of Āryaṇ origin, one would expect it to occur in the *Ṛg Veda* or be associated with the Avestan tradition rather than the Sumerian. The legend relating to the genesis of a people is after all of prime importance. Considering the close contacts between the Harappa culture and the Sumerians, it is possible that the same legend may have been used as a genesis in both cultures and the Puranic genealogies may therefore contain a pre-Āryan tradition. R.C. Hazra's very able studies of the Puranic sources point to some non-Vedic religious contents in the *Purāṇas*.

As regards the mythological sections, the initial legend alone raises a host of interesting ideas: the concept of the Flood as genesis, the use of the sun and the moon as the symbol of the two royal lineages, (*Sūryavaṁśi* and *Candravaṁśi*) and the association of these in the tribal mythology of India and elsewhere; the fact that the Aila lineage derives its name from the sole daughter of Manu, Ilā who married the son of the moon deity (Soma), suggests a matrilineal-cum-mother goddess tradition.

42. Magadha in the period from 400 B.C. to A.D. 400 saw the rise of the Mauryas and the Guptas; the Raichur-Bijapur region in the period from 500 to 1200 was the nucleus of Cālukya and Rāṣṭrakūṭa power and the Kanchi-Tanjore region in the same period was the homeland of the Pallavas and Colas. Other areas also gave rise to important dynasties, but generally to only a single dynasty in a shorter period, e.g. Kannauj under Harṣa, Bengal under the Pālas, etc.

43. We know that various groups were recruited to the *brāhmaṇ varṇa* and that their status within the *varṇa* could change; thus the Kuru-Pañcāla *brahmaṅs* looked down upon the Magadha *brāhmaṇs* (*Jataka* II.83 *Aitereya Brāh.* VIII.14), the Gandhara *brāhmaṇs* are described with contempt in the *Rājataraṅginī* (I. 306 ff) yet are regarded as respectable in the *Bhaviṣya Purāṇa*. It is also evident that families of non-*kṣatriya* origin became rulers or were given *kṣatriya* status through fabricated genealogies. Thus the Nandas are described as *śūdras* in the Purāṇas. The Candella kings claimed Candravamśi lineage and *kṣatriya* status in spite of obscure origins and having acquired the status continued to marry into the local Gond families. There is an absence of any reference to the *vaiśya varṇa* in certain parts of India. The composition of the *śūdra varṇa* varied from region to region and its role was different in south India as compared to the Ganges valley. When we cease to look at early Indian society as a static, rigid structure stratified into immobile castes, we then begin to see considerable evidence to suggest the contrary. R.S. Sharma, *Social Changes in Early Medieval India* (1969), has shown the emergence of various new castes in the period A.D. 500-1200. A recent study using social anthropology, that of N. Wagle, *Society at the Time of the Buddha* (1966), is a pointer to the possibilities not only in the field of interdisciplinary studies, but also the extraction of a more realistic picture of the times from the sources.

Purāṇic Lineages and Archaeological Cultures

At a seminar in Poona in 1964, Professor Sankalia initiated discussion on the subject of Traditional Indian Chronology and Carbon-14 Dates of Excavated Sites by stating that his paper was an essay in speculation. The speculation continues. In the absence of contemporary written records or deciphered scripts any attempt to correlate archaeological material with traditional accounts of the past becomes a venture into speculation. This is particularly so as the literary sources represent accretions over a period of many centuries and the archaeological evidence is partial, supported more by exploration than excavation, and ultimately based on vertical rather than horizontal excavation. It is therefore again very much as a speculative enterprise that an attempt is being made here to compare the excavated material with the historical tradition in the general time bracket of the second and early first millennia B.C. The attempt arises not from a need to insist on a correlation of tradition and archaeology but is more in the nature of an investigation of the tradition which may perhaps be carrying an element of historical memory for which archaeology might provide some evidence.

Earlier attempts to correlate archaeology and the literary sources have in the main focused on the question of identifying the Āryans (and inevitably the Dravidians as well), and trying out a variety of archaeological cultures—perhaps the most plausible identification being with the Painted Grey Ware culture.[1] But the term 'aryan' covers a wide range of groups and geographical distribution, quite apart from its ethnic connotation of its distinctiveness as a geographical culture being ambiguous in the texts.[2] Nor are we clear about the nature of 'aryanisation' at this time and the channels through which it proceeded. More recently the focus has been narrowed to that of examining particular cultures in the light of a single literary text. Here the use of epic literature raises some fundamental problems, since epic literature in

From *Purātattva,* vol. 8, 1975, pp. 86-98.

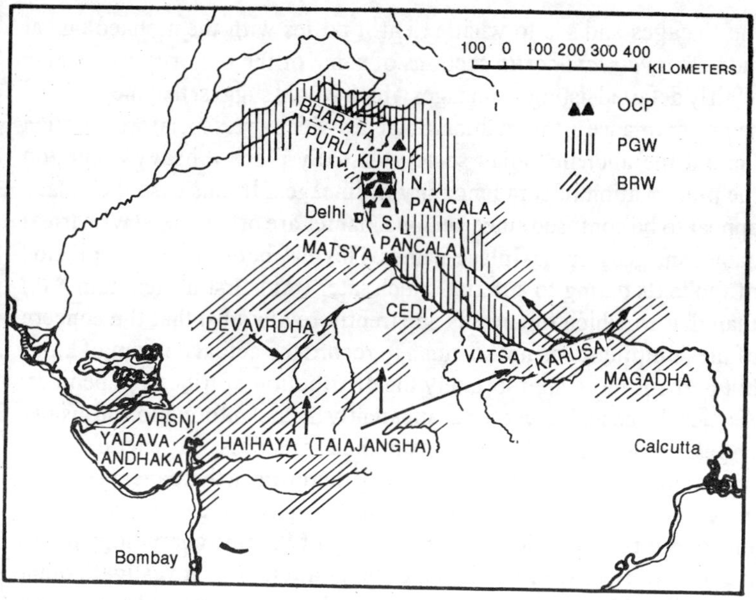

particular in all societies is the survival of many encrustations in the form of events and locations introduced through interpolations. If ever higher criticism and textual analyses manage to unravel the original *Rāmakathā* and *Bharata-kathā* the result may be somewhat startling to those who take even the critical editions of the *Rāmāyaṇa* and the *Mahābhārata* as the earliest, original epics.[3] A more promising investigation has been the attempt to correlate some aspects of the Painted Grey Ware culture with the Later Vedic Literature where the emphasis has not been so much on the identity of the geographical distribution as on the correlation of the social and economic data from both the literary and the archaeological sources.[4]

The attempt in this paper will be to narrow the literary focus still further although the framework of archaeological cultures relates to virtually the whole of northern India. It has been suggested in the past that some of the archaeological cultures may be linked to the major lineages of the early tradition and in this connection the Painted Grey Ware (hereafter referred to as the PGW) has been associated with the Pūrus and the Chalcolithic Black and Red Ware (hereafter referred to as the BRW) with the Yadus/Yādavas.[5] The suggestions have largely been casual and there has been little attempt to use the history of the lineages and see to what extent it tallies with the archaeological data. The *vaṃśānucarita* sections of some of the mojor *Purāṇas* give a fairly detailed listing of lineages which would suggest that they carried some importance in the tradition. Societies which stress social organization (as did the ancient Indian society) usually place a heavy accent on the preservation of some memory of lineages. In this case the details appear to be confused since personal names are often mixed with tribal names and geographical place-names. This may be due to the compilation of the texts dating to a period much later (mid-first millennium A.D.) than that to which the events apparently relate: also that the concern of the compilers was not so much to record the actual descent of kings but perhaps more appropriately the distribution of tribes and peoples. As such the genealogies are not apparently factual information on history and chronology but they can be examined as records of a general pattern of settlements and migrations. I am not therefore in this paper primarily concerned with the chronology of the lineages since that is an almost insurmountable problem. The reliability of Purāṇic chronology per se has yet to be proven.[6] This paper is an attempt to investigate other types of evidence which lineage records can supply and which can perhaps be examined in the light of archaeological data.

The *vaṃśānucarita* sections, describing as they do the two major descent groups—the *Ikṣvāku/Sūryavaṃśa* and the *Aila/Candravaṃśa*—and the fanning out of these groups, include as their geographical framework the whole of northern India.[7] The archaeology of the Ikṣavāku areas, essentially Ayodhyā, Videha and Vaiṣālī, is substantially unknown as yet for this period. This paper will therefore be concerned only with the *Candravaṃśa* lineages; and in that too the discussion will be limited to the obviously more significant lineages, that of the Pūru and the Yādava, which also happen to relate to the area where fairly substantial archaeological material is available.

The lineage commences with Ilā the daughter of Manu born from a sacrifice performed by Manu, which in some texts is associated with the termination of the Great Deluge from which Manu was saved by the Matsyāvatāra of Viṣṇu.[8] Ilā gives birth to Purūravas whose great-grandson is Yayāti. Of Yayāti's five sons, the eldest is Yadu and the youngest is Pūru, the middle ones being Anu, Druhyu and Turvaśa. Yadu, the rightful successor, displeases his father and is banished to the south/west and Pūru the youngest inherits the *madhya-deśa*. The descent of the Paurava line is geographically concentrated and relates to the Indo-Gangetic divide and the Ganga-Yamuna Doāb and its environs, whereas the Yādavas spread out over the Aravalli region, Gujarat, Mālwā, the Narmada valley, the northern Deccan and the eastern Ganges valley. The descent groups of the three middle sons are relatively unimportant according to the texts. The line of Turvaśa merges with the Pūru fairly early and that of Druhyu associated with Gāndhāra and the extreme north-west is referred to as producing the *mlecchas* after a few generations. The descendants of Anu survived in central Punjab and Sind and one branch is said to have migrated to the extreme east, Aṅga, Vaṅga, Puṇḍra, etc.; only the lineages of Pūru and Yadu are listed in detail and at great length (see Genealogical Table at the end).

The Flood is in many historical traditions a time-marker, clearing away the past as it were and initiating a new era. It need not therefore refer to an actual flood.[9] It is however a useful point for our purposes since it also provides a possible archaeological correlation with the decline of the major cities of the Indus civilization. The attempted correlation here will therefore be with the archaeological cultures which succeed the Harappan. Until recently the Flood would have been acceptable as a useful starting point for the cultures of the western Ganges valley as well; but now there is a debate on this question involving the explanation for the peculiar characteristics of the Ochre Colour Pottery (OCP).[10] Even if one of the theories regarding the possibility of a flood in the upper Doāb is accepted, it could still not be correlated with the legend, for, in order to do this, the flood would have to be dated to the end of the third millennium B.C. and have occurred prior to the OCP culture, whereas the argument is that the rolled condition of the OCP sherds is due to the settlements suffering from a flood in the mid-second millennium B.C. However, whether or not there was a massive deluge, there seems to have been a major disturbance in the river systems of the Indo-Gangetic divide and this may have taken the form of flooding in some areas and desiccation in others. The two predominant cultures of the post-Harappan period (during the second and early first millennia B.C.) are quite unmistakably the PGW and the BRW. The antecedents and evolution of these two will therefore have to be considered. The keeping of lineages and genealogical records (in howsoever garbled a form) is also associated generally with societies at a stage which would be regarded as Chalcolithic in archaeological terms, since the motivation for maintaining lineage records stems from kinship organization and property relations, both of which would become more complex in Chalcolithic societies as compared to earlier societies.

Evidence of the late Harappan culture in the northern area is available at sites along the river-bed of the Sarasvati (especially in Ganganagar district), in the watershed between the Indus and Ganges systems and in the upper Doāb (in Saharanpur, Meerut, Bulandshahr and Gurgaon districts). The latter two regions are areas of relatively uniform elevation (200-500 m.) and suggest a movement generally along the river lines. The suggested Carbon-14 dates for the peripheral sites of the late Harappan are 2200-1700 B.C.[11] It is also in these two regions that there is now growing evidence of other cultures, either co-existent with the Harappan or else continuing into the post-Harappan period. Of the first there appear to be a continuity of pre-Harappan cultures into the second millennium B.C. at sites in the Sutlej valley and the upper Sarasvati (e.g. Bara and Siswal A).[12] Of the second, the OCP begins during the Harappan period and continues into the post-Harappan, with a mean date of 1880 B.C. Variations in the OCP culture suggest some affinities with the Harappan (as at Bara and Bahadarabad) with a noticeably more independent development in sites further south in the Doāb (as at Atranjikhera, Lal Qila and Saipai).[13] However, the concentration of the OCP is strikingly heavier in the upper Doāb in Saharanpur district. This would suggest a more cohesive geographical settlement in the upper Doāb with a diffused movement southwards, thinning out towards the southernmost site at Noh. Eastwards it extends to Saheth-Maheth but the region to the east of the Ganges has not so far produced much evidence of the OCP. Earlier associated with nomadic groups, the recent excavations at Lal Qila, Mitathal and Saipai indicate fairly settled peasant communities.[14] If the Copper Hoards are to be associated with the OCP then the Chalcolithic nature of this culture would be well-established. Furthermore, since the OCP was in contact with the Harappan settlements some survivals of the latter into the OCP culture are possible even if the OCP was not a degenerate form of the Harappan culture.

With the termination of the OCP in the late second millennium B.C. there appears to be a hiatus between it and the succeeding PGW culture. This is evident from those sites where the PGW settlers occupied the earlier OCP sites and which register a break in occupation between the two cultures. The earlier date for PGW, *c.* 1100 B.C. would have indicated a short break in occupation, but the more recent date of *c.* 800 B.C. suggests a longer period. If the contention is correct that the weathering of the OCP sherds is due to extended exposure then a long hiatus between the OCP and the PGW will be further supported. It does however seem unlikely that there should be a uniform date for the PGW, considering the extensive area over which the culture is distributed, an area which includes the Rāvi and Sutlej valleys, the erstwhile Sarasvati valley, the Indo-Gangetic divide and the entire Doāb and its environs extending eastwards to the Gomati (Bahraich and Varanasi districts) and westwards to Rohtak, Hissar, Ajmer and Jaipur districts. The distribution of PGW sites in the Doāb tends to adopt a pattern of settlement closely following the banks of rivers and their tributaries.[15] It may well turn out that the Rāvi and Sutlej valley PGW is a little earlier and that of the Doāb, associated with iron, a little later. The sites along the southern fringes of the Doāb appear to be of a later date than those of the upper Doāb, and places still further south (e.g. Ujjain, Broach, etc.) register the arrival of the PGW even later, as an immediate prelude to or in association with iron and the Northern Black Polished Ware.[16] The predominance of the PGW over the OCP is based not merely on the substantially larger area of distribution, but also on individual settlements being larger, with a well-defined material culture, and the increasing use of iron technology. The latter appears to have been introduced gradually with a shift from copper to iron.[17]

The association of PGW sites and the places mentioned in the *Mahābhārata* has been discussed at length.[18] But the events of the *Mahābhārata* focus on the last part of the Pūru lineage. Taken as a whole the Pūru lineage seems to have three distinct phases.[19] The first phase is from Pūru to Bharata, the second sees the segmentation of the main lineage into four groups with a consequent expansion of the territory held by the lineage and the third is the descent from Kuru to the period of the *Mahābhārata* war (see Genealogical Table at the end).

The first phase is probably reflected in some of the hymns of the *Ṛg Veda* where the Pūrus are described as a tribe dwelling on the two grassy banks of the Sarasvatī and associated both in war and friendship with the Bharatas.[20] There is the curious use of the epithet *mṛdhra vāc* for the Pūrus in the *Ṛg Veda* suggesting that they spoke insultingly or discordantly; and the *Śatapatha Brāhmaṇa* refers to Pūru as an ancient king who was an Asura Rākṣasa and was overthrown by the Bharata.[21] This could be a reference to the famous Daśarājña battle described in the *Ṛg Veda* or else to the coalescing of the Pūrus and the Bharatas to form the Kuru-Pañcāla. In terms of the Pūru lineage these events would relate to the last part of the first phase of the lineage just prior to the segmentation. It is interesting that the inclusion of Bharata in the Puranic genealogy is immediately followed by a curious story. We are told that Bharata was dissatisfied with his own sons and therefore adopted the son of Bhāradvāja to succeed him. Could adoption be the mythological symbol of the amalgamation of tribes? The etymology of the name Bhāradvāja is explained as 'one who is borne (*bhara*) by two progenitors (*dvija*)'.[22] The archaeological association of the first phase of the Pūru lineage, i.e., from Pūru to Bharata, could be with either the OCP or may have been carried as part of the surviving tradition into the early PGW. At the end of this phase there was a break represented by Bharata adopting sons in the genealogy, after which there was a commencement with the PGW correlated in the genealogy with the second phase of segmentation after Hastin.

At the start of what we have called the second phase the city of Hastinapur is said to have been founded by Hastin and thereafter the Pūru lineage divides into segments with each segment controlling a distinct area of territory. The segmentation is in effect an augmentation of the lineage and would reflect an increase in numbers which required migration into the neighbouring areas. What appears to have been the main line continued at Hastināpur. The other segments consisted of the line established in North Pañcāla, South Pañcāla and the successors of Dvimīḍha whose geographical base is not clear.[23] What is interesting about the distribution of these segments is that the Pūru now covers a wider geographical area and this area tallies fairly closely with that of the distribution of PGW sites. The watershed region and the upper Doāb would constitute what later came to be known as the land of the Kurus. North Pañcāla (north of the Ganges and east of the upper Doāb) with its capital at Ahicchatra has produced PGW sites as has, to an even greater degree, South Pañcāla (south of the Ganges as far as the junction of the Chambal and the Yamuna) with its capital at Kāmpilya. The Dvimīḍha line may have been located in the Rohtak and Hissar region which is also associated with PGW. The break in descent after Bharata and the segmentation may well indicate a new cultural element in terms of the lineage record. The ceramic tradition of the PGW is from every point of view—fabric, firing, shape, design and function—a new feature and does not have any connections with the earlier ceramic tradition of this region. The associated wares and other artefacts from PGW sites suggest a materially far more prosperous people than the authors of earlier cultures of the Doāb. It would seem feasible that this material culture provided the base for the emergence of states with a monarchical system of government in which the control of agricultural land and rights to succession would play a major role. The excavation at Hastināpur shows an OCP occupation followed by a break and then the very substantial PGW occupation. It is clear that the potentiality for urbanization came with the PGW culture and not the earlier one. The segmentation and consequent migration of the lineage would coincide not only with the diffusion of PGW but also the consolidation of the emergent kingdoms beginning to exploit the newly introduced iron technology.

The third phase of the genealogy is marked by the name of Kuru in the descent list. By now, relations between the Kurus and the Pañcālas were established both through lineage connections as well as the occasional rivalry of neighbouring kingdoms. We are told that soon after this one of the Kuru kings, Vasu, branched off and conquered Cedi (on the southern fringe of the Yamunā) and Magadha (southern Bihar), both areas said to be previously in the hands of the Yādava tribes.[24] If the Bhind district can be identified with the Cedi kingdom there is some evidence of the inter-mixture of PGW and BRW from surface collections; but the stratigraphical sequence awaits excavation.[25] In Magadha, however, although BRW is known, PGW is absent. We are further told that Vasu's five sons carved out new kingdoms, with Bṛhadratha founding a dynasty at Magadha, Kuśa ruling the territory of Vatsa from Kauśāmbi and the other three ruling the kingdoms of Cedi, Karūṣa and possibly Matsya. The sequence at Kauśāmbi from the excavator's reports suggests that the earliest levels show an affinity with pottery from Navdatoli and western India and that the PGW marks the second culture phase.[26] The date suggested for the founding of Kauśāmbi by the excavator has been questioned as being too early.[27] The important point for our purposes however is that the PGW should post-date the BRW, however small be the evidence of either. A late date would fit better with the lineage account. Karūṣa, generally identified with the Shahbad district of Bihar, provides evidence of a BRW settlement but no PGW. The Matsyas, often located in the Alwar-Jaipur region, may be indicated by the mixed BRW and PGW evidence but the stratigraphy is not clear,[28] although the arrival of the PGW at Noh in the adjoining area appears to be late.[29] If the lineage correlations with archaeological cultures referred to so far have any validity then these kingdoms should relate to the period just prior to the NBP since they are mentioned late in the lineage.

The suggested correlation of the Yādava lineage with the Chalcolithic BRW[30] also needs to be examined closely. BRW unlike PGW had a much earlier start, in *c*. 2000 B.C., and in some of the sites in Saurashtra and Kutch is associated with the late Harappan (e.g. Surkotada, Amra, Bhatiravdi). If the white-painted BRW is of the same genesis as the plain BRW, then it can be said to have travelled from western India in two directions. One was along the Aravalli Hills, with a base in the Banas valley (*c*. 2000-1800 B.C. at Ahar), continuing in the direction of the Ganga-Yamuna Doāb where plain BRW dates to *c*. 1200 B.C. or later (Atranjikhera Noh). At sites in this region where the BRW and the PGW occur mixed in the same stratum, either the BRW date will have to be made later or the PGW date somewhat earlier than *c*. 800 B.C. In the few sites in the Doāb itself where BRW occurs it is generally mixed with PGW.[31] An unpainted, plain BRW is also found along the Yamunā as far north as the Indo-Gangetic divide and dating to the end of the second millennium B.C. The second direction in which the BRW appears to have travelled was along the Narmada valley and into Malwa and central India, largely following the river valleys and later going eastwards to Bihar, the middle Ganges valley and, ultimately, to the eastern Ganges valley (*c*. 1650 B.C. at Navdatoli, *c*. 1500 B.C. at Eran and *c*. 1200 B.C. at Mahisdal and Chirand). That there was a diffusion of the technique seems apparent. The further southward extension of the BRW via the west coast and through Vidarbha seems to have occurred later. The BRW therefore essentially skirts round the Doāb and the substantial concentrations of this culture occur in Kutch, Kathiawar, and in the districts of Udaipur, Bhilwara, Bharatpur, Indore, Bhind, Ghazipur, Mirzāpur and Vārāṇasi.[32]

This geographical distribution in terms of the traditional lineages would evidently point to the Yādavas. The association of the Yādavas with Kathiawar is mentioned more than once. The *Purāṇas* state that Raivata, the grandson of Ānarta, was established at Kuśasthali (Dvārkā as it came to be called later) but, on having to be away at the court of Brahma, he returned to find that many centuries had passed.[33] In the interval Kuśasthali had been conquered by a Rākṣasa and Raivata's brothers had fled in various directions. The Andhaka-Vṛṣṇi were now ruling at Dvārkā. This story which suggests an original dispersal in various directions from the Kathiawar region would agree with the archaeological pattern. But the story of Yadu in the *Purāṇas* suggests that he came from the *madhya-deśa* although he finally established himself in western India.

The *Ṛg Veda* refers to Indra helping the Yadus across the flood.[34] In one hymn they are said to have come from across the sea and in another from afar. This could be explained as their having come from Gujarat near the sea. The *Ṛg Veda* also associates them with wealth in cattle and horses and it is significant that among the earliest evidences for the horse are the remains from Surkotada.[35] The *Harivaṃśa* states that Yadu had his capital at Ānarta (Kathiawar) and that his maternal grandfather was the Rākṣasa Madhu whose territory, which extended from Ānarta to Mathura, was conquered by the Yādavas.[36] This would suggest a movement along the Aravallis towards the Doāb. It would also imply that the Yadus had control over a part of the *madhya-deśa,* namely Mathura, which control in the *Purāṇas* is suggested as being of a late period with the emergence of the Andhaka-Vṛṣṇi segments. One of the important segments of the Yādava lineage was that of the Sātvata from whom were descended three major clans—the Andhaka, the Vṛṣṇi and the Devavṛdha. The emergence of these clans occurs fairly late, just prior to the third or Kuru phase of the Pūru lineage, which, on the basis of the archaeological correlation suggested with the PGW, would date it at approximately *c.* 1000 B.C. or even a little later. The Andhaka and Vṛṣṇi are closely linked with the Mathura region from where they are said to have fled when attacked by Jarāsandha of Magadha and finally settled in Dvārkā. For this there is little archaeological confirmation since the presence of BRW is, so far at least, virtually absent at Mathura (barring a small amount at Sonkh) and the excavations at Dvārkā have not as yet reached possible BRW levels.[37] The lineage of Devavṛdha is said to have been connected with the Parṇāśā river (the modern Banas) and the Mt. Abu region.[38] In terms of archaeological correlation, the occupation of the Banas region by the Yādavas should have occurred earlier.

The more adventurous group of Yādava lineages are those which come under the title of the Haihaya clans. These were in the main, five, all of whom called themselves Tālajangha (perhaps with the palm tree as totem?).[39] Among these were included the Saryāta (whose ancestors had fled from Kuśasthali), Bhoja, Vitīhotra, Avanti and Tuṇḍikera. The Haihayas moved along the Narmadā and are believed to have captured

Mahiṣmati from the Karkoṭaka Nāga and fortified it as an important settlement.[40] According to the tradition the Haihayas are credited with attacking Kāśi, presumably making their way through central India to the Son-Yamuna Doāb. The BRW presence is attested to in these areas often at the earliest level. The Haihayas are also said to have overrun Ayodhyā and to have come into conflict with Vaiśāli and Videha.[41] From all these places, as from Kāśi, the Haihayas are said to have been driven back. The evidence of BRW is not as yet available from Ayodhyā and Vaiśāli but the extension of BRW to eastern Uttar Pradesh and Bihar is of a later date than its occurrence in Rajasthan and Madhya Pradesh. It was also a Yādava prince who is said to have wandered in the upper reaches of the Narmadā and finally settled in the hills where the Ken rises. His son Vidarbha went in a southerly direction and established the kingdom of Vidarbha. The BRW from sites in Vidarbha (e.g. Paunar and Kauṇḍanpur) is later than that from sites along the Narmadā.[42]

Thus the Yādava lands were Kathiawar and the areas drained by the Banas, Chambal, Betwā, Ken, Narmadā and pockets along the Yamunā, all of which are areas associated with the migration of BRW people, provided that the north Indian variants in the BRW ceramic type can all be said to belong to one cultural foundation. The record of the Yādava lineage in the *Purāṇas* virtually terminates with the events of the Mahābhārata war. The association of the Yādavas with Kathiawar however continued as late as the seventh century A.D. with the epigraphical reference to a Yādava family ruling at Simhapura.[43] The medieval period sees a revival of the seeking of connections with the Yādava lineage. This is perhaps most insistent in the thirteenth century A.D. with the reference in the south Indian tradition to the eighteen Yādava clans who are believed to have migrated from the north to the Deccan and further south under the leadership of Agastya.[44] The date for this 'event' has been calculated to the eighth century B.C. The Yādavas are said to have settled initially mainly along the west coast as far south as Kerala. It has been argued that the eighteen clans of the Veḷir of the Sangam period were Yādavas.[45] A number of medieval dynasties of the western half of the peninsula—the Tulūvas, Rāṣṭrakūṭas, Hoysalas, Yādavas of Devagiri—claim Yādava descent.[46] The Āy chiefs of Āykkuḍi of the ninth century A.D. claim to be of the Vṛṣṇikula as also the Mūṣaka kings who link themselves with Haihaya origins.[47] Is this sheer fantasy, or is it an attempt to acquire status, or does it reflect the persistence of descent (or supposed descent) even in very changed historical circumstances? The interest in this tradition lies in the coincidence of the diffusion of BRW associated with the megalithic culture in the peninsula during the first millennium B.C., an association which is a new feature. A detailed technical and comparative investigation of the BRW ceramic industry associated with the northern Chalcolithic and the southern Megalithic would go a long way towards clarifying the problem. As it stands there is at least a superficial similarity between the two ceramic industries but this may not be found viable on further analysis.

The Yadu lineage has a greater tendency to branch off into segments and this process takes the segmented lineages over a larger geographical area than that of the Pūrus. The branching off starts earlier in the Yadu lineage with the Haihayas emerging in the eighth generation whereas the first segmentation of the Pūrus takes place as late as the fifty-first generation.[48] This may in part be accounted for by the fact that the alluvial plains of the Doāb could contain a larger population and the exploitation of agricultural resources could be confined to a more limited area as compared to Rajasthan and Madhya Pradesh where movement along the river valleys would be necessary for a growing population and demands on agriculture. The Yādava lineages do subscribe to a higher degree to one of the chief functional purposes of segmentary lineages, namely, predatory expansion.[49] In a pastoral-cum-agrarian society pastoralism would be more conducive to movement and would also provide the motive in the search for new grazing lands. The ability to segment suggests political flexibility and an economy not too deeply embedded in sedentary plough agriculture. Political flexibility and the absence of the social hierarchy of monarchical systems is reflected in the seemingly more egalitarian inter-clan relations of the Yādava lineage. Their pastoral economy is frequently referred to. Possibly the bull cult, evident from some sites linked with the BRW (Kayatha, Eran, Banas) may also have been a part of this.[50] In the movement from Kathiawar and Kutch via the Banas valley to the edge of the Doāb the migration might have been along the copper producing areas of the Aravallis especially as the Ahar copper artefacts appear to have been produced from local ore.[51] The culture may have lost its momentum when it arrived in areas already familiar with copper technology such as the Ganga-Yamuna Doāb. The search for new settlements would also have brought them into conflict with microlithic and neolithic cultures already occupying these lands, such as the Bagor culture or the earliest phase of the Mālwā culture. These would be food-gathering and herding groups or agriculturalists at a pre-metal age. Can these be identified, as has been suggested, with the Nāgas, Pulindas, etc., which are mentioned in the literary sources?[52] The archaeological remains of these would be difficult to locate as most of them would have been absorbed into the Chalcolithic culture.

The ecological context of most BRW sites, barring those of eastern India, suggests a more generalized reliance on a subsistence economy, with pockets of a more advanced economy. There appears to be a tendency to remain within a similar ecological bracket, with settlements on elevated plateau regions of lightly wooded vegetation cover, huts with pot-holes and wattle and daub walls, large-sized or multiple hearths and a substantial meat diet. This would in part explain the gradual succumbing of the BRW Chalcolithic to the iron-using PGW in the mid-first millennium B.C. and it would be worth investigating whether the extension of the BRW into a new ecological area in the eastern Ganges valley was due to association with iron technology. Indeed it might also explain, in reverse, how the more advanced iron technology of the peninsula Megalithic cultures (whatever may have been their origins) withstood for a considerable period the advance of the northern cultures. Was the migration of the Yādava clans into the peninsula (if the tradition is correct) carried out on the backs of the newly emergent Megalithic culture, or can the continuity of the Yādavas and their traditions be explained by assimilation into the existing megalithic culture?

The attempt to link the Pūru and Yādava lineages with certain archaeological cultures as examined in this paper has resulted in some echoes of identification, but nothing more definite than that can be said at this point. The identification remains speculative and requires both more information and more analyses before anything conclusive can be stated. Even this suggested identification raises a number of problems. The first of these is the problem of chronology. The start of the lineage is indirectly connected with the Flood. If the flood referred to is to be related to the only known major flood of the protohistoric period, the flood on the Indus, then it would date to *c.* 2000 B.C. and, even assuming a MASCA correction for Indian sites, can, at most, be taken back to 2400 B.C. This is still very much later than one of the dates which is associated with the start of the lineages, 3102 B.C.

Was the flood in the lineage records mythical and borrowed perhaps from the Sumerian king-lists where the flood plays a dominant role and is archaeologically not entirely speculative?

Further, if the Kuru section or the third phase of the Pūru lineage is to be identified with the PGW, then the date of the Mahābhārata war cannot be earlier than *c.* 800 B.C. and was probably later. This would again conflict with the traditional chronology where the minimum time-span between Mahāpadma Nanda and Pariksit is 1050 years which would place Parikṣit in approximately the fifteenth century B.C.[53] This lack of fit between chronology, archaeology and genealogy can perhaps be partially resolved if it is assumed that the listing of the generations was not meant to be a precise time-reckoning (in which case regnal years would have been mentioned), but rather a means of providing an approximate notion of the chronological framework. This is also indicated by the fact that not all the names listed in the genealogies are personal names (or even used in later times as personal names): some are quite clearly geographical place names and others are tribal names. Furthermore, it is as well to keep in mind that the tradition was compiled as a conscious attempt to record the past many centuries after the events referred to. As in all such records there would be a strong element of reorganizing the material to suit contemporary needs. The tradition itself therefore needs to be looked at more analytically. Many scholars have pointed out that the tradition is the end result of a series of encrustations and until these can be prised apart the tradition cannot be accepted as an entity. With reference to the *Mahābhārata* war, one view among scholars maintains that the original war was fought between the Kurus and the Pañcālas.[54] It is not impossible that the original *Bharata* referred to in Vedic literature[55] and differentiated from the *Mahābhārata* may have concerned an earlier section of the Pūru lineage and may have referred to a battle fought some time in the second millennium B.C. and that this *kathā* may have been appropriated by a later epic concerning the Kuru-Paṇḍava conflict. Sukthankar's analysis of the Bhṛguisation of the *Mahābhārata,* for example, shows clearly that attempted synchronisms from traditional sources are not as simple as they may seem at first glance.[56]

The second major problem raised by the identifications examined in this paper is the inevitable question of identifying the Indo-Aryan speakers. Undoubtedly the simplest solution would be to say that all the archaeological cultures were Indo-Aryan speaking: yet the contradiction is that the language of the *Ṛg Veda* shows evidence of non-Āryan elements, which evidence grows stronger in the later Vedic literature, suggesting that the substratum cultures were non-Āryan speaking.[57] The older Pūrus (whom we have tried to identify with the OCP) are described as Asura Rākṣasa, yet it is their descendants (if the lineage is correct)—the Kuru-Pañcālas—in whose land the best Sanskrit is spoken.[58] If Pūru was a distant figure of the past as he appears to have been to the Later Vedic literature and there was a break in the lineage after Bharata, then Pūru may well have been called an Asura Rākṣasa by more recent cultural groups such as the people of the PGW. The PGW could well reflect the arrival and settlement of a group such as the Indo-Aryan speakers since there is a hiatus between the OCP and the PGW and the latter is technologically and otherwise more advanced. This could be a neat hypothesis but for two problems: firstly, the *Ṛg Veda* would have to be dated to the start of the PGW period (*c.* 800 B.C. unless an earlier period can be suggested for the Punjab river valleys), which would seem late for the *Ṛg Veda;* and secondly, the origin of the PGW culture would have to be traced and this remains an enigma. Links with Iran suffer from an absence of any well-defined migratory route. So far, the possible link seems to be via the Swat Valley Grave cultures (Ghaligai V and Timargarha II and III),[59] and that too assuming that there was a major change in pottery type and other cultural facets on arrival in the Punjab, a change conditioned by local needs. This remains very tentative evidence at best. (In tracing such migrations or cultural continuities it might be worthwhile to examine the substratum pottery such as the grey ware and the red ware which occur as associated wares with more noticeable ceramic types.)

If the *Ṛg Veda* is sought to be equated with the post-Harappan cultures of the second millennium B.C. (and on linguistic grounds it cannot be taken any earlier) with a geographical focus in north-western India conforming to the *sapta-sindhava* of the text, there is a striking absence of uniformity in any of the cultures variously identified as 'Āryan', i.e. the Jhukar, Cemetery H and the Gandhāra Grave Culture.[60] Apart from lack of uniformity there is also an absence of any group of common traits—settlement patterns, artefacts, weapons, burial customs—which could be said to indicate a related culture. There are only isolated artefacts suggesting connections with west Asia. On the question of the diffusion of the Indo-Aryan language there are two other possibilities which merit attention. One is the very useful distinction drawn by

Hawkes between primary diffusion and secondary diffusion.[61] The first refers to the physical entry of a new people bringing an assemblage of new cultural traits. The second refers to the assimilation of the cultural traits of one group by another contiguous group without the first physically imposing itself on the second. The assimilation of cultural traits can be the adoption of the material culture where artefacts would register a difference, or the adoption of selected items such as language where the difference would not be easily recognizable, or both. In such an understanding of diffusion the element of invasion could be quite limited and it would be some aspect of dominance through technology, trade or some similar feature which would lead to the acquisition of new cultural traits. Another possibility is that the diffusion of Indo-Aryan in India followed a pattern similar to that of Hittite and Phrygian. The Hittites adopted the higher material culture of the people whom they conquered but kept their own Indo-European language.[62] Thus the material culture of Anatolia during this period does not declare the arrival of a new people to the extent that the cuneiform inscriptions indicate the arrival of a new language.

From recent work in linguistics it is clear that invasion is not the only method of accounting for the spread of a language. On the diffusion of Indo-European for instance, the earlier model of Indo-European replacing the existing languages in many parts of west Asia is now giving way to the notion of there being periods of bilingualism and relationships between the various languages of a particular language area. Thus it has been suggested that Uralic is cognate with Indo-European and also with Dravidian and more recently the theory has been put forward that Elamite is cognate with Dravidian.[63] If these relationships can be finally established then the nature of the diffusion of Indo-European will undergo a change and it may not be necessary to look for uniform, superimposed cultures in the archaeology of north-western India to identify the arrival of Indo-Aryan speakers.

If language diffusion is seen in these terms, then it would be possible to argue that there could have been small nuclei of Indo-Aryan speakers prior to the PGW who may have adopted the material culture of the previous settlers but retained their own language, thus initiating a period of bilingualism.[64] The continuity of cultures contemporary with Harappan, such as the OCP and the white-painted BRW, indicate that elements of survival from the Harappan have to be conceded. Against this background the introduction of the new technology of iron if controlled by the Indo-Aryan speakers, would have provided this group with the required political and economic edge, reducing the need for extensive conquest. Some of the religious rituals and practices of the indigenous culture would be Sanskritized and the new rulers would seek social legitimisation by being incorporated into the earlier elite lineages (a process which, incidentally, occurs repeatedly in later centuries of Indian history). The lineages would then be recorded as continuing in an unbroken line of descent from the earlier to the later period (which is again a characteristic of the *vaṃśāvalis* of the early medieval period). New ruling groups would thus 'latch-onto' the existing lineages and become socially acceptable as well. The archaeological culture of the PGW and its literary counterpart the Later Vedic literature would then be an evolved culture reflecting the indigenous as well as the later elements,[65] and 'aryan' would refer not to an ethnic group but to a social group identified by status, language and conformity to a particular cultural pattern, which certainly seems much closer to the connotation of the word *'ārya'* as it occurs in the Later Vedic literature. The heartland of the PGW where it had the maximum impact, i.e. the Doāb and its fringes, would remain the *āryāvarta*.

This process of acculturation can perhaps be more clearly visualized with reference to the BRW cultures. The association of BRW sherds with late Harappan levels in the same site and its subsequent diffusion would have made it a carrier of Harappan survivals to a far greater extent than the cultures contemporary with the Harappan in the upper Sarasvati and upper Doāb. In the case of the BRW there was no hiatus either. The movement of the white-painted BRW culture along the copper route in Rajasthan may further suggest that despite the decline of the Harappan cities there may still have been a modicum of the copper trade with west Asia of which the BRW culture of Rajasthan and Kathiawar was the inheritor. The movement into the Narmadā valley may also have been in continuation of an earlier source of timber and carnelian for the west Asian trade.[66]

However, should the identity of the Chalcolithic BRW with the Yādava lineage be acceptable, it raises its own problem, namely, that the Yādavas were unlikely to have been Indo-European speakers. The occurrence of black and red ware in the ancient middle east is generally not associated with Indo-European speakers. Similar pottery is found in Egypt and Nubia (going back to fourth millennium B.C.) and some traces in the Arabian peninsula have been suggested.[67] Archaeologically there is until now no connection between Egypt/Nubia and the west coast of India, apart from some traits in the first millennium megalithic culture of the peninsula. It is also not certain that the black and red of Egypt/Nubia is of the same ceramic type as the Indian megalithic black and red. It has been suggested that references to the Land of Punt in the Egyptian sources may be to trade connections with India, but even these were very sporadic, with long time intervals and the maximum contact was during the fifteenth century B.C.[68] A variety of what seems to be the black and red ware, the Khirbet Kerak ware, reported from Palestine, northern Syria and Anatolia has been under discussion as a possible ware associated with Indo-European speakers.[69] But the dates of this ware, *c.* 2600-2400 B.C., precede the earliest indications of the arrival of possible Indo-Europeans in Anatolia, the Luwians in *c.* 2300 B.C. In any case, the distribution of this ware ceases east of the Euphrates. Once again the links between the BRW in India and in west Asia remain enigmatic. There is a single shape which might indicate some connection and that is the channel-spouted bowl which occurs in white painted BRW and resembles in form a type from Sialk, Tepe Hissar and Tepe Giyan.[70] But this is again tenuous evidence.

Even from literary evidence the Yādavas are clearly not a primarily Indo-Aryan speaking group. The Vṛṣṇi and Andhaka are referred to as *vrātyas*.[71] The inhabitants of Ānarta and Surāṣṭra are described as belonging to the *sankīrṇa jātis*.[72] The Yādava kinship system shows traces of a matrilineal structure which is alien to the Indo-European kinship system.[73] If the *nīla-lohita* referred to in the *Atharvaveda* is to be taken as BRW as suggested, then it is evident that the text disapproves of the practices of those who use this pottery.[74] It would seem that the continuity and survival of cultures going back to the early second millennium B.C. in Gujarat would not only have preferred more of the third millennium culture but would also have modified the impact of linguistic and cultural Sanskritization in these areas. It is significant that the survival of the Harappa script, in the form of a few recognizable pictograms, occurs, so far as is known to date, as graffiti on the black and red pottery of the peninsula megalithic.[75] It is also curious that Gujarat is listed as one of the *pañca-drāviḍa* lands in a late Buddhist text.[76]

Attempts at correlating Purāṇic lineages and archaeological cultures are beset with speculation and suppositions. It would seem that the identification of the Yādava lineage on the whole appears to fit the archaeological evidence better, provided that the white-painted and plain Chalcolithic BRW cultures can be said to emanate from a common source or at least be closely related. The identification of the Pūru lineage is far more complex owing to the more pronounced changes in the archaeological cultures of the OCP and PGW. With the literary sources there is not only the problem that the Purāṇic texts were compiled many centuries after the events referred to, and even in the most meticulously maintained oral tradition chronological discrepancies are bound to enter thereby changing the concordance of the event and its record; there is also the problem that the Vedic and Purāṇic texts are sometimes in serious disagreement even with regard to the order of succession of the various descent groups. For example, Divodāsa and Sudāsa are mentioned in the *Ṛg Veda* as approximate contemporaries of Purukutsa and Trāsadasyu. Yet in the Purāṇic genealogies the latter two occur fairly early in the list of kings of Ayodhyā and the former two are listed late as kings of North Pañcāla, thus indicating a substantial time difference between the two.[77]

If archaeological evidence suggests that the Āryan speaking people settled in India in the post-Harappan period, then a more fundamental question connected with the historical tradition has to be posed. Does the tradition record personalities and events related only to Āryan culture or has it assimilated into its own tradition those names and events which might refer to non-Āryan and pre-Āryan times? In a period of bilingualism for instance, it could be assumed that non-Āryan names from an earlier tradition would be rendered into Sanskrit. If there is evidence of archaeological survivals from the Harappan culture, then some survivals within the tradition must also have persisted and these may not have been confined only to religious practices.

Perhaps at this stage it would be best to work towards a more precise definition of the evolution of archaeological cultures through more intensive excavation in an attempt to give greater clarity to the chronology, distribution and socio-economic structure of the various groups of people who were the authors of these cultures. Once the archaeological picture is more clearly defined and the information arrived at placed on a firmer footing, then the correlation with the historical tradition from literary sources might be more meaningful.

REFERENCES AND NOTES

1. B.B. Lal, 'Excavations at Hastināpur', *Ancient India*, nos. 10 and 11, 1954-55. H.D. Sankalia, 'Traditional Indian Chronology and C-14 Dates of Excavated Sites', in V.N. Misra and M.S. Mate (ed.), *Indian Prehistory: 1964*, (Poona, 1966), pp. 219-35. B. and R. Allchin, *The Birth of Indian Civilisation*, (Harmondsworth, 1968) p. 144 ff. D.H. Gordon, *The Prehistoric Background of Indian Culture*, (Bombay, 1958) pp. 59 ff, 83 ff.
2. H.W. Bailey, 'Iranian *Arya* and *Dahā*', *Transactions of the Philological Society*, 1959, pp. 71-115.
3. C. Bulcke, *Rāma-kathā* (Allahabad, 1950), V.S. Sukthankar, *On the Meaning of the Mahābhārata*, (Bombay, 1957).
4. R.S. Sharma, 'The Later Vedic Phase and the Painted Grey Ware'. *Proceedings of the Indian History Congress*, Calcutta, 1974.
5. D.D. Kosambi, *Introduction to the Study of Indian History* (Bombay, 1956), p. 139; H.D. Sankalia, op. cit.
6. Many attempts have been made to work out the chronology and perhaps among the most detailed is that of S.N. Pradhan, *Chronology of Ancient India* (Calcutta, 1927).
7. *Viṣṇu Purāṇa* IV. I am using this text as the basic text for the lineage correlations. In many ways it is the most standard of the *Purāṇas*.
8. *Matsya Purāṇa*, I. 11-34; *Śatapatha Brāhmaṇa* I.8.1. 1-10; *Mahābhārata* III.185 (all references to the Mahābhārata are to the Critical Edition).
9. Mircea Eliade, *The Myth of the Eternal Return* (New York, 1959).
10. B.B. Lal, 'A Deluge? Which Deluge? . . . . *American Anthropologist*, 1968, LXX, pp. 857-63. Dr. B.B. Lal, 'The Ochre-Coloured Pottery—A Geochronological Study', *Purātattva*, 1971-72, no. 5, pp. 49-58. R.L. Raikes, 'Kalibangan: Death from Natural Causes', *Antiquity*, 1968, no. 42, pp. 286-91.
11. D.P. Agrawal and Sheela Kusumgar, *Prehistoric Chronology and Radiocarbon Dating in India* (New Delhi, 1974), p. 103.
12. Y.D. Sharma, 'Value of Common Painted Ceramic Designs . . .' in D.P. Agrawal and A. Ghosh (eds.) *Radiocarbon and Indian Archaeology* (Bombay, 1973), pp. 222-30, Suraj Bhan, 'The Sequence and Spread of Prehistoric Cultures in the Upper Sarasvati Basin' in *Radiocarbon and Indian Archaeology*, p. 252 ff.
13. Y.D. Sharma, comments on OCP Seminar. *Purātattva*, 1971-72, no. 5, p. 21.
14. It would be worth plotting the OCP sites on a topographical map to see whether they at all reflect one of the modern characteristic uses of the flood plain in the upper Doāb, namely, the partial trans-humance between the *khadar* and the *bhangar* where the flood-plain is used as grazing ground by pastoral communities such as the Gujars. If the sites are substantially in the flood-plain it might explain in part the condition of the pottery as well as what superficially appears to be the nomadic nature of the culture. R. Ramachandran and S.C. Thakur, 'Human Perception and Adjustment to Flood Hazard in the Ganga Flood Plains'. Paper presented at the Twenty-second International Geographical Congress, 1972.
15. Information based on a map of the sites of the Doāb prepared by Roshan Dalal.
16. N.R. Banerjee, 'The Iron Age in India', in V.N. Misra and M.S. Mate (eds.),

Indian Prehistory: 1964, p. 177ff.

17. This is indicated by a comparative study of copper and iron finds from Hastināpur, Atranji-khera and Noh.
18. B.B. Lal, 'Excavations at Hastināpur', op. cit.
19. The phasing of the Paurava lineage is suggested by Pargiter, *Ancient Indian Historical Tradition*, (London, 1922), p. 110, but my preference is to take the first phase from Pūru to Bharata rather than Ajāmīḍha as Pargiter suggests because of the myth associated with the succession after Bharata to be discussed further in this paper.
20. *Ṛg Veda* VII. 96.2; VII.8.4; VII.18.13
21. The phrase *jeṣma pūram vidathe mṛdhravācām*, occurs in *Ṛg Veda* VII.18.13 and is sometimes understood to mean hostile or scornful speech and on other occasions speech which is alien or incorrect and therefore grating on the ears. The *dāsas* are generally characterized by the epithet *mṛdhravāc*. The comment of the *Śatapatha Brāhmaṇa* on this specific verse of the *Ṛg Veda* suggests the latter meaning.
22. *Viṣṇu Purāṇa*, IV.19. The same text clarifies in another section (II.1.) that the Bharata after whom Bhāratavarṣa was named was Bharata the son of Ṛṣabha.
23. F. E. Pargiter, *Ancient Indian Historical Tradition*, p. 146, *Viṣṇu Purāṇa* IV.19.
24. Pargiter, op. cit., p. 118.
25. *Indian Archaeology—A Review*, 1958-59, p. 26. *IA*, 1961-62, p. 98 (sites at Barata and Akoda). Cedi is sometimes identified with the Suktimati river but this seems too far from the Yamuna with which Cedi had connections. B.C. Law, *Historical Geography of Ancient India* (Paris, 1954), p. 313.
26. G.R. Sharma, *The Excavation at Kausambi, 1957-59* (Allahabad, 1960), pp. 6-7. V.D. Misra, 'Pottery of Kausambi' in B.P. Sinha (ed.), *Potteries of Ancient India*, (Patna, 1970), p. 203 ff.
27. A. Ghosh, *The City in Early Historical India*, (Simla, 1973) pp. 11, 62, 80-81. K.K. Sinha, 'Stratigraphy and Chronology of Early Kausambi' in *Radiocarbon and Indian Archaeology*, pp. 231-39.
28. *IA*, 1958-59, p. 45.
29. B. and R. Allchin, op. cit., p. 211.
30. D.P. Agrawal, 'Protohistoric Chronology and Technology and Ecological Factors. ', *Purātattva*, 1967-68, no. 1, pp. 17-23. D.P. Agrawal and Sheela Kusumgar, op. cit., pp. 103-13, give the revised dates for the Chalcolithic BRW from the sites discussed here.
31. *IA*, 1962-63, p. 30 (site at Bharatpur, Aligarh district); *IA*, 1965-66, p. 41 (site at Khalaura, Agra district); *IA*, 1965-66, p. 47 (rite at Bishnupur, Farrukhabad district); *IA* 1958-59, p. 50 (site at Alamgirpur, Meerut district); *IA*, 1969-70, p. 43 (site at Kasu, Meerut district).

    The excavation at Atranji-khera, however, does not conform entirely to this pattern. Here the BRW occurs as a distinct cultural level on the south side lying between OCP and PGW levels. But on the north side it is the earliest occupational deposit. R.C. Gaur, 'An Appraisal of the Protohistoric Problems of the Ganga-Yamuna Doab', *Purātattva*, 1970-71, no. 4, p. 42 ff.
32. Information collated from *Indian Archaeology*.
33. *Viṣṇu Purāṇa*, IV.1

34. *Ṛg Veda,* I.174.9; IV.30.17; V.31.8; VI.20.12; VI.45.1.
35. *Ṛg Veda,* VIII.6.46. J.P. Joshi, 'Excavation at Surkotada' in D.P. Agrawal and A. Ghosh, *Radiocarbon and Indian Archaeology,* p. 181.
36. *Harivaṃśa,* 54.
37. M.S. Mate and Z.D. Ansari, *Dwarka Excavations.*
38. Pargiter, op. cit., p. 279.
39. *Viṣṇu Purāṇa,* IV.1.
40. Pargiter, op. cit., p. 266.
41. *Viṣṇu Purāṇa,* IV.3.
42. S.B. Deo and M.K. Dhavalikar, *Paunar Excavation (1967),* (Nagpur, 1968), p. 6; *IA,* 1961-62, pp. 29-30.
43. *Epigraphia Indica,* XI, p. 18.
44. B. Saletore, *Ancient Karnataka,* (Poona, 1936), pp. 245, 247.
45. M. Raghava Aiyangar, *Vēḷir Varalāru.* (This reference was mentioned to me by Dr. R. Champakalakshmi.)
46. P.B. Desai, *Ancient History of Karnataka,* (Dharwar, 1970), pp. 112-13, 305.
47. Gopinatha Rao (ed.), *Travancore Archaeological Series,* no. 1, p. 191.
48. Pargiter, op. cit., p. 146.
49. Marshall D. Sahlins, 'The Segmentary Lineage: An Organisation of Predatory Expansion', *The American Anthropologist,* 1961, vol. 63, no. 2, pp. 332-45.
50. M.K. Dhavalikar, 'Some Aspects of the Chalcolithic Cultures of Central India', *Purātattva,* 1970-71, no. 4, pp. 24-30.
51. K.T.M. Hegde, 'Early Stages of Metallurgy in India' in *Radiocarbon and Indian Archaeology,* p. 401 ff.
52. H.D. Sankalia, op. cit., p. 223.
53. D.C. Sircar, *The Bharata War and Puranic Genealogies,* (Calcutta, 1969), p. 19 ff.
54. N.N. Bhattacharya, 'The Kurukshetra War and the Pandavas' in D. C. Sircar (ed.), *The Bharata War and Puranic Genealogies.* p. 37 ff, argues in support of the earlier theories of Lassen, Weber and Monier-Williams that the original war was a Kuru-Pañcāla war.
55. *Aśvalāyana Gṛhya Sūtra,* III.4.4.
56. V.S. Sukthankar, 'Epic Studies', *ABORI,* XVIII, pp. 1-76. P.K. Gode (ed.), *Sukthankar Memorial Edition,* vol. I.
57. T. Burrow, *The Sanskrit Language,* (London, 1965), pp. 373-88. B.M. Emeneau, *Collected Papers,* (Annamalai, 1967), pp. 148-55.
58. *Śatapatha Brāhmaṇa,* III.2.3.15.
59. Stacul, 'Exacavation near Ghaligai (1968) and chronological sequence of protohistorical cultures in the Swat valley', *East and West,* 1969, vol. 19, pp. 44-92. A. H. Dani, 'Timargarha and Gandhara Grave Culture', *Ancient Pakistan,* III, 1967, p. 1 ff.
60. D.H. Gordon, op. cit., pp. 59, 83. A. H. Dani, op. cit.
61. C.F.C. Hawkes, *The Prehistoric foundations of Europe to the Mycenaen Age.*
62. H. Hencken, 'Indo-European Languages and Archaeology, *American Anthropological Association,* December 1955, vol 57, no. 6, part 3, Memoir no. 4, pp. 2 ff, 41 ff.
63. S.A. Tyler, 'Dravidian and Uralian: The Lexical Evidence', *Language,* 1968,

no. 44, pp. 798-812. D.W. McAlpin, 'Elamite and Dravidian· Further Evidence of Relationship', *Current Anthropology*, March 1975, vol. 16, no. 1, p. 105ff.

64. B.M. Emeneau, *Collected Papers.*
65. I have discussed the possible mechanism of such a cultural evolution in the Presidential Address—Section I of the Indian History Congress, Varanasi, 1969. See Proceedings and pp. 211-39 of this volume.
66. Romila Thapar, 'A Possible Identification of Meluhha, Dilmun and Makan', *Journal of the Economic and Social History of the Orient*, 1975, vol. XVIII, part I, p. 30 ff.
67. S.P. Gupta, 'Gulf of Oman: The Original Home of Indian Megaliths', *Purātattva*, 1970-71, no. 4, p. 7.
68. M. Murray, *The Splendour That was Egypt*, (London, 1954), pp. xxi, 20, 49, 98.
69. I am grateful to Mr. B.K. Thapar for drawing my attention to this discussion. E. Anarti, *Palestine before the Hebrews*, p. 101 ff and L.C. Wooley, *A Forgotten Kingdom*, (London, 1938), p. 32 ff, both associated the ware with barbarian invasions. More extensive excavation has modified these views. B. Maisler, et al., 'The Excavation at Beth Yerah', *Israel Exploration Journal*, 1944-46, 1952, vol. 2, nos. 2, 3, 4. In the same journal, Ruth Amiran, 'Connections between Anatolia and Palestine in the Early Bronze Age.' R. Braidwood, *Mounds of the Antioch Plain*, p. 55. S. Hood, 'Excavation at Tabera al Akad, 1948-49', *Anatolian Studies*, 1951, vol. I, pp. 113 ff. More recent views on this discussion are given in brief in the *Cambridge Ancient History*, vol. I, part 2, pp. 213 ff.
70. K.V. Soundara Rajan, 'The Iron Age Culture Provinces of India', *Bharatiya Vidya*, 1963, vol. XXIII, nos. 1-4, pp. 1-21.
71. *Mahābhārata*, VII.143.15.
72. *Baudhāyana*, I.1.2.13
73. The main feature is the mention of cross-cousin marriages which is particularly prohibited in the Indo-Aryan kinship system. For a discussion of this see T.R. Trautman, 'Cross-cousin Marriage in Ancient North India' in T.R. Trautman (ed.), *Kinship and History in South Asia*, (Michigan, 1974). For Indo-European kinship structure see P. Friedrich, 'Proto-Indo-European Kinship', *Ethnology*, 1966, V, pp. 1-36.
74. *Atharvaveda*, IV.17.4 and cf. V.31.1. The reference is discussed in A. Ghosh, *The City in Early Indian History*, p. 6 and Shivaji Singh, 'Vedic Literature on Pottery' in B.P. Sinha, op. cit., p. 305 ff. The reference to *sūtra nīla-lohita* in the Paippalada text can perhaps be explained as a late recension in a distant land (Kashmir) being totally unfamiliar with black and red pottery and associating it with *sūtra*.
75. B.B. Lal, 'From the megalithic to the Harappa: tracing back the graffiti on the pottery', *Ancient India*, 1960, no. 16, pp. 4-24.
76. *Khuddakanikāya, Apādāna*, II, p. 359.
77. *Ṛg Veda*, I.63.7; IV.42.8; VI.61.1 ff; V.16.4; VII.18, 25; VII.191.3. Pargiter, op. cit., pp. 145-46.

The Tradition of Historical Writing in Early India

It has long been maintained that the ancient Indians were a people lacking in a sense of history, since they do not appear to have kept an accurate record of past events. Comparisons are made with the ancient Greeks, whose history was recorded by a series of historians, and the Chinese who have traditionally maintained chronicles of various dynasties and rulers. The Indian tradition until the seventh century A.D. lacks any literature which can be specifically described as historical writing. Historical records are embedded in various kinds of literature which are not historical documents *per se*. From the seventh to the twelfth centuries A.D. there are a number of historical biographies and some histories of kingdoms, which can certainly be included in the category of historical literature. But many of these are not treated as serious historical documents, since the required critical assessment of events is often lacking, and, except on rare occasions, it is said that historical causality in these texts, is not frequently based on rational, empirical argument.

Since much of the argument hinges on the definition of a sense of history, let me begin by suggesting a definition. A sense of history can be defined as a consciousness of past events, which events are relevant to a particular society, seen in a chronological framework and expressed in a form which meets the needs of that society. It may be argued that this is too restricted a definition and that history implies a concern with political events and, in addition, involves the analysis of past events by suggesting causal relationships based on rational explanation and which, therefore, assumes a critical judgement on the past by the historian. It is, however, debatable whether this extension of the definition of an historical sense is not a product of modern thinking, and where such historical writing does exist in ancient cultures (as indeed it does even in the Indian tradition at a later period),

From *Indian Church History Review*, vol. VI, no. 1, 1972, pp. 1-22.

it is not a consciously thought-out philosophy of history but the result of an individual and rather analytical mind applying itself to historical narrative.

If the above definition of a sense of history is acceptable, then the historical tradition can be culled from existing literature, whether specifically historical or not. Every society has a concept of its past and therefore no society can be called a historical. Furthermore, historical memory is frequently recorded in a chronological order. Therefore, the most significant aspect in studying the historical tradition of a society is to understand why certain events are regarded as the most relevant and worth recording. The form in which the record is maintained (and this can range from mythology to critical narrative) will depend to a large extent on the type of events recorded. I would like to suggest in this paper that the Indian historical tradition, particularly in the period prior to the seventh century A.D., was not concerned primarily with keeping a record of essential political events, since they were not always believed to be the most relevant by those who were responsible for maintaining the historical tradition. To this extent, the form in which a sense of history was expressed in ancient India must be judged by the literature of other ancient classical cultures. What is perhaps more important is to try and understand what was regarded as relevant and why.

The first part of this paper is a survey of the sources and literature which either include the historical tradition or form part of it. The latter part of the paper deals with the three main constituents of the historical tradition, namely, mythology, genealogy and historical narrative. An attempt is made to explain why these three factors constitute the historical tradition and the way in which they can be related to a sense of history. This will also serve to reveal the patterns and meanings in the flow of events as seen in ancient India. A distinction is made between the existence of a historical tradition and a philosophy of history. It is perhaps as well to keep in mind that although an awareness of a philosophy of history may make historical narratives more meaningful, they do not necessarily thereby express greater historical veracity. The historical tradition may not concern itself primarily with purpose in history but may well be an equally authentic record of the past.

Sources and Literature of Historical Tradition

The nearest equivalent term for history used in Sanskrit literature is *itihāsa*—which literally means 'thus it was' or 'so it has been'. By extension, the term came to refer to legend, history and accounts of past events. The purpose of *itihāsa* was to refer to the events of the past in such a manner as would relate them to the goals and purposes of the Hindu tradition.[1] The historical tradition grew out of a variety of literary forms current during the Vedic period. Of these the most significant were the *gāthās* (songs), *nārāśaṃsi* (eulogies of heroes), *ākhyāna* (dramatic narratives), and *purāṇa* (ancient lore). These were very often the compositions of the priest-poets attached to the various tribes. The original tradition was oral and the compositions were recited at gatherings. The written records of the tradition came considerably later.

The two epics, the *Rāmāyaṇa* and the *Mahābhārata*, include elements of the historical tradition which arose largely from attempts to provide antecedents in order to connect the origins of tribes and geographical locations with the heroes of the epics and, in the genealogical sections, to indicate relationships at various levels between the gods and the heroes.

The work of collecting this information and composing it in a literary form was the special function of the *sūtas* and the *māgadhas*, the bards and the chroniclers. They were probably originally drawn from the priest-poet families of the Vedic period and were at this time accorded an important status.[2] Their work was to preserve the genealogies of the gods, the kings, the *rsis* and the heroes, and to compose the royal panegyrics and eulogies as the occasion demanded. In a context of new settlements and inter-tribal warfare, the genealogies of kings became the nucleus of the historical tradition, since these were maintained, among other things, for the functional purpose of proving legal rights and social status, not to mention the preservation of tribal identity.

Throughout the period from the rise of the Mauryan empire in the fourth century B.C. to the establishment of the Gupta kingdom in the fourth century A.D. there is, as far as we know, no evidence of any purely historical writing, and this, in spite of the fact that the period was germane to the evolution of the major political and social institutions in ancient India. We can only assume that the *sūtas*, the *māgadhas* and the official archivists quietly pursued their activities. For it is the material which they collected and put into literary form which is incorporated in the Purāṇic texts which were compiled or rewritten from the time of the Guptas, i.e., the fourth century A.D. The word

Purāṇa literally means 'old' and was used for a body of literature consisting largely of traditional history and aspects of social and religious life which it was thought should be preserved. It was claimed by the authors of the *Purāṇas* that Purāṇic literature was handed down from very ancient times.

The earliest surviving written evidence of at least a part of the *itihāsa* tradition such as is found in the *Purāṇas* therefore dates to the fourth century A.D.[3] This is a period much later than that of the original composition and relates to a changed socio-cultural milieu. The original material must have undergone considerable modification in the process of being incorporated into the *Purāṇas*. If, as Pargiter suggests, the genealogies were preserved originally in Prakṛt and when rewritten in the *Purāṇas* were translated into Sanskrit with occasional metrical and grammatical lapses which give a clue to their Prakṛt origin, then clearly the original was further diluted. Moreover, in the days when the tradition was still an oral one, various mnemonic devices were used—the most common being legends—and these were also the most easily incorporated into the tradition. It is to the *Purāṇas* that we must turn next in our search for the historical tradition. In this paper the *Viṣṇu Purāṇa* has been used as a model.

The historical material in the *Purāṇa* is not to be found in a clearly defined and separate section. The genealogical matter is certainly kept distinct, but it is seen in the context of mythological and cosmological material, not to mention laws relating to social behaviour and ritual. The historical value of the *Purāṇa* as records of the past is limited by the fact that they were consciously and deliberately rewritten at a particular period subsequent to the events described and the rewriting was not by the *sūtas* and the *māgadhas* who had earlier been the custodians of the tradition. Authorship was now ascribed to a variety of ancient and almost legendary sages. In fact the texts were compiled by various *brāhmaṇ* families. The attempt was to collect from the heralds and chroniclers, 'the scattered traditions which they had imperfectly preserved.'[4] This material was largely the genealogies of royal dynasties and descriptions of the universe. It is interesting that by now the social status of the *sūta* and the *māgadha* had been considerably reduced, for both are described in contemporary law-books as the offspring of a mixed-caste marriage and therefore very low in social scale.[5]

As long as the tradition was oral it would require professionally skilled memorizers; once it was written down, then the work of these bards became less valuable. Those with access to formal education tended to take over the records. Thus the *brāhmaṇs* who had access to formal education appropriated the genealogies and became the keepers of the records. The fact that the records were rewritten in the Purāṇic form was, however, the result of a variety of historical reasons.

Clearly there was a realization at this time of the importance of the historical tradition and it had therefore to be incorporated with the priestly function and not left to mere genealogists and chroniclers. This in turn was the consequence of the delicate balance of sacred and secular control. The concept of divinity was no longer a dominant aspect of the Indian political tradition. During this period, status by birth became a much more important factor. Within the caste structure, political power, although theoretically confined to the *kṣatriya* caste, was in fact open to all. This is evident from the number of dynasties drawn from the non-*kṣatriya* castes, to which even the legal texts had to admit. Had this continued unchecked, the status of sacerdotal power would have been reduced to a minimum in political functioning. With the increasing importance of the *brāhmaṇs* in the Gupta period it became customary for dynasties of the non-*kṣatriya* castes to seek legitimization by acquiring a fabricated genealogy from a *brāhmaṇ* author. The same process of legitimization was also utilized by foreign dynasties aspiring to roots in India. The *brāhmaṇs* took over the records and genealogies of the *sūtas* and the *māgadhas* and provided the new rulers with legitimate links with the gods and kings of antiquity. The keeping of genealogies provided social status to both the subject of the genealogy and the record-keeper.

The attribution of the authorship of the *Purāṇas* to the sages was an attempt to claim both antiquity and authority for the texts. This is further emphasized in the genealogical sections where the dynastic lists are given in the form of a prophecy using the future tense. This has the advantage for us today of providing a rough clue to the date of compilation of the *Purāṇas* since the prophecy would have to terminate with contemporary events. The geographical location of the *Purāṇa*, though theoretically extending over the entire sub-continent, was in fact largely focused on the Ganges valley and the fringe areas of this valley, with the central point being the kingdom of Magadha.

Although historical material is woven into the various sections of the *Purāṇa*, this is not done in a totally arbitrary manner. The format of the *Purāṇa* does suggest a framework which reflects a fairly integrated view of the past, in spite of the fact that this view is somewhat obscured by mythology, cosmology and the unfolding of the Vaiṣṇavite tradition. The aim of the *Purāna* was to consider subjects relevant to the nature of creation, the relationship between men and gods, the maintenance of social institutions, the genealogies of kings and heroes, the legends relating to the *Kṛṣṇa-avatāra* of Viṣṇu and the eventual destruction of the world at the end of the *Kaliyuga*. The *Purāṇa* therefore presents an integrated world-view from a Vaiṣṇavite brahmanical perspective. Seen in this light, the historical tradition becomes a part of this world-view. The limitations ensuing from the rewriting of this tradition and the consequent weakening of its historicity, are perhaps compensated for by its having now acquired a socio-cultural context and a philosophical base. The *Viṣṇu Purāṇa* may not reveal a critical and causal analysis of the past but it certainly does provide evidence of a consciously formed image of the past.

From the seventh century A.D. onwards the historical tradition as expressed in the idea of *itihāsa* and *purāṇa* underwent a process of enlargement. The genealogical aspect of the tradition was not only maintained but intensified in the various *vaṃśāvalis* or family chronicles maintained in many kingdoms. In addition, the tradition gave rise to a new genre of historical writing, the historical biography. This was due to a number of reasons. The emergence of small, regional kingdoms, based on a feudalistic pattern of functioning, led to the development of local loyalties and interests and a more strongly defined association of a locality with its history. Together with this, the centre of historical interest had moved from the tribe to the king and his court. The heroic tradition had given way to the court and the focus of the court, the king. The *sūta* receded into the background and the court poet became central to historical writing.

A number of historical biographies of royalty were written in the period from A.D. 600 to 1200. Among these the better known are the *Harṣa-carita* of Bāṇa, the *Vikramānkadevacarita* of Bilhaṇa, the *Kumārapāla-caritas*, and the *Prithvi-rāja-vijaya* attributed to Jayānaka. Occasionally the biographies of important ministers were also written. These clearly demonstrated an increasing interest in secular power. These works were written within the framework of the Indian courtly perspective on the world, emphasizing the values of chivalry, heroism and loyalty A recognizable literary form, with well-defined phases of introduction and climax of plot and theme, was used. The authors being sophisticated court poets, they did not hesitate on occasion to sacrifice historical veracity to an elegant turn of phrase or to dramatic analogies. Furthermore it was often frankly admitted that the purpose of the biography was eulogistic. The author was seeking patronage and the subject was seeking immortality. The departure from the earlier historical tradition lay in the fact that these works focused attention on a particular person or on a single dynasty and therefore covered a far smaller time-span and concerned themselves with a precisely defined geographical area. The historical frame was now much smaller and allowed of greater detail. The link with the *itihāsa* and *purāṇa* tradition was maintained both indirectly when the court poets used these earlier texts as source material and more directly by associating the subject of the biography with the earlier heroes and legends. This was largely an attempt at literary ornamentation, and at continuing the *itihāsa* tradition.

The authors of the biographies were familiar with the historical tradition. The heroic tradition may have given way to the courtly one but it had not died. Unfortunately, modern historians have tended to dismiss the historicity of these biographies largely because of the literary ornamentation. The close affinity between the *Purāṇa* and the historical biography was also due to the fact that the authors of these texts, generally Brāhmaṇs, not only came from the same social background but had an almost identical education. Sections of the earlier *Purāṇas* would have formed a part of the syllabus in the education of the court poets.

The last of the major works which can be included in this survey is the famous history of Kashmir, the *Rājataraṅgiṇī* written by Kalhaṇa in about 1149. Kalhaṇa's historical writing, although it owes a great deal to the *itihāsa* and *purāṇa* tradition, is nevertheless a departure from it. It covers the history of Kashmir from the mythical past to the twelfth century A.D. Kalhaṇa uses as evidence not only the earlier tradition but much more so the local religious and secular literature, inscriptions and historical remains from an earlier period. From the point of view of Kalhaṇa's handling of historical events, the *Rājataraṅgiṇī* can be divided into three main sections. The first, dealing with the mythical past, borrows heavily from the *itihāsa purāṇa* tradition. In the second section, he begins to gather information from a variety of sources and there is a greater degree of historically verifiable material. The last section deals with the history of Kashmir from the eighth to the twelfth centuries and is by far the most accurate and interesting. It is largely on the basis of this section that Kalhaṇa's significance as a critical historian can be established. Here his concern is not merely with chronicling events but also in seeking for causal explanations ranging over a wide variety of factors. There is a noticeable change in the character of causal relationships between the first and last sections, where super-natural elements give way to rational, secular explanations, sometimes based on empirical observation. The fact that Kalhaṇa and his family were intimately associated with the politics of Kashmir during the eleventh and twelfth centuries may in part account for this change. The *Rājataraṅgiṇī* is often regarded as somehow outside the Indian tradition because of its highly developed historical sense. Attempts are made to try and explain this by attributing it to the influence of the Greeks—a thousand years prior to the writing of the book—or to the influence of the Turks in Central Asia who, because they were converted to Islam, are immediately endowed with a historiographical tradition. The fact remains that if the *Rājataraṅgiṇī* is seen in the context of the evolution of early Indian historical writing, then it appears well within the Indian tradition. If however indirect influences have to be found, then perhaps it would be more worthwhile to consider the influence of the Buddhist tradition on Kalhaṇa.

Historical biographies in Sanskrit declined after the conquest of many parts of northern India by the Turks and Afghans. Now the majority of the court poets were Muslims who wrote in Persian. Nevertheless, even in these areas poets continued to write biographies of the Sultans in Sanskrit, but since many of them were not court poets of the first rank, these biographies often degenerated into vapid works of little literary or historical interest. In other parts of the country the historical tradition was continued in Sanskrit with greater success. Perhaps the most impressive work of the twelfth and thirteenth centuries were those of the Jaina teachers of western India.[6] These were mainly historical biographies stylistically favouring the model of the courtly tradition mentioned earlier. However, in these works by Jaina authors the courtly values were subservient to a strong moralistic under-pinning in the narrative. The historical tradition was preserved by the Jainas in two categories of literature. One was the continued writing of the *prabandhas*, connected narratives relating to royalty, which were maintained by itinerant Jaina monks who made these texts the excuse to moralize on the actions of reigning kings. This writing coincided with an attempt by Jaina teachers to reform the Jaina religion during this period. The other literature consisted of genealogies and chronicles pertaining to the local kings and states. In fact it would not be incorrect to say that the Jaina religious teachers and monks displayed a considerable and particular interest in the historical tradition.

The mention of monks associated with the historical tradition brings me to the final category of literature which I would like to include in this survey—the Buddhist Chronicles of Ceylon, commonly known as the Pāli Chronicles. These were written in an area outside the geographical limits of India proper, nevertheless their association with the Indian historical tradition justifies their inclusion. Although smaller in number than the Sanskrit texts, in the context of historiography they are equally important as they reflect the Buddhist attitude to history or, to be more precise, the attitude of the Theravada Buddhist sect. Of the many chronicles, the ones most pertinent to this survey are the *Dāpavaṃsa* and the *Mahāvaṃsa*. These chronicles began as an oral tradition and were recorded in writing at a later period, their present form dating to about the fifth and sixth centuries A.D. Of the two texts, the *Dāpavaṃsa* is more narrow in its interests as it narrates the history of the island. The *Mahāvaṃsa* on the other hand claims to be the introduction to the chronicle of the *Mahāvihāra* monastery—an important Buddhist monastery in Ceylon and its authorship is attributed to a monk called *Mahānāma*. The narrative winds its way through both the history of Ceylon and the history of Buddhism on the island, with cross-references to important events in the history of Buddhism taking place in India. A variety of sources are used such as royal records, monastic records, histories of relics and shrines, legends, folk-lore and the personal experience of those who have witnessed events. The *Mahāvaṃsa* is given to literary embellishments and a ready incorporation of mythological and legendary material. The destruction of the *Mahāvihāra* monastery in the fourth century A.D. disrupted the records. It has been suggested that the material was then collated from various monastic sources. The purpose in writing the chronicles was partly historical and partly didactic since they were also intended for the edification of the Buddhist Order, the *saṅgha*.

Main Concepts of the Historical Tradition

So much for a survey of the historical tradition and its manifestation in various types of literature. I would now like to examine the various concepts which went into the making of this tradition and to consider whether such concepts constitute an idea of history. These concepts were based on a wide range of assumptions acceptable to Indian society. Before discussing these assumptions it may be as well to look at the characteristic forms of the historical tradition in which the concepts are implicit. There were three major forms, genealogies, myths and historical narrative, and these three are frequently interwoven in the texts.

The core of the historical tradition was the genealogical records. These have remained constant in the Indian scene throughout the centuries and in fact up to the present day. In the *Purāṇas*, the genealogies are carefully preserved and follow an historical order. With the kingdom of Magadha as the base and extending to the fringes of the Ganges valley, an attempt is made to trace the antecedents of the more important dynasties. The record begins with the great flood from which only Manu and his family and seven sages survive. Manu returns to Jambudvīpa—after the flood has subsided. Of his many children, the tenth is an hermaphrodite. This child gives birth to the two royal lineages. From the female half comes the Lunar family and from the male half comes the Solar family. From this point on most later dynasties are said to belong to either the Lunar or Solar line. The text then provides us with the genealogies of the three major dynasties, the Pauravas of Hastināpur, the Aikṣvākus of Ayodhyā and the Bṛhadrathas of Magadha, and these form the bed-rock of the genealogical records. The geographical movement eastwards from the upper Ganges valley to Magadha follows a historically attested direction, although the details of the king-lists cannot always be verified by cross-evidence. The records continue with the more important dynasties of Magadha, for whose historical existence, there is cross-evidence, such as the Śiśunāgas, Nandas, Mauryas, Śuṅgas and the Guptas, with others such as the Āndhras, Śakas, Yavanas, mentioned in the outlying areas.[7]

Had the *Purāṇas* been only a series of genealogical records, they would have received more respect as historical documents from modern historians. But since these genealogical sections are embedded in a larger whole made up of myths, cosmological theories and social and ritualistic laws, there is a tendency to dismiss the entire text as fanciful. It is interesting that the formal structure of the *Purāṇas* appears to have been maintained in modern Indian genealogies such as the *vahivaṃśas* and the *pothis* or the caste *Purāṇas* maintained in many parts of India today, by both bards and family priests. These generally consist of two sections: the factual, where the genealogies are recorded and brought up-to-date at regular intervals, and the mythical.[8] The latter consists partly of traditional mythology drawn frequently from the classical *Purāṇas* and partly of what has been called the 'mythical-historical section', where the bard tries to relate his patrons to the heroes and historical events of the past. Whereas the mythical section is kept fairly intact, the genealogical section is continually 'telescoped' in order to make its preservation more manageable. This telescoping inevitably results in the pruning of the record, where often only the bare bones of names and relationships are left: these being regarded as the most significant to social needs. Thus where once there might have been a narrative or an explanation accompanying the genealogy, in its final form it was pared down to just the genealogy. The same 'telescoping' process is used by the family priests who maintain family records in the various Hindu centres of pilgrimage. Taken as a whole, the *Purāṇas* came to be regarded both as historical records preserving information on the continuity of dynasties and as socially necessary documents establishing a community's roots in the past and, more narrowly, becoming the basis for the enforcement of legal claims and providing status and antiquity to those seeking political and social status.

Genealogies are also useful as records of time. The span of time can be calculated through the generations in the genealogies. Similarly a record of regnal years can indicate the time-span of a dynasty. The 'telescoping' of the genealogical material did not affect the calculation of the time-span as long as the relationship between generations was clearly maintained. In cases where the regnal years of a succession of kings are mentioned, as is often the case in the *Purāṇas*, the genealogy becomes the basis of the dating system as well.

The process of 'telescoping' does however raise one obvious problem. Unless a very careful check is maintained in recording names and relationships referring to earlier parts of the genealogy, there is a possibility of names lapsing and getting dropped out. Only the record of the generations remains and this has then to be completed with a fabricated genealogy. It is not surprising that in the genealogies of both the *Purāṇas* and the Pāli Chronicles, the more recent genealogies are the most accurate. The genealogical information in the *Mahāvaṃsa* can be divided into two parts. The early genealogies upto the period of king Devānampiyatissa in the third century B.C. appear to be largely fabricated. We are even told of one group of kings who ruled for the mystic number of 84,000 years (7 X 12 X 1000). With the accession of Tissa, the record becomes much more accurate and reliable. The king lists are more carefully maintained from this period until the destruction of the monastery. In all these genealogies the major concern from the point of view of historical records was with the immediate past and not the remote past.

The second characteristic of the early Indian historical tradition was the inclusion of myths. Here the pertinent question is that of the relevance of the myths to the historical world-view of the authors of these texts.

The Purāṇic myths referring to the origin of the two royal lineages has a fairly obvious meaning. The great flood caused the total destruction of the world and this is a recognized stage in the cyclic time concept. The beginnings of history therefore emerge from a condition which has no antecedents: it is in fact symbolic of the very beginning. The birth of the two royal lines from a hermaphrodite suggests a variation of idea of twins as parents, indicating the purity of the lineage. The choice of the two lineage names—the Sun and the Moon—is equally significant. Perhaps a structuralist would see in this the bi-polarity of male and female, day and night, and a series of other opposed pairs. Perhaps the myth was a memory of the dividing of the tribes into two rival groups. Alternatively, it was an attempt to weave the many dynastic strands into two main currents and finally to a single origin. It is not surprising that the word Manu provided the generic base for *mānava* meaning 'mankind.'

Let us briefly consider a well-known myth from the opening section of the *Mahāvaṃsa*—the story of the birth and arrival of Vijaya in Ceylon—and see whether it contains any historical assumptions.[9] There was once a princess in the land of Vaṅga (eastern India) whose father had her married to a lion. She gave birth to a son and a daughter. But she remained unhappy and homesick. So when her son grew up she talked him into killing his father the lion. The princess with her two children returned to her home. But the children soon left her and wandered away to a place where they got married to each other, built themselves a city, and soon established a kingdom. The marriage resulted in sixteen pairs of twin sons of whom the eldest was Vijaya. He was so evil that he had to be exiled but was allowed to take 700 attendants with him. He travelled at first to western India and finally arrived in Ceylon with his 700 attendants on the same day as the Buddha's death. He eventually subdued the demons which inhabited the island, sent to India for wives for himself and his followers and became a virtuous king.

The geographical area of the story is very wide, starting with eastern India, going to western India, whence Vijaya takes ship and sails for Ceylon. This may well have been the normal route taken by people travelling south. The overland route certainly went via western India. The fact of his unusual and supernatural origin is amply emphasized. He is the grandson of a lion, the son of an incestuous marriage, the eldest of sixteen twin brothers, and the conditions of his birth serve to underline the purity of his ancestry. His social status is well taken care of by his royal antecedents both in the animal and human world. Royal antecedents also provide him with the economic wherewithal to travel the long distance from Vaṅga to Ceylon together with his attendants. The exile was presumably necessary to explain why anyone would travel all that way to an island inhabited only by demons. It is appropriate that the man who founded the human population of Ceylon should arrive on the auspicious day of the Buddha's *parinirvāṇa*.

From the more narrowly historical point of view, the legend attempts to explain the derivation of the name of the island—Sinhala—associated with lion. It strongly hints at an early and close connection with India. This connection is also seen at another level. It is interesting that some of the important events narrated in this myth appear to be stereotypes in myths referring to the origins of certain republican states in northern India in the seventh century B.C. as described in other Buddhist literature.[10] The incest theme and the reference to the sixteen pairs of twins are common to many of these origin-myths, a case in point being the origin of the Śākyas as described in the *Mahāvastu* of the northern Buddhist tradition. The Śākyas being the tribe which produced the Buddha, it is possible that the author of the *Mahāvaṃsa,* being familiar with this myth, wished to associate similar conditions with the emergence of Ceylon. That the Buddhist monks were not only familiar with the northern Buddhist literature but also with the legends of a Hindu cult is evident from the story of the birth and life of Pāṇḍukābhaya in a further chapter of the *Mahāvaṃsa.*[11] This story approximates to that of the birth and life of the god Kṛṣṇa-Vāsudeva so closely, that one wonders whether the author of the *Mahāvaṃsa* may not have been well-acquainted with the *Viṣṇu Purāṇa*. The details of the story are too similar even to allow of any Jungian explanation of the identical myth.

Unlike the *Viṣṇu Purāṇa.* with its limited amount of historical narrative, the *Mahāvaṃsa* provides a reasonably equitable balance between myth, genealogy and historical narrative. The narrative is partly fanciful and partly factual. But the logic of events is maintained and there are comparatively few inconsistencies once the assumptions are accepted. It has to be kept in mind that the chronicle is the work of Buddhist monks and is concerned with the history of Buddhism in Ceylon. Thus the Buddha is brought to Ceylon. This may be factually incorrect but in the historical perspective of the Buddhist monks it makes sense since the Buddha was the pivot of their history. The arrival of the Buddha is almost completely enveloped in supernatural occurrences which may suggest that the author was aware of the dubious historicity of this event. However, having made this concession to an ideological position, subsequent events develop in a more probable manner.

In the early part of the chronicle the location moves alternately between northern India and Ceylon since events significant to the early history of Buddhism took place in India. The Buddhist Councils held in India to clarify the doctrine are described presumably as a background to explaining why a particular doctrine came to be the accepted one in Ceylon. The broad outlines of Mauryan history are indicated, since it was a Mauryan prince in the third century B.C. who first initiated the people of Ceylon into Buddhism. The scene then shifts to the island itself with the coming of Vijaya and the establishment of his rule and the narrative is brought forward to the reign of Tissa in the third century B.C. with a cross-reference to the Third Buddhist Council held in northern India. At this point the two locations and the many facets of the story meet with the arrival of Mahinda, the Mauryan prince at the court of Tissa, sent by the Third Buddhist Council to propagate Buddhism in Ceylon. From this point on the history is essentially that of Ceylon and the references to persons and events in India, although frequent, are essentially subordinate. There are historical inconsistencies, but these are on the whole minor as compared with the overall logical framework within which the narrative unfolds.

Historical narrative often contains the core of historical explanation. In seeking to understand the nature of historical explanation it is necessary to examine some of the ideological assumptions implicit in historical narrative. For our purposes, perhaps the two most significant assumptions are first the notion of time, and secondly the role of man in shaping history, and the two are inter-related.

The measurement of time changes and evolves in keeping with the historical changes in a society. In its earlier phases time is measured on the basis of natural phenomena which occur regularly. It is generally cyclical and the lunar reckoning becomes the obvious basic measure. For purposes of historical memory, genealogies are maintained where the chronology relates to regnal years and not to a central date. Time periods are often reckoned not according to a calendar but by some important event. Even when the measurement of time becomes more precise with advances in mathematical and astronomical knowledge and the adoption of the solar calendar, a variety of time-reckonings can continue to co-exist within a society. Such was the case in ancient India, where the lunar calendar was frequently used for everyday activity, and the solar calendar was used by the priests for keeping accurate records and ascertaining dates, etc. A luni-solar calendar comprising both systems of reckoning was also known. The lunar calendar continued to be used widely perhaps because it is easier to use and perhaps because much of the ritual associated with time-reckoning had already been established on the basis of the lunar calendar.

In historical terms the use of a calendar also suggests the use of eras. In India the earliest evidence of the use of an era dates to first century B.C., the previous reckoning having been in regnal years. The two commonly used eras of this time were the Krita or Vikrama of 58 B.C. and the Śaka of A.D. 78. From the Gupta period onwards there is flowering of eras all over the subcontinent. This was no doubt due to the emergence of numerous feudalistic kingdoms as well as the proliferation of knowledge in mathematics and astronomy. The reference to the Mahābhārata war in the Hindu tradition, generally calculated by modern historians to *circa* 3102 B.C., appears to have been a late attempt at finding an historical focus which could be used as the basis of an era. The fact that even this date was seldom used as an era date is obvious from the continued reckoning in regnal years and generations in texts such as the *Purāṇas*. The Buddhists, on the other hand, did have a recognizable central point in time—the Buddha's death—which even if it did come into use somewhat later was nevertheless regularly used as an era date. The selection of a particular date for an era is in itself interesting. In India both religious and secular events were used as the basis of eras, and these eras were used concurrently.

Calendars and eras are the more functional aspect of time reckoning.

The wider question is that of the concept of time. In early India the concept of time was generally a cyclical concept, where the movement of time according to some was in the form of a circle and according to others in a series of waves. The Hindu tradition as recorded in the *Purāṇas* saw time as moving in a cycle—the *Mahāyuga*—the great cycle which lasts for 43,20,000 years. The cycle was divided into four parts decreasing in size according to arithmetical progression. These four are the *krita, tretā, dvāpara* and *kaliyuga*, of which the last is the smallest consisting of 4,32,000 years. The *kaliyuga* is the current period of time in which we are living and it began, if modern calculations are correct, in about 3102 B.C. At the end of the great cycle comes total destruction and out of this destruction arises a new, fresh cycle.

The most commonly used word for time is *kāla*. This is derived from the root *kal*—'to calculate', and was therefore originally used in the sense of a means of measurement. By extension and presumably under the influence of the cyclic theory it also came to mean 'destruction'. It is interesting that by the first century B.C. when the *Bhagavad Gītā* was composed, *kāla* is described in this text as 'the imperishable'.

The figures given for the cycle and the parts thereof are not entirely arbitrary. They are based on the numbers 7, 12, 27 and 72, which are frequently used in the study of astronomy.[12] Furthermore, the fact that many of these figures had counterparts in the astronomical calculations of the time suggests a borrowing of at least the numbers from astronomy. In spite of the fact that the concept of the great cycle is mythological it was nevertheless of the highest concern to the authors that in its details it should be, '. . . a mathematically ordered, astronomically referred notion about the relationship of man and the rhythms of his life on earth not simply to the seasons, the annual mysteries of birth, death and regeneration, but beyond those to even greater, very much larger cycles—the great yyears . . . [13] At heher end of the scale meticulous care for the exact moment in time measurement was maintained in the association of ritual with time. The measurement of time was frequently in spatial terms.

The theory of the *Mahāyuga* was not merely a concept of cyclical time. It also subsumed the idea of changing morals as is sometimes the case with cyclical time theories. The beginning of the cycle is a period of pristine bliss and an abundance of virtue. But gradually virtue gives way to evil until finally the *kaliyuga*, the last of the four parts of the cycle, becomes an evil age *per se*. Evil is uprooted in the final destruction and the new cycle starts afresh with a period of virtue. The usefulness of such a theory to society is that the existence of evil can be, if necessary, explained away in a fairly simplistic manner. Evil must be tolerated since it is inevitable in the *kaliyuga*. But there is hope and succour for those battling against evil, for Viṣṇu manifests himself in a series of incarnations and comes to the aid of the genuinely virtuous. Taken literally, the immensity of the time span leading to the eventual uprooting of evil would tend to dwarf man and make human activity almost meaningless. This was, however, countered by the dominant religious belief that salvation—freedom from rebirth—was available to every human being within a life-time.

Comparisons have been made between the Hindu cyclical concept of time postulating a golden age at the start of the cycle and retrogressive movement into time, with the Judaeo-Christian and Islamic concept of time, which is seen as a linear movement where the messianic tradition and the symbolism of the new heaven and the new earth provide a forward looking perspective with Divine Will giving a progressive direction to historical events.[14] It has been suggested that the association of time with destruction and with retrogressive movement inhibits the idea of a purpose in history. This is partially true. But the Hindu cycle concept is essentially a cosmological concept. It did not prevent the recording of the past in a form considered socially relevant and necessary to the present and the future. Such a cyclic concept emphasized continual change. Thus there was an implicit rejection of the idea that history repeats itself: or to be more exact, that history can repeat itself within the time-span of one cycle. Nevertheless, it was maintained that the past can and does teach lessons, usually moral lessons. Since the individual is concerned with his own salvation, the lessons of history may be of some use.[15]

According to the Buddhists, time was also seen as being of incalculable length.[16] The Buddhists presupposed as movement of time in waves, beginning with a golden age and utopian condition and gradually degenerating into evil which is finally overcome by a slow return to a utopian state. The continual stress was on escape from rebirth which was seen as the only and ultimate release. The death of the Buddha became the focal point in time and this also placed the Buddha himself in a historical process. The concept of the Buddha Maitreya—the Buddha to come—with its messianic undertones gave a forward looking perspective to Buddhist historical thinking. Buddhism became a proselytising religion with a sense of mission. This underlined the idea of its historical role. The major institution of Buddhism was a well organized monastic system. The need to maintain chronicles of the monasteries, of the succession of monks, as also the need to maintain records of sectarian groups, all heightened the idea of historical continuity. Attempts are made to align the history of Ceylon with the more important events in the wider world of the history of Buddhism. The authors of the Pāli chronicles maintained that Ceylon had been intended by the Buddha for the propagation of Buddhism, which would necessitate historical events moving in this direction—surely an excellent example of theological determinism. The understanding of the historical role was emphasized by the idea of causality which was basic to much of early Buddhist thinking.

Had the theme of causality been allowed free play, the nature of historical explanation would have been different in the Indian tradition. But into historical explanation were interwoven the two concepts of *dharma* and *karma* which at two levels introduced elements of historical determinism as well as the idea of the responsibility of the individual in history. *Dharma* was seen in the historical context as the socio-religious ordering of society. Society was theoretically supposed to be so well-regulated that historical events should almost automatically follow the laws of the social order. Events were thus illustrations of the religious, moral and social maxims which went into the making of the *dharma* system.[17] In a scheme where each man has a place and each man should be in his place, theoretically, historical inevitability would tend to overrule the search for varied historical explanation. However, this concept was an ideal model and consequently the application of the deterministic explanation was rare.

The concept of *karma* concerns the actions in the life of an individual which condition his next birth. It is closely associated with the idea of *puṇya* or merit, for the merit accumulated from the activities of the previous births can provide an explanation for the facts and events of the present birth. Thus the continuity from the past is both relevant and significant. The historical purpose of man is to perform merit-earning actions and thus arrive at salvation. The most meritorious actions are those which are carried out in conformity with the laws of *dharma*. This relationship between *dharma* and *karma* could well have degenerated into fatalism, but interestingly enough, this rarely happens. The concept of *karma* frequently provides the channel for historical explanation.

From the perspective of historical explanation the concept of *karma* holds an almost dialectical position vis-a-vis that of *dharma*. No model of social structure can be so rigid as totally to exclude human free-will, for it would then be too unrealistic even for theoretical functioning. By conceding the concept of *karma*, ultimately man's control over his own actions was also conceded. The significance of this attitude in relation to the question of purpose in history can perhaps best be demonstrated by the fact that the period which saw the popularization and widespread acceptance of *bhakti* teaching (which emphasizes the relationship of the individual to his deity and the idea of *karma*) coincided with an increasing output of historical literature. There were, as has been suggested earlier, other reasons as well for this development in the post-Gupta period but the influence of this teaching cannot be ignored.

The acceptance of the more extreme idea of Fate or Destiny over which man has no control is interestingly enough not usually attributed to the belief in *karma*, but to the direct intervention of the supernatural. Men die and on occasion are restored to life by the will of the gods.[18] Famines, pestilences and times of trouble can also be attributed to the will of the gods.[19] Divine retribution against evil actions or divine intervention in battle are not unknown.[20]

One of the more significant applications of the theory of *karma* in a political sense is the belief that the *karma* of the king is integral or else intimately related with that of his people. Thus a people gets the king it deserves. This is particularly relevant in a society where the office of the king was nearly co-extensive with the functions of the state.

Theories concerning the origin of government and forms of political structure have a bearing on historical explanation, since historical records are most often concerned with political power. Here the difference between the Hindu and Buddhist tradition is worth commenting upon. The Buddhist tradition postulates a remote utopian period when there was a natural social harmony and the necessity for government did not exist. However, the desire for possessions resulted in disharmony and confusion. Therefore people gathered together and elected from among themselves one man who would maintain law and order.[21] Thus the primary political institution is man-made and in origin is contractual. The contractual element was an important factor in the forms and institutions associated with the Buddhists.

The early Hindu theories explain the origin of kingship as being essentially the need for a tribal leader, particularly in war.[22] Although the contractual element is implicit, and in some sources it is actually stated, this element is counter-balanced by the equally strong stress on divine intervention in the appointment of the king: and indeed the implicit divinity in the office of the king cannot be overlooked.[23] Where kingship is associated with some form of divine interest, there historical explanation presumably must also make concessions to divine interests. Where kingship evolves out of entirely human attempts at political organization, there the option to associate the gods with historical explanation is open to the historian.

Conclusion

To sum up: In the first part of this paper I have attempted to describe the texts which can be said to constitute an historical tradition. The core of this literature consists of the *itihāsa-purāṇa* tradition which is scattered and largely undocumented in the pre-Gupta period, but which is re-written, modified and enlarged in the post-Gupta period. In spite of its continuity it is not a static tradition, for the form in which it is used changes over the centuries. It was an important part of the Hindu cultural form of the *Purāṇas* which ensured its preservation and transmission, since the *Purāṇas* acquired the status of sacred literature. Historical changes of various kinds in the post-Gupta period led to the emergence of historical writing which was always regarded as secular literature although it had links with the *Purāṇa* tradition.

The *itihāsa-purāna* tradition had three main constituents—myth, genealogy and historical narrative. The remote past was described in the form of myths and probably fabricated genealogies. There is so far no means of checking the authenticity of these genealogies. The more immediate past was recorded almost entirely in the form of genealogies filled out with historical narrative. Some of these genealogies can be checked with other sources to establish their historical authenticity. The historical literature of the post-Gupta period is almost exclusively historical narrative, but the authors of this literature show a familiarity with the *itihāsa-purāṇa* tradition which is frequently used as the source for references to myths and genealogies. Inscriptions of the post-Gupta period referring to the antecedents of local kings also make the connection with the *itihāsa-purāṇa* tradition.

History is generally seen as the record of the activities of socio-political status groups. In societies where political power was the criterion of status the sequence of political events was of prime importance in recording the past. Individuals became historically important when they acquired political status. In Indian society, the criterion of status was birth, and mobility was possible only through a group. Historically therefore what was relevant was the lineage and chronicle of the group: hence the importance given to genealogies. Continuity was seen not in the sequence of political events but more often in the sequence of a lineage. Political history was not therefore the pivot of the Indian historical tradition as it was perhaps in the Greek historical tradition. It did however gradually become important in the historical literature of the post-Gupta period.

Historical explanation was influenced by certain ideological assumptions current in the society and which tended to produce historical thinking rather different from that in other classical cultures. In discussing the historiography of ancient India a distinction has to be made between the historical tradition and historical literature. The historical tradition is that which I have called the *itihāsa-purāṇa* which is available to us now in the *Purāṇas* and which has been placed in an essentially socio-religious context by priestly authors. The sources which they used are no longer available to us. Historical biographies, family chronicles and regional histories, later in date, are the more secular extension of this tradition and form the main corpus of historical writing. This, however, is not the only distinction. A further distinction has to be made between the Buddhist and the Hindu tradition vis-a-vis historical writing. Clearly the Buddhists were familiar with the *itihāsa-purāṇa* tradition, but their historical literature takes on a different development. Both these distinctions are relevant to the earlier question—that of the relation between the historical tradition and a philosophy of history. In the context of early India it can be said that the concept of meaning in history appears to be rudimentary and the evidence for a well-developed philosophy of history, as compared for example to the Judaeo-Christian tradition, is certainly limited. Nevertheless, this does not preclude a historical tradition which forms a significant part of the cultural ethos.

REFERENCES AND NOTES

1. *Arthaśāstra*, I.5.
2. V.S. Pathak, *Ancient Historians of India*, p. 21 ff. (Bombay, 1966).

3. Pargiter, *The Ancient Indian Historical Tradition*, p. 77 ff. (London, 1922).
4. H.H. Wilson, *The Viṣṇu Purāṇa*, p. xi. (Calcutta, 1961).
5. Cf. *Atharvaveda* 15.2.1 and *Taittirīya Brāhmaṇa*, II, 4.1., with the later texts of *Gautama* IV, 17; *Manu*, X, 11 and *Nārada* 110.
6. *Pariśiṣṭaparvan* of Hemcandra, *Prabandha-cintāmaṇi* of Merutuṅga and the *Hammira-mahā-kāvya* of Nayacandra Sūri.
7. *Viṣṇu Purāṇa* IV.
8. Milton Singer (ed.), *Traditional India*, (Chicago, 1958).
9. *Mahāvaṃśa* VI.
10. *Mahāvastu*, I. 348-52.
11. *Mahāvaṃsa* IX and X.
12. J. Campbell, *The Masks of the Gods*, II, p. 128 ff. (New York, 1959).
13. *Ibid.*
14. Patrides, *The Phoenix and the Ladder*, p. 3.
15. Kalhaṇa, *Rājatāraṅgiṇī*, *V.211.*
16. *Samyutta Nikāya*, 2.180-1.
17. *Rājatāraṅgiṇī*, (Stein ed.) p. 32.
18. *Ibid.*, II, 92.
19. *Ibid.*, I, 179; II, 17-55.
20. Bilhaṇa, *Vikramānkadevacarita.*
21. *Dīgha Nikāya*, III, 90-93.
22. *Ṛg Veda*, VII.18.
23. *Mahābhārata*, Śānti Parvan, 59.

Origin Myths and the Early Indian Historical Tradition

The organization of a historical tradition revolves around two related components—the purpose of action and the agency of action. Both of these are implicitly present irrespective of the form which the tradition may take, whether it is expressed as a myth or as an historical narrative. These components are by no means of equal importance but an element at least of each resides in all historical traditions. By the purpose of action is meant that the recording of what is believed to be history has an aim, either to moralize, as was often the case with traditional historical writing, or else to explain why and how past events happened, as is frequently the case with modern historiography. The agency of action is ultimately human (even if sometimes claimed to be divinely inspired); but it is of interest to discover which group of men are regarded as the actors in history and to what extent they function independently of any other agency, as for example, the gods.

Past events have to be related in a chronological order but the time sequence can be part of a much larger concept of time. Events concerning the more remote periods often take the form of a myth. Myth is in a sense a prototype history since it is a selection of ideas composed in narrative form for the purpose of preserving and giving significance to an important aspect of the past. Although myths cannot be used as descriptive sources on the past, their analysis can reveal the more emphatic assumptions of a society. Myths record what a people like to think about their past and to that extent even some modern histories are not always free of an element of myth-making.

Mythos is defined as an 'utterance', often a tale recited in association with a religious ceremony. In that sense the narratives of the Purāṇic tradition were myths, since the *ākhyāna* was recited on ritual occasions and the *purāṇa* is explained as relating to an ancient lore which would

D. Chattopadhyaya (ed.), *History and Society*, (Calcutta, 1978), pp. 271-94, Essays in Honour of Professor Niharranjan Ray.

tend to be preserved in mythical form. The myth involved archetypal or elemental characters, themes and symbols. It may be differentiated from the folk-tale by its focus on the 'grand events' of the past—the creation of the world, the origin of man and of the gods, the justification of kingship—whereas the folk-tale is concerned with more restricted social pre-occupations generally not involving any grand designs.

The interpretation of myths has resulted in diverse explanations.[1] Early interpreters saw in them symbols of natural phenomena and most myths were nature myths.[2] Others tried to see them as attempts at explaining the real world but couched in symbolic form.[3] Another view held that myths had an intrinsic relationship with ritual and could only be explained in terms of ritual origins, a view which conjured up the world of Frazer's *Golden Bough*.[4] A major re-orientation came about with Malinowski's view that myths were essentially charters of validation in which the aim was very often to provide a sanction for current situations.[5] This analysis encouraged an interest in the social underpinnings of myth. The notion of myth as charter was reconsidered later when the emphasis shifted to the structural study of myth and the relation of this to the structural study of society.[6] The notion of myth as an archetype and as a primary cultural force has also remained a dominant trend.[7] Partially associated with this is the theory of Mircea Eliade that myths reflect a nostalgia for the origins of human society and try to evoke a return to a creative era.[8] More recently it has been suggested that myths are connected with liminality and arise in transitional situations, thus explaining how one state of affairs became another, or how things came to be what they are.[9] Specific to Indo-European mythology have been the attempts of Georges Dumezil to analyse these myths on the basis of the 'tripartite ideology', a pattern which even for Vedic myths is not always beyond question.[10]

This brief survey of the possible range of paradigms which can provide interpretations of myths is not an attempt to establish any priorities of interpretation. It is provided only to emphasize that in choosing to limit this study to origin myths, and that too in the context of the *itihāsa-purāṇa* and related historical tradition, there will implicitly be a delimiting of the range of interpretation.

Myth is at one level a straightforward story, a narrative; at another level it reflects the integrating values around which societies are organized.[11] It codifies belief, safeguards morality, vouches for the efficiency of the ritual and provides social norms. It is a rationalization of man's activity in the past although the expression may take on non-rational forms. It remains socially important as long as it is a charter of belief, but becomes ineffective when seen as a myth. As a charter of belief it serves to protect cultural continuity and provides through its theme a point of cultural equilibrium. In a historical tradition therefore the themes of myths act as factors of continuity.

The analysis of the structure of a myth can reveal (to a lesser or greater extent) the structure of the society from which it emanates. The analysis may centre on one of two perspectives: either the sequence and the order of events or the schemata and organization of the sequences at different levels. Ultimately the myth is concerned with the quest for understanding the significance of nature and culture. The action of the myth is usually the narration of sacred history which is believed to be a true event which has taken place in the past. Since these primordial events are often associated with supernatural beings they also tend to take on the character of models for action and for ritual. Most myths being explanatory (whether explicitly stated as such or not) they are related to the origin or the commencement of a particular event or action. Myths made the past intelligible and meaningful, but it was intelligibility and meaningfulness which related to the present, for the continuity of myth is largely with reference to the present.

In societies (and this would include most pre-modern societies) where the oral tradition rather than the use of literature is the more functional means of communication on a large scale, myths become one of the means of passing on information. There is therefore a process of constant adjustment, and myths from earlier periods are recast in conformity with the social assumptions of later periods. The repetition of the same myth, with perhaps some modifications, from age to age is partly to ensure 'the message' getting through and partly to indicate new nuances. Myths therefore have a widely over-arching relationship to all aspects of society and each major myth could be the subject of an expansive analysis. The attempt here is not to provide a complete analysis of each myth but to recognize and point up the historically significant aspects of certain myths, i.e., those aspects which had some role in the propagation and continuity of the *itihāsa-purāṇa* tradition and its main concerns. But this is not to deny that even within those aspects there may well be other layers touching on different facets of early Indian society. Further, the attempt is not to ascertain the historical authenticity of the myth but rather to probe the reason for its acceptance in as much as it relates to social validation. As validating charters myths have a close connection with social organization, not only representing, as they do, the assumptions about the past but also underpinning the social relationships of the present.

The myths which are the most closely related to the *itihāsa-purāṇa* tradition are available in the core of the tradition, that is, the genealogical sections, *vaṃśānucarita,* of the major *Purāṇas*. A variant of these may be seen from the somewhat different perspective of the Buddhist historical tradition, the sources for which have to be culled from various texts. These will form our primary sources. In both cases the earliest occasion for the recital of these myths would be in association with rituals and ceremonies. The *Purāṇas* were recited over a period of many days in connection with a religious ceremony. The genealogical sections in particular were preserved by the *sūta* and the *māgadha,* the professional bards and chroniclers, who recited them in association with the epics and the heroic ballads at royal courts. In the Buddhist case too the literature would initially be preserved as part of the oral tradition of monastic centres. This does not however imply that there was any integral correlation between the ritual and the purpose of the myth. It seems more likely that the association with ritual occasions would serve to heighten the importance of what the myth was meant to convey, for with the compilation of the texts in a literary form, making them accessible to literate members of society, the association with ritual perceptibly weakens. The texts referred to above were in the main compiled and edited by about the middle of the first millennium A.D., but earlier versions of the myths and narrative stereotypes are known from earlier texts, some of which go back to the first millennium B.C. There was therefore both time and incentive to recognize the narrative and the symbols of the myths for changing social contexts. The texts drew in the main from the earlier oral tradition and were transferred to a written form in the first millennium A.D. In spite of this *Purāṇas* were frequently treated as part of the oral tradition with the reciting of the texts to large audiences. Both categories of sources came into prominence during the period when Buddhism and Vaiṣṇavism, in addition to their religious role, were performing the function of being agencies of acculturation for those for whom the Great Tradition had hitherto been inaccessible. Such texts reflected the social concerns of the present even though they treated of the social concerns of the past. The significance of this lies in the fact that it is also by the mid-first millennium A.D. (and in later centuries) that these texts—and the *Vaṃśānucarita* section of the *Purāṇas* in particular—are used for the more secular purpose of providing lineage links and genealogical connections for the families which gave rise to the multiple dynasties of the time.

In a historical tradition origin myths play a crucial role as they provide a point of commencement. In the *itihāsa-purāṇa* tradition the origin myth referred to or implied is that of the Flood. It occurs first in the *Śatapatha Bhāhmaṇa* and is found again in the *Mahābhārata* and *Purāṇas*, there being a substantial difference of time between the first and the last version.[12] The *Śatapatha Brāhmana* version relates that Manu, primaeval man, was performing his morning ablutions when a fish came into his hands. It is asked to be reared and protected and promised Manu safety from the deluge in return, explaining to Manu that the gods had decided to punish mankind by unleashing a massive flood to destroy all creation. The fish grew larger in time. On the eve of the flood it commanded Manu to build a ship for himself, in which Manu escaped from the flood. The ship was tied to the fish who swam through the waters and lodged it on the northern mountain. When the water subsided it glided down the mountain slope and returned Manu to Jambudvīpa. Manu being alone and desirous of sons performed a sacrifice to the gods from which a woman was born as a result of which she was called Iḍā (or Ilā in other versions). Through her Manu generated this race.

The story is repeated in some of the *Purāṇas* but with certain significant additions. In the *Matsya Purāṇa* the fish is described as an incarnation of Viṣṇu—the *Matsya-avatāra*. Ilā is a hermaphrodite, hence called by the cognate Ila-Ilā, and is the progenitor of one of the two royal lineages, the *Candravaṃśa* or lunar lineage. Manu's eldest son Ikṣvāku was the progenitor of the *Sūryavaṃśa* or solar lineage. In some texts however the male Ila is referred to as the eldest son who was inadvertently changed into a woman, Ilā. To these lineages belonged all those who came to be regarded as legitimate *kṣatriyas*. Manu being the originator of the lineages framed the rules and laws of government and collected one-sixth of the produce of the land as tax. The *Viṣṇu Purāṇa* omits the story of the flood in the *vaṃśānucarita* section but refers to the birth of Ilā as the daughter of Manu and states that through the goodwill of the gods she was able to switch her form from female to male and back as occasion demanded.[13]

The flood assumes the primary precondition of water from out of which the known creation arises. The great flood caused the total destruction of the world and this is a recognized stage in the cycle of the time concept, what Eliade would call the abolition of profane time.[14] The beginnings of history therefore emerge from a condition which has no antecedents: it is in fact symbolic of the very beginning. However, the negation of antecedents is not absolutely total since Manu is not created out of the flood but exists prior to it. Further creation follows from the flood. Repetition occurs frequently in myths of renewal such as the story of the flood and in such cases the abolition of profane time is a marker separating mythical time from historical time. The latter emerges from a condition of renewal where the vestiges of the old have been destroyed.

The choice of the fish as the saviour is obvious since the fish alone could survive the flood and this is used to good effect in the Purāṇic version where it is referred to as the *Matsya-avatāra*. The myth is brought into service as a means of exalting the deity Viṣṇu and introducing him into what was an old and well-established myth through the mechanism of the *avatāra*. This endows Viṣṇu with antiquity and enhances his image as the deity who was willing to take on the lowly form of the fish in order to save man. It might be worth mentioning in passing that the Sumerian god Enki, who in the Sumerian version of the flood myth saved Ziusudra, the Sumerian counterpart of Manu, is often represented as a fish in later Mesopotamian mythology in which capacity he acts as a saviour deity.[15]

That Manu procreates through his daughter possibly reflects a patrilineal emphasis known from other myths of such societies where an incestuous relationship also occurs in origin myths.[16] More plausibly it may indicate the symbolic insistence of the purity of lineage, that ultimately the mother-father of the founders of the lineages was the child of Manu and created from a sacrifice. The derivation of the Candravaṃśa lineage from a hermaphrodite suggests a variation on the idea of twins or siblings as parents, stressing again the purity of lineage. It is significant that in the widely accepted description of the utopia, the land of the Uttara Kurus, people are born as couples, thus eliminating the need for physical procreation.[17] The *Purāṇas* repeat the idea in the story of the evolution of society where it is said that Brahmā created the earth and then four sets of human beings, each consisting of a thousand couples.[18] Life was idyllic and easy. But this did not last, for ultimately decay set in together with the emergence of the four *varṇas* and a general falling off from the utopian beginnings. Yet in a late section of the *Ṛg Veda* the theme of rejecting sibling incest is associated with the god of death, Yama, and his sister, Yami, suggesting that the idea was being questioned by some.[19] However, in Purāṇic sources Yama is sometimes contrasted with Manu (associated with life), both being sons of Vivasvat.[20] That one of the royal lineages was born from a female form was obviously rather galling in later times when women were of low social status and on par with the *śūdras*. This is sought to be explained away in the *Viṣṇu Purāṇa* by the statement that during the course of the sacrificial ritual there was an inaccuracy and, although Manu had been performing the sacrifice for the obtaining of sons, a daughter was born.[21] The situation was retrieved somewhat by Mitra and Varuṇa permitting the daughter to become an hermaphrodite. In actual fact the male-female distinction was necessary for the purpose of the myth and was required as a distinguishing feature of the two lineages.

In terms of the bi-polarity of symbols the lineages were separated by the one being associated with the sun and the other with the moon.[22] Evidently the lineages had to be kept distinct. This is evident from the structure of the lineages for the two groups. The *Candravaṃśi* or Aila appears to be a segmentary lineage system where each male child and his male progeny is treated as a separate segment of the lineage and the descent group of each is recorded.[23] Such a record inevitably covers a wide geographical area—central, western, northern and parts of eastern India. The *Sūryavaṃśi* or Ikṣvāku lineage on the other hand records only the descent by primogeniture of a few lines and is far more limited in area as well as being confined chiefly to the middle Ganges valley. The difference in the structure of lineages may also indicate the more sedentary settlement of the Ikṣvāku as against a society more given to migrating groups among the Aila.

The choice of the two lineage names, the Sun and the Moon, are significant as the dominant planetary pair. Perhaps the myth refers to a belief in an early division into moieties of the tribes or two rival groups. Alternatively it could have been an attempt at orderliness on the part of the compilers of the *Purāṇas*, to weave the many dynastic strands into two main currents and finally to a single origin. It is not surprising that the word Manu provided the generic base for *mānava* meaning mankind.

The variation between the early and later version of the myth as in the *Śatapatha Brāhmaṇa* and the *Purāṇas* shows the manner in which it was used for two purposes pertinent to the new concerns of the later period. The readjustment of the myth to Vaiṣṇava religious purposes is self-evident in the idea of the *Matsya-avatāra*. The latching on of one of the two royal lineages to Ila-Ilā and Ikṣvāku, the children of Manu, and thereby indirectly to the flood story, was an effective means of giving both antiquity and prestige to the lineages. The historically attested dynasties from the fourth century B.C. onwards appear to have had little interest in proclaiming their lineage origins. The concern with lineage and genealogical connections involving either the *Sūryavaṃśa* or the *Candravaṃśa* are more marked in the early centuries A.D. and become quite obsessive in some parts of India after the mid-first millennium A.D. This concern may have necessitated the adaptation of earlier myths to new interests. Information on what was believed to be the 'history' of the lineages would have been preserved as part of the oral tradition by the *sūta* and the *māgadha*. It is believed that this oral tradition was taken over, probably by priestly authors, in the process of the compiling of the *Purāṇas*, some of which date to the middle of the first millennium A.D.[24] The neat arrangement of the lineages and their segments could well have been worked out in the process of adjusting the earlier myth and the new version would then provide the validation for the new lineage connections. The reference to Manu framing the laws and collecting the tax would have underlined the legitimacy of these two functions for those who were the descendents of Manu.

Curiously, there is a striking parallel to this in the Mesopotamian tradition. The story of the flood from Sumerian texts is remarkably similar to the version of the *Śatapatha Brāhmana* in its details. Deluge myths as the genesis of cultures are by no means rare. What is of interest however is the particulars in which the versions seem to agree. It is now well-known that the Sumerian myth found its way via the Babylonian version into the Bible story of Noah's ark.[25] It has also been argued that the Greek version in which Zeus sends a flood to punish mankind and the survivor from the flood is Deucalion, the son of Prometheus (or in later versions Ogygus), is a myth derived from the Mesopotamian original, since the occurrence of the flood and the attitude of the gods towards man are not in keeping with the Greek stereotypes regarding natural calamities and the deities.[26] The Sumerian flood myth is sometimes associated with the archaeological evidence of the massive flooding of a group of cities in the delta of the Tigris-Euphrates valley, an event generally dated to the end of the fourth millennium B.C.[27] Is it possible that the Sumerian myth found its way to the Harappans and via the Harappans entered the Vedic tradition? What is even more curious is that in the late third millennium B.C. the Sumerian flood myth is worked into the story of the king-lists of ancient Mesopotamia.[28] These refer to the mythical seven pre-diluvian kings, then the coming of the flood and the survivor who is associated with the descent of kingship on the various cities of ancient Mesopotamia. Indian sources also refer in sequence to the seven pre-diluvian Manus, the flood and then the royal lineages which succeeded. It would seem that the Mesopotamians made the same use of their earlier Sumerian flood as did the Indians in searching for an earlier sanction to an existing situation of a later period.

The genealogical sections of the *Purāṇas*, with their recital of king-lists and descent groups, are punctuated with myths relating to the supposedly more important personalities. The narration of the *Candravaṃśi* lineage in the *Viṣṇu Purāṇa* is a case in point and is interspersed with stories. This was in part a mnemonic device as well as an attempt to embellish the otherwise rather dry narration of succession-lists. What is more important from our point of view is the fact that the two ancestral figures from whom the main *Candravaṃśi* lineage segments trace their origin—Purūravas and, of a later generation, Yayāti—are in each case introduced through a well-known and frequently repeated myth.[29] Purūravas has the female Ilā as his mother and Soma, the moon-god, as his grandfather. That his descendents were the progeny of Soma would further strengthen the nomenclature of *Candravaṃśa*. This idea is echoed in at least one *Candravaṃśi* royal family of the early medieval period, the Candella, who claim the moon-god as one of their original ancestors.[30]

The legend of Purūravas and Urvaśi is rèlated in full, following in detail the version earlier recorded in the *Śatapatha Brāhmana* in preference to the variant in the *Mahābhārata*. The earliest version of the myth in the *Ṛg Veda* reads as an inversion of the Cupid and Psyche story.[31] The king Purūravas falls in love with the *apsarā* Urvaśi who has been banished to earth for a temporary period. She agrees to live with him on condition that she should never see him in the nude. After some time the Gandharvas decide to call her back to the celestial regions and arrange one night for her pet rams to be stolen. As Purūravas rushes after the thief there is a flash of lightning which reveals him in his nudity to Urvaśi, whereupon she vanishes. The distraught king wanders for many years in search of her and eventually finds her. She does not return to him but does bear him a son. The Ṛgvedic version appears to be incomplete and there may have been more to the story. In the version recorded in the *Śatapatha Brāhmaṇa*, Purūravas is anxious to join the Gandharvas and thereby live permanently with Urvaśi.[32] The Gandharvas require him to kindle three fires and perform some sacrifices, after which he is accepted into their world. In the *Mahābhārata* the king is killed by the *brāhmans* whom he disturbs during their sacrificial rituals.[33]

The myth has in the past been interpreted as a solar myth with Purūravas representing the sun and Urvaśi the vanishing dawn.[34] A more plausible interpretation suggests that the latter two versions are mythological variants of each other, the significance of the action being that Purūravas is being sacrificed.[35] The sacrifice of the male, symbolized by his kindling three fires and then being taken to the world of Gandharvas, was associated with certain matriarchal mother-goddess cults. The myth therefore would represent the transitional phase to patrilineal society. It is further argued that Purūravas having a hermaphrodite parent is not only an attempt to link him with Manu via Ilā but is also indicative of a transition to a patrilineal society from an earlier matrilineal one. But as we have seen, the symbolism of a hermaphrodite does not necessarily indicate such a transition. The repeated occurrence of the myth in a variety of texts points to the mythological significance attached to Purūravas as the founder of the *Candravaṃśi* lineage. Its occurrence in a lineage context as well gives added status to the descent of Purūravas's progeny from an *apsarā*. Of the many sons whom Urvaśi bore to Purūravas, two received particular attention. The eldest was Āyus through whom the main lineages of the *Candravaṃśi* descended; and the other was Amavasu whose line included Paraśurāma, the destroyer of the *kṣatriyas*, suggesting thereby a balancing of lineages.

Of Purūravas's sons, the main lineage goes via the eldest son Āyus to his eldest son Nahus whose eldest son Yati declined the throne, whereupon it went to his younger brother Yayāti, the emphasis being on primogeniture. At this point there is the famous myth of Yayāti who in old age seeks to exchange his years for the youth of one of his sons.[36] He asks each one in turn, starting with the eldest, Yadu, who refuses, as indeed do each of the next three, Druhyu, Turvaśa and Anu. These three are cursed by Yayāti with the statement that none of their progeny shall possess dominion. The youngest, Pūru, readily agrees to the request of his father and takes upon himself his old age. Ultimately, after many years, when Yayāti is exhausted with his youth, he accepts his old age from Pūru. Before dying he appoints Pūru as his successor and gives him sovereignty over the main kingdom, the *madhya-deśa* (in the main the Ganga-Yamuna Doāb), which should otherwise by rights have gone to Yadu. The eldest son Yadu is sent to territories to the south-west of the *madhya-deśa*, and the other three to the south-east, the west and the north. The *Viṣṇu Purāṇa* states that Pūru was made the supreme monarch of the earth and his brothers governed as viceroys.[37] The *Mahābhārata* has an elaborate version of the myth and explains further that from Yadu there descended the Yādavas, the Turvaśa produced the Yavanas, the Druhyu produced the Bhojas and the Anu a variety of *mleccha* peoples, i.e. those regarded as socially inferior.[38] This version takes the story further, involving Yayāti's attempt to enter heaven.

The Yayāti myth has been the subject of a lengthy analysis in which the emphasis has been on an explanation of the symbolism of not only the youth-age syndrome associated with the Yayāti-Pūru relationship but also the expression of values such as valour, sacrifice, riches and, above all, truth.[39] A more narrow interpretation linked to the requirements of the historical tradition indicates two obvious emphases. Firstly, the myth explains the lack of observance of the rule of primogeniture where the eldest son is sent to a distant area and the youngest son succeeds to the throne. Secondly, it highlights the supremacy of the Pūru lineage as being the superior one among the *kṣatriyas* since Pūru inherits the sovereignty. The Druhyu, Turvaśa and Anu lineages tend to die out or else get merged with the Pūru and this takes care, genealogically, of an otherwise impossibly wide distribution of descendants. Significantly, the superiority of the Pūru lineage is contrasted with the low status of the others where in the *Mahābhārata*, as we have seen, they are regarded as *mlecchas*. The Yayāti myth also provides an explanation for why non-*kṣatriya* groups are not recorded in the genealogies. Subsequent to this myth, the narrative of the Candravaṃśi lineage becomes substantially that of the descendants of Yadu and Pūru. In a sense, the events of the *Mahābhārata* war suggest a kind of reversal of the relationship between these two descent groups, where it is the offspring of Pūru who seek the help of the offspring of Yadu and the latter play the dominant role. The myth also serves to explain the migration and settlement of tribes. The Pūrus in Vedic literature are associated with the Sarasvati region and the Punjab.[40] The Yayāti myth would account for a possible migration into the *madhya-deśa* and perhaps the reorganizing of the settlement in that area. Similarly the Yadus are also associated with the Punjab and their appearance in western India would have to be explained.[41]

The emphasis on primogeniture is continually underlined in many texts. This after all is the crux of the events which form the core of two epics, the *Mahābhārata* and the *Rāmāyaṇa*. Where the law is not observed the breaking of the law has to be justified. This is clearly set out in an earlier section of the *Viṣṇu Purāṇa* in the myth of Pṛthu the son of Vena, a myth which also occurs in other texts.[42] We are told that among the early kings of the earth was Vena who obstructed the sacrifices. His opposition to the Vedic *sūtras* and *yajñas* provoked the antagonism of the *ṛṣis* who put him to death by piercing him with stalks of the *kuśa* grass. In the absence of a king there was now a threat of total anarchy. So the *ṛṣis* churned the left thigh of Vena and there sprang up a short, dark, ugly man whom they called Niṣāda, a name derived from the command of the *ṛṣis* who told him to 'sit down' (*ni-ṣada*). The *ṛṣis* were unhappy with what they had produced so they banished him and he became the ancestor of all the *mlecchas* and the wild tribes such as the Kirāta, Pulinda and Śabara. The *ṛṣis* then churned the right arm of Vena and there sprang up a beautiful man whom they called Pṛthu (the broad or expansive one). He was righteous in his manner, introduced cattle-rearing and the plough, and his reign was so prosperous that the earth was named Pṛthvī in memory of him.

The wickedness of Vena is ascribed to the usual reason that he objected to the teaching of the Vedas. It is significant that he can be put to death only by the *ṛṣis,* who alone have the power to assassinate kings. His death is caused by the *kuśa* grass used in the sacred rituals of Vedic ceremonies. The fear of revolt against and assassination of legitimate kings is evident from the fear of resulting anarchy. This sentiment is in conformity with the concept of *matsyanyāya* as explained in the *Mahābhārata* where, in a condition of anarchy, the large fish devour the small fish.[43] The legitimacy of succession has to be maintained by producing a successor from the body of Vena. It is the left side of Vena which produces the ungainly, primitive successor who has to be exiled and the right side which produces the appropriate successor, conforming to the symbolism of the left being impure and the right pure. The association of Niṣāda with the wild tribes, food-gatherers perhaps, is juxtaposed with the introduction of agriculture by Pṛthu and it is through the latter that the earth prospers. That the elder son was banished in favour of the younger could only be justified by pointing to the inadequacies of the elder. The contrast however is so extreme that one almost suspects an association of guilt with the usurpation by the younger son. Could this myth have symbolized the overpowering of the legitimately settled food-gathering cultures by the agriculturalists, in a period which saw the gradual encroaching of agriculture into new lands via the grants of land to religious donees and secular officials, when the former cultures would henceforth always be associated with the dark and the ugly and the latter with that which is beautiful and prosperous? Vedic sources mention Niṣāda and Pṛthu but in unrélated contexts. Niṣāda appears to have been the general term used for non-Āryan tribes and Pṛthu was the first of kings and associated with the invention of agriculture.[44] It is from the sacrifice performed at the birth of Pṛthu that there emerged the *sūta* and the *māgadha* who are told that their function is to eulogize the king and praise his actions.[45] Perhaps historical consciousness (to the extent that this is embodied in bards and chroniclers) was believed to coincide with the development of agricultural society.

Another myth relating directly to primogeniture occurs at a later stage in the *Candravaṃśi* lineage, in connection with the brothers Devāpi and Śantanu of the Pūru lineage.[46] For twelve years there has been a drought in the kingdom and this is explained as arising from Śantanu, the younger brother, ruling in place of the elder, Devāpi who has gone into the forest. The situation can be righted only if Devāpi can be brought back. When Śantanu's minister hears this he despatches some heretics to the forest who instruct Devāpi in anti-Vedic doctrines. This annoys the *brāhmaṇs* who declare that Devāpi is degraded and unfit to rule, whereupon there is rain. Earlier versions of the myth in the *Ṛg Veda* and *Nirukta* attribute the supercession of the elder brother to his becoming an ascetic or his suffering from a skin disease, both perfectly legitimate reasons for supercession.[47] In these versions Devāpi rejects the throne when offered to him and performs a ritual which results in rain. In the Purāṇic version the Vedic story is readjusted so as to highlight the importance of primogeniture.

Myths emphasizing primogeniture are relatively rare in the *Sūryavaṃśi* sections of the genealogies for these record descent only of the eldest son or the legitimate successor. In the *Candravaṃśi* lineage the stress on primogeniture was required from time to time so that the senior descent group in the segmentary system could be clearly demarcated. Where the procedure was reversed it had to be explained. The myth would serve both to legitimize a junior line which might have become more powerful, as is suggested by the Yayāti myth, and also to ensure that technically at least the core kingdoms remained with the 'senior' lineages.

Mythology in the Buddhist sources relates essentially to two main areas, origin myths of tribes and places and the legend of the life of the Buddha. In later Buddhist texts there are myths connected with the Theras and the Saṅgha, but these are often derivative of the earlier myths. The earlier myths tend to be fairly traditional and are often either borrowings from the Purānic tradition or come from a common source of myths which supplied both the Purāṇic and the Buddhist texts. What is of interest are the similarities in the origin myths as recorded in the two traditions as well as the deviations.

The most important of the tribes is of course that of the Śākyas to which the Buddha belonged. The Śākyas are traced back to the Ikṣvāku lineage or the Okkaka as it is called in the Pāli sources.[48] In one text we are told that king Okkaka had five sons and four daughters by his chief queen. On her death the king married a young woman who, when she bore the king a son, wanted her son to be the heir. The king was persuaded to exile his elder children and the five brothers and four sisters travelled to the Himalayan foot-hills. Here they met the sage Kapila who advised them to build a city and settle in that region. The city therefore was called Kapilavastu. The eldest brother remained unmarried and the other four brothers married their four sisters and from them there descended the tribe of the Śākyas. The *Mahāvastu*, a text of a later period, has a variation on this, in that there are five brothers and five sisters, the name of the Okkaka king is Sujāta, and it is his concubine who wishes her son to be king.[49]

The Śākyas had a close relationship with the Koliyas according to another version of the origin myth of both.[50] The Śākyas in this case consisted of five sisters and four brothers. Since the degradation of the race had to be prevented it was decided to appoint the eldest sister as the mother and the remaining brothers and sisters paired off. The eldest sister developed leprosy and was therefore put into a deep pit in the forest where she was one day threatened by a tiger. She was rescued by Rāma, the king of Banāras, who had also been exiled because of leprosy but had managed to cure himself. He therefore cured her as well and married her and they lived in a city which they had built. They sent their sons to Kapilavastu so that they could marry their maternal uncles' daughters. The young men kidnapped the Śākya princesses and were not prevented from doing this since they were related to the Śākyas and the kidnapping was almost customary. It was from these marriages that the Koliya tribe descended and was so called because their city of origin was established at a place where a large *kol* tree was growing. The *Mahāvastu* version states that the princess suffering from leprosy was left in a forest where she was discovered by the royal sage Kola who took her to his hermitage.[51] Sixteen pairs of twin sons were born and were called the Koliyas and were sent to Kapilavastu from where they obtained their brides. The settlement of the Koliyas adjoined that of the Śākyas and the two were separated by the river Rohiṇī, the waters of which, used for irrigation, were the cause of dispute between the Śākyas and the Koliyas.[52]

In a late text the Moriyas (Mauryas) were also associated with the Śākyas.[53] They are described as those Śākyas who fled from Kapilavastu when Viḍuḍbha, the king of Kośala, attacked the Śākyas for having deceived him into marrying a maid-servant rather than the princess who was promised to him. This group of Śākyas settled in a *pipal* forest, the Pipphalivana, which abounded in peacocks—*mayura/mora*—from which their name was eventually derived. This appears to have been a later attempt to link Aśoka Maurya with the family of the Buddha.

The origin of the Licchavis again relates them to the royal family of Banaras.[54] The chief queen gave birth to a lump of flesh which was put in a box and floated down the river. It was picked up by a hermit who nurtured its contents until eventually the lump of flesh changed into a twin boy and girl. They had such a translucent beauty that they appeared to have no skin, hence the name, *nicchavi*; or alternatively, everything seemed to get absorbed into them and thus they were called *linacchavi*. Eventually they came to be called Licchavi. The children were adopted by local cowherds but as they proved to be totally undisciplined they had to be abandoned (*vajjitabba*). An area was demarcated and given over to them and this was called Vajji, an obvious attempt to explain the name of the confederacy of eight clans commonly referred to as the Vṛjji or Vajji confederacy. The boy and girl were married and had sixteen pairs of sibling twins. Since the city in which they lived had to be continually enlarged (viśālikata) they came to call it Veśāli/Vaiśāli. The Licchavis were to become a powerful tribe and were the main contenders for the control over the Ganges valley against the kingdom of Magadha. Although defeated at this juncture they continued to maintain their status in the Terai-Nepal area, for not only does Candragupta I make much of his marriage to Licchavi princess[55] but they also provided an early and important dynasty in Nepal. In some of the later *vaṃśāvalis* of Nepal the lineage of the Licchavis is not only linked to the Ikṣvākus but the actual descent is given via Raghu, Aja, Daśaratha, eight other kings and then the Licchavis, but the Buddhist origin myth is not repeated.[56]

The origin of the Śākyas is related in fuller detail in the biographies of the Buddha from the northern Sanskrit Buddhist texts, some of which have been collated in a Chinese version.[57] This version makes the same points as the earlier one but underlines the emphases more strongly. In the dynasty of the Fish king was born a ruler called Ta-man-tso. Not having a son he became an ascetic and gave his kingdom to his ministers. When he was old and incapable of looking after himself, his disciples, if they had to leave him alone for any length of time, would place him in a basket and bang the basket from a tree. This would safeguard him against wild animals, snakes and the like. One day a hunter shot him by mistake. His disciples, full of grief, cremated his body. But two drops of blood had fallen from the wound onto the ground. Out of these drops of blood sprang up two stalks of sugarcane (*ikṣa*) which on maturing burst asunder and revealed a boy in one and a girl in the other. The children were taken to the ministers who agreed to recognize them as the children of the late king. The boy was called Ikṣvāku and Sūryavamśa and girl Subhadrā. They were married and a son Janta was born to them. Ikṣvāku had four sons by a later, second marriage, all of whom were fine, manly young men. Subhadrā was now concerned that her son, who was not as attractive, would be overlooked for the succession. She therefore plotted to have the four boys banished. They went into exile and travelled north across the Bhāgīrathī and into the Snowy Mountains, accompanied by their four sisters. They arrived in a beautiful valley where the sage Kapila dwelt and settled there. So as not to pollute their race they married their sisters and founded the city of Kapilavastu. Because they were able (*śaknoti*) to govern well they came to be called Śākyas. The story then continues to trace the lineage of descent from the princes down to Śuddhodana, the father of the Buddha.

This sample of origin myths indicates certain characteristics which provide some clues to social concerns. In each case the myth attempts to explain not only the origin of the tribe but also the city associated with that particular *janapada* or territory where the tribe eventually settled. The inclusion of the city seems to have almost equal importance as indeed the cities of the *janapadas* in the latter part of the first millennium B.C. had considerable political and economic importance. In the *janapadas* with the *saṅgha* or *gaṇa* system of government (i.e. what is generally described as oligarchic government or republic in modern writing on that period), the city was the nucleus of political life and would inevitably be seen as arising almost coterminously with the *janapada*.

The attempt to explain the name of the tribe is a striking feature of these myths if only because the etymologies are so patently false. The survival for example of the extremely far-fetched etymology for Licchavi is quite remarkable. It would seem that the original etymology for these names was either forgotten or lost and clumsy attempts were made in a later period to invent an etymology. This would also account for the variation in the explanation. Thus Śākya is derived from *Śaknoti* (to be able), the *śaka* tree and *sakahi* (with reference to their marrying their sisters). Totem worship may be suggested as a possible explanation but this would be a plausible theory only if there had been a consistency of association with a single object in each case.

The selection of tribes whose origin and genealogy are considered worthy of record are invariably those *janas* which had *saṅgha* and *gaṇa* systems of government. These gave prominence to the *kṣatriya* families of the *jana* since they were the ones who had the right to be represented in the *santhāgāra* or assembly-hall. The *kṣatriya* members of these *janapadas* were frequently inter-related and their territories lay in geographical proximity to each other. The *kṣatriya* families were again those who were associated with the Buddha, Mahāvīra and other heterodox teachers. None of these origin myths are concerned with the genesis of the neighbouring kingdoms where monarchy prevailed, even though the Buddha after his enlightenment preached more frequently in the kingdoms of Magadha and Kāśi.

The insistence on siblings or, even better, sibling twins as the procreators of the *jana* is explained in the myths as necessary for maintaining the purity of lineage, where the lineage can be traced back to those of identical blood. Related to this was possibly also the idea that sibling marriages would be the closest simulation of the situation which prevailed in the Uttara-Kuru utopia, which utopīa was equally acceptable to the Buddhists and to the *brāhmaṇs*. Periods of genesis would inevitably be associated with the earliest golden age or utopia from where the origin myth would begin. The occurrence of the sixteen pairs of twins makes a rather special number. It may perhaps be explained as a multiple of two (2 x 2 x 2 x 2) where the base of two would again covey the sense of a twin or couple. The sibling marriage symbolism is so strong that in the *Daśaratha Jātaka*, Rāma and Sīta are described as brother and sister and finally marry each other, a distinctly Buddhist transformation of the *Rāma-kathā*.[58]

The prevalence of cross-cousin marriage would also seem apparent, especially that involving the maternal uncle's daughter. This may reflect an actual social situation or it may be symbolic. In the Chinese account, the marriage is not only mentioned but is explained as being prevalent by the pointed reference to there being no objection to it. This might perhaps indicate that in later periods the sytem of cross-cousin marriage had to be explained or that the audience for this particular text was unfamiliar with the system.

The reference to cross-cousin marriage in the Pāli texts and that in the Epics, *Purāṇas* and other literature, raises the question of the prevalence of the system. These references are a contradiction of the śāstric rules on the observance of *sapiṇḍa* and *sagotra* limitations with regard to marriage. Some late *dharmaśāstras* refer to the legitimacy of cross-cousin marriages by quoting a few ambiguous passages from Vedic literature, but far more forcefully by arguing that where it was a customary practice, as for example in the southern regions, it was a permitted relationship even for *brāhmaṇs*.[59] It has recently been suggested that the references to cross-cousin marriage in texts pertaining to northern India may be traces of an earlier Dravidian substratum culture, particularly as the texts appear to have been composed in areas where cross-cousin marriage was the prevalent pattern, as in the case of the Pāli canon edited and compiled in Ceylon.[60] That the acceptability of the system was doubted in cases other than those occurring in the

Buddhist texts is evident from the attempt to find an explanation for it or to treat it somewhat contemptuously.[61] In such cases the reference to cross-cousin marriage may well be a memory of an earlier social custom which gave way later, under the powerful impact of Indo-Aryan social structure, to the *sapiṇḍa* and *sagotra* observances, at least among the elite groups of northern India.

In the Buddhist tradition however there appears to be more than either the memory of a substratum culture or the influence of southern social usage. There is a deliberate attempt to associate cross-cousin marriage with elite groups. This would heighten the antiquity of the custom as well as the exclusive character of the groups involved. It has been argued that, in order to prolong the relationship established by marriage between kin-groups, two techniques were used to record the relationship.[62] One was that the original relationship could be traced back to sibling incest, thereby emphasizing the close blood tie; the other was the frequent introduction of cross-cousin marriage at appropriate points in the genealogy among the related lineages. It is evident that at least the Śākyas and Koliyas were closely connected by kinship and the use of both these techniques in their records may have been an attempt to emphasize the connection. The techniques would be identical for both matrilineal and patrilineal groups so that cross-cousin marriage need not indicate, as it was once thought to, the precondition of a matrilineal society. At another level incest is a logical explanation of how two people could found a lineage. That the questioning if not the tabu on incest had crept into some of the later Buddhist texts is evident for example from the reference to the Śākyas being rebuked by the Koliyas for cohabiting with their own sisters.[63]

The *kṣatriya* status of the tribe is both assumed and made implicit in the fact that the origin is always from an established royal family either of the Ikṣvāku lineage or from the king of Banaras. The Ikṣvāku lineage would make these tribes off-shoots of the Sūryavaṃśi. The repeated theme of exile would either point to their being dissident groups or else that they migrated from the family base, generally a kingdom along the Ganges river or the middle Ganges plain, to the foothills of the Himalayas. The theme of exile would also become necessary where a major social tabu, that of sibling incest, was being broken even if only symbolically. Possibly, these were groups of cultivators in origin, belonging to the *jana* (but perhaps not to the *rājakula* or the landowning groups), who had migrated in search of new land and, on becoming prosperous, adopted the *kṣatriya* genealogy of the *jana* from which they came. Equally possibly, they could have been local tribes, who, on becoming agriculturalists and acquiring landownership and status, sought links with the prestigious Ikṣvāku tradition and invented the myth of exile.

That there was some element of discordance is evident from the fact that, in spite of the Buddhist insistence on their *kṣatriya* status, these tribes are never listed in the Puranic genealogies. If it was merely a question of discounting those who were the fountain-head of heterodox movements, then surely the Puranic genealogies would have deliberately included them and described them either as *vrātya kṣatriyas* or else given them *śūdra* status.[64] The disavowal of monarchy as the accepted political system may in part explain their exclusion from the Puranic lists. In the case of Vaiśāli for example, the period of monarchy is referred to in the Puranic genealogies but there is silence with regard to the period when it was the nucleus of the Vṛjjian confederacy. Even though the Śākyas and Koliyas in their myths emanate from royal families, they do not appear to have repeated the experience of monarchy and their political organization seems more often to have been oligarchic, the emphasis being on political egalitarianism extending to at least the *kṣatriya* families. The reference to sixteen pairs of twins can be interpreted as an attempt at the symbolic diffusion of power within a small but powerful social group. In a monarchical situation, presumably, there would have been a single pair of twins. That substantially the same myth is related for all these *janas* suggests that they formed a separate group; probably in origin an extended kin group settled in geographical proximity of each other. Alternatively, the use of a similar origin myth may have been deliberate; to emphasize a similarity of political and social culture and an exclusivity which separated them from the more common monarchical *janapadas*.

The expanded version of the myth in the *Mahāvastu* seems much more elaborate with an implicit attempt at providing explanations. Thus the name Ikṣvāku is introduced through the reference to the sugarcane stalks and the association with the *Sūryavaṃśa* lineage is also made clear. The location of Kapilavastu is more explicitly described as being north across the Bhāgīrathī and into the Snowy Mountains, presumably the proximity to the Himālaya. This explanation would be necessary for the new audiences for Buddhist literature who would be unfamiliar with northern India.

The theme of the exile of princes carries echoes of the *Ramāyaṇa*. It would seem from the frequent references to this theme and to that of the abduction of princesses in Buddhist literature that exiled princes may well have been a stereotype of the folktale. The *Daśaratha Jātaka* suggests the possible existence of an earlier *Rāma-kathā*, the events of the *Jātaka* being a Buddhist version of the story of Rāma. It is not without significance that the events of the *Rāmāyaṇa* also concern the members of the Ikṣvāku-Sūryavaṃśi lineage.

The importance of the *kṣatriya* in society is also apparent from another myth which relates to the origin of government.[65] When the Buddha was asked about the origin of government he explained that to begin with the world was of a utopian order where no one laboured and time was passed in pleasant leisure. Gradually this golden age began to tarnish and evil crept into the ways of man. The cause of the decay was man's desire for possessions and this was reflected in the emergence of the family as a social institution with the possession of woman by man, and in the notion of personal property where fields were demarcated and were claimed by individuals. Ultimately the situation became so chaotic that people gathered together and elected one from among them (the great elect or the *mahāsammata*) in whom they invested the power to make laws and maintain order and to whom as recompense for performing this unenviable task they agreed to pay a percentage of their produce.

The story apart from its strikingly rational assumptions reflects early thinking on the origin of the *kṣatriyas*. A demarcation is made between the period of common ownership of land and the later evolution of private ownership. Out of a non-stratified society there first arose the stratification of occupations. Subsequent to this, those who owned land were set apart and the establishment of the family is also associated with the cultivation of land. Ownership of land accelerates dispute and disequilibrium which can only be tentatively corrected by the imposition of an authority which lay above and beyond that invested in ordinary persons. The crux of the story relates to the two areas of *kṣatriya* interest, landownership and the exercise of political authority.

The readjustment of the format of the Buddhist origin myth of the Śākyas and the Koliyas to changed social conditions in a later period becomes apparent in the myth regarding Vijaya and the early history of Ceylon as recorded in the *Mahāvaṃśa*.[66] A princess of Vaṅga, too arrogant to accept a human husband, is married to a lion. She gave birth to a son Sīhabāhu and a daughter Sīhāsavali but remained unhappy and homesick. Ultimately she persuaded Sīhabāhu to kill his father, the lion, whereupon the princess with her two children returned to her father's kingdom. But soon after this the children left her, wandered away to a distant place where they married each other, built themselves a city and established a kingdom. The marriage resulted in sixteen pairs of twin sons. Among these Vijaya was regarded as the eldest. He was however so evil that he had to be exiled but was permitted to take seven hundred attendants with him. He travelled at first to western India and finally arrived in Ceylon together with his attendants on the very day of Buddha's *nirvāṇa*. The island was inhabited only by *yakhas* and *yakhinīs* whom he subdued. He sent to India for wives for himself and his attendants and not only made the island fit for human habitation but became himself a virtuous king.

The myth seeks to introduce all the elements of the traditional origin myth of the Buddhist texts. There are also, underlying the story, many levels of assumptions. The geographical area of the story is very wide, starting with eastern India, moving to western India and from there to Ceylon. This is not the compact region of the earlier myths. At the time of the compilation of the text both eastern and western India were in close contact with Ceylon. The western contact is attested to linguistically, the Pāli of the Chronicles having an affinity with the western *prākṛt* of India. The eastern link may have been introduced to established as close a connection as possible with the Buddhist homeland. The myth is replete with assumptions regarding the social order. Vijaya's unusual and supernatural origin is amply emphasized: he is the grandson of a lion, the son of an incestuous marriage and the eldest of sixteen pairs of twin brothers. Incest in this case again points to purity of descent. Uniqueness is further stressed by the sixteen pairs of twin brothers, although here the eldest stands out since the context is monarchy and not oligarchy. His social status is indicated by his royal antecedents both in the animal world and in the human. Royal antecedents also provide him with the economic means to travel the long distance from Vaṅga to Ceylon together with his attendants. The story of the exile was necessary to explain why anyone would travel such a long distance to an island inhabited only by demons. It is appropriate that the man who founded the first human colony in Ceylon should arrive on the auspicious day of the Buddha's *parinirvāṇa*. Such a connection would be virtually inevitable in the *Mahāvaṃśa* which after all was the Chronicle of the major Buddhist monastery of Ceylon, the Mahāvihāra. The etymological interest is also clear from the attempt to explain the derivation of the name of the island—Sinhala— associated with a lion. The earlier origin myths had by now almost become archetypes. The story of Vijaya does not occur at the start of the *Mahāvaṃśa* but in the sixth chapter. Nevertheless it marks the commencement of the narrative of the history of Ceylon. Earlier chapters relate the story of the Buddha's visit to Ceylon and the conversion of Aśoka which prepares the ground for the arrival of Buddhism. This structure makes the narrative more purposive and strengthens the notion of the mission of Buddhism to Ceylon.

The social function of these origin myths in the context of the early Indian historical tradition appears to be four-fold: to establish kinship links, to emphasize the legitimacy of succession, to indicate the migration of important groups and to provide social status to those who had acquired political power. The recognition of kinship links among the *kṣatriya* families in the mid-first millennium B.C. was central to the question of rights of land-ownership and ultimately political authority. In the first millennium A.D., with new claimants to *kṣatriya* status and political power in the many dynasties of the period, the kinship links were revived through the search for actual or fabricated genealogical connections.[67]

The legitimacy of succession was implicit in the genealogical links requiring *kṣatriya* antecedents. In the monarchical system there was the additional need to stress primogeniture. That this was a real concern is evident from other literature which stresses not only the need for hereditary succession but also the rights of seniority within it.[68] It is not surprising that this question crops up repeatedly in the literature of the mid-first millennium A.D. and later, wherein plays such as the *Devicandraguptam* and in historical biographies such as the *Harṣacarita* and the *Vikramānkadevacarita*, there is an elaborate justification for the transgressing of the rule.[69]

The theme of migration, often disguised as exile, sets the geographical dimensions of the social group and can be used to establish the rights and priority of a particular group over a particular region. This assumes significance in periods when new groups are moving in as entrepreneurs in either previously occupied areas or in newly opened up lands: the entrepreneurs in the mid-first millennium A.D. being the recipients of grants of land. Those who succeeded in establishing new dynasties would either have to link themselves genealogically with the descent groups, who were already associated with the area or else would have to introduce the idea of migration. The Sisodia Rajput link with the *Sūryavaṃśi* lineage and the migration of one of their ancestors from Lahore (associated with Lava the son of Rāma) to Rajasthan would form a case in point.[70] Puranic sources refer to the dispersal of the Haihayas (a sub-lineage of the Yādavas). This provided a useful peg for many early medieval dynasties to hang their genealogies on, such as the Kalacuris of Tripuri[71] and the Muṣakavaṃśa of Kerala.[72] Exiled princes also provide one of the mechanisms by which local tradition can be hooked onto the 'classical' tradition and vice versa.

In both the *itihāsa-purāṇa* tradition and the Buddhist tradition, as far as origin myths are concerned, it is in the main the *kṣatriya* status which is sought to be validated. The origin myths of the *kṣatriya* tribes in Buddhist literature are attempts to provide status for those who played an important part in the events relating to the establishment of Buddhism, and are the counterparts to the lineage myths in the Puranic tradition, both sets of myth endorsing the groups in political authority at the time. Nor is it coincidental that this search for validation through myth is systematized and recorded at the time when dynasties claiming *kṣatriya* status rose to political control and, in the Buddhist case, sectarian institutions of the Buddhist *saṅgha* were involved, albeit not always directly, in political authority.

REFERENCES AND NOTES

(I am grateful to my colleagues Dr. Satish Saberwal and Dr. B.D. Chattopadhyaya who read an earlier draft of this paper and discussed it with me).

1. G.S. Kirk, *The Nature of Greek Myths*, (Harmondsworth, 1974), p. 31 ff.
2. Max Müller, *Chips from a German Workshop*, vols. I & II (London, 1867, 68).
3. A. Lang, *Custom and Myth* (London, 1884); *Myth, Ritual and Religion* (London, 1887).
4. W. Robertson Smith, *The Religion of the Semites* (London, 1894); J.E. Harrison, *Themis*; (Cambridge, 1912).
5. As in *Magic, Science and Religion* (New York, 1948).
6. C. Levi-Strauss, *The Raw and the Cooked* and *From Honey to Ashes*, being the first two volumes so far translated into English of a longer work, *Mythologiques* (Paris, 1964-72). The more successful applications of the structural analysis of myth have been in the myths of pre-literate societies. E. Leach (ed.), *The Structural Study of Myth and Totemism* (London, 1967), and T.A. Sebeok (ed.), *Myth: A Symposium* (Indiana, 1955). Changes introduced in myths over a period

of time in literate societies could add a worthwhile dimension even to structural analysis.

7. The notion of the archetype as developed by S. Freud, *The Interpretation of Dreams* (New York, 1965), was of considerable influence. But the names of Jung and Cassirer are more closely associated with the growth of this idea. C.G. Jung and K. Kerenyi, *Introduction to a Science of Mythology* (London, 1963), and E. Cassirer, *The Philosophy of Symbolic Forms*, vol. 2, 'Mythical Thought' (New Haven, 1955).
8. Eliade has touched on this theme in many of his writings but more especially in *The Myth of the Eternal Return, Myth and Reality*, and in *Patterns in Comparative Religion* (New York, 1963).
9. V. Turner, 'Myth and Symbol' in *The Encyclopaedia of Social Sciences*, vol. X.
10. Georges Dumezil's *Mythe et Èpopée* in three volumes is not as yet available in an English translation but an attempt has been made to represent his ideas in C. Scott Littleton, *The New Comparative Mythology* (London, 1973). Dumezil uses the theory of the three functions (which can be approximately translated as sanctity, coercion and fecundity) as the basic pattern of Indo-European symbolism and myth. None of the functions are precisely defined and the overlapping makes for a rather ambiguous analysis at times. Also associated with these ideas are the writings of Stig Wikander, especially the paper entitled 'La Legende des Pandavas et la substructure mythique du Mahabharata' in Georges Dumezil, *Jupiter, Mars, Quirinus IV.*
11. K. Thomas, 'Anthropology and History' in *Past and Present*, no. 24, April 1963, p. 1 ff.
12. *Śatapatha Brāhmaṇa*, I.8.1.1-10; *Matsya Purāṇa* I. 11-34; *Mahābhārata*, Vanaparvan, 185.ff.
13. *Viṣṇu Purāṇa*, IV.
14. M. Eliade, *Myth and Reality*, p. 5 ff.
15. This point came up in a discussion with Professor A. Kilmer.
16. Sally Falk Moore, 'Descent and Symbolic Filiation', *The American Anthropologist*, no. 66, VI, pt. 1, 1964, pp. 1308-20.
17. *Aitareya Brāhmaṇa* VIII.14.23; *Śatapatha Brāhmaṇa*, III.2.13.15; Āṭānāṭiya Sutta, *Dīgha Nikāya*, III. 199.7.ff.
18. *Vāyu Purāṇa*, VIII. 176 ff.
19. *Ṛg Veda* X. 10.
20. Sukumari Bhattacharji, *The Indian Theogony* (Cambridge, 1970), p. 217-18.
21. *Viṣṇu Purāṇa*, IV.1.
22. The symbolism of the sun and the moon occurs frequently in Yoga and in Tantric texts although in these the sexual association is reversed: the moon is associated with the male and the sun with the female. M. Eliade, *Yoga* (Princeton, 1971), p. 239.
23. For a description of the segmentary system which fairly approximates some of the features of the Candravaṃśa see Marshall D. Sahlins, 'The Segmentary Lineage: An Organisation of Predatory Expansion', *The American Anthropologist*, vol. 63, no. 2, 1961, pp. 332-45.
24. F. E. Pargiter, *Ancient Indian Historical Tradition* (London, 1922), p. 15 ff.

25. A. Heidel, *The Babylonian Genesis* (Chicago, 1963).
26. G.S. Kirk, *The Nature of Greek Myths*, p. 261 ff.
27. L. Woolley, *Excavations at Ur* (London, 1954), pp. 34-6; *Ur of the Chaldees* (London, 1950), p. 29 ff. *The Cambridge Ancient History,* vol. I, pt. I, p. 353 ff. Reliable evidence on substantial floods in India during this period (as available so far) would point to two areas and time brackets. The first would be the flooding of Mohenjo-daro and the lower valley in the early second millennium B.C. (G. Dales, 'New Investigations at Mohenjo-daro', *Archaeology*, 1965, no. 18). The second would be that of the Ganga-Yamuna Doāb and particularly Hastināpur in the early first millennium B.C. (B.B. Lal, 'Excavations at Hastināpur', *Ancient India*, 1954 and 1955, nos. 10 and 11). The second is certainly too late in time to have been the original of such a myth. More than likely the myth was not referring to any particular flood but rather to the possibility of a flood as a cataclysmic point of time and change and this notion may have arisen from the observation of recurring floods in the area.
28. Th. Jacobsen, *The Sumerian King-List* (Chicago, 1939).
29. *Viṣṇu Purāṇa*, IV.6 and 10.
30. N.S. Bose, *History of the Chandellas of Jejakabhukti* (Calcutta, 1956); E. Zannas and J. Auboyer, *Khajuraho* (The Hague, 1960), p. 30 ff.
31. *Ṛg Veda*, X.95.
32. *Śatapatha Brāhmaṇa*, XI.5.1.1ff.
33. *Mahābhārata*, Ādiparvan, 16ff.
34. Max Müller, *Chips from a German Workshop*, IV, (London, 1968), p. 109 ff.
35. D.D. Kosambi, *Myth and Reality* (Bombay, 1962), p. 47 ff.
36. *Viṣṇu Purāṇa*, IV.10.
37. *Ibid.*
38. *Mahābhārata*, Ādiparvan, 80.
39. Georges Dumezil, *The Destiny of a King* (Chicago, 1973).
40. *Vedic Index*, II, pp. 11-12.
41. *Ibid.*, p. 185.
42. *Viṣṇu Purāṇa*, I.13.
43. *Mahābhārata*, Śāntiparvan, LXVII, 16-24.
44. *Vedic Index*, vol. 1, p. 452; *Ibid.*, vol. II, p. 16.
45. *Viṣṇu Purāṇa*, I.13.
46. *Ibid.*, IV.20.
47. *Ṛg Veda*, X.98; *Nirukta*, II.10; *Bṛhaddevata* VII.155, 156 ff.
48. *Sutta Nipāta*, 420 ff; *Sutta Nipāta Commentary* I, 352 ff; *Sumaṅgalavilāsinī*, I, p. 258-60.
49. B.C. Law, *Some Kṣatriya Tribes of Ancient India*, p. 162 ff. (Varanasi, 1975 reprint); *Mahāvastu*, I, p. 348-52.
50. Ambattha Sutta, I.16 in *Dīgha Nikāya*, I; *Kuṇāla Jātaka*, no. 536, (vol. V, p. 219).
51. H.C. Raichaudhury, *Political History of Ancient India*, (Calcutta, 1952), p. 192 ff.
52. *Kuṇāla Jātaka*, no. 536.
53. *Mahāvaṁśa Tīkā*, p. 180 ff.

54. Buddhaghosa, *Paramatthajotika*, Khuddakapatha, pp. 158-60.
55. S.R. Goyal, *A History of the Imperial Guptas*, (Allahabad, 1967), p. 81 ff.
56. Paśupati inscription of Jayadeva, quoted in B.C. Law, *Kṣatriya Clans in Buddhist India*, pp. 28-29; J.F. Fleet (ed.), *Corpus Inscriptionum Indicarum*, III, pp. 155, 133, 136.
57. S. Beal, *Romantic History of Buddha*, (London, 1920), p. 18 ff.
58. *Daśaratha Jātaka*, no. 461 (vol. IV, p. 78).
59. P.V. Kane, *History of Dharmaśāstra*, II.1, (Poona, 1941), p. 460 ff.
60. T.R. Trautmann, 'Cross-Cousin Marriage in Ancient North India' in T. R. Trautmann (ed.), *Kinship and History in South Asia* (Michigan, 1974).
61. *Bhāgavata Purāṇa*, X.54.18.
62. Sally Falk Moore, op. cit.
63. *Sutta Nipāta Commentary*, I.357; *Kuṇāla Jātaka*, no. 536.
64. *Manu*, X.22, does however refer to the Licchavis as *vrātya kṣatriyas*.
65. *Aggañña Sutta in Dīgha Nikāya*, III.93.
66. *Mahāvaṃśa* VI.
67. For some references to fabricated genealogies see D. C. Sircar, *Indian Epigraphy*, (New Delhi, 1965), p. 24 ff.
68. *Arthaśāstra* I, 17.34; *Majjhima Nikāya*, II. 75; *Manu*, IX.105-09:
69. The first of these texts justifies the succession of Candragupta II, who, owing to cowardly act of his elder brother Rāmagupta, had finally (it would seem from other sources) to kill his elder brother and usurp the throne. Both biographies concern the succession of younger brothers and here again an elaborate argument is produced to prove the justification for the younger brother. In the *Harṣacarita* the elder brother is killed by the enemy so that the justification is not so elaborate. In the *Vikramānkadevacarita* we are told that the god Śiva himself commanded the younger brother to usurp the throne for the sake of the well-being of the people and the prosperity of the kingdom.
70. J. Tod, *Annals and Antiquities of Rajasthan*, I. p. 176.
71. F. Kielhorn, 'Kalachuris of Tripuri', *Epigrahia Indica*, II, pp. 300-05.
72. T. Gopinath Rao, 'Extract from the Mūṣakavaṃśa. . . . , *Travancore Archaeological Series*, II, 1, no. 10, pp. 87-113. M.G.S. Narayanan, 'History from the Mūṣakavaṁśa', *P.A.-I.O.C.*, Jadavpur, 1969.

Genealogy as a Source of Social History

Historical interest in the genealogical sources of the ancient period of Indian history became a serious concern with the publication in 1922 of what has since come to be regarded as the classic work of F. E. Pargiter, *The Ancient Indian Historical Tradition*. This was essentially an attempt to ascertain the chronology of the beginnings of Indian history by correlating the genealogical information from the *vaṃśānucarita* material from the various *Purāṇas*. Having worked out what he thought was the most acceptable chronological and genealogical reconstruction, Pargiter then tried to identify the various lineages with what were believed to be the predominant racial-linguistic groups of the time—the Āryans, Dravidians, Mundas, etc. Later work on the same subject has, on the whole, continued to emphasize chronological and dynastic reconstruction[1] which inevitably has led to a considerable juggling with the lists of descent groups and succession.

It is proposed in this paper to move away from chronological reconstruction, on the assumption that traditional genealogies are rarely faithful records of times past. Their primary function and purpose perhaps lies elsewhere. This is not to deny their chronological dimension for, obviously, in a measuring of generations, the element of time is important; but, rather, to suggest that genealogies provide elements of other facets of society as well[2] and these facets have often been ignored in the study of genealogical material from Indian sources. Genealogies relate to the past and claim to be records of succession, yet very often their preservation (or even their fabrication) is dependent on the social institutions of the period when they were put together and for which they provide legitimizing mechanisms. They are often encapsulations of the migration and movement of peoples in time and to that extent are associated with a geographical locale. However, the

From *The Indian Historical Review*, vol. II, no. 2, January 1976, pp. 259-281.

genealogical record is not based on a region but on the distribution of the lineage[3] which may or may not coincide with geographical region.

As records of social relations, they were concerned only with particular social groups, namely, those who were members of the lineages and had access to political and social status. Lineages of those in authority even in tribal society had to be maintained with as much concern as those of kings. This was even more pertinent in conditions of frequent warfare or in new settlements of land where the genealogy became a reference point for legal rights and status. When other groups began to participate in social and political power, such as religious teachers and priests, then their genealogies had also to be maintained. Thus, lists of succession do not pertain only to dynastic descent of kings.

The keeping of genealogies becomes important with the emergence of property, for the right to ownership or participation in property can be proved by lineage links. In pre-agricultural food-gathering societies the right to ownership of property (other than personal) was, for a variety of reasons, faintly defined and flexible. The right to property was subordinate to the right to status. In agrarian societies, particularly with the emergence of ownership of land, whether group or individual, the notion of property became stronger. Whereas in non-agrarian or early agrarian societies it is largely the lineages of the clan chiefs which are remembered, in more developed agrarian societies other groups may also come to be recorded in lists of succession. The record of ownership and status can extend not only to rights over land and livestock but also rights to women in the form of marriage alliances between lineages, and to other resources.

Succession is another form of the transfer of property and office from one person to the next and therefore involves a small segment of society through a hierarchy of restricted and inter-linked roles.[4] What is recorded in the genealogy is the social system of succession, namely, the office to which succession is made, the relationship between the successive office holders, the procedure of selection, and the time when it occurs. The choice of the successor is often determined by the social system.

Since genealogies are arranged chronologically this provides the dimension of the measurement of time.[5] This may be represented either by reference to cyclical occurrences or much more directly by reference to age groups, kinship (father-to-son or uncle-to-nephew) or by regnal years. Reckoning by generations also provides an approximate time scale. But regnal years and generations should not in every case be taken literally. Significant spans of time are usually demarcated by some important event and are pointers to the historian that the interrelationships recorded have undergone some fundamental change.

Most traditional genealogical records carry two types of information. The core of the genealogy consists of the succession lists or the lists of the descent groups and this has been called 'the fixed tradition'. However, even this is subject to considerable fluidity should the situation demand it. Interspersed with this is the narrative tradition which is added to and changed by the genealogist more freely. The 'fixed tradition' was perhaps less tampered with, although it was often 'telescoped' where only the essential names and events were memorized and other matter dropped as long as the genealogical record was an oral one.[6] The narrative tradition, consisting of legends or the description of incidents, inevitably changed more easily when the social norms changed or when new requirements demanded fresh comment. Into the Puranic genealogies are interwoven such narratives. The inclusion of genealogies in a body of literature reflects both a desire to freeze the tradition on the assumption that it will continue to serve a social purpose as well as the taking over of the tradition from professional memorizers by literate groups. It has also been suggested that where a number of genealogies are coalesced this indicates the collation of various literary traditions.[7] That genealogies become a part of literature at some point is inevitable. The keepers of such records in the oral tradition were respected as sources of sanction for status. When the record was embodied in literature, not only this respect and power transferred to those who were keeping the written record but, by collating the different segments of the tradition, it facilitated the control over these records as well.

Keeping these aspects of genealogical records in mind, the ancient Indian tradition can be seen as a useful source of data. The earliest attempts at lineage records and succession lists are to be found in Vedic literature. Those relating to kings are almost incidental since they merely refer to connections of about two or three generations and that too not in any genealogical form. The two dominant tribes of the Ṛgvedic period—if we are to go by the mention of lineages—were the Bharatas and the Pūrus in whose families it is possible to trace minimal descent links.[8] In Later Vedic literature these two families are replaced by reference to the Kuru-Pañcāla descent groups and a more eastern centre of interest, Videha, is also introduced.[9] These two regions, the Ganga-Yamuna Doāb and its fringes and the middle Ganges plain, remain the focus of much of the earlier genealogical material of the *Purāṇas* as well. What are however referred to with greater interest in the Later Vedic texts are the succession lists of Vedic teachers.[10] The preservation of these lists was due to the need for the ritual to be handed down orally and the record of those connected with it in the past was maintained by recording the names of the teachers and the *brāhmaṇ gotras*. These succession lists were made a part of the sacrificial ritual to ensure that they would be memorised.[11] It is significant that, whereas the succession lists of those in political power went almost unrecorded, there was a deliberate formulation of lists of those who had status through ritual actions and the careful maintenance of such lists.

The proliferation of the ritual may also have required its demarcation by association with particular groups of teachers and priests. Further, the *Vaṃśa* or succession lists help to maintain a record of *gotra* and *pravara* relations and these were of fundamental importance to the *brāhmaṇs* as an indication of social and ritual identity. The *gotra*, a patrilineal, exogamous, sibship whose members trace their descent to a common ancestor, was, to begin with, an institution recording kin and social relations only among the *brāhmaṇs.*[12] Later, it extended to other *varṇas* as well.[13] The *pravara*, a stereotyped list of names of ancient *ṛṣis* believed to be the remote founders of families, had a similar function. The *gotra* was crucial to marriage and property since members of the same *gotra* (*sagotra*) were not permitted to marry within the *gotra* but they could, in the absence of an heir, claim rights to the property owned by one of their fellow members. The lists of *vaṃśas* and *gotras* therefore served a distinct social function and underlined the status of the *brāhmaṇs* and indicated that the knowledge of ritual was a crucial aspect of social status if not (indirectly) of property. By the period of the *śrauta-sūtras* there are systematic lists of *gotras* and *pravaras*, but sometimes subject to inconsistencies and contradictions.[14] Notwithstanding the latter, it would seem that at the point where it became socially necessary there was probably a rush to systematize the lists and connections. For the *brāhmaṇs* the maintenance of such a system was necessary when new members had to be recruited who were not from the old kinship groups. Thus tribal priests in new areas or the conferring of *brāhmaṇ* status on the priests of cults assimilated into Vedic religion would require the records of such families of priests.[15] Doubtless the *gotra* system was useful both to incorporate the new *brāhmaṇs* into the *varṇa* and assist in their being absorbed into kinship groups where this was desired, or equally, the preservation of a subtle barrier between the new and the old if this was preferred.

The major texts for the recording of lineages were the *Purāṇas* with their *vaṃśānucarita* sections claiming to be authentic records of the *kṣatriya vaṃśas*. Not all the *mahā purāṇas* record the genealogies in detail. In most of the standard ones, such as the *Viṣṇu, Brahmāṇḍa, Vāyu, Matsya* and *Bhāgavata*, there is broad agreement in most sections of the genealogies.[16] An attempt was evidently made to arrange and organize all the *vaṃśas* and *janapadas* which, as tribes and states, were known in northern India and provide them with a history via the genealogies. That the genealogies agree broadly suggests that it was a concerted effort. It is not unlikely that some sections of the lists were historical and others were added to fill out the genealogy and to cover the known geographical regions. Some were contemporary and others were given antecedents so as to introduce an order into the structure, which is in fact extremely orderly. That genealogical information was a well-known part of the tradition and that the genealogies at least were maintained in the fourth century B.C. if not the *Purāṇas* is evident from the statement of Megasthenes quoted by Pliny[17] that the Indians count one hundred and fifty-four kings up to the time of Alexander.

The original oral tradition was kept by the bards and chroniclers, the *sūtas* and the *māgadhas*. There are various myths describing how Vyāsa taught the *itihāsa-purāna* tradition to his disciple, the bard Lomaharṣaṇa.[18] The latter in turn taught it to his disciples who were *brāhmaṇs*. Does this perhaps indicate the taking over of the tradition by the *brāhmaṇ* authors of the *Purāṇas*? Originally the *sūta* and the *māgadha* had a high social status and were seated in proximity to the king on ritual occasions.[19] Curiously, with the incorporating of the genealogical records into the body of literature, the *Purāṇas,* in the early first millennium A.D., the social status of the original keepers of the tradition was lowered.[20]

For a detailed analysis, the *vaṃśānucarita* section of the *Viṣnu Purāṇa* (Book IV) provides the necessary source material. The genealogy covers a long span of time, starting with Brahmā and continuing as far as the dynasties of the early first millennium A.D. It appears however to be divisible into three distinct sections which seem to represent social and political changes (see Table at the end). The first is avowedly mythical and acts as a preface to the later sections. The details are not given in the genealogical section but are discussed in the earlier part of the text concerning primary and secondary creation (the *sarga* and *pratisarga* sections). Descent is traced from the gods, starting with Brahmā and continuing via Dakṣa, Aditi and Sūrya to Manu Vaivasvata. Earlier in the text we are told that there were six Manus prior to him, the earliest being Manu Svayambhu.[21] In the *Matsya Purāṇa* the Great Flood occurs at the time of Manu Vaivasvata and Viṣnu in the form of the Matsya incarnation saves Manu.[22] The period of the Manus has no specific geographical location except that of Jambudvīpa in a general way and the time spans associated with the Manus are enormous. In all this there is a distinct echo of the Sumerian king-list.[23] The pre-diluvian list is recognizable in that virtually no attempt is made to try and give it authenticity.

The children of Manu, born after the flood, initiate the second section (which is described in *Viṣṇu Purāṇa* IV. 1-22) which, whether historical or not, is clearly carefully constructed and probably represents the collation of many floating genealogical traditions as kept by the *sūtas* and *māgadhas*. It is concerned primarily with the distribution and descent of the Ikṣvāku and Aila lineage and terminates in the Mahābhārata war. The lineages descended from the other children of Manu are referred to but tend to be dismissed after a brief description. Ikṣvāku, a son of Manu, is the progenitor of the Sūryavaṃśa lineage in direct line of descent from Aditi and Sūrya. The Caṇdravaṃśa lineage was descended from the daughter of Manu, Ilā. She was created from a sacrifice offered by Manu who desired a son, but owing to a mistake in the ritual a female child was born.[24] The situation was somewhat ameliorated by her ability to change her sex on occasion and she is therefore referred to by the cognate Ila-Ilā.[25] Ilā gave birth to a son fathered by Budha the son of the moon deity, Soma. Thus the lunar element in the name of the lineage is introduced. The second section covers a span of approximately ninety-six generations as computed by Pargiter.[26] The Mahābhārata war at the end of this period is for genealogical purposes quite evidently a time-marker, virtually terminating the record of the descent of the two lineages. Almost all the lineages are involved in the war and the ultimate victory of the one is bitter in the light of the destruction of the many. In the second section of the genealogy, the lineages are not cordoned off into dynasties and are recorded merely as descent groups. The term used is *vaṃśam rājñyam* where *vaṃśa* should be seen more appropriately as lineage rather than as dynasty or royal family or race. There is a reference in the opening section of the *vaṃśānucarita* to the members of the lineages being *bhupālas* or kings, but the term *vaṃśa* is used more frequently in other chapters of this section. The same term *vaṃśa* is used for lists of teachers and therefore it may be taken to mean a descent group or lineage not always related by blood. Thus the second section is a record of lineages, some of which may have been royal lineages, others those of the *kṣatriyas* in the sense of landowning clans. The definition which we are assuming for *kṣatriya* is the one given by Pāṇini as referring to the ruling clans both in monarchical and oligarchic systems.[27] We hope to show that the structure of the *vaṃśas* as described in this section makes it apparent that it is politically important lineages which are being recorded and not dynasties.

In the third section of the genealogy (*Viṣṇu Purāṇa* IV.22-24) which follows the Mahābhārata war, dynasties are mentioned by name and their members are listed. The geographical focus shifts to Magadha. Regnal years are introduced for the successors of Vṛhadratha of Magadha in some of the *Purāṇas* and this is a new feature. The assassination of Ripuñjaya by the minister Sunika terminates the lineage of Vṛhadratha and one suspects that the assassination was yet another, less dramatic time-marker. Sunika usurps the throne and there is a succession of dynasties at Magadha, which are listed. Ultimately the genealogical record includes other dynasties of northern India.

There is of course a continuing debate on the historical authenticity and chronology of these genealogical sections. In this paper we are not primarily concerned with either. It is assumed that the genealogical section was constructed at the time of the compiling of the *Viṣṇu Purāṇa* and it is this construction which needs to be analyzed. It is not the veracity of the lineages which is being investigated but the social and political forms which they reflect. As regards chronology it can only be suggested that one may go from the known to the unknown. Of the dynasties, the Śiśunāgas are the earliest attested from other sources as well and date to *circa* fifth century B.C. They are preceded by approximately twenty kings which would give a rough date of the early part of the first millennium B.C. for the Mahābhārata war. (The regnal years given for the kings could well be arbitrary.) This is of course assuming that such a date was of any significance to the makers of the genealogy. The importance of the war seems more symbolic than chronological. The distance of a round sum of a hundred generations prior to the war would substantially relate to the second millennium B.C. and a little earlier. But the chronological reconstruction remains at best extremely tentative.

The three sections of the genealogy which we have described are of course not demarcated clearly in the text but seem to us to be implicit in the way in which the genealogy has been put together. Of these three sections, the first can be set aside as not providing any worthwhile evidence on the social background. But the second and third sections offer a series of contrasts and are suggestive of recording a major shift in emphasis through social and political change. The most obvious indication of this is in the form of the genealogical record itself. It claims to have been recorded immediately after the termination of the Mahābhārata war, during the reign of Parīkṣit. The references to descent groups prior to the war are in the past tense. Subsequent to this the record is in the form of a prophecy and therefore uses the future tense.

This grammatical change has a further interest. In the past tense the succession is listed in four different ways, thus:[28]

B was the son of *A*

B was 'of *A*' (the use of the genetive)

B was 'from' or 'after' *A* (the use of ablative)

B was heir of *A*

In the first two cases it can be assumed that *B* was the child of *A*. The most commonly used phraseology runs thus,

Turvasor-vahnir-ātmajo-vahner-gobhānu-statca-traisamba-stasmāccakarandhama . . .[29]

The son of Turvasu was Vahni, Vahni's son was Gobhānu, his son was Traisamba, his son was Karandhama . . .

The second two cases are however ambiguous and leave the relationship in doubt; all that is certain is the succession of *B* after *A*. Such a form would be more appropriate to non-monarchical systems, where hereditary succession was not inevitable, or in tribal systems, where adoption is very often the only form of recruitment into the tribe.

After the Mahābhārata war the statements are made in the future tense, thus,

ataḥ paraṃbhaviṣyānahambhūpālān kīrtayiṣyāmi...[30]

I will now enumerate the kings who will reign in future periods... This enumeration takes a form such as,

...*asyāpi-putro-bindusārobhaviṣyati-tasyāpyā-śokavardhahastataḥ-suyaśas-tatśca-dośaratha-*. . .[31]

. . . his son will be Bindusāra, his (son) will be Aśokavardhana, his (son) will be Suyaśas, his (son) will be Daśaratha...

The change to the future tense and the prophetic form points to a major event in time and the past being viewed as essentially the period before the Mahābhārata war. This might explain the attempts to shift the start of the Kaliyuga from the time of Manu Vaivasvata to the period after the Mahābhārata war. The inconsistency in the prophetic form is evident. All the *mahāpurāṇas* profess to be prophetic, yet their standpoint in time is not identical.[32] The *Viṣṇu Purāṇa* makes it clear that the genealogy is being narrated by Pārāśara to Maitreya in the reign of Parīkṣit. But Pārāśara was the father of Vyāsa and was therefore dead long before the battle or the birth of Parīkṣit. The purpose of the prophetic form coming at this point was to draw attention to the *Candravaṃśa* lineages in their peak period of glory, prior to their supersession by the emergence of powerful dynasties. In the case of the *Viṣṇu Purāṇa* the attempt may also have been to highlight the role of Viṣṇu (as Kṛṣṇa Vāsudeva) both at the battle and subsequently. The genealogy was in any case organized with a certain bias in favour of the *Candravaṃśa* lineage since the central event which separates the historically verifiable section with what came before is the war.

The second section of the genealogy records the distribution and descent of the *Sūryavaṃśa* and *Candravaṃśa* lineages, both ultimately claiming Manu as an ancestor. The choice of names is curious. Vedic literature refers to Ikṣvāku and to Ilā in separate contexts and the former is associated with a lineage. But the more commonly used terms, *Sūryavaṃśa* and *Candravaṃśa*, occur in the epics and the *Purāṇas* and appear to be later appelations, perhaps of the period when the genealogies were being collated. To name the lineages after the planets seems in no way peculiar and was probably an obvious choice. It may however be mentioned in passing that the symbolism of the sun and the moon reaches across to a number of cults and groups of early Indian society. Its frequency in Tantric and Yogic texts, together with the reference to Agni which in the early medieval period was adopted as the appelation for another group of lineages, might suggest some connections in the symbolism. The sun and the moon are said to symbolize the two main nerve centres to the right and the left of the human body and their union is sought in certain yogic practices.[33] The construction of the lineages is suggestive of this pattern. Might the inclusion of the ancestors for the *Candravaṃśa* also be attributed to similar influences? One of the characteristics of the *Purāṇas* was the assimilation of certain substratum cults.

The connection of the epics with the two major lineages is also of some interest. The *Rāmāyaṇa* focuses on the *Sūryavaṃśa*-Ikṣvāku lineage and the *Mahābhārata* on the *Candravaṃśa*-Aila lineage. The structure of the epics relates closely to the social formation suggested by the lineages. This would in part account for the popularity of the epics which would be associated with those who in later periods as well linked themselves to the earlier lineages. It is perhaps also worth keeping in mind that early epic literature, constructed out of the fragments of bardic traditions, is often the literature of the transitional phase of the declining of tribal society and the emergence of kingdoms.[34]

The most striking feature of the *Sūryavaṃśa* or the Ikṣvāku lineage is not only the fullness of the names where practically every generation is represented but also the relatively stable location for these lineages with little evidence of branches migrating in various directions. Ikṣvāku we are told had three sons, Vikukṣi who established the kingdom at Ayodhyā, Nimi who established the kingdom at Videha, and Daṇḍaka who migrated south to the Daṇḍakāraṇya. Daṇḍaka appears to have been a later addition and was probably included when some contact was established between the *janapada* of Kośala with the lands to its south-west. This may have originally been a migration from Kośala to what came to be called Dakṣiṇa Kośala.[35] Basically the Ikṣvāku lineage consists of the ruling families of Kośala and Videha. These were contiguous regions perhaps settled at the same time by groups which had either travelled along the Himalayan foothills or up from the Ganges river along the northern tributaries of the Gandhak and the Gaghra. At one point, therefore, the families of Raghu and Janaka were seen as moieties. The Ikṣvāku lineage would conform to what has been called a linear descent group with descent going from father to eldest son. Younger sons are not mentioned, barring certain exceptional cases such as Purukutsa, the son of Mandhātri, the sons of Daśaratha or the mention of Kuśadhvaja, the brother of Sīradhvaja (Janaka) whose descendents are listed as the inheritors of that branch of the *Sūryavaṃśa*. Even in cases where younger sons are mentioned it seems that they did not migrate to new areas but remained as junior members of the family in the two states. The emphasis therefore was on genealogical seniority where the first-borns are given highest rank. In such a system the right to succession of the eldest son would be unchallenged and thus the events of the *Rāmāyāṇa* take on many different levels of meaning, even within the sphere of social and political life. Patrilineal descent would also be heavily underlined in such a system.

The *Rāmāyaṇa* preserves lengthier lists for the descendants of both Vikukṣi and Nimi as compared to the *Viṣṇu Purāṇa*.[36] Clearly the latter has resorted to telescoping for the first few generations, whereas the *Rāmāyaṇa* tends to reduce the generations immediately preceding Daśaratha. The Puranic list also suggests a connection between Ayodhyā, Kāśi and the Narmadā region. Purukutsa, the younger son of Mandhātri marries Narmadā and the main lineage then descends through him. This is also the geographical locale of the epic. That the Puranic list may have been conflated is suggested by the repeated occurrence of some names, such as Yuvanaśva, and the use of other names such as Sindhudvīpa, Aśmaka, Ilavilā which do not inspire much confidence as the personal names of *kṣatriyas*. The need for conflating was probably to emphasize the stability of the lineage as well as to relate it chronologically to the other major lineage of the *Candravaṃśa*. The line of Nimi in the *Purāṇa* is very sparse as compared to the epic until the period of Janaka, after which the epic lineage stops but the Puranic continues. The lineage is traced through Kuśadhvaja ruling at Kāśi, thus suggesting a connection between Kāśi and Videha.

The linear descent of the Ikṣvāku lineage may indicate a stable political system probably based on a developed agrarian economy, the existence of the state and an established monarchical system. This is of course clearly reflected in the *Rāmāyaṇa* where the kingdoms of Ayodhyā and Videha stand in contrast to the Daṇḍakāranya, Citrakūta and Kiṣkindhā where the technology is relatively primitive.[37] The contrast may well have been motivated in part by poetical fancy but the consistency with which it is adhered to in the many versions of the story would suggest that it carried some implicit notions of a technically more advanced society being associated with the *Sūryavaṃśa* lineage. It is also strange that the Puranic genealogy eliminates totally any reference to the *gaṇa-saṅgha* tribes and oligarchies in the regions adjoining Kośala and Videha and whose lineages are referred to at some length in Buddhist and Jaina sources. The only trace of any of these is the inclusion of the names Śākya, Sudodhana and Rāhula, towards the end of the Ikṣvāku lineage.[38] Curiously the Videha lineage also seems to terminate with Sīradhvaja (Janaka), after which the record of descent shifts to his brother Kuśadhvaja who is associated not with Videha but with Kāśi. Was this an indication that, after Sīradhvaja, Videha also changed to a *gaṇa-saṅgha* form of government? Buddhist literature mentions Videha as one of the two important principalities of the Vajjian confederacy.[39]

The connection between Videha and Kāśi is also referred to in the *Jātaka* literature.[40] This would also point to the *Purāṇa* recording only those lineages in the middle Ganges valley which conformed to a monarchical system of government. The early termination of the lineage of Vaiśāli in the *Purāṇa* may reflect the change which occurred here from monarchy to oligarchy.[41]

The *Candravaṃśa* lineage presents a different pattern of descent and has a wide geographical background. Unlike the *Sūryavaṃśa* it records the descent of all the sons and each forms a segment of the main lineage. The migrations of the various segments take them over a large geographical region including central, western and northern India. Of the sons of Purūravas the eldest, Ayus, inherits Pratiṣṭhāna (Prayāg) and two others rule from Kanyākubja and from Kāśi. The latter two gradually merge into the first. The main line goes from Āyus to his eldest son Nahuṣa and again to his eldest son Yayāti. At this point the listing by primogeniture is dropped and the segments are recorded. Yayāti has five sons of which the eldest Yadu and the youngest Pūru are the most important. Their lineages are described at length and form the major part of the *Candravaṃśa*. Pūru inherits the *madhya-deśa* (the core and hence the most important part of the kingdom) from his father and since this is contrary to the rule of primogeniture a myth is invented to explain how this happened.[42] The Yadus move to the south-west and from this point onwards there is a considerable migration of segments in various directions. One line of Yadus via Satvata, Andhaka and Vṛṣṇi migrate to Dvārkā in Kathiawar. Another line through the Haihayas (whose descendants included the five Tālajhanga lineages) settles along the Narmadā valley (with possible branches going up to Mālwā) and finally spreads through central India to the mid-Ganges valley where its advance is stopped by Sagara of the *Sūryavaṃśa* lineage. A third group taking the name of Cedi and Vidarbha migrate to those regions (Bundelkhand and Berar). The main line of the Pūrus were more sedentary and remained in *madhya-deśa*. There seems however to have been a break in the main line after Bharata who is said to have adopted the son of Bharadvāja.[43] Was this perhaps a reference to the amalgamation of tribes in the formation of the Kuru-Pañcāla *janapadas*? The only migrations are to contiguous areas by the descendants of Hastin who founded the states of North Pañcāla and South Pañcāla. The main line rules at Hastināpur and after the Mahābhārata war and the flooding of the city moves south to Kauśāmbi.

Of the segments descended from the other sons of Yayāti, Anu and Druhyu move northwards, and the Turvaśa fairly soon merge with the Pūru line. The Druhyu are associated with Gandhāra and the line terminates within a few generations. The Anu continue for longer and divide in an interesting fashion. One branch, the Uśinara move to the Punjab and Sind and their descendants are the Yaudheyas, the Krimi, the Ambaṣṭha and the Śivi. The latter in turn give rise to the Sauvīras, Kekeyas and Madras. The other branch of the Anus descended from Titikṣu move into eastern India (carefully by-passing the middle Ganges valley) and are known as the Aṅga, Vaṅga, Kaliṅga, Puṇḍra and Suhma. The latter seems almost obviously an attempt on the part of the Puranic genealogists to fit eastern India into the main genealogical pattern, as indeed the distribution of the Haihaya lineages in central India seems to be motivated by the same concern.

The *Candravaṃśa* genealogy is less a listing of kings and more a description of tribes and clans. Many of the names are of tribes and were later bequeathed to the regions where the tribes settled. The *Sūryavaṃśa* list in comparison has far fewer tribal and place names. The *Candravaṃśa* therefore includes references to the migration of tribes. The major migrations are those of the Pauravas and Yādavas. There is mention of at least one conflict between them concerning the acquisition of Magadha where ultimately the descendant of the Paurava lineage succeeds with the establishment of Vṛhadratha as the founder of the kingdom of Magadha. On the whole however the areas settled by the two main lines are distinct and the conflicts among them are few.

The nuclear area is that of *madhya-deśa*. The expansion is along the rivers and more so in the fringe uplands along the Yamuna from where the migrations move out in widening circles to the north-west, the west and the south-west. The north-east remains walled off, presumably because the Ikṣvākus were settled in that area. The Haihayas, incorporating the Surasena, the Tālajhanga and the Cedi are ultimately associated with the Narmada region. The Mādhavas and the Satvatas span out into the Andhaka and the Vṛṣṇi who are finally based in Kathiawar. The Mahabhoja are also associated with the Andhaka but their location seems to have been a little closer to the Malwa region. In areas where cultivable land is not freely available (and this would be the case in elevated regions of low scrub) to those who could claim it by rights of lineage or kinship, there would either be a redistribution of land which may involve a conflict or else the need for junior segments to settle new lands. The central Indian region would tend to see quick migrations whereas the Doāb would encourage more sedentary groups with smaller geographical extensions. The Pūru lineage remains remarkably compact until the splitting off into the Ajāmīdha, the Dvimīdha and the two Pañcāla segments which seem to suggest a major change (perhaps technological) or a population pressure requiring expansion into contiguous areas. Elsewhere I have suggested that this may have coincided with the introduction of iron in the western Ganges valley.[44] In the case of the Pūrus the area of migration is relatively limited and it is possible that the area was settled by branches of the main lineage. In the case of all those claiming (ultimately) Yādava descent, the distribution is so wide that one is led to believe that some of the central Indian lineages associated with the Haihayas were perhaps not actual segments of the Yādava lineage but were separate groups who were either conquered or else were later integrated into the Yādava lineage in a period when such integrations became a means of acquiring social status. This part of the Yādava lineage could then be seen as an attempt to include central India into the political geography of northern India. The segmentary lineage system would then apply more to the other lineages of Yādava descent than of those from the Haihayas.

A comparison of the Pūru lineage as given in the *Purāṇa* with those of the *Mahābhārata*[45] again suggests that either the epic has telescoped the generations or else the *Purāṇa* has conflated them. The list from the *Purāṇa* is more detailed and carries a number of intermediate names. Telescoping would be expected in the literary text where the tendency would be to record only the important names. The order of names is also not identical. But the main discrepancy is a block of names which, as a group, occur earlier in the epic list. This again is not a major difference.

The Yādava-vaṃśa presents certain features of what has been

called the segmentary lineage.[46] This is essentially confined to societies at a tribal level for it is absent both in small bands as well as in a state system. Its main thrust is predatory organization in conflict with other tribes. It is most suited to tribes which are both pastoralists and agriculturalists but not advanced agriculturalists. The transition to the formation of a state and the decline of the tribal structure leads to the collapse of the system. Tribal segments such as those of the Haihaya and the Andhaka and Vṛṣṇi tend to be equal in status with political and economic autonomy. The legends interspersed in the genealogy suggest that leadership remained in the segment. Thus the authority of Kṛṣṇa Vāsudeva is largely restricted to the segments relating to the Andhaka and Vṛṣṇi and does not effectively extend to those of the Haihayas. Relationships between the groups are very often determined by lineage links—as is evident from the story of the Syamantaka jewel.[47] The Satvata segment is more closely related to the Vṛṣṇi both in the lineage and in the narrative and this permits of easier political consolidation and closer sociability. In situations of conflict segment alignments are carefully balanced and this is reflected in the participation of the lineage in the Mahābhārata war. The strength of the lineage depends on the number of segments identifying with it. The pattern of the segmentary lineage system is one of expansion outwards and the conquest and assimilation of other tribes which requires the continual adjustment of new tribes in the lineage. In theory therefore the lineage has a wide geographical reach. The conquests of the five Tālajhangha segments of the Haihayas, in the Narmada valley against the Nāgas, in central India and in the middle Ganges valley against the *Sūryavaṃśa*, is eventually contained by Sagara of the latter lineage.[48] One of the most remarkable features of the Yādava lineage is precisely its wide geographical reach, both in terms of segments distributed over northern India, which according to the *Purāṇa* are ultimately traced back to the Yādava ancestry, as well as the number of tribes and royal families in the peninsula which in the historical period claimed Yādava connections.[49] Clearly many of these were tribes adopted into the Yādava lineage. As against this the Pūru lineage remains noticeably compact.

The distribution of the segments suggests a period prior to the emergence of stable kingdoms and the political forms would be more in the nature of chiefdoms. The economy appears to have been pastoral-cum-agrarian with references to the tending of large herds of cattle. Both the search for fresh pasture lands as well as potentially cultivable lands would lead to migrations. It is perhaps worth noting that the distribution of the lineages follows river valleys and areas of optimum elevation and fertility for cultivation, such as the west bank of the Yamuna, the Malwa plateau, the Banas valley, Gujarat, Kathiawar and the Narmada valley. It reflects a period of intrusion into new areas, some of which may have already been inhabited although probably by people with a more primitive technology. Inter-segment conflict is therefore reduced since there is an outlet in migration. Political consolidation becomes possible through identity with a lineage without the need for an over-arching state.

With the increasing adoption of agriculture and the emergence of sedentary societies the rights over land assume greater proportions in social and political life. The records of status groups then primarily pertain to recording which families had rights over which land; the name of the land owning clan and the geographical region of its ownership become the prerequisites of historical and legal records. This more or less conforms to the kind of evidence contained in what we have called the second section of the genealogy. In a society moving from a fairly flexible tribal organization to an agrarian structure incorporating caste, records of kinship would have to be kept since kinship relations among exogamous and endogamous groups would have to be known. Cutting across the kinship line was the notion of ritual ranking (*varṇa*). The sanctioning of the rank was dependent on proving a kinship connection. Thus the Puranic genealogies listing lineages came to be seen both as historical records preserving information on the continuity of succession, as well as socially necessary documents establishing a community's roots in the past. More narrowly, they also become the basis for legal claims apart from providing status and antiquity to those seeking such status. The sanction of rank could always be drawn upon by new groups who had acquired political power but lacked the appropriate social rank. Thus the genealogies were not limited to actual lineage relations of the past but also included the listing of those who had successfully 'latched onto' a lineage and thereby succeeded in claiming status and power.

It has also been suggested that the segmentary lineage system allows for the easy accumulation of cults and deities. The cult of every segment is sooner or later incorporated into the all-encompassing religion of the lineage. On an impressionistic view at least it would certainly seem that Bhāgavatism, so closely associated with the Yādavas, was an assimilative religion facilitating the process of absorbing cults and deities. Taking this argument a step further one might suggest that the epic of the *Candravaṃśa*, the *Mahābhārata*, in which the Yādavas play the role of one of the protagonists but at the wings, could perhaps be regarded as a compendium of the many bardic epics and fragments of the various Yādava segments, and other *Candravaṃśa* descent groups.

Since the movements of the lineages are recorded in the form of genealogies there is a time dimension as well. Pargiter has computed ninety-five generations from Manu to the Mahābhārata war.[50] In the first decade of generations, Videha and Ayodhyā are established, the sons of Yayāti are aligned in various directions and the Haihayas have branched off from the main Yādava line. The second decade sees their positions in the north-west and in eastern India. In the fourth decade the Kanyakubja line comes to an end. The Cedis break away from the Yādavas and the Druhyu and Turvaśa lines are terminated in the fifth decade. The Pauravas split into the Dvimīḍha, Ajāmīḍha and the Pañcālas in the sixth decade. In the seventh decade the Cedi line comes to an end, the Andhaka and the Vṛṣṇi become prominent and the lineages of the north-western Ānavas are terminated. The next decade sees the establishment of Vṛhadratha at Magadha and the emergence of the Kurus in the Paurava lineage. In the last decade the major event is the war.

The *Viṣṇu Purāṇa* lists the lineages as *vaṃśam rājñyām* but some of these are ranked as distinctly low in the *smṛti* literature. Thus the Āndhras, the Satvatas and the Ambaṣṭhas are placed by Manu in the category of *Śūdras*.[51] The Āndhras are particularly despicable even though they are a respected clan in the *Purāṇa*. Pāṇini refers to the Andhaka and the Vṛṣṇi as being of the *kṣatriya gotra* and having a *saṅgha* form of government.[52] Other groups mentioned in this context include the Bharatas (although the Kurus are associated with a kingdom), the Yaudheyas, the

Daśārha and the Sātvata.[53] The distribution is therefore in northern and western India and includes some of the segments of the *Candravaṃśa*. The *Mahābhārata* describes the Anus as the ancestors of the *mlecchas* and the Yavanas (who are also *vrātya-kṣatriyas*) as the descendants of the Turvaśa.[54] It would seem that these groups ranked as *sankīrna-jātis* (mixed castes) in the *dharma-śāstras* were politically important and had been inducted into the *jāti* structure since their *śūdra* status indicates a *varṇa* ranking. A lineage system based on a segmentary structure would have facilitated this process. The genealogies therefore also reflect the transition from *jana* to *jāti* since the reference to them as *ksatriyas* was a concession to their political power and the conferring of legitimacy. Thus the spread of a social system was also being recorded. Assignment to a particular lineage would probably have depended on geographical proximity, the political authority and status of the new group and the loyalty and closeness to the group of the *brāhmaṇ* who was making the lineage link.

Not surprisingly, therefore, this section of the genealogy also refers, although somewhat obliquely, to the distribution of priestly families and their links with the various segments. The most powerful of these families were the Bhṛgus and the Vasiṣṭhas.[55] The relationship between the Haihayas and the Gujarat Bhṛgus for example, even if highly exaggerated, still suggests close ties. The genealogy therefore becomes a record of both the *kṣatriya* family, using *kṣatriya* in the sense of clans owning land and moving towards the creation of states, and motivated *brāhmaṇs* involved in the acculturation of these clans.

The problem of legitimacy can be seen not only in the discrepancy between the Puranic lineage and the caste ranking of these in the *dharmaśāstra* literature, but in two other areas as well. One is the concern for primogeniture and the second is the almost inadvertent references to what appear to be non-patrilineal systems. Primogeniture refers both to the eldest son as well as to the rights of the senior-most descent group in a segmentary system. The right of succession to the eldest son is claimed in a variety of sources.[56] It is applied relatively easily in the *Sūryavaṃśa*. That there were some problems with primogeniture in the *Candravaṃśa* is indicated by the legends interposed in the genealogies relating to the succession by the younger brother, where, in each case, elaborate justifications had to be invented for this seeming departure from the norm, as for example, in the story of Yayāti and the succession of his youngest son Pūru rather than the eldest Yadu,[57] or the story of Devāpi and Śantanu[58] or indeed the central events in the two epics which revolve around the attempted supersession of the eldest son. Primogeniture is closely associated with societies where land rights have been established and ambiguities relating to this form of succession would suggest a flexible situation in relation to land rights. Primogeniture has also been seen as necessary in a situation where there is a divergent inheritance/descent system such as the establishment of a patrilineal system in a matrilineal region.[59] In the matrilineal system, lateral succession would be acceptable and the ousting of the elder brother may carry a memory of such a succession.

It is perhaps worth noting that there appear to be traces of matrilineal, or at least non-patrilineal, elements in the *Candravaṃśa*. Ilā, the ancestress of the lineage, was regarded as sufficiently unconventional for the *Viṣṇu Purāṇa* to have to provide an explanation. Was this a reflection of the integrating of a matrilineal descent system, where the original ancestress could not be replaced by a male ancestor, and had to be retained in the story and, therefore, an explanation was required for an audience more familiar with the patrilineal system? Incest prohibitions include the younger sister of the wife and this may in part explain the problem which Yayāti had with his wife Śarmiṣṭha when he begat children on Devayānī, although they were not actual sisters but had once been as close as sisters.[60] The major evidence however which has been frequently cited is that of cross-cousin marriages among the lineages. These have recently been collated and discussed in detail.[61] It has been argued that most of these references come from texts which have originated in south India or Ceylon or which were re-edited and compiled in the southern region. Therefore the incidence of cross-cousin marriage, which is characteristic of the Dravidian kinship system and therefore quite normal to these regions, was introduced into the texts. The frequency of this form of marriage in the *Bhāgavata Purāṇa* can be explained by the text having a southern location, and the references in Buddhist literature are due to its having been edited in Ceylon. Or, alternatively, mention is made of this form of marriage in relation to Gujarat and western India, which also subscribed to this custom, being included in the area of the Dravidian kinship system. In *dharmaśāstras* cross-cousin marriage is prohibited except to the people of the south where it is recognized as customary practice and therefore legal.[62] In the *Viṣṇu Purāṇa*, the Vṛṣṇis are associated with cross-cousin marriage[63] and this has been explained as due to their location in western India.[64]

In the unexpurgated version of the *Mahābhārata* there is a reference to matrilineal succession in the land of the Āraṭṭas associated with the Vahikas on the north-western borders of the Indian sub-continent.[65] This certainly would not come into the geographical area demarcated for the normal practice of cross-cousin marriage and matrilineal descent. There are two other practices which are sometimes suggestive of matrilineal societies and these are referred to fairly frequently in connection with the *Candravaṃśa*. One of these is bride-price which is essential to the Asura form of marriage (one of the eight forms recognized by the *dharmaśāstras*) and the other is forceable abduction or the Rākṣas form of marriage.[66] Of the bride-prices mentioned the most interesting was the demand from Ricika of a thousand white horses each with one black ear for the hand of Satyavatī the daughter of Gadhi.[67] The event is followed by the narration of a story involving Satyavatī and her mother in which there is a veiled reference to the rivalry between the son and his mother's brother. Interestingly, Satyavatī is the mother of Jamadagni and the grandmother of Parśurāma. What is significant is that the *Purāṇas* generally associate the Yādava lineages with cross-cousin marriage (irrespective of the provenance of the text). Whereas there is no conclusive evidence on this point, it would certainly seem that the Yādava lineage retained some features of matrilineal descent.

The discussion on the possibility of matrilineal descent is often vitiated by the notion that there was an evolutionary development from matriliny to patriliny, or alternatively that there has been a consistent practice of either one or the other. That the two systems can be juxtaposed and maintain separate practices or can act on each other and can modify each other, is also a possibility.[68] Perhaps the Yādava lineages retained matriliny for a longer period in western India than elsewhere and that both systems continued to exist at various levels in different parts of western India at this time, if the genealogical section of the

Purāṇa is seen as a reflection of the social systems of the period. It may also be suggested that forms of descent may vary among different strata in the same society. Thus if some of the elite follow a patrilineal system but matriliny is common in the rest of society then there may well be traces of the latter in the former.[69] The gradual erosion of cross-cousin marriage would be expected not merely because of the increasing influence of the patrilineal society but also because migrating groups require a wider network of kinship. Interestingly, the occurrence of cross-cousin marriage is most frequent in those Yādava segments which are located in Saurāṣṭra suggesting that this was the area of concentrated settlement. The system weakens as the segments migrate away from it. If the geographically more distant segments were not originally of the lineage but were 'latched on' to the lineage then their social system would have currency. Saurāṣṭra may have retained the custom, whereas the assimilation of tribes to the east with the Yādava lineage would have brought in those who were not familiar with the custom. It is not surprising that the Vṛṣṇi and Andhaka are referred to as *vrātya* in the *Mahābhārata*[70] or that the inhabitants of Saurāṣṭra are described as *ṣankīrṇa-jātis*.[71] One of the features often associated with matrilineal descent is absent, namely, the use of matronymics. This is noticeable in view of the fact that the *vaṃśas* of the teachers in the *Bṛhadāraṇyaka Upaniṣad* list forty sages with matronymics.[72] The association of matronymics with western India is however attested to in later historical sources with reference to the names of some of the kings of the Sātavāhana dynasty.[73]

The *Sūryavaṃśa* shows hardly any trace of such customs. Yet, the Buddhist literature of the post-Buddhist period when speaking of the origin of the tribes of the middle Ganges plain and the Himalayan foothills, has unmistakable references to the matrilineal system. We are told that many of these tribes, e.g. the Śākyas and Licchavis, originated from Ikṣvāku lineages (the term *Sūryavaṃśa* is not used), generally associated with Kāśi, and migrated north where they settled.[74] The references to sibling incest among the ancestors of the tribe and the custom of cross-cousin marriage points to matrilineal influences. The *Mahāvaṃśa* version may well have been influenced by the prevailing social system in Ceylon. But the same features are to be found in the Chinese version of the *rājavaṃśa*, or the genealogy of the Śākyas.[75] Later historical references to the genealogy of the Licchavis describes them as *kṣatriyas* of the *vasiṣṭha gotra*, as of the Sūryavaṃśa, and their descent is traced from the Puranic Ikṣvāku lineage—even though they are excluded from mention in the *Purāṇas*. The consistency with which matrilineal features are associated with these tribes in the Buddhist tradition suggests that their social organization may have had to do with a matrilineal structure and that this cannot be explained only as due to the imposition of a southern social structure onto these texts. If this is so, then this may have been an additional reason for excluding these tribes from the Puranic genealogies. Their social structure and mythology, as evident from Buddhist texts, being so markedly non-patrilineal, it would not have been so easy to explain it away as in the relatively lighter traces of the same in the *Candravaṃśa* lineages. The Buddhist genealogies indicate an Ikṣvāku origin for these tribes but make no attempt to try and associate them with the Ikṣvāku lineages. This association, where it occurs, comes from the later non-Buddhist literature of Nepal, as in the case of the Licchavis.[76]

The termination of the second section of the genealogy revolves around the Mahābhārata war. This was inevitably a turning point in social and political life, for its immediate motivation is the claim to land rights, and not merely the claim to ownership of land but the right to rule. The monarchical system had by now come to stay and this was one of the crises in the system. Monarchy involved the right to enforce law and order and the right to collect revenue, as the many explanations on the origin of government indicate.[77] It involved therefore much greater control over the economy and political authority. The law of primogeniture as applied to kinship was stressed in order to prevent frequent battles over succession. Legitimate succession was dependent on seniority of birth and purity of blood, a deviation from either having to be justified by a myth. That the reference to the war in the genealogical record has a strong symbolic content is suggested from the fact that the two contenders for the right to rule the kingdom, the Kauravas and the Pāṇḍavas, are neither of them related by blood to the Pūru lineage. The lineage as a patrilene ends with Bhīṣma. Both Dhṛtarāṣṭra and Pāṇḍu are of lesser stock, claiming their connection with the Pūru lineage via their grandmother Satyavatī, who was associated with the fisher-folk. The legitimacy of their connection with the Pūru lineage is sometimes defended by reference to the custom of *niyoga*: that Kṛṣṇa Dvaipāyana was a half-brother to Vicitravīrya. However, it is significant that he was a half-brother on his mother's side and could not be regarded as a *sapiṇḍa*.

The third section of the genealogy lays less emphasis on lineages (*vaṃśa*) and speaks more often of kings (*bhūpāla*). The centre of interest shifts to Magadha which by the middle of the first millennium B.C. was emerging as the pre-eminent kingdom of northern India. Doubtless, hindsight on the part of the authors of the Puranic genealogies must also have accounted for this shift in geographical area. Dynasties are mentioned by name, in many cases the kings of each dynasty are listed and in some *Purāṇas* (such as *Vāyu* and *Matsya*) the regnal years of individual kings are given. Clearly the interest is different from that of the earlier section. Regnal years and the time-span of individual dynasties gave the impression of greater precision (whether accurate or not) and provided better data for historical accounting. Many of the dynasties are historically authenticated. The dramatic use of changing from the past tense to the future provides an excellent device for indicating change on a bigger scale. However, the prophetic form of the genealogy was not only to suggest a time-marker but also to bestow distinction on the authors and keepers of the tradition who could claim thereby that they could foresee the future.

The stability of the state as a form of political organization was well-established by the time of the Mauryas. Such states relied less on the charisma of ritual and traditional sanctions and more on the mechanics of administration and political organization. It was also a period which saw the ascendencies of the heterodoxies. Legitimacy was based on political strength and not on lineage connections or, as stated in the *Purāṇa*, property alone confers rank, the earth is venerated only for its mineral resources and the strongest rules.[78] None of the major dynasties claimed to be *kṣatriyas* and yet the legitimacy of their rule was not doubted. The *Purāṇa* when referring to these kings expresses what it regards as the decline of society by describing it as the coming of the *kaliyuga*. The kings are of *śūdra* origin as is clearly stated for the Nandas and implied for the Mauryas.[79] Even the Śuṅga dynasty (elsewhere claiming to be of *brāhmaṇ* origin) introduces a name such as Pulindaka in its list of kings.[80] The Āndhras again are of low origin where the term Bhritya is literally taken to be a servant in the text.[81] *Brāhmaṇs* as kings seem to be disapproved of since this would be contrary to *varṇa* rules. The picture depicted in this section continues to get more and more depressing with various references to dynasties of *śūdra, mleccha* and other castes coming to power and ousting the *āryas*. There will be a widespread rejection of *kṣatriya* values by these kings we are told. Ultimately, however, the Kalkin *avatāra* of Viṣṇu will restore order and start a new *kritayuga*.

The first millennium A.D. saw the increasing emergence of states in the form of kingdoms and the gradual decline and extinction of tribal groups. Many of the states emerged from erstwhile tribal areas and the ruling elite sought to strengthen its political authority by associating itself with the dominant cultural tradition as expressed in Sanskritic culture. One of the means of doing this would be the acquisition of a high status lineage. The dynasties in the third section of the genealogy being of low status would not have been very useful. Inevitably therefore the links were sought with the *kṣatriya vaṃśas* of the second section of the genealogy. This process was emphasized in the political decentralization of the post-Gupta period. The social insecurity of *sāmanta* families scrambling for independent status and the frontier psychology of those moving into new lands and claiming rights over these lands, gave rise to the need for the recording of genealogies, the validating of family connections and the legitimizing of new royalty. For all of this the second section of the genealogy came in very useful, particularly with Sanskritization emphasizing the *varṇa* system. The tradition was now recorded in the *Purāṇas* which facilitated its use. Since the lineage links were with the second section, the third section could not be up-dated. It was more appropriate for each family to maintain its individual *vaṃśāvali*, indicating its origins and including the historically more authentic events since its rise to power. As semi-legal documents it was also necessary that separate and independent charters be maintained by each family.

Furthermore, the *Purāṇas* were by now sacred texts and obvious interpolations could not therefore be permitted.

It may be suggested that the genealogies in the *Purāṇas* were constructed on a careful structural base in the period when the Puranic tradition was recorded in the form of the *mahāpurāṇas*, i.e., in about the mid-first millennium A.D. The concern at that time was not necessarily with the authenticity of the descent and the lists of succession in the various dynasties but with collating genealogical fragments which could be used for providing social status to those groups which had come into positions of authority by the early centuries A.D. In a society which had accepted the *varṇa* system, adequate social status meant *kṣatriya* status. The genealogies were therefore constructs providing *kṣatriya* status to a large number of tribes or castes who had produced ruling families. To that extent the genealogies represent the view of the dominant castes of mid-first millennium A.D. looking back on what they came to believe was their social history. It was possible now for any ruling family to pick up a connection with this vast network of lineages covering virtually every area of the northern part of the sub-continent. The antecedents were now organized and functional. Within the construct of the genealogy the kinship relations may have been fictional but the incorporation of the lineages and their geographical location do appear to reflect some historical authenticity. Thus the genealogies should be seen as an attempt to plot the settling of lineages in various areas at a point in time when they were moving towards forming states. State-formation seems to be a concern of some significance to the genealogist (though perhaps subconsciously) as the identification of a lineage, and this is more apparent in the third section. Thus the Ābhīras are mentioned only when they establish a kingdom and their equally if not more prestigious contemporaries, the Mālavas and Arjunāyanas, are omitted. The pre-condition of monarchy for the use of such genealogies is self-evident. Families claiming royal status would be far more in need of genealogical validation than a politically more diffuse system such as government by an oligarchy or rudimentary republics.

We have attempted to suggest in this paper that three types of information can be gathered from the *vaṃśānucarita* sections of the *Purāṇas*. There is first of all the geographical distribution of lineages. Some are relatively sedentary such as the Ikṣvāku in Kośala and Videha and the early Pūrus in the Doāb. Others tend to migrate and fan out as for example in the extensive network of the Yādava lineages in western and central India and the less extensive network of the Ānavas. One possible means of cross-checking these settlements would be to try and correlate them with the archaeological cultures of the area. Such an attempt has been made elsewhere,[82] working on the hypothesis that the Late Harappan and Ochre Colour Pottery cultures may represent the early settlements of the Pūru lineage in the Doāb and the Indo-Gangetic divide and that the Painted Grey Ware culture represents the period after the emergence of the Kuru and Pañcāla lineages; the distribution of the Yādava lineages may be correlated with the Black and Red Ware cultures. Unfortunately no definite correlation can be worked out, partially because the chronology of the lineages is unclear from the texts. A convincing correlation would therefore be extremely useful in calculating the chronological bracket of the lineages.

The second type of information pertains to social structure. The early Pūru and Ikṣvāku lineages are of unilineal descent based on exogamous patrilines. (Although the evidence from Buddhist sources may indicate the existence of other patterns in the region.) The Yādava lineages on the other hand appear to conform more to the segmentary lineage system and the segments associated with western India carry traces of matrilineal forms. The major problem in this investigation is whether the lineages were descent groups consanguinially related, or groups which had over the years been assimilated into earlier lineages. Where otherwise low status groups are given *kṣatriya* status in the genealogy, it may be seen as a successful social improvement of such groups.

The third category of information concerns economic and political status. A distinction can be suggested between the pastoral-agricultural societies of western and central India and the more advanced agricultural societies of the Doāb and the middle Ganges valley. The latter suggests stable agriculture and the establishment of the state. The accounting of dynasties coincides with the rise of Magadha as an important state in northern India. The genealogies would appear to record the movement from tribal and oligarchic forms to the more complex monarchical states.

One of the problems which has confused the study of these genealogies has been the attempt to equate them with Āryans, Dravidians, Mundas and the like, on the assumption that the *vaṃśas* were distinct ethnic groups with primarily ethnic identities which were being recorded. It is essential to keep in mind that these genealogies were compiled many centuries after the events which they purport to have taken place and should therefore be seen as the historical appreciation of a later age of what it believed were its earlier antecedents.

REFERENCES AND NOTES

1. The most detailed of these was the study of S.N. Pradhan, *Chronology of Ancient India*, (Calcutta 1927), until the very recent publication of R. Morton Smith, *Dates and Dynasties in Earliest India* (Delhi, 1975). The latter had already published some of his results in the form of articles, in *JAOS* and other journals. One of the major drawbacks in attempting a chronological reconstruction is the absence of critical editions of the *Purāṇas*. Morton Smith has attempted such an exercise in his study but has limited it to collating and commenting on the variants in the genealogical material from the *Purāṇas*.
2. The general points discussed in the next few paragraphs relating to the use of genealogies are drawn mainly from anthropological work carried out in the last few decades on the function of genealogies in various cultures. In this connection mention may be made of the following studies, E.E. Evans Pritchard, The *Nuer*, (Oxford 1940); J. Middleton and D. Tait, *Tribes Without Rulers*, (London, 1958); J. Goody, *Succession to High Office*, (Cambridge, 1966); M. Fortes, *Kinship and the Social Order* (Chicago, 1969).
3. The term 'lineage' will occur frequently in this paper and therefore requires definition. Lineage is the unilineal descent, actual or fictional, claimed by a group. It consists of a group of unilineal kin, has a recognized system of authority, has rights and duties, carries a name and may be divided into segments, where each segment takes on the character of a lineage.
4. J. Goody, *Succession to High Office*, pp. 1-8.
5. J. Vansina, *The Oral Tradition*, (London, 1965), p. 102 ff; P. Nilson, *Primitive Time Reckoning*, (London, 1937), p. 99 ff.
6. A.M. Shah and R.G. Shroff, 'The Vahavanca Barots of Gujerat: a case of genealogists and mythographers', *Journal of American Folk-Lore*, (Philadelphia, 1958), 71, pp. 246-76.
7. M. Noth, *A History of Pentateuchal Traditions*, (New Jersy, 1972), pp. 214-19.
8. The Bharatas are referred to in *Rg Veda* III.53; III.33; VII.8; VII.33; VI.16; III.23. The pūrus are mentioned in I.108; VII.18; VII.8; VII.96; 1.59; I.130; I.108; IV.21, IV.38; VI.46; VII.5; VII.19.

9. *Gopatha Brāhmaṇa* L.2.9, *Kaṭhaka Samhitā,* X.6; *Kauśītaki Upaniṣad* IV.1. Videha is referred to in the *Śatapatha Brāhmaṇa* L.4.1.10 in connection with the legend of Videgha Māthava.
10. As for example in the *Bṛhadāraṇyaka Upaniṣad,* II.6; IV.6; .VI.5.
11. U.N. Ghoshal, *Beginnings of Indian Historiography,* (Calcutta, 1944), p. 6.
12. J. Brough, *The Early Brahmanical System of Gotra and Pravara,* (Cambridge, 1953), pp. 1-4.
13. Pāṇini refers to *kṣatriya gotras,* II.4.58..
14. e.g. *Aśvalāyana Śrauta-sūtra* II.6.10.15, *Āpastambha Śrauta-sūtra* XXIV.5.10.
15. One of the most interesting legends suggestive of this process is the story of Śunaḥśepa *Aitareya Brāhmaṇa* VII.13.
16. It is useful to relate the Purāṇic genealogies with those occurring in the epics. The genealogies of the Ikṣvākus as given in the *Rāmāyaṇa,* I.69 and I.70 differ somewhat from those of the *Purāṇas* as also do the Aila genealogies as given in the Ādi Parvan of the *Mahābhārata.*
17. Pliny, *Natural History,* (New York, 1962), VI.21.4-5.
18. *Vāyu Purāṇa* 42.137-48; *Padmá Purāṇa* V.1.27.
19. *Atharvaveda* V.3.5.7; *Śatapatha Brāhmana* V.3.1.5; XV.2.1 V.22.14 *taittīrya Samhitā* IV.5.2 grants inviolability to the *sūta (namo sūtāya ahantyāya.)*
20. *Vāyu* I.31-32; *Manu* X.11. The term *sūta* came to mean a charioteer and his status was low.
21. III.1.
22. I.10-33 ff.
23. T. Jacobsen, *The Sumerian King-List,* (Chicago, 1939), p. 57 ff. The god Enki, the deity of the powerful city of Eridu, also takes the form of a fish to save mankind and, after the deluge, the list of kings commences. The syntactical and stylistic form of the ante-diluvian king list is different from the rest and therefore it has been suggested that this was a later addition. The astronomical figures for the regnal years of the earlier kings of the ante-diluvian period are in contrast to the more acceptable figures of later periods. The motivation for the Sumerian king-list may have been the political revival under Utu-hegal who was celebrating his victory in *c.* 2400 B.C. The number of ante-diluvian kings varies from seven to ten. In the *Purāṇas* the genealogy is linked with the seventh Manu and we are told that there will be a total of fourteen Manavavatāras. It is curious that in Indian mythology a deity in the form of a fish as a mythological symbol of significance occurs only in association with the Flood. It was not therefore a frequent item in the list of Indian religious symbols. Where it does occur frequently is in the Harappan pictograms, but in later iconography it is not so common. The Sumerian genealogies also inter-link descent groups with legends and narratives. There seems to be a deliberate attempt at organizing the material which may of course have stemmed from a common original. Similarities between the Sumerian and Indian material could be accidental, but the emphasis on the Flood and the difference between the ante-diluvian and post-diluvian records does suggest a nagging sense of connection.
24. *Viṣṇu Purāṇa* IV.1.
25. S. Bhattacharya, *The Indian Theogony,* (Cambridge, 1970), p. 95.
26. F.E. Pargiter, *The Ancient Indian Historical Tradition,* (Oxford, 1922), p. 146.

27. IV.1.168. Discussed by V.S. Agrawal, *India as Known to Pāṇini*, (Lucknow, 1953), pp. 427-28.
28. Pargiter, op. cit, p. 89.
29. *Viṣṇu Purāṇa* IV.16.1.
30. Ibid., IV.21.1.
31. Ibid., IV.24.28ff.
32. Pargiter, op. cit., p. 50 ff.
33. S.B. Das Gupta, *Obscure Religious Cults*, (Calcutta, 1946), p. 235 ff.
34. This has been effectively demonstrated for the Homeric epics in M.I. Finley, *The World of Odysseus*, (Harmondsworth, 1962), and G.S. Kirk, *Homer and the Epic*, (Cambridge, 1965).
35. The geographical focus of the Ikṣvāku lineage is in the main confined to the middle Ganges valley. The extension goes to Daṇḍakāraṇya and no further. There is no trace of the exile of Rāma to the southern part of the sub-continent or any links with regions that far. It may therefore be said in passing that the genealogical evidence would tend to support those who argue that the events narrated in the *Rāmāyaṇa* probably took place in central India, at least when the story was first put together.
36. *Rāmāyaṇa* I.70-71, The Genealogies occur in Book I, the Bālakāṇḍa, which is believed to be a later addition.
37. Dev Raj Chanana, *The Spread of Agriculture in Northern India* (As depicted in the *Rāmāyaṇa* of Valmiki), (Delhi, 1964).
38. *Viṣṇu Purāṇa*, IV.22.
39. *Majjhima Nikāya* I.225. Dr. B.D. Chattopadhyaya has drawn my attention to this point.
40. *Suruci Jātaka*, IV, no. 489.
41. Ibid., IV.1.18.
42. Ibid., IV.10.
43. Ibid., IV.19.
44. 'Puranic Lineages and Archaeological Cultures', *Puratattva*, no. 8, 1975, pp. 86-98. See also pp. 214-236 in this volume.
45. *Ādi Parvan*, 90 ff.
46. Marshall D. Sahlins, 'The Segmentary Lineage: an organisation of predatory expansion'. *American Anthropologist*, (Chicago, 1961), vol. 63, no. 2, pp. 332-45.
47. *Viṣṇu Purāṇa* IV.13.
48. According to the *Viṣṇu Purāṇa* (in what is obviously an anachronistic reference), Sagara is also said to have destroyed the Śakas, Yavanas, Kambojas, Paradas and Pahlavas, the foreign tribes who inhabited northern and western India. The location of these would be in accordance with the distribution of the Candravaṃśa lineage. Interestingly this event is also made the basis for explaining why these foreign tribes came to be regarded as *vrātya-kṣatriyas*.
49. B. Saletore, *Ancient Karnataka*, (Poona, 1936), pp. 245-47; P.B. Desai, *A History of Karnataka*, (Dharwar, 1970), pp. 112-13, 305.
50. Pargiter, op. cit., p. 144 ff.
51. *Manu*, X.23.
52. VI.2.34.

53. V.S. Agrawala, *India as Known to Pāṇini*, p. 445 ff.
54. *Ādi Parvan*, 80.1.ff.
55. Pargiter, op. cit., pp. 193 ff, 203 ff.
56. *Śatapatha Brāhmaṇa V.4.2.8; Arthasastra* 17.1ff.
57. *Viṣṇu Purāṇa* IV.10. See also the analysis of the myth in Georges Dumezil, *The Destiny of the Warrior*, (Chicago, 1970).
58. *Viṣṇu Purāṇa*, IV.20.
59. David Schneider and Kathlene Gough, *Matrilineal Kinship*, (Berkeley, 1974), p. 26 ff.
60. *Mahābhārata*, Ādi Parvan, 70-79; D. Schneider and K. Gough, op. cit., p. 453.
61. T. R. Trautmann 'Cross-cousin Marriage in Ancient North India' in T.R. Trautmann (ed.), *Kinship and History in South Asia*, (Michigan, 1974), p. 61 ff.
62. *Baudhāyana Dharma Sūtra* I.5.11.2; I.1.2.2.2-3.
63. IV.16.38-40.
64. Trautmann, op. cit., p. 65.
65. Karṇaparvan, VIII, 44-45.
66. Kane, *History of Dharmaśāstra*, (Poona 1941), II.1, pp. 517, 519.
67. *Viṣṇu Purāna* IV.7.
68. J. Goody, *Comparative Studies in Kinship*. (London, 1969), p. 133 ff.
69. The continued existence of these two systems is reflected in the social structure of the Mers of Saurashtra (H.H. Trivedi, *The Mers of Saurashtra*, Baroda 1961, p. 38 ff). The existing cross-cousin marriage has been adopted even by those lineages which claim Rajput origin and status and who believe themselves to have arrived relatively recently in Saurashtra. The kinship terminology is consistent with bilateral cross-cousin marriage and even where this marriage is not possible the terminology remains.
70. VII.143.15.
71. *Baudhāyana Dharmasūtra*, I.1.32-33.
72. II.6; IV 6; VI.5.
73. *Epigraphia Indica*, VIII, p. 60, 88; X. p. 108; XX. p. 6.
74. B.C. Law, *Kshatriya Clans in Buddhist India*, (Calcutta, 1922), p. 1 ff; *Papañca Sudani*, I.258. The origin of the Śākyas is described in the *Mahāvaṃśa*, II.1-24.
75. S. Beal, *Romantic History of Buddha*, (London, 1907), p. 18 ff.
76. E. Senart, *La Mahāvastu*, (Paris, 1882-97), I, pp. 283-300; D. Regmi, *Ancient Nepal*, (Calcutta, 1969), p. 65; Pasupati Inscription of Jayadeva, quoted in B.C. Law, *Kshatriya Clans in Buddhist India*, pp. 28-29, *Corpus Inscriptionum Indicarum*, III, (ed.) J.F. Fleet, pp. 133-36, 155.
77. *Śatapatha Brāhmaṇa*, XI.1.6.24; *Mahābhārata*, Śānti Parvan. 59.14-27.
78. *Viṣṇu Purāṇa*, IV.24.74-93.
79. Ibid., V.20' ff.
80. Ibid., V.35-36.
81. Ibid., V.43.
82. 'Puranic Lineages and Archaeological Cultures', *Puratattva*, no. 8, 1975.

The Scope and Significance of Regional History

I am indeed extremely grateful to the Punjab History Conference for this great honour which has been done me in asking me to preside over this session. I am only too well aware of my inexperience in the study of regional history and my inadequacies. I assume therefore that the decision symbolizes a policy of encouraging those of lesser experience to participate in the responsibilities of the profession. I am, therefore, doubly grateful for this gesture.

At a gathering such as this discussion naturally revolves around the study of regional history. I thought therefore that I would use this opportunity to place before you some of the problems which I have felt may have a relevance to this study. In many parts of the country regional history is being taught as an important segment of the history syllabus. As such, it merits the attention not only of the specialist in the region but also of historians working on other aspects of Indian history. I shall, in the course of what I have to say, refer to the history of the Punjab, not because of any expertise of my own on the subject but to derive the benefit of your expertise.

What I shall be saying is not out of any pretensions to specialization on the Punjab, but more in the spirit of placing before you the kinds of problems which I think we are now facing when we work on the history of a region. The substance of the problems would be the same for any region. Much of what I have to say is in the nature of hypotheses, initial to analyses. Perhaps in the working out of such hypotheses we may arrive at a clearer comprehension of the region and its history.

The initial interest in India in regional history grew out of nationalist historical writing. It was motivated to some extent by a search for new source materials, a search which has resulted

Address to Punjab History Conference, Patiala, 1976.

in an abundance of sources—archaeological, epigraphic, historical literature, religious literature, archival records and family papers—all of which have added to the body of information available on the history of many regions of the sub-continent. It is however at the interpretational level that the interest in regional history assumes greater historiographic potential, a potential with which we are perhaps as yet not altogether fully familiar.

The historical interest in regions such as south India, Bengal and Maharashtra, coincided with the new sources providing information particularly on what came to be regarded as the inter-empire periods of Indian history, or, alternatively, complementing the information available from records outside the region. It began to be seen that the supposed 'dark ages' stressed by the historiography of the nineteenth century were far from dark and that the lacunae could be eliminated by using local source material. Further, that it was in these inter-imperial periods that the nature of historical change at the regional level could be seen more clearly. Regional history thus became a corrective to the earlier tendency to generalize about the subcontinent from the perspective of the Ganges Valley.

The spread of nationalism into the various states increased the interest in regional history. This brought its own perspective with the emergent professional groups who participated in the national movement and at the same time sought for an identity from the past; a process which has continued into the post-independence period. It might be argued that historical writing often takes the form of a desire to establish an identity on the part of the social group to which the historian belongs. Thus, Ganesh Das writing his *Char Bagh-i-Punjab* in 1849, was, as a member of the social elite, projecting the known history of the *khatris* of the Punjab, a form of legitimization of the *khatri* status. Groups in power, therefore, sometimes tend to see the history of their community as the history of the region or even of the nation. This is further emphasized in contemporary historical writing by the equating of the present-day state boundary as the boundary of the region; and this is held to be viable for all periods of history.

These trends are in many ways parallel to those of nationalist historical thinking in the early decades of this century. As such there are both the negative and the positive side of the impact of nationalist historical thought. Of the former, I would like to draw attention in particular to three trends. There is, firstly, the all-too-ready acceptance of the conventional periodization of Ancient, Medieval and Modern. Periodization does not merely imply time-brackets; it also involves historical assumptions (which is why the nomenclature at least was changed from the earlier Hindu, Muslim and British). The acceptance of this periodization imposes assumptions on the historical data from regional sources, and it seems to me that the evidence from the Punjab supports neither the assumptions nor the time-brackets. Admittedly there is a certain convenience in this periodization but a convenience should not be allowed to become an intellectual truth.

Secondly, certain theories current in earlier historical writing and believed to be almost axiomatic are endorsed even for regional history. For example, the theory of the Āryan origin of culture and of social stratification is projected even in those regions where it is obviously untenable. In the Punjab the social stratification based on the four-caste division presents its own problems. *Brāhmaṇs* rarely play a dominant role in the society of this region, the *kṣatriyas* fade out after a while and the *khatris* who claim to be *kṣatriyas* are invariably associated with professions more akin to the *vaiśya*. Clearly there is a deviation from the prescribed norm and this deviation can only be explained by investigating the actual caste stratification at various historical times.

Thirdly, there is the almost inevitable search for a golden age, often identified as the period to which the currently dominant group traces its roots, and it is described in the glowing tints of cultural resurgence. The protagonists of this age became the heroes of history and act as eponymous ancestors to those in power. In ancient historiography the golden age was generally in the distant past, in the beginnings of time; so distant and so mythological that none could question the historicity of the age and it was imbued with whatever values the historian wished to propagate. Gradually the utopias were brought forward into historical times and eventually into recent periods, when the social and political function of history became more important. Golden ages have to shift as new social groups come to the fore and they have the disadvantage that they focus on a particular series of historical events often to the near exclusion of others of equal importance.

Enfolded in the writing of regional history is also the positive side. The earlier nationalist school, despite its weaknesses, succeeded in generating a debate on the historical assumptions of the historians of the nineteenth century concerning the nature of the Indian past: a debate which has opened up many new dimensions. Regional history in the context of Indian history could play a similar, catalytic role. This however does not mean the substituting of the concerns of Indian ideology by those of regional ideology. On the contrary it would require the analysis of the historical patterns of the region and the relating of these patterns to the generalizations of Indian history. Here again, I do not mean the acceptance of the theories of Indian history and their application to the region, but, rather, the juxtaposing and comparing of the analysis of the regional patterns which would indicate the generalizations required to be made at the wider level. The testing of these generalizations would involve the understanding of the patterns of historical change at the regional level.

I would like at this point to consider some of these patterns for they give rise to the problems which I spoke of earlier.

One might begin with the historical point at which the awareness of being a region, and having a history, is first expressed. In the case of the Punjab it has been suggested as having evolved during the Mughal period. The historian's interest lies in analyzing the roots of this consciousness—whether they result from an administrative or political coherence, or from linguistic or religious urges or a combination of many factors. In analyzing this consciousness it is equally imperative to consider that which preceded it and that which came subsequently. In order to do this we arrive at the second important problem, namely, what were the geographical boundaries of the region.

The question of boundaries has its own complexities since man-made boundaries change frequently and rapidly with each political change. The only stable boundaries are geographical and even these are liable to be substantially modified by ecological changes. The definition of a region requires the correlation of many facets in the study of historical evolution, as is amply demonstrated in the Punjab.

On the face of it the Punjab is easy enough to define. It is the land of the five rivers and the inter-fluvial regions, the

Doābs. Yet the coinciding of this geographical definition with a political and cultural entity has occurred only for a brief period of its history. Prior to that the area contained more than one geographical and social identity. What seems significant, therefore, is not just the brief period when the larger frontiers coincided but the investigation of the interaction and relationship between the sub-regions and this constitutes a major part of the history of this region.

The sub-regions within the larger area can be listed as follows: firstly, the Potwar plateau and the Salt Range constituting the northern part of the Sind-Sagar Doāb, the southern half being mainly desert; secondly, what I shall refer to as the Upper Doābs, those of the Chaj, Rachna, Bari and Bist, lying at an elevation of 200-500m and stretching into the sub-montane tracts and with which the Potwar area had close contacts; thirdly, the upper reaches of the rivers leading into the hill valleys at the forefront of the Himalayas; and fourthly, the Lower Doābs forming the hinterland of Multan. Both the plain of Peshawar and the watershed of the Indo-Gangetic divide, although historically very significant, remain geographically marginal to the main area. Even though the sub-regions can be approximately demarcated, their historical interaction has been complex and any history of the Punjab will have to take both the interaction and the complexities into account. The pattern of relationships has not been consistent and similar through time. One of the more obvious reasons for these changes has been the extreme hydrographic disturbances, such as those involving the Sarasvati, the Beas and the Rāvi. But the complexities are also due to other reasons.

Evidence of settlement in this area during the third and second millennia B.C. show a distribution of pre-Harappan and Harappan sites along the Indus (particularly the trans-Indus region) and along the Bari Doāb and Sutlej and Sarasvati valleys. Archaeological explorations in Pakistan and India point to a particularly heavy concentration of population at the confluence of the rivers, in the Bari and Bist Doābs and in the Sarasvati valley. It has been plausibly argued that there were major ecological changes in this area during the second millennium B.C. which appear to be accompanied by a decline in settlements in the Multan area and a concentration in the Indo-Gangetic divide. References to the occupation of the

Upper Doābs, as for example the *janapadas* of the Kekeyas and the Madras, come from sources of the first millennium B.C. Was there a migration of people from the gradually desiccated Multan region to the Upper Doābs? A slow ecological change would encourage migration. If Harappan agriculture was based on inundation irrigation then hydrographic changes would virtually necessitate a migration. Or, were the new areas settled by fresh migrants from elsewhere? The distribution of the Painted Grey Ware culture suggests that the settlers, whether indigenous or alien, may have moved along the Sutlej and Sarasvati valleys. The further distribution of this culture extends from the Indo-Gangetic divide to the Ganges valley itself, the link between the two areas having been previously established through the Ochre-Colour Pottery Culture. In subsequent centuries the people of the latter region regarded those of the Upper Doābs with some disdain. The Madras are accused not only of forsaking brahmanical rites but of unconventional behaviour and the breaking of social taboos. For the orthodox of the *madhya-deśa* this region was always on the brink of the social pale if not actually outside it. It is also worth remembering that two linguistic systems seem to have been in operation since Vedic Sanskrit carries evidence of the assimilation of Proto-Dravidian elements.

More precise information on the condition of the Punjab comes to us from the accounts of Alexander's campaign in the late fourth century B.C. Alexander's initial route was from the Peshawar plains across the Doāb—rich, fertile lands supporting monarchical kingdoms such as those of Āmbhi, Pūru and Saubhūti, and a relatively sophisticated culture. In contrast to this was the stark, primitive habitat of the Śibi in the Shorkot region. Further south in the Bari Doāb, the oligarchies of the Mālava and the Kṣudraka presented a more cheerful picture. It seems that the Lower Doābs were not as prosperous as the Upper Doābs, nevertheless, the agricultural base of the latter was not substantial enough to support a powerful state. That the desiccation in the Lower Doābs was spreading seems probable from the fact that by the first couple of centuries A.D. the Mālava (among others) had migrated to Rajasthan and Avanti.

For the Mauryas the significance of the Punjab seemed to focus on Taxila which became the administrative seat of the northern province. This, in a sense, introduces a new dimension to the patterns discussed so far. Taxila was the meeting point, on the one side, of the royal highway and the trade route running from the Ganges valley via the watershed and through the Upper Doābs and, on the other, the route from west Asia via the Khyber Pass. Mountain passes accentuate communication and the Khyber has always been the route of migration, trade and invasion, with cities such as Taxila and Begram flanking either end of the pass and giving way in time to other cities (ultimately Peshawar and Kabul), but always in the same vicinity.

The role of invasions in the history of the Punjab is mentioned so often that it hardly bears repeating. But it might be as well to consider also some of the other factors contributing to the history of this region, as, for instance, trade. One easy index to the growth of trade is an increase in the number and size of towns. Sources such as Ptolemy list a large number of towns in the Upper Doābs, far exceeding those in the Lower Doābs. Can it be argued that the prosperity of the Upper Doābs was based primarily on trade rather than on agriculture? Is it possible that the peak periods of affluence coincided with the political control of this region extending its reach into Afghanistan and possibly Kashmir, since Kashmir also had links with central Asian trade routes? The earliest references to Taxila as a commercial and cosmopolitan centre relate to the period when Gandhāra was included as a satrapy in the Achaemenid empire. Post-Mauryan dynasties in this region frequently straddled the Khyber Pass and this period also saw a sharp rise in trading activities and commercial income. One has only to compare the Mauryan settlement of Bhir Mound at Taxila with the post-Mauryan city of Sirkap at the same place to see the difference. The political importance of Śākala during this period may also have been due to its location on the trade route. The attempt of empire builders from the Mauryas to the Mughals, who, if their empires included the Punjab, tried to annex eastern Afghanistan as well, may in part have been motivated by the wish to control not only the strategic entrances into the sub-continent, but also the trade routes.

Gupta rule appears to have made scant impression on the Punjab in spite of Samudragupta having 'uprooted' as he claims, the tribal republics of the Mālavas, Yaudheyas and Ārjunāyanas in Rajasthan and the watershed and the Mādrakas in the Upper Doābs. If the control of the trade route involved the conquest of the Potwar plateau and beyond and if the Upper Doābs were not agriculturally very developed, this might have acted as a disincentive to further conquest in the region. It would seem that effective Gupta control stopped at the watershed which in later times, as Sirhind, was regarded as the frontier to the Ganges valley. The persistence of tribal republics in this region, despite the Mauryan and post-Mauryan conquests, suggests a relative autonomy from interference by strong political powers which interference would have been inevitable had it been a rich, agricultural region. Interestingly, some of these tribal states are said to have provided soldiers in lieu of revenue, in the true frontier tradition. The Indo-Gangetic divide seems more frequently to have been drawn into the vortex of the Ganges valley. Harṣavardhana, although originating from Thanesar, moved the centre of his kingdom into the Ganges valley rather than up into the Punjab.

Hsüan Tsang, visiting India in the seventh century A.D., travelled from Taxila through the towns of the Upper Doābs to Thanesar and the Ganges valley. It is significant that when he visited Multan he approached it from Sind, suggesting that its accessibility and association with Sind was stronger. Multan itself was a commercial centre of great importance, but its hinterland to the north and to the east called for little attention. In his description of the Upper Doābs, Hsüan Tsang refers mainly to towns, some of which are surrounded by fertile country. But his more glowing references are to grain fields and fruit orchards in the sub-montane areas and the hill valleys spanning out along the mountain reaches of the rivers.

One of the most puzzling problems in the latter part of the first millennium A.D. is the surprising absence of land-grant inscriptions from the Punjab plains. If agriculture was of primary importance in this region, then there would have been some record either of the bringing of waste land under cultivation or of the granting of cultivated land to religious or secular grantees. The absence of these records would either suggest a low priority for agriculture or else an agrarian and administrative system which did not require the kind of changes taking place in neighbouring regions. Land-grant inscriptions are available from the hill areas, as for example from Kangra, as early as the seventh century and from Chamba a little later. The extension of agriculture into the hill valleys must have taken place in the latter half of the first millennium A.D. to allow of the granting of land during this period. Does this reflect a migration from the Upper Doābs into the hills and the creation of the hill states? Or was this due to a natural migration caused by shortage of land and an increasing population? The pressure of revenue collection was probably not a causal factor as this would have led to agrarian changes in the plains. If insecurity resulting from invasions was the cause, then the accusation of creating this insecurity would have to be levelled against the Hūnas rather than the Turks, since the migration to the hills predates the Turkish invasions by a few centuries. Alternatively, one may have to argue that, given the existing agricultural technology, cultivation was easier in the hill valleys. Access to these higher valleys also introduced new commodities and trade connections especially with the increasing use of mountain passes into Kashmir, Ladakh and Tibet. The proximity of the main trade route of the plains to the hill states doubtless facilitated these connections. Absence of evidence is not a conclusive argument but it is indeed strange that records of land grants should be a rarity in the Punjab plains when such records are available for many other regions of northern India. This would also imply a corresponding rarity of at least one aspect of such grants, the instituting of *agrahāras* and brahmanical settlements and endowments to temples. Hsüan Tsang refers to 'deva' temples in the cities of the Upper Doābs but none as spectacular as the one at Multan. There are few early temples in the Punjab plains and one wonders whether their lack of survival was due to insufficient endowments or to the conventional explanation of Muslim invasions destroying temples. The sub-montane and hill areas, however, which were also at the receiving end of such invasions, although admittedly not on the direct route, do have surviving examples of early temples, many of which are well-endowed. The absence of land-grants would have further implications not only for the role of brahmanism in the religion of the area but also for the pattern of caste formation and caste structure, given that the acculturating role of brahmanical settlements noticed in certain other parts of the subcontinent was absent. Brahmanism never seems to have had a deep social root in the plains. But in the hill states it had a firm foothold and the process of acculturation is more evident.

It has been suggested that, at the end of the first and in the early half of the second millennia A.D., there appears to have been a population movement with the Jats of Sind settling in the Punjab mainly in the area between the Chenab and Sutlej rivers, as also in the watershed and extending further into eastern Rajasthan and western Uttar Pradesh. This was not merely a population movement for the Jats were converted from pastoralism to agriculture; and crucial to the change was that they brought with them the technology of the Persian wheel. This resulted in a rapid extension of agriculture, particularly in the Upper Doābs. The *Ain-i-Akbari* records the presence of Jat *zamindār* castes and well-irrigation in the Doābs of the Punjab. Had there already been a large agricultural population in these areas such a movement would have created a massive unrest; but for this there is no evidence: unless one argues that the migration into the hill states had something to do with this movement. The Jat migration was probably a slow .movement not causing much displacement. The hinterland of Multan was in any case sparsely populated. At most, the Jats may have pressurized the cultivators of the Upper Doābs and the sub-montane area to move further up into the mountain valleys. By the time of Akbar, the Subah of Lahore is described as agriculturally very fertile and yielding a healthy revenue. One has the impression that agriculture was more in evidence now with possibly more land under cultivation than before, judging by the relatively infrequent references to agriculture in this region from pre-Mughal sources. The numerically larger *zamindār* castes included the Jats, Bhattis, Rajputs and various others.

The *zamindār* castes were however distinct from the trader and administrator caste, that of the *khatris*. The references to *khatris* associated with land are very few. The post-Gupta period is seen as one of a decline in trade in northern India. However, a modicum of commercial activity must have continued, as is suggested by the ninth century inscription from Pehoa, which refers to a body of horse-dealers coming from various places and agreeing to contribute to a donation to temples at Pehoa and Kannauj from every sale of their animals. The emergence of the *khatris* seems to coincide with the period of the Turkish invasions, perhaps because the invasions had the supplementary effect of opening up the trade routes to central Asia which were under the control of Mahmud of Ghazni. His armies certainly marched through the towns of the Upper Doābs, but his prize targets were cities elsewhere—Multan, Kannauj, Thanesar and Somanath.

Agricultural technology was perhaps to play a further role in historical change in the Punjab. It is somewhat startling to read in the *Ain-i-Akbari* that the Bet Jalandhar Doāb in the *sarkar* of Dipalpur yielded a very high revenue, until one remembers that Firuz Tughlaq built a canal in this region in 1354. The upper Bari Doāb becomes a key area of the Punjab from the seventeenth century. Was this also related to the canal built by the Mughal administration in this period? The Multan area was sought to be controlled by the administration of Ranjit Singh in the early nineteenth century through the building of inundation canals. The British policy of canal networks and canal colonies in the under-developed areas of the Lower Doābs had its antecedents. The extension of agriculture in the Punjab made it possible to extend the natural frontier northwards.

Whatever the reasons, involving agricultural technology, new commercial possibilities, invasions and migrations, there appears to be, in the Mughal period, a change in the relations between the sub-regions of the Punjab. The upper Doābs and the hill states impinge on each other to a greater degree than before. Lahore and Multan seem to be in closer contact, although not always well-disposed towards each other. The ambitions of the Governors of Lahore extended in their geographical reach to more distant areas such as Kabul and Kashmir, doubtless motivated by the trading network.

Evidence of a more general economic stabilization, probably due to the extension of agriculture, is apparent from the appearance of land-grants and endowments to various religious sects. The sects are largely heterodox, irrespective of whether they conform to the Hindu or Islamic tradition. The core of the religious tradition comes from groups of renouncers, such as the Nathpanthis, Bairagis, Sufis. The earlier groups of renouncers, the Buddhists, had also once been important in this region. Although they had now disappeared, possibly some of the earlier social requirements which had led to the support of Buddhism may have been remanifested in the support for the renouncers of this later period. The creation and diffusion of the Punjabi language is also tied up with religious sects. They adopted the language of the towns-people and villagers in preference to that of the courtly elite, and gave both form and status to the language.

A variety of sects were recipients of land-grants. The Upper Bari Doāb furnishes examples of such grants (as for instance, the Jogis of Jakhbar and the Vaishnavas of Pindori). They appear to have had fairly easy access to revenue-free land, exemption from irrigation cesses and a variety of perquisites. Their patrons changed over the centuries but the status of the patrons remained the same. They were all members of the ruling order—the Rajput rulers of the hill states who patronized the shrines, the Mughal emperors who endowed them with land, the governor of Lahore and later the Sikh rulers of the kingdom of Punjab and the British. In spite of the sharp differences in the religious persuasions of this cavalcade of rulers they were all making grants to these and similar sects. The documents of the Punjab kingdom refer to the grants as being in accordance with the practice of the times of the Mughal rulers: a strange continuity among those otherwise believed to be antagonistic to each other on religious grounds. Doubtless, most believed that they were acquiring religious merit by making these grants, but one wonders if other more mundane reasons did not encroach upon the decision. Perhaps such endowments would help to stabilize the area politically since the sects would develop into centres of political loyalty as long as the grant was forthcoming. Some of the documents of the later period describe the location of the land granted and judging by the continuity of the villages it would seem that the Upper Bari Doāb was by now well populated. The continuity of the grants from the Mughal period by later rulers may also have been regarded as a status symbol. Many of these sects had a network of connections via itinerant members and monastic establishments over large geographical areas. The Nath sect was well distributed in northern India by now. These connections could also have served as trading networks, as they were known to do, for instance, with the Gosain sects of other parts of northern India. It is interesting that eventually market centres develop on some of the lands thus endowed. Gradually the religious institution evolved into a body of land-owners. Income from the endowments was spent on the maintenance of the institution and the order. Often this involved investing the income in land or commerce. Thus the renouncers came to perform administrative and entrepreneurial functions, assisted by secular agents. Perhaps the religious teaching of such sects did not remain unchanged and took on the nuances of their new role in society.

Did the acquisition of the new status breed political ambition among these religious groups? The hostility between them was not invariably over religious differences though this may have been presented as the apparent cause. Hostility could equally well arise from a competition for patronage or from the need to protect property which in part explains the organization of para-military sections among such sects.

Popular support for religious sects involves the question of the link between them and the various castes. This is crucial not merely to the history of a religious movement but also to the social pattern of the region. It is often said that the initial support for Guru Nanak came from the *khatris* but that gradually Sikhism drew greater support from the Jats. This may suggest that the evolution of Sikhism be seen in two phases, since the social base would differ in each case. At the same time it would be relevant to examine why the initial *khatri* leadership gave way to the increasingly effective Jat participation. Urban groups may find universalistic teaching more acceptable. Peasant groups would require the assimilation of their own cults into the new religion. Would this in part explain Guru Govind Singh's tendency to use Hindu symbols, particularly those relating to the Śakti tradition? Does it also reflect political concerns, either hostile or friendly, between the Hinduized hill states and the Sikhism of the plains? It has been suggested that the Jats, as a low status group, were drawn to use this for improving their social status. Such a group would, on consolidating its position, tend to introduce a hierarchical separation between itself and others. Is it a coincidence that it was also at this time that the demarcation between the *sardar* and the *mazhabi* Sikhs enters the movement?

The emergence of the kingdom of the Punjab was not a sudden development of the eighteenth and nineteenth centuries. It has, as I have tried to show, a long gestation period. It incorporates in its development the various connections which I have referred to: the changing links between the sub-regions where the changes are indirectly man-made or directly so; the two economic thrusts of agriculture and trade, technology as a factor in these; the emergence of caste relations; the growth of religious sects; and the crystallization of political identities. The contribution which regional history can make is in seeking to connect these elements at a more precise level. If the focus on the pattern of historical change in the region can be sharpened it contributes to the quality of generalizations at the broader level as well as makes for more valuable comparative studies with other regions. In terms of comparative studies mention is often made of the kingdoms of the Punjab and the Marathas. They are said to have been motivated by an anti-Muslim sentiment which helped them to be rid of central, imperial authority. As a mono-causal explanation this can be traced to communal historiography where the tension between imperial authority and regional pressures was seen at the single plane of religious differences. A careful examination of the mainsprings of these developments however suggests a multitude of factors, not least of them the crisis within the Mughal empire itself. Comparative studies would suggest the similarities within the two regions, thereby enabling a wider generalization. Dissimilarities would indicate the particular regional factors and would lead to the modification of the broader generalization.

I began with the suggestion that there are three trends in regional history which need to be reconsidered. I have tried to show that the accepted periodization on the large scale seems to be inapplicable to the Punjab. Medievalism, with its attendant social and economic changes, would have to be placed later than is normally done. To date the modern period to the mid-eighteenth century would create its own problems in the history of the Punjab. The assumptions on which this periodization is based would in any case require serious reconsideration. Secondly, the deviation from the standard picture of caste society also needs careful investigation. With the third trend, the search for a golden age, one treads on soft ground, for this is also tied up with the attempt to suggest a regional periodization, but without changing the assumptions of the existing periodization. Thus the history of Maharashtra is equated with the rise of the Maratha kingdom, that of Rajasthan with the emergence of Mewar and Marwar, that of the Punjab with Sikhism and that of Tamil Nadu with Sangam culture. I have attempted to suggest that even a movement as powerful as that of Sikhism and the emergence of the kingdom of the Punjab can become a viable historical study only in the context of the totality of the history of the Punjab. Historical events are not isolated phenomena, suspended in space and time, and the historical matrix in which they are embodied is as important as the events.

Great Eastern Trade: Other Times, Other Places

(Maritime Trade In The First Millennium A.D.)

Perspectives on the history of India have tended to be landlocked and the arrival of the European trading companies is often viewed as the induction of India into what some historians call the global economy of the eighteenth century. But in recent years the shaping of the history of coastal areas in pre-colonial times has come into focus. Given the lengthy Indian coastline this study becomes a major enterprise. Maritime trade was not only crucial to coastal areas but also to economies further inland. The profits it brought were attractive enough for traders from elsewhere to new communities. They also brought commodities that captured the Indian imagination and led to the cultivation of new tastes and fashions.

Maritime trade, since it traverses seas and oceans, can locate Indian history in the wider context of more distant societies. The argument now being made is that there was in pre-colonial times a commercial economy that incorporated many societies of Eurasia and Africa. The economic impact of this trade was not incidental, as indeed also its imprint on varying cultures and its linking of Roman, Arab, Indian and Chinese centres.

Networks of sea trade had tentative beginnings with a cautious hugging of the coastline in a looping trade from one small port to the next. This exchange was routinely of consumables and necessities and such ships have been referred to as 'travelling bazars'. But with advances in the understanding of winds, ocean currents and astronomy, navigation became daring and mid-ocean crossings, regular. This permitted more than routine exchange and

The Fourth Vasant J. Sheth Memorial Lecture delivered in Mumbai on 10 January 2002.

allowed for a regular trade in luxury items over long distances. Nevertheless, bulk goods, such as grain and onions, continued to be carried since their saleable value was an insurance against the fluctuating demands for luxuries. Gradually some areas became centres, investing in and controlling exchange. The commodities came either from other such centres or from the peripheries where they were produced. But these were not permanently either one or the other, and among the more interesting aspects of the history of commerce is the shift in centres and peripheries.

Maritime trade in India linked multiple centres. The focus in this chapter would be on just one of these links. We shall limit ourselves to the trade between the west coast of India and the eastern Mediterranean, the trade that used the sea lanes of the Arabian Sea and the Red Sea. The examples of trading activities will be illustrated by three groups of traders from the west, each of which had different relations with Indian societies. The link began with those who traded within the parameters of the early economic development of the Indian peninsula, and it communicated with centres that were initially part of the Roman empire. It then shifted to the Arabs. Eventually it incorporated a network of Jewish traders. There is as yet less known of the reverse direction although the evidence of the Indian presence in the Red Sea is increasing. The time span of this chapter starts in the Christian era and continues to the early second millennium A.D.

As is often the case, trade became viable when travel over distances became easier. For maritime links, this meant mid-ocean crossings. Attempting a mid-ocean voyage across the Arabian Sea brought the western seaboard of India within easier reach of the Red Sea. Ships would dock in the Egyptian ports of the Red Sea such as Myos Hormus, Berenice, and Leucus Limen, and would take on cargo for India. Consignments would be collected at Alexandria, taken down-river on the Nile to Coptos—the emporium for this trade, and then transported across the Egyptian desert to the ports. The first stop of the sea voyage would have been near Aden, to collect water and other necessities before the mid-ocean crossing. Some of these ports were gathering points for ships, sailors and navigators—Greeks,

Egyptians, Arabs and Indians—the mix of peoples and cultures that comes naturally to centres of exchange. From here ships would sail annually and most frequently in late July to cross the Arabian Sea and arrive in India in September. The winds of the south-west monsoon, somewhat abated by then, facilitated this crossing. Local navigators probably knew about these winds but when ships carrying cargo for the Indo-Roman trade began to sail with the winds, the quantity and quality of trade changed. The more common danger in such voyages was less from a possible untimely ferocity of the monsoon winds, and more from the pirates who combed the seas, and remained a menace throughout the millennium.

This calendar of sailing coincided with activities along the west coast. The port of Bhrighukachchha—the Bharuch of today and Barygaza to the Greeks—was a major commercial centre. The range and variety of coinage that was legal tender at this port is impressive. Near Mumbai other ports such as Sopara, Kalyan and Semylla/present-day Chaul, were also mentioned. Equally important was the port at Muziris, often identified with modern Kodungallur/Cranganore, near Kochi. Arriving at these ports meant a stay of some weeks to off-load cargo and sail with the return cargo. The waiting period was calculated both for the procurement of cargo and the return monsoon. The most substantial Indian export was of pepper which ripened after the monsoon. By the time the pepper was dry and packed, the north east monsoon also became due and this facilitated the return journey. It is said that initially there were about twenty ships sailing to India in a year, but as the volume of trade picked up, mention is made of up to one hundred and twenty ships. This maybe an exaggeration but nevertheless the frequency is apparent from the increase in India of objects from distant places and the presence of pepper from the excavations of the Red Sea ports.

What has come to be called the Indo-Roman trade was first noticed through references in Greek and Latin texts dating to around the Christian era. The contents of these texts varied. Some were geographies of the Greco-Roman world, such as those of Strabo and Ptolemy, and included descriptions of the eastern lands. More unusual was the *Periplus of the Red Sea,* a manual for navigators and traders, with useful comments on local products and commerce and hints of political conditions. The itinerary stretched in an arc from the horn of Africa, along the entire west coast of India and Sri Lanka, and then up the east coast of India.

The focal point of the trade was the port of Alexandria in Egypt, the entrepot of the Mediterranean. Greek, Egyptian and Jewish merchants invested in this trade, functioning under the control of the Roman administration in the eastern provinces of the empire. These traders may well have had Indian partners as in later times. Possibly some may also have settled in India, and although modern communities do not claim them as ancestors, there are traces of their presence. Perhaps the small bronze statuettes of gods and heroes—Atlas, Eros and Poseidon found at Kolhapur, or the Roman lamps, metal cups and vessels, mirrors, cameos and seals, found at various places in India, belonged to these traders. Alternatively were they souvenirs brought back from Egypt and the eastern Mediterranean by Indian traders? The Tamil poem, the *Shilappadikaram,* refers to 'the foreign quarter' as it were, inhabited by the prosperous Yavanas at the southern Indian port of Kaveripattinam. The term Yavana, originally used for the Greeks, was now used for all those who came from the west.

The early Roman imperial system is discussed by the Roman historian Pliny, and not unexpectedly it refers to the trade with India. His perspective is that of an administrator and includes what would today be regarded as a cost-benefit analysis. Pliny complained that the trade was a financial drain on the Roman treasury. However, the notion of a drain may be exaggerated. The customs duties and the taxes on the profits of the Indian trade, collected by the Roman administration, were so large and so rigorously controlled, that they amply compensated for the initial investment. The criticism it is thought, reflects the view of some Roman senators who objected to the luxurious life of the Roman patricians with their eagerness to flaunt exotica, such as exquisite textiles, semi-precious stones and spiced food, not to mention apes and peacocks in their gardens. Other factors, largely unconnected with maritime trade are more likely to have been critical to the decline of the Roman economy. Nevertheless, even speaking impressionistically, the profits for the Indian traders seemed to have been sizeable.

It was earlier argued that the initiative for this trade came from the west and Indian participation was restricted to producing the goods. The redefinition of who traded with whom and how, has undergone a change in recent years. Archaeological evidence from the Indian peninsula at this time, indicates an extensive distribution of impressive megalithic burial sites, with an assortment of grave goods. It registers a network of exchange in various items—paddy, beads, and iron objects. Many megalithic sites were located along important routes. Ports such as Arikamedu near Pondicherry or Alagankulam further south were linked to hinterlands through megalithic activity. In their late levels, these sites sometimes have Roman artifacts confirming a contact dating to the Christian era or even somewhat earlier. Buddhist sites located in the Deccan, drew their patronage substantially from merchants, artisans and small scale land owners. The locations of Buddhist monasteries became staging points along trade routes.

Excavations at Arikamedu have revealed a range of Roman objects such as glass, tableware, cameos. It was earlier described as a Roman trading station where textiles were produced to Roman specification. This description evokes later European colonial settlements. However the comparison is of a limited kind since the Roman trade did not replace local networks of exchange nor was there an acquisition of territory. Among the potsherds found in various places were those of amphorae from the Mediterranean. These were the large jars used for storing and transporting liquids, most frequently wine. The sediment deposit on most such potsherds is of wine, and the stamp on the amphorae is often of Koan wine from southern Italy and the Greek islands. The consumption of wine was not limited to visiting traders and there was a local demand. The Tamil Shangam poems speak of the fragrant wine brought in elegant jars by the Yavanas, in their beautiful ships that stir the foam on the Periyar river. Other potsherds, smaller in number, have a sediment of olive oil and garum—a liquid fish paste. Since neither of these became popular in Indian cuisine, it is likely that olive oil and the fish paste catered to those from the eastern Mediterranean, living in India. The amphorae incidentally served a double purpose. The cargo of wine was used as ballast to steady the ship during the sea voyage in the same way as sacks of pepper were used on the return voyage.

Evidence from excavations, suggesting that the megalithic sites were centres of distribution and exchange, has clarified the picture. There is also now a more analytical understanding of the patterns of pre-modern trade. We no longer assume an identical pattern everywhere. Barter as a system of exchange co-existed with sophisticated markets, and differences depended on the items to be exchanged, their transportation and the outlay of capital in buying and selling. These varying patterns also provide clues to the political economy of different regions. The economic intrusion of the trade through the Red Sea and into the eastern Mediterranean does not appear to be due to a dominating Roman presence as was previously assumed, although the presence in itself is of historical interest.

Nevertheless, what is striking and remains a little puzzling is the discovery literally, of hoards of Roman coins in various places, but mainly in south India. A scatter of such coins occurs elsewhere in the sub-continent wherever the trade with the eastern Mediterranean impinged. But the coin hoards in the peninsula point to more complex possibilities than just buying and selling. With the exception of a small number of coins that go back to the Roman Republic, a large part of the coins are of the early Roman emperors—Augustus and Tiberius and are prior to the debasement of coins introduced by Nero. These would date therefore to the late first century B.C. and the first half of the first century A.D., which was also the peak period of the trade. Such coins were legal tender in the world of international commerce. The Roman imperial coins found in India have a high content of gold or silver, and carry the usual superb portraiture. Some are even in mint condition. Jars containing such coins are found along the main routes, as for instance, from the Kerala ports, across the Palghat gap near Coimbatore and along the Kaveri valley to the ports of the eastern coast.

The puzzling question relates to the use to which the coins were put. Normally coins go into circulation as a medium of exchange, as in the case of the punch-marked coins, also found in these parts and associated with Mauryan administration and trade. But hoards of coins can have other functions. Did the hoard constitute the capital for further exchange? Since they are located in the peninsula we presume that the local traders used them as capital and in the production of commodities for trade. This gives a rather different complexion to the role of the local trader in relation to the visiting trader. A small percentage of the coins are however, overstruck by a bar, or have a tiny but visible nick. This would make them defective for circulation and the marking may have been deliberate in order to use them as bullion. Possibly in some localities barter was the more effective exchange and coins used as bullion would facilitate barter, unlike ports and markets where high value coins were in commercial circulation.

The locations of these hoards of coin are often in areas governed by chiefs, or else, chiefs in the process of becoming kings. Such societies lay great store by exchanging high value gifts among themselves. The giving and receiving of these gifts, often through a ritual, are seen as indicators of status. So were some Roman coins put out of circulation and used for this purpose? The impact of this trade may have been a catalyst in the mutation of the Chera, Chola and Pandya chiefdoms into kingdoms.

Clearly the coins were a major item of export from the eastern Mediterranean and may explain why Pliny feared a financial drain on the Roman economy. Of the other exports, wine was marginal to the Roman economy as also was the enormous export of coral. For the Greco-Romans, red coral was a talisman and possibly this notion took root in India or strengthened similar associations.

The returning cargo from India consisted substantially of black pepper, spices, semi-precious stones—especially beryl and pearls, textiles in cotton and silk, and special timber of teak, ebony and sandalwood, all items activating energies in the Konkan and south India. Chinese silk was now available in India and its export to the west may have been the start of what was to become a fashionable demand in Europe. However, pepper and spices were to remain the predominant items brought to Europe from India even as late as the time of the Portuguese. They were widely used in Europe as preservatives, condiments and medicinally. It is thought that the search for more spices was what initially took Indian traders to south east Asia. Pepper sold for such a high price in Alexandria that there are complaints that local merchants adulterated it with mustard seeds. A second century papyrus in Greek, documents a contract between a financier and a merchant and refers to a cargo from Muziris coming to the customs house in Alexandria. A large consignment of spices and textiles doubtless involved a heavy investment of capital.

The identity of Indian traders in the Red Sea trade is becoming clearer from inscriptions. These are written in the widely used *brahmi* script and the languages are Tamil and Prakrit. Some inscriptions are scratched on potsherds, identifying the owner, and turn up in the excavations at ports along the Red Sea. One of these carries a fragmentary name ...atan, which has been identified with Tamil-brahmi inscriptions referring to the name Catan, both on potsherds and rock engravings. An inscription near a cave in Coimbatore refers to a Catan who was a dealer in semi-precious stones and made a large donation to the local monks. Perhaps he was one of those who provided beryl to the merchants of Alexandria. Other potsherds from Red Sea ports carry Prakrit inscriptions with names such as Halaka, Vinhudatta and Nakada, suggesting a home base in the Deccan.

Longer inscriptions at Buddhist places of worship in the peninsula are generally votive. Interestingly, some record donations by Yavanas, as for instance, at the rock-cut monastery at Karle near Lonavala. The Yavanas appear to have had a settlement in the vicnity of Karle at Dhenukakata, described appropriately as a *vaniya-gama.* This raises the question of whether some Yavana traders became Buddhists. Large donations by some Yavanas from north Indian towns are recorded, and with names such as Indragnidatta the son of Dhammadeva. The Yavana conversion to Buddhism was doubtless motivated by an attraction for the religion, but there may also have been a wish to participate in the culture and rituals of their Indian counterparts. Donors to the Sangha at places such as Junnar, Kanheri and Karle include merchants among others, and some of these sites were located on the passes in the western Ghats leading down to the ports.

Buddhism was open to accepting people of alien cultures. The early Buddhists expressed a curiosity about other societies. They commented on the dual division of Greek society into masters and slaves and the absence of caste among them. The rules of *varṇa* by way of contrast, required that Yavanas be treated as *mlecchas*—outside the pale of caste society and impure. If applied, this would hardly have been conducive to a camaraderie of merchants, Indian and foreign.

Greek writing had earlier focused on the strangeness of man and animal in India. There were men who curled up and slept within their ears, others who were nourished merely on the smell of food without having to eat; or among animals, the fierce 'matrikhora' with its three rows of teeth. Gradually with the accounts of visitors and traders, a more realistic picture emerged. Indians now became more familiar but their society was organized differently from the Greco-Roman. India was therefore seen as what we would now call 'the Other' of Europe. Otherness can he pointed to in many ways and perhaps the most persistent was a rather mixed up Greek view of caste.

Indian society was said to have seven main divisions—philosophers, which was the smallest group; cultivators and soldiers, which were the largest; herdsmen, artisans, administrators and councillors. Occupation and marriage it is said were determined by the rules of the group one was born into, thus giving these arbitrary divisions, a touch of caste. This was the description originally recorded by Megasthenes when he visited India in the Mauryan period. It is interesting that this view remained unchanged in later Greek writing from the eastern Mediterranean, even when there was enough familiarity with the west coast and its hinterland, to know that the seven-fold division did not fit. Such is the power of stereotypes!

Yet at the same time, systems of knowledge benefited by these diverse contacts. Advances followed particularly in medicine and astronomy. Indian medicinal plants are even referred to in Greek

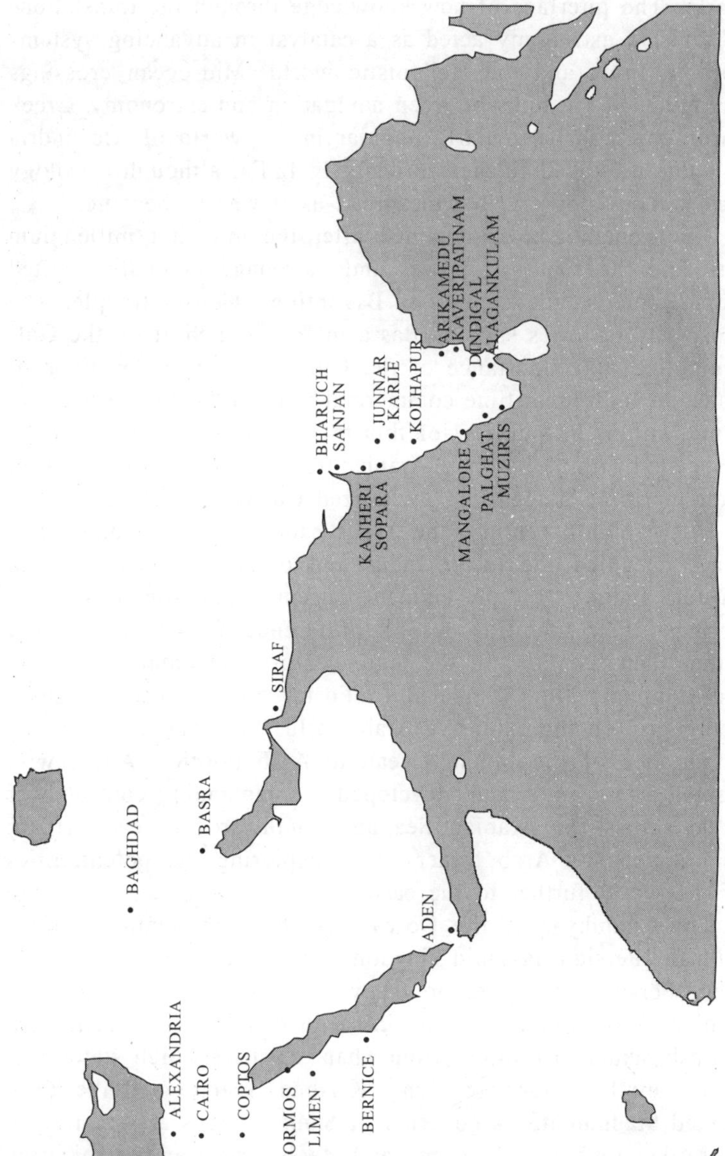
ALEXANDRIA
CAIRO
COPTOS
MYOS HORMOS
LEVCUS LIMEN
BERNICE
BAGHDAD
BASRA
ADEN
SIRAF
BHARUCH
SANJAN
KANHERI
SOPARA
JUNNAR
KARLE
KOLHAPUR
MANGALORE
PALGHAT
MUZIRIS
ARIKAMEDU
KAVERIPATINAM
DINDIGAL
ALAGANKULAM

works. The interface of new knowledge through the translations of texts in astronomy acted as a catalyst in advancing systems both in India and the Hellenistic world. Mid-ocean crossings strengthened the links between navigation and astronomy. Greek horoscopy was particularly popular in the world of Alexandria and this provoked further curiosity in India, although astrology was perhaps not yet so widespread as it was to become.

The Roman empire declined after the mid-first millennium A.D. and the focus of power and patronage gradually shifted from Rome to the capital of Byzantium, Constantinople. The prosperity of cities such as Basra in Iraq and Siraf on the Gulf symbolize the importance of the Gulf to the new locations of trade. In India, maritime commercial interests of the west coast, came within the purview of this trade. But it also came to be associated with the southern Arabian traders whose gradual control over maritime navigation, revitalized earlier trade links.

In the eighth century, the Arabs campaigned in Gujarat and Sind, occupied the lower Indus and organized themselves in western India as the pre-eminent entrepreneurs from west Asia. Perhaps their ambition was a preference for trade in India rather than territory. In the tenth century the Fatamids moved the Caliphate from Baghdad to Fustat / Old Cairo, to get a better grip on the extensive Arab world. This was a hint of the importance of the Indian Ocean to Arab politics. Aden, with Yemen as its hinterland, developed a commanding control over trade across the Arabian Sea and southwards to east Africa. Simultaneously, Arab traders were exploring the potentialities of the world further to the east.

The Chalukyas of the Deccan had had diplomatic relations with the Persian Sassanid kingdom and Zoroastrian communities from Persia had settled on the west coast, as for instance in Sanjan. A simultaneous Arab link with this area is evident from a Rashtrakuta inscription from Thana District which states that in the ninth century, the king, Krishna II appointed the Tajik named Madhumati, as governor of Sanjan. Arabs are referred to as Tajiks in many inscriptions, and Madhumad is an Indianization of Muhammad, also known from other Konkan inscriptions. The Arab governor, acting on behalf of the Rashtrakuta king, conquered the ports in the neighbourhood and appointed his men as port officials. One wonders why the Rashtrakutas chose Arab officials to man their ports. Was it because the Arabs were more familiar with the trade coming to these ports; or that the Arabs were anxious to cultivate Rashtrakuta authority to facilitate their commercial transactions; or were the Rashtrakutas suspicious of their own feudatories such as the Shilaharas, who later superseded them? Whatever the reason, the choice is interesting.

The purpose of this inscription is to record a grant of land to a *brāhmaṇ matha*. The *matha* was established by a *brāhmaṇ* and at his request, and, with the permission of the Rashtrakuta ruler, Madhumati/Muhammad gave the revenue of a village to the *matha* and to the temple dedicated to the goddess Durga. The grant also required the feeding of the *pancha-gaudiya-mahaparshad brāhmaṇs* settled in Sanjan.

Al Mas'udi, in the tenth century, mentions numbers of Arab merchants and sailors resident on the west coast and Alberuni writes that most were from southern Arabia. A Shilahara inscription of the eleventh century again from the Thana District, records the grant of an oil-mill to a *matha,* and refers by name to merchants, officials and *brāhmaṇs*, who were involved with recording the grant. The governor of Sanjan was now a certain Chamundaraja and therefore not an Arab. But among those listed as local dignitaries, there are three Arab names, pointing to the importance of the local Arab community and their participation in local affairs.

Arab traders settled on the west coast largely to facilitate their trade with India and to extend it to China. The Khojas, Bohras, Navayats and Mapillas claim connections with these settlements. Yet each was in many ways culturally distinct, perhaps because there had been some inter-marriage with local families or the adoption of local customary law, and some intermingling of religious and social practice. Or alternatively they happened to have evolved differently in India from the ways of the land from where they had migrated. Their ways of life also differed from each other yet they had emerged from similar historical processes. For the historian therefore their early history provides invaluable insights into processes of cultural integration. This is not to suggest that the integration was either entirely harmonious or given entirely to conflict, but to underline the need to examine the process, and to ascertain the nuances of the negotiations that are essential to the emergence of social identities. The cultures of maritime communities differ from hinterland cultures, and a single identity, be it religious or linguistic, or whatever, cannot be presumed as uniform for all.

The Indian trade was important to the Arabs who were also sending merchandise to Europe, largely pepper, sandal-wood, Chinese silk and porcelain. The Chinese items, whetted the Arab appetite for going further afield and establishing commercial bases in China. It has been argued that a direct voyage from the Gulf to Canton in south China would have been difficult given the shipping technology of the time. Therefore the journey was undertaken in segments. The Indian coasts provided convenient stopping points, linked to local hinterlands, as did ports in Sri Lanka and south east Asia. Nevertheless, there was competition from Indian traders going to China. Rajendra Chola's naval raid on Shrivijaya in the early eleventh century was largely to safeguard the south Indian trade to China traversing the seas between Malaya and Sumatra controlled by the kingdom of Shrivijaya. But apart from this there was perhaps a still more important reason for closer Arab ties with India and among these was the extremely lucrative trade in horses.

India had problems breeding thoroughbred horses. It is thought that the climate and the pastures were not of the right kind. Consequently quality horses were imported either from central Asia for use in north India, or from the Arabs for use elsewhere. The degree to which the import of horses became a significant item in the Arab trade is also a comment on activities in India at this time. Many new kingdoms were being established, sometimes in new areas, with each defining its boundaries and battling over territory. The horse became increasingly essential to the army and new equestrian technologies—metal stirrups, saddle shapes, bits—were more effective in battle. Thoroughbred horses were therefore imported even at exorbitant prices.

The merchant, Abdullah Wassif, writes that the quality of the Arab horses was such that even the legendary steeds of the ancient

Persian hero, Rustam, would, in comparison, be as worthless as the horse of the chess board. Not surprisingly, the average price of a horse is quoted as 220 gold *dinars*. The regular import, if credible, was said to be over ten thousand horses annually. This was because as both Wassif and Marco Polo maintain, Indians were inept at looking after horses. Wassif adds, and this needs investigation, that the cost of importing these horses, namely two million two hundred thousand *dinars* annually, was met from the overflowing revenues of the estates and endowments of the Hindu temples, and that no charge was incurred by the public treasury. The involvement in trade of religious institutions in various parts of the world is of course well-known, but this quantity of investment, would have required financing of an unusual kind—hence the need for historical investigation.

The Arab explorations to the east are reflected in the writings of merchants and geographers, such as Suleiman, Al-Mas'udi and Al-Idrisi. Unlike Indians who rarely wrote about where they had gone and what they had seen, the Arabs, inheriting the tradition of the Greeks, expressed their curiosity about the world they knew and commented copiously on the places they visited. Incidentally such accounts became the kernel of a genre of wonder tales, many drawing on fantasies about India, and some eventually taking shape as the stories familiar to us of Sinbad the Sailor.

Arab visitors to India seem to have been intrigued by ascetics. Suleiman writes that he saw a man dressed in a panther's skin, standing with his face to the sun; and after sixteen years he saw him again standing in the same stance. Al-Idrisi from Morocco writing in the eleventh century repeats the theory that Indian society had seven divisions. The king's status is the highest. Then come the *brāhmaṇs* who worship idols and drink no alcohol. The *ksatriyas* drink three litres of wine at a sitting. The farmers and the artisans form the next two categories and the final two are musicians and magicians. There are forty-two sects he says, and they variously worship ancestors, stones, fire, trees, snakes, or else deny every form of worship. The inclusion of sceptics and atheists is interesting. Multiple castes and sects seem to have been a source of curiosity to visitors. Such descriptions need not be taken literally, but the historian has to figure out what may have occasioned these statements.

The shift of the Caliphate from Baghdad to Fustat/Cairo led to the revival of trade through the Red Sea. Among the more fascinating documents on this trade are the recently deciphered Genizah letters, composed in Arabic but written in the Hebrew script. These were discovered in a chamber adjoining a synagogue in Old Cairo and had been preserved, not because they were religious literature but because they mentioned God in passing, and therefore such documents could not be destroyed. They date to the eleventh and twelfth centuries and a small number were written by those who were called the 'India traders'—Jewish merchants trading with India. Copper-plate inscriptions from Kerala confirm the presence of Jewish traders. One refers to a grant and privileges given by the Chera king to Joseph Rabban, the head of the local Jewish community of traders. The earlier arrivals from the west already settled in south India, were the Syrian Christians.

The 'India traders' came from families as distant as from Morocco, Tunisia and Spain. Their networks followed the areas conquered by the Arabs with extensions into Europe and into China. These links were somewhat shaken by the Crusaders, who, although ostensibly organizing the defence of Christianity, were nevertheless competing for the control of the eastern trade. The Genizah letters are the correspondence of the Jewish merchants writing home from distant places where they had their commercial connections.

Many of the letters begin with eulogies directed to the recipient, frequently to soften the blow of news about lost cargo, either wrecked at sea or looted by pirates. Piracy was rampant as would be expected when the volume of maritime trade increased appreciably. Large memorial stones from the Konkan, some now housed in the Goa museum, depict heroes in battle with pirates, and date to approximately this period. But for the most part the letters are business-like and set out the deals and exchanges, the shipments, prices and the sending of presents to secure favours. Some are more personal, and sound quite contemporary. A trader writes to his wife from India, asking her to refrain from accusing him of neglecting her and assuring her that he constantly thinks of her and yearns for her, and wishes to fulfill all her desires. There was always the danger that wives left alone for long periods would demand a separation. Women sometimes became bankers and brokers and thus participated in the trade, a practice that went back to Roman times.

Consignments of merchandise headed for India consisted of coral which continued to be in considerable demand, textiles such as Russian linen which was fashionable in India, and silver vessels, herbs, aromatics, incense, medicines and newly minted gold *dinars.* The use of gold and silver coins varied according to the transaction. Although coins moved from west to east, the scale was now far smaller than that of the Roman coins. The cargo to be sent home consisted substantially of pepper, lac and iron. In the mid-eleventh century the market price of 45 Ib. of pepper was roughly equivalent to a moderate annual salary of 35 *dinars*, and a house in Cairo cost 300 *dinars*. So the price of a thoroughbred Arab horse at 220 *dinars* was pretty steep.

Aden was not merely a port at the nodal point of sea lanes. It was the centre for this trade. The Rabbinical court where Jewish merchants could bring their disputes for settlement was also located at Aden and at Fustat/Old Cairo. Disputes ranged from compensation for shipwrecks or the sharing of profits, to making a settlement on a slave and her child abandoned by an 'India trader'. A major figure was the trustee of the merchants, the *wakil,* who negotiated with princes and pirates, was a banker, had jurisdiction over Aden and India in the India trade, and was highly respected in the eastern Mediterranean. One among these based in Aden and mentioned more frequently was Madmun. He also invested in his own trading ventures, including a partnership with the ruler of south Yemen to build ships to carry cargo to Sri Lanka. The most impressive of such persons was the famous Moses Maimonides, living in Fustat, one of the most respected religious scholars and philosophers of the Eurasian medieval world.

Sometimes the letters refer to legal problems as in the case of Joseph Lebdi. He collected consignments from as far away as Tunisia to exchange for profit in his India trade. The agreement at Aden was that half the consignment was to be left there and exchanged for pepper from Malabar, and the other half was to be taken to an inland town in Gujarat. Lebdi spent a few years in Gujarat doing business and exchanged his coral for lac and semi-precious stones. On the return journey two of his shipments were wrecked. The legal questions then were, who should bear the losses, was the book-keeping in order and did his takings match what he had sold? Eventually the law-suit was settled by negotiation between three Jewish courts located in Aden, India and Tunisia, an accomplishment that would be difficult today.

Of those that lived in India, Abraham bin Yiju was the best known and ran a bronze factory for seventeen years in Dindigal near Madurai. But he seems to have spent more time in Mangalore. He made his fortune importing scrap metal and recycling it into vessels and exporting them to Aden. This enabled him to live a good life in India. He also used his wealth to rescue his extended family in Tunisia from deportation to Sicily after an attack on Tunisia by European Crusaders. The letters mention the Indian Ashu who bore his children. There is a hint that she might have been a Nair and possibly their relationship was a form of *sambandham.*

But the Jewish involvement was not at the commercial forefront. Arab trade prospered as did the growing exchange with China. Chinese porcelain surfaces at coastal locations in India and confirms the increasing presence of Chinese trade in the Indian Ocean, referred to in texts. This brings us to the cusp of the arrival of Europeans from western Europe and their trading companies, which were to radically change the pattern of the earlier trade.

The rippling out of the trading circuits provides the geographical dimensions to what was viewed as almost a global commerce at that time. Connections over the centuries moved from the hub of the Red Sea and the Arabian Sea to a much larger rim. Tunisia and China came within the same trading circuit. Indian history of the first millennium A.D., came to be set in wider horizons. In this expansion there was inevitably a shift in centres and peripheries, occasioned either by changing demands for goods, or the emergence of new investors or even new navigational methods affecting routes. The intervention of the European trading companies was initially a further extension of this geography and a capturing of the existing trade. But what ultimately changed the pattern was the emergence of capitalism in Europe and its impact on the economy of maritime trade and colonies.

As a factor in economic change, trade varies in its effectiveness. Some exports such as pepper and textiles continued throughout the centuries. The import of horses in large number was costly. If the export of pepper brought in gold and silver, the import of horses drained away some of this income. Would this have restricted economic growth? The Indo-Roman trade may have brought about a qualitative change in some south Indian economies. The Arab trade had a more marked impact on the kingdoms of the peninsula. The Jewish India trade was marginal to Indian political economies.

Indian traders were not merely at the receiving end of these enterprises; they were successful both as entrepreneurs and as middlemen. But apart from overland trade especially to central Asia and northern China, their maritime concentration seems to have been eastwards to south east Asia and China. They had a dominant presence in south east Asia, but their visibility was evident in southern China as well. Analytical studies of these links and the role of a mercantile Indian culture have still to find a place in the understanding of Indian civilization.

The Indo-Roman and Jewish trade faded out. The Arab trade left a deeper imprint with a stronger interface in the form of communities and innovative religious and social observances in both Islam and Hinduism. If global exchange can be said to have transmuted cultures, then perhaps the most meaningful result of these contacts, were contributions to the advancing of knowledge, both in India and in centres outside India. Indian mathematics, astronomy and medicine became independent areas of knowledge, their critical enquiries releasing Indian and other scholars from the constraints of orthodoxy. The ensuing knowledge was reformulated in Baghdad and other Arab centres as it had been earlier in Alexandria and the eastern Mediterranean. Eventually it reached Europe. Eastwards, exchange of information on alchemy in India and China, triggered an exploration not only of material substances but also in the transmutation of ideas as part of philosophical speculation. These were remarkable demonstrations of how systems of knowledge have grown and progressed in the past, not in isolation, but through the interface of many cultures.

The intention is not to suggest that these patterns could only have emerged from maritime links, for there are parallels in the patterns of overland trade. But maritime history can provide a variant perspective from different kinds of evidence, and the forms that evolved through this trade need to be recognized. Acquainting ourselves with our ancestral societies can be salutary, for it tells us that we were different in the past and points up the difference. If carefully reconstructed, such history can also provide an image of how others from diverse societies saw us. Such mirrors from the past provide glimpses of what we were, and maybe, these can also provide invaluable insights into what we are today.

REFERENCES

Chakravarti R. (ed.), *Trade in Early India* (Delhi: Oxford University Press, 2001).

Chaudhuri K.N., *Asia Before Europe* (Cambridge, 1990).

De Romanis F. and A. Tchernia (ed.), *Crossings*. Early Mediterranean Contacts with India (Delhi, Manohar, 1997).

Goitein S.D., *A Mediterranean Society* (Barkeley: University of California, 1999).

A. Gunder Frank, *Reorient*: *Global Economy in the Asian* Age (New Delhi: Vistaar Publications, 1998).

The Museum and History[1]

The museum as we know it today had its genesis in India a couple of centuries ago. Collecting objects specifically of past times and locating them in a designated place as was done in China and in Europe, was not an activity of noticeable interest among Indians in previous times. Nevertheless, although there may not have been museums, there were many occasions when a bronze sculpture of a deity or a miniature painting was thought about, talked about, written about and appreciated. Manuscripts were collected and carefully preserved, not for their antique value but for their contents or as votive objects. Royal decrees on various matters were inscribed either on stone or on copper-plates and were located in a public place or were held by families. Other antiquities, barring of course coins, rarely found a location separate from where they had been initially placed.

Buddhist monks inhabited monasteries that were either free standing or often rock cut caves in peninsula India and especially the Deccan where the volcanic rock was suitable for cutting. These date to the urn of the Christian era. Their walls were painted with murals depicting the life of the Buddha and events important to the mission of the Buddha.[2] When they fell into disuse, the paintings were damaged. Where living in cave monasteries was discontinued and the caves deserted, there the entrances got blocked by rock fall and this helped preserve the painting. In later periods some sanctums of Hindu temples had murals.

What did survive and underwent changes of style and aesthetics was sculpture. Stone sculpture was profuse as it was frequently an adjunct to the architecture of the place of worship. In a few places where stone was sparse, brick and clay were used. Buddhist sacred places had icons of the Buddha as well as panels depicting narratives of the biography of the Buddha and scenes of secular life.[3] Hindu sculpture tended to be images of deities and scenes from mythology and a depiction of narratives from the better-known epics. However, free-standing images in stone were also made for placing in the sanctum. Bronze icons were taken out in procession on ritual occasions.[4] Icons also had a political significance, when, at the end of a campaign the victor brought home the icon worshipped by his defeated enemy and claimed acknowledgement from its deity.[5]

These were made by professional craftsmen in accordance with the Sanskrit manuals on sculpture and architecture—the *shilpa-shastras*. They described in minute detail how each variant icon of a deity and other figures were to be sculpted. Icons under worship that were thought to be somewhat worn out after a time, were replaced with new ones. It was recommended that the old ones be ritually submerged in rivers. More often however, lesser divinities were placed in the precincts of the temple or under a tree, for continuing worship along with other deities.

Folk deities were of course worshipped in larger numbers, but were frequently of wood or terracotta and placed in small shrines. Their iconography sometimes overlapped with the orthodox stone images but more often was different. Because they were made of biodegradable material, these icons did not survive over long periods and had to be replaced more frequently than those in stone and metal. Recognizing the importance of these images, both ritually and aesthetically, is a recent development and they still tend to be segregated and kept in "Craft Museums".

From about the eleventh century A.D. manuscripts on birch-bark and palm leaves began to be illustrated. Many of these were written by Jaina and Buddhist monks, or by scholarly *brāhmaṇs* and kept in the *bhandara*, or repository attached to the place of worship, or else they were kept by the families of royalty, priests, merchants and wealthy householders. The gifting of manuscripts and hence their being written in large numbers was a pious act among some religious sects such as the Jainas.[6] Illustrated manuscripts were in a distinctive style different from the painting that had preceded them. They did not feature in the discussions on aesthetics among erudite Sanskrit scholars, their use being largely in religious discourse; but they would nevertheless have been discussed in other circles. The adoption of paper for manuscripts, from about the twelfth century tended to change the format and size of the illustrations.

These miniature paintings, illustrating manuscripts on a variety of themes, were the opposite of the earlier murals stylistically and thematically. As a genre they became an important item of royal patronage in the courts of the Sultans, the Mughals and lesser rulers up until the eighteenth century. In some ways they were the counterpart to the extensive articulation in sculpture of the earlier period. The paintings included illustrations of the Indo-Persian epics such as the *Hamza-nama* and the *Tuti-nama,* narratives from the Sanskrit epic especially the *Mahābhārata,* and semi-historical texts such as the *Padshah-nama* depicting events at the imperial court.[7] Miniature painting was a link to earlier Indian and Persian book illustration.

This change in style and medium gave prominence to well-established royal ateliers and the painters who worked there. Judging by their names they came from a range of social castes and artisan families, and from various religions—Hindu, Jaina and Muslim. Representation of activities of kings and nobles and their portraits became a central feature, or else there was a focus on the special interests of a particular emperor. Jahangir being something of a naturalist employed artists who excelled in detailed paintings of flowers and birds.

Miniature paintings when collected and kept as albums and distinct from book illustrations, further encouraged royal and private collections. These collections were in part a parallel to the royal treasuries, going back to early times. They housed a variety of objects—some of it had been gifted to the king and others were kept in storage to be given as gifts.

From the sixteenth century onwards Europeans belonging to religious missions such as the Jesuits or merchants in trading companies, settled in towns that were political and commercial centres in order to facilitate their proselytizing or their ventures in trade. Those holding office in trading companies started a fashion for albums of paintings depicting everyday scenes of street life in the towns and in the households of the newly rich

Europeans, imitating an Indian life style. The Kalighat paintings of Bengal represented one style among these.[8] The style however was different from that of the miniatures. Inevitably, collecting antiquities for commercial use was not far behind. By the eighteenth century, entrepreneurs such as Antoine Polier and Claude Martin, had substantial personal collections.[9] Claude Martin for example, made a fortune in business transactions and knew that there was a demand for oriental antiques in Europe where both royalty and the wealthy bourgeoisie were now interested in exotica. Like others, he too shipped these collections to Europe where they were sold for an impressive profit. The collections took on the character of private museums although they were not referred to as such.

The East India Company treated such collecting as the hobby of gentleman traders. Its officers were not averse to trading privately and accumulating wealth both in the form of money and of objects that had a market in Britain. The increasing availability of such exotica raised the demand for Indian antiquities in the markets of Europe.

However, some officers of the East India Company, were, apart from their usual functions, seriously interested in investigating the Indian past. But they could not recognize histories that might have helped them in this investigation, barring only one—*Kalhana's Rājatarangini* which being a twelfth century history of Kashmir could not provide evidence for an all-India history. They argued therefore, that India was an a-historical civilization and lacked a sensc of history. It was thought incumbent upon these officers to discover the Indian past. Sir William Jones established the Asiatic Society in Calcutta in 1784 for precisely this purpose.[10]

Later, after 1857, when the East India Company's control over its Indian possessions was taken over by the British Government, India became a directly administered colony. Administration moved from the private officers of a trading company to the representatives of the British government in India—the Viceroy and his Council. This included officers of the Civil Service who supervised the administration of various state activities, including those related to antiquities. There was a shift from collecting antiquities for sale on the European market to collecting antiquities to reconstruct the early history of India. From being exotic objects, antiquities now became factual data in the knowledge system pertaining to the colony.

The colonial state believed that furthering knowledge about the colony was one of the means of exercizing power over the colony. Lord Curzon regarded it as what he called, the necessary furniture of empire. But antiquities when seen as art, raised other problems. For instance, the aesthetic of 'the Other', the colonial society, was different and unfamiliar. Pre-Islamic Indian art was viewed as over-decorative and unrealistic with the many armed anthropomorphic deities being described as somewhat monstrous.[11]

Unearthing the past became a major activity among some officers of the British Indian Government. Alexander Cunningham consulted, among other sources, the itinerary of a Chinese Buddhist pilgrim, Hsuan Tsang, who came to India in the seventh century A.D. This helped Cunningham in discovering a number of early Buddhist sites in northern India rich in antiquities.[12] These discoveries increased knowledge about the past but also required decisions about the custody and control over the sites. And so, an Archaeological Survey was established in 1861, to dig, to discover and to conserve. Engineers and surveyors such as Francis Buchanan and Colin MacKenzie, not only gathered data but started collections of manuscripts and artifacts. Private investigators too were not lagging behind. James Fergusson, who made his wealth in the indigo trade, was interested in the historical remains of the land in which his factories were located. He traveled widely, making sketches and later taking photographs of architectural ruins of Buddhist *stupas*, Hindu temples and Islamic mosques.[13] This helped in the study of the history of architecture in India with attempts to systematize the data. Hindu and Buddhist monuments elicited greater enquiry since the Islamic monuments were viewed as alien to India, despite their carrying the imprint of pre-Islamic elements. This approach followed from the interpretation of Indian history by James Mill who had projected a dichotomy between what he called Hindu and Muslim civilization in India, an interpretation which by now had become a hegemonic concept. Antiquities from what was called the Hindu period were further divided into the pure Aryan styles and the supposedly more adulterated non-Aryan styles, although the definition of neither was clear. It is curious that none of these people thought of discussing their formulations with the Indian master craftsmen who were still both active and knowledgeable.

The nucleus of a modern museum in India was in the premises of the Asiatic Society in Calcutta where in the early nineteenth century some collections came to be housed and exhibited. This was virtually a private museum since the Asiatic Society was not open to Indians or the public until later. The collection was intended for historical research. Eventually the Indian Museum was established in Calcutta in 1866. This was a major enterprise. It was not limited to antiquities of art historical interest since it also housed material from ethnological fieldwork and later from archaeological excavations. Even beyond that it was intended to include specimens of flora, fauna, fossils and minerals as well. The Indian Museum was where the representations of all things Indian were to be gathered and then exhibited according to a defined pattern that drew on the colonial perceptions of how the Indian past and its environment was to be understood.

Similar categories of collections were placed in museums in Britain. Other European museums, particularly those located in countries which had colonies in Asia such as France and Holland, and whose antiquities had affinities with those from India, were also anxious to build collections of objects from India especially those from the pre-modern period. In India, the idea of a museum was gradually implanted in other important towns such as Chennai, Mumbai, Patna and the like, where antiquities had been gathered from the region. Some decades later, University Departments of History began to house small collections of local finds used mainly in teaching art history. The controversy over whether significant objects should remain in local museums or be transferred to the central museum is a continuing debate. With the recognition of regional cultures in the sub-continent there is support for regional museums.

The artifacts in Indian museums were initially unfamiliar to the official collectors. Nevertheless, they had to be placed in a cultural context comprehensible to those who organized the museum, even if this format was not drawn from the way in which these objects were viewed by the societies that made them. Museums in India did not grow out of the collections of Indian royalty or individual Indians. They grew from the colonial government wishing to discover, interpret and order a past for its own understanding of India and for its Indian subjects. The backdrop was provided by events of great magnitude—empire and conquest, colonialism, industrialization and the Enlightenment. These were baffling events at that time, both for the colonizers and the colonized. The last half century has not seen much essential change in this approach.

Placing antiquities in a museum imbued them with additional monetary value. By the late nineteenth century there was a greedy market for such antiquities outside India and the plundering of archaeological sites began to be noticed. This occasioned the Treasure Trove Act passed in 1889 by which the British Indian government declared its right over all antiquities.[14] The removal of these from the site where they had been found was made illegal. However, this Act did not protect Indian antiquities from the official removal of such antiquities to Britain, as for example, the sculpted stone panels from the *stupa* at Amaravati. The Treasure Trove Act is incidentally reminiscent of the treasure trove clauses in the *Arthashastra* of Kautilya written in the fourth century B.C., and the references in many early inscriptions to the king's right to treasure troves—except that in these texts the treasure was gold and not antiquities.[15]

As in Europe, so too in India, Indians of the middle class began to take an interest in collecting antiques and artifacts that had a curiosity value. Private collections tended to focus on objects of daily use, as well as textiles, jewellery and weaponry. An example of this was Bhau Daji Lad, a doctor and a public figure in Bombay, whose collection dates back to the latter half of the nineteenth century and is located in the recently renovated house where he lived.[16] Nevertheless, a nexus was formed between collectors and museums. Gradually collecting began to include antiquities of art-historical value and became a status symbol with the new bourgeoisie imitating the old aristocracy.

Museums established by the government were invariably called the *ajaib-ghar*, literally, the House of Curiosities but also translated as the Wonder House. This was in some ways reminiscent of the *wunderkammer,* the room of marvellous objects in European houses, encapsulating curiosity about unfamiliar objects and the wish to collect them and to know more about them. Colonial curiosity in the Indian context referred more to natural history and ethnographic displays but the term included art history museums as well. The past was atomized and each object was treated as something unusual. However, the current names for art museums refer to the obvious—literally, the collections of art, antiquities and artifacts.

Surprisingly there has been little outcry about placing religious icons of deities in a secular space, and thereby in a sense, making them secular objects. One reason for this not becoming an issue was that although the icons came from places of worship, many were no longer actually under worship, although some visitors to museums today make a gesture of worship before such an icon. The deity when placed in a museum evoked the narrative of its mythology rather than its being an object of worship. The mutation of an object of worship into an object admired for its aesthetic appeal gives it a more secular meaning and an additional context. This also hints at the debate elsewhere on the concept of a museum veering between temple and forum.

The displacement from a context of ritual was in part achieved by converting the object into an individual item and giving it a label with a minimal but clear statement on its provenance, its period in history and its style. There were major debates among art historians on the aesthetics of variant styles. For example, Indian Buddhist sculpture from Gandhara in the north-west of the sub-continent which scholars have labelled variously as Greco-Roman, Greco-Bactrian, Greco-Bactrian-Indian, was marginal to the Indian aesthetic. Nevertheless there was a debate as to whether this style was aesthetically superior to the more recognizably Indian style of Buddhist sculpture in central and south India,[17] or was it merely a hybrid style that happened to be familiar to the modern European eye and therefore more easily appreciated by the European. That the antiquities of

Gandhara represent remarkable cultural intersections which needed to be investigated was lost in battling the question of which was the superior aesthetic. The use of dynastic labels for antiquities suggested a homogenous artistic expression. It diverted attention from the obvious difference between the polished stone sculpture of an imperial Mauryan style and the terracotta folk deities of the same period. Such debates reflected the growing discipline of art history and the much wider debate on the interpretation of early Indian history and projected the imprint of both Orientalism and Nationalism. The formulation of a national history had advanced with the clearer perspective of history helping to construct a national identity as a prelude to integrating the subcontinent. But this national identity was subverted by the partition of the sub-continent into the two nation-states of India and Pakistan.

In 1947, the erstwhile colony became independent. In the following year an important exhibition was held in Delhi. The finest objects of art-historical value were brought together from various Indian museums. It was projected as symbolizing the cultural heritage of the nation and as an essential component of defining national culture.[18] Since there was no national museum at that time, it had to be housed in the Rashtrapati Bhavan, the residence of the erstwhile Viceroy which became the residence of the President of India. Some regard this as a symbolic conjoining of the highest state authority with national culture. The exhibition became the nucleus of what was to be established as the National Museum. This Museum differed from the earlier nineteenth century Indian Museum in as much as it was intended to represent the cultural heritage and to educate the public. More recently it has become a focus of tourist interest.

Sculpture in stone and metal was given prominence above other arts. This was understandable since historically sculpture in India has been of an extraordinary quality. There was a profusion of Hindu images, with Buddhist images being fewer but perhaps equally if not more aesthetically impressive, as were some Jaina images. This again tended to emphasize the Hindu idiom being the dominant cultural achievement of the Indian past. The recognition of miniature painting particularly of the

Mughal period as first order art would have given appropriate attention to Islamic, Jaina and other articulations. The nationalist discourse had argued that ancient Hindu India had been the golden age of the past stretching from the fourth century B.C. to the fifth century A.D. The location of the post-Gupta period in this scheme was a later addition. To some extent therefore the National Museum illustrated the standard histories of India and the concept was replicated in the smaller museums.

Gradually however the function of the National Museum began to be viewed from other perspectives. In the late twentieth century an institute of art history became a part of the Museum. This raised other problems. Was the Museum to continue to project a visual representation of Indian civilization to the public, and thereby educate the public, or should it also convert itself into a centre for collating and conserving data on art history and thus become an institution with an additional specialization? In either case, museums would require to be properly equipped with a library, a photo-tech, and laboratories for conservation and restoration. These in most museums are either lacking or are inadequate.

Educating the public through an art-historical museum has its own problems. The context of an object is annulled when it is exhibited in isolation and its meaning in terms of its origins and historical dimensions is curtailed. What remains for the public to view is partial, limited to something of its aesthetic quality. Walter Benjamin has argued that the object exhibited is embedded in a tradition and if one is seeking for the aura of the object it lies in the tradition. Yet some others would argue that the museum liberates the object from its tradition. This may introduce many more facets in its appreciation than if it were still embedded in its tradition. However the basic problem remains that of defining the tradition and definitions can be contentious.

The word culture is now often replaced by heritage and a museum is said to encapsulate a heritage. Again the definition is complicated. Heritage draws from a constellation of historical events. But what we regard as our heritage today need not be the same as what our ancestors believed to be their heritage.

The complexity deepens when the discussion is about national heritage because this can shift when the contours of national culture change in accordance with the emergence of new nations. Where once the Indian national heritage was viewed as sub-continental, there are now multiple notions of national heritage pertinent to each nation-state of the subcontinent. This multiplicity increases further when we realize that there are many strands to each national heritage with unequal meanings for the various communities of the nation. Ministries of Culture tend to annul cultural differences in multi-cultural societies by projecting a homogenized packet as a national culture which does not always reflect the sensitivities of multi-culturalism. The western world is only on the threshold of this problem with the pressure of large immigrant communities bringing in their own notions of heritage.

If the museum is to encapsulate a civilization, Indian in this case, there has to be much more discussion on what this term means. In popular usage, civilization is still tied to its nineteenth century meaning, and this also reflects the way in which it was played out in the colonies. The priority of exhibiting icons of deities as symbols of a civilization continues. These relate largely to the world of various orthodoxies and elites and although the objects remain familiar the understanding of their historical context has changed. The context could be made visible by juxtaposing other items from the same period, especially where artifacts are plentiful or have special qualities. Objects of art historical interest need not always be viewed in splendid isolation. The juxtaposition of art and artifact would introduce on occasion a required corrective to the priority of the one over the other. The ordering of the art historical and archaeological museum should ideally invoke new ways of looking at the past. Rather than seeing a single object as representing an entire age it might be more meaningful to see it as one among multiple facets of a moment in time. Given the technical facilities now available this should not be a problem. It would need ways of approximating the virtual reality of the context of the object, and attempting to go beyond the vision of Andre Malraux towards that which technology today is likely to make possible.

Matters that relate to museums in the developing world in particular have their own problems. The antiquities exhibited are generally those from the life-ways of elite groups with little effort to put them into a wider social and cultural context. This in part conditions the perspective of the audience, the visitors to the museums. The living patterns of societies generally draw, and have drawn, on symbiotic social relations and representing this would require a radical rethinking of some concepts. For example, the concept of civilization would need to be more inclusive of what have been set aside as marginal or minority cultures. How does a museum exhibit the artifacts of these cultures not in separate galleries but as part of an integrated heritage? Should we not rethink the priorities implicit in what we highlight and how we order and systematize the representation of objects? In a sense this is a continuing problem since visitors to museums constantly change and make new demands on what is to be exhibited and what can be ignored. When going to a museum becomes a matter of interest to those who have not visited a museum before—as often happens in South Asia—then the accessibility of objects in terms of understanding them often requires a refocusing on the display so as to communicate with new categories of visitors. Sometimes this involves having to display objects different from the usual but of interest to the new visitors.

An issue that comes to the forefront intermittently is that of the repatriation of antiquities taken away from sites and placed in distant museums. This was most obviously done during the colonial period. Arguments flow back and forth. For some there is acrimony over the manner in which objects were displaced even if it is conceded that they might be better maintained in the museums of the developed world? Others maintain that all antiquities are part of the universal cultural heritage and involve all of humankind and not just a single nation. Therefore, they can be placed in any museum anywhere and if need be accessed through the internet.

There has been insufficient discussion of the inter-disciplinary nature of the concept of what is referred to as the universal museum and some see it as merely a way of not returning antiquities forcibly removed from their place of origin even if now claimed as part of the national heritage of where they came from. A universal museum does not simply mean a juxtaposition of, and a larger collection of superior quality objects from all over the world. The concept would first require a redefinition of the categories used, such as, historical, traditional, indigenous, ethnographic, and so on. There would also have to be an attempt to explain how a range of objects from different cultures have come to be exhibited in one place, how they relate to the cultures they have come from and the other cultures in the midst of which they are now located. This would require some radical redefinitions of the categories currently used.

The tendency to homogenize cultures would also come under question and would have to be reconsidered especially because in many discussions of heritage such homogenizing is not acceptable. Hierarchies in evaluating cultures using the earlier definitions as for example of 'civilized' and 'primitive' have now been discarded in the social sciences and would have little relevance for art-history. The most difficult problem for a universal museum as visualized so far would be that of not giving priority to what goes under the label of western civilization since universal museums so far are situated largely in Europe and North America. The museum was created from political acts and social concerns and assumes the superiority of certain cultures. How should this be corrected?

Further, whereas the world of the ex-colonies is asked to let go of the antiquities taken from them, the world of the ex-colonizers is not willing to share the antiquities from its own past with other parts of the world. This creates an asymmetrical situation. How do other countries, less gifted with objects, acquire antiquities from richer cultures to enable them to become universal museums?

If antiquities are truly a universal cultural heritage then major museums all over the world should be made trans-national. How is this to be done? In today's world this means that those museums that wish to increase their range would have to depend on an exchange or a donation of objects. The exchange of antiquities would have to be of the same status as those taken away. It would not apply to antiquities that were bought by the museum although looted or stolen, objects so bought raises other awkward questions. The donation could be from museums that have a surplus of particular antiquities.

For example, could antiquities from the west, not necessarily of the first order, be donated to museums outside the developed world and particularly through museums that have high value objects acquired during colonial rule? The presence of such objects in non-western museums might encourage the study of cultures that are currently perceived as too distant and too alien. Such studies could also result in framing questions about various cultures from a different perspective. Museums in the developed world have extensive collections from various places and particularly from their ex-colonies. By contrast most museums in developing countries focus on their national culture and do not have collections to support the study of antiquities and artifacts from other parts of the world. This can be overcome to some extent by technical facilities. It would help if the vision of museums could be moved from the specific to the more universal.

This is also a matter of discussion within the larger countries of the developing world. Site museums are important to understanding the nature of a site and of the object. The best antiquities from a site are removed and taken to the national museum where they are exhibited outside of their context. There are also complaints that not everything can be exhibited in the national museum and a fair amount goes into storage. Such reserve collections are not always easily viewable even by those researching on them. Would it not be better then to leave them at the site museum or in important local museums where they would be on exhibition. But would they be secure in a small site museum or even in a local museum? The saga of the Kabul Museum in recent times has made such discussions pertinent.

With the increasing collection of antiquities by private persons there will soon be private museums—as indeed there are some already. Private and state museums can become contenders for the best on the art market. State museums are dependent on state funding and this tends to be small and not consonant with the demands of the art market. There are however, many agencies, such as private collectors and art dealers, and patrons of various kinds, involved with either assisting the museum or competing with it. The prices of antiquities on the art market are determined for the international market and have little relationship to the domestic market in developing countries. This commercialization makes it difficult for museums to purchase outstanding objects and such objects then go to private collectors. In countries such as India, collectors do not have tax benefits to nudge them into eventually donating their collections to museums. Converting an antique into a commodity is as good as destroying it for purposes of historical and cultural research.

The future of the museum points us in the direction of thinking anew about what is being displayed and how. The museum, as also the writing of history is the mediation between the past and us. The past is not something out there, it is a part of us. We therefore need to understand it, and to understand it not in isolation but in context. One can only repeat the often repeated sentiment that a museum should make the invisible, visible.

If the object in the museum or if the monument at a site is allowed to be stripped of its multiple meanings, and made into a symbol of a new concept, then, as it has been said, it can become an object of political contestation. We cannot assume that museums and monuments are protected by the sheer fact that they are articulations of what is past and gone. It is precisely the past that is now being politicized and therefore contested. Situations of political confrontation, expressed through the idiom of religion for instance, have caused as much damage to antiquities and monuments as have time and neglect. We are likely to experience these traumas more frequently in the future, for we live in a world characterized by the aftermath of all varieties of colonialisms, and by political contestations pretending to be religious assertions or statements of civilization. We who are historians, art-historians and curators might well have to go beyond just understanding and presenting the past and have to involve ourselves in protecting the testimonies that come from the past.

If culture is universal then its universality has to be protected.

Economic globalization seems to be furthering all fundamentalisms—be they Christian, Islamic, Hindu, or Buddhist. It seems to me that the delegitimizing of each of these fundamentalisms is ultimately more important than the confrontations between them.

Museums can assist in continually emphasizing the obvious—that cultures are not isolated, monolithic, uniform and unchanging. Cultural articulations emerge from the intersection of ideas and forms. If it can be shown that cultures have continuously been involved in giving and taking then to insist on the isolated evolution and identity of a single culture is not viable. The museum may evoke collective memory which is not just an aggregate of individual memories nor is it history, but it is an interaction of these. The interaction as a process needs to be reflected. This may change many perspectives, involving systems of classification, the context of the display and an emphasis on the elements of creativity and cultural crosscurrents that may have gone into the making of the object. Such reformulations are current in historical writing.

Definitions of culture start with the question of who defines culture and whose cultures are we exhibiting and thereby evaluating and why. The notion of classicism has changed and historians are now giving more space to cultures earlier believed to be marginal, cultures that might even tell us about the other side of the classical. The nineteenth century was rich in its attempts to define culture, but these definitions need to be re-analyzed, re-contoured. As a historian I would like to see a far greater dialogue between the reading of the object and of the text. An object is fundamentally important since it is the only tangible testimony of past reality. The text helps to explain the reality.

And finally there is the question of chronology. The past has its own genealogy. When we speak to the past in the sources we use—be they antiquities or texts—we are tapping into points of time that have experienced their own pasts before we have even reached out to them. Fernand Braudel spoke of the three dimensions of time relevant to every historical event. Initially there is the *longue durée* that over many centuries moulds the landscape of the event. Then there is its shorter social and economic background. And lastly there is the moment when the event happens. To this some have added the fourth perspective—the moment when the observer becomes aware of the historical event, as for instance, in the form of an object in the museum. I am not suggesting that every object displayed should be set in geological deep time. But if the context of the antiquity or the artifact could evoke the historical process that went into its making, could provide a glimpse at least of what came before and what came after, then such an insight might give a different meaning to our currently contested notions of tradition, identity and culture. The museum could then become the focus of a new discourse.

NOTES

1. Based on a presentation at a conference at the Vatican Museum in December 2006 on "The Future of the Museum."
   I would like to thank Michael Meister, Brian Kennedy and Gene Garthwaite for their useful and helpful comments on this talk and for the time and trouble they took to discuss the contents with me.
2. The foremost examples of these are to be found in the Ajanta caves in the vicinity of Aurangabad in western India. Benoy K. Behl, *The Ajanta Caves* (London, 1998).
3. Vidya Dehejia, *Discourse in Early Buddhist Art: Visual Narratives of India* (New Delhi, 1997).
4. C. Sivaramamurti, *South Indian Bronzes* (New Delhi, 1963); Douglas Barett, *Early Cola Bronzes,* (Bombay, 1965).
5. Richard M. Eaton "Temple Desecration and Indo-Muslim States", in Richard M. Eaton, *Essays on Islam and Indian History* (Delhi, 2000), pp. 94-132.
6. Shridhar Andhare, "Jain Monumental Painting"; John Guy, "Jain Manuscript Painting" in Pratapaditya Pal (ed.) *Jain Art from India* (London, 1994), pp. 77-100.
7. Jeremiah R. Loosty, *The Art of the Book in India* (London, 1982); Stuart Gary Welch, *Imperial Mughal Painting* (New York, 1978).
8. Jyotindra Jain, *Kalighat Painting: Images from a Changing World* (Ahmedabad, 1999).
9. Maya Jassonoff, *Edge of Empire* (London, 2005), pp. 45 ff.
10. Soumen N. Mukherjee, *Sir William Jones: A Study in Eighteenth Century British Attitudes to India* (Delhi, 1983).

11. Partha Mitter, *Much Maligned Monsters: A History of European Reaction to Indian Art* (Oxford, 1977).
12. Abu Imam, *Sir Alexander Cunningham and the Beginnings of Indian Archaeology* (Dacca, 1966).
13. James Fergusson, *A History of Indian and Eastern Architecture*, 2 vols. (London, 1879), (Delhi, 1972 reprint).
14. Tapati Guha-Thakurta, *Monuments, Objects, Histories: Institutions of Art in Colonial and Post-Colonial India,* (Delhi, 2004), pp. 198-99.
15. Kautilya, *Arthasastra,* 4.1.51-55. Text edited by R.P. Kangle as *The Kautiliya Arthasastra* (Bombay, 1972).
16. J.V. Naik, "Dr. Bhau Daji Lad", in *Gallery of Excellence* (Mumbai, 1996), pp. 29-35.
17. Ernest B. Havell, *Indian Sculpture and Painting* (London, 1908), pp. 83-109; Ananda K. Coomaraswamy, *Essays in National Idealism* (New Delhi, 1981 reprint).
18. Tapati Guha-Thakurta, op. cit, pp 175-84.

The Future of the Indian Past

In a seemingly contradictory way, looking into the future requires an understanding of the past. Such an understanding can illumine the present and enable one to think more meaningfully about the future. History as a commentary on the past becomes essential to this process. How the past is to be understood is one among the many alternatives for the future that Indian society is facing in present times. In this chapter, are discussed the choices before us that will determine the future if the Indian past. Such choices are dependent on our understanding of the *past,* but among other things, are also tied to the shape that we wish to give to the future society. What is sometimes referred to as the controversy over history is an indicator of this connection.

The tradition of liberal, independent historical writing in India is now under attack from an official interpretation of Indian history. Many historians are currently opposing the attempt to use history in support of an ideology of religious nationalism. The opposition was sparked a couple of years ago by the government condemnation of existing school textbooks in History published by the NCERT. These textbooks were discredited so as to justify their being replaced in 2003 by a history that would endorse the current political ideology. Historians have been troubled not just by the content of the new textbooks but also by the manner in which these changes have been made.

The school curriculum was changed by government fiat, without consulting the educational bodies that had earlier routinely been consulted, such as, the Central Advisory Board of Education. Such a consultation would have prevented the implementation of what many now regard as a substandard curriculum for schools, quite apart from the rather drastic re-orientation of history.

The Seventh D. T. Lakdawala Memorial Lecture, New Delhi, 21 February 2004.

Middle School students are to be taught the following subjects: a package entitled "Social Studies" consisting of potted versions of history, economics, civics and geography; Vedic Mathematics; Simple Sanskrit; and Yoga and Consciousness. On the completion of Middle School they will be tested to ascertain whether they go into the academic stream or the vocational stream and the tests will draw on the Intelligence Quotient, Emotional Quotient and Spirituality Quotient—whatever these may be.

An immediate action was the arbitrary deletion of passages from the existing history textbooks. The government claimed that various religious organizations had demanded these deletions. Their objections were not discussed by any committee or organization of professional historians prior to the passages being deleted. Discussion in school of the deleted passages was also prohibited. These passages included seminal questions, among them the origin and evolution of caste society in India. In a society where caste remains hegemonic, it is ironic not to allow a discussion on how social hierarchies came about. Other deletions referred to the eating of beef in early India, to the difficulty of dating the *Mahābhārata* and the *Rāmāyana* because of later additions to the texts, to the mention of a brahmanical reaction contributing to the decline of the Mauryan empire, and so on. The rationale for these deletions remains unclear. It would seem that these were random objections made by anyone who chose to and were used to discredit the books. A year later these textbooks were replaced by hastily put together new ones, some of which were pedagogically incompetent, apart from their slanted history.

One is not arguing against the periodic revising of textbooks but rather, one is insisting upon such revisions observing accepted pedagogic procedures such as were observed in earlier years; and also urging that textbooks should provide updated, refereed knowledge, and in a manner that encourages students to think critically and independently. In other words, to perform the role expected of textbooks. At the best of times, textbooks raise pedagogical problems as they did even in the last fifty years. But one had hoped that educational policies would keep addressing these problems and improving on the process of educating students. Unfortunately what is happening now is a series of retrograde steps in terms of structure and content.

One possible amendment to this would lie in the availability of a range of professionally vetted textbooks. Together with this, examining boards concerned with school education, in prescribing such books, should be made responsible to regularized procedures of discussion among schoolteachers and historians. There is furthermore, an urgent need for transparency in and information on, what is being taught in schools run by organizations that describe themselves as religious and cultural, be they the Shishu Mandirs of the RSS, the Madrassas, the schools run by Gurdwara Committees or Church mission schools. As for state schools there is an additional fear that a sub-standard curriculum will intensify the current bifurcation in education: where quality education is available in private schools for those that can afford such schooling, and a near worthless education for those that cannot. We have been far too casual about what is taught in school and are reaping the consequences of adopting a system that is politically malleable.

Textbooks are not just learning manuals. They are also the media through which societies transmit the definition as well as the rights and obligations of citizenship, and these in turn help formulate identities. Future citizens have to learn to assess the institutions that constitute their state and society, an assessment linked to encouraging a critical enquiry in the young mind. Far from making it an investment, education is being reduced to a rather meaningless game of scoring marks. When to this is added a doubtful content in what is taught, the system of education begins to annul education.

Not satisfied with changing school textbooks, the government has also claimed the mandate to propose a uniform history syllabus for colleges and universities throughout the country. This has been done through the funding body, the University Grants Commission. There is a hint that non-compliance may affect funding. The proposed syllabus is seriously deficient as it ignores developments in methodology and historiography of the past half-century. Some universities are currently teaching far more advanced history courses.

There is now a greater interference in the autonomy of universities, with attempts to centralize admission procedures, exams, syllabi and funding, not with the intention of raising standards but to exercise maximum governmental control. The state will of course demand the right to intervene in state-funded institutions, but the intervening should not violate the professional autonomy of the institution. Legitimizing obscurantism through introducing Departments of Astrology cannot be a unilateral decision. It has to be seen in the context of whether the same funding could be used more effectively in other areas, as for instance, in developing libraries for students. It is claimed by the University Grants Commission that introducing Departments of Astrology at University level will prove that astrology is India's contribution to world science and that it can solve the problems of the world. That many Indian scientists have described it as a leap backwards did not deter the UGC.

Dismantling the autonomy of universities is being permitted by academics, who either out of apathy, or a wish to conform to government directives, do not protest against the changes. One remembers the words of Miguel de Unamuno, rector of the University of Salamanca in 1936, that at times silence is a lie for it can be interpreted as acquiescence. The latest attempt of the Government has however, met with some resistance. Various university teachers' associations have rejected the UGC's proposed Model Act for Universities of the Twenty-first Century in India. It is seen as an attempt to introduce control by the government and corporate houses and to eliminate democratic procedures, not to mention the responsibilities of the state for funding higher education.

Attempts are also being made to dismantle specialized institutions of technology (IIT) and management (IIM) by changing the fee structure and the syllabus. Since this impinges in a more observable way on the future prospects of the middle-class, a small protest is beginning to be heard. But now that the court has validated the Government's objective, the protest may become ineffectual. The objective is that the degree of self-financing of these institutions—which is considerable—to be drastically reduced so that they become dependent on heavy Government subsidies. There is little logic in this. The funds for these subsidies would be better spent by the Government on financing primary and secondary education and on providing full scholarships for impoverished students to be trained in the IITs and IIMs. Nor is the element of greed altogether absent in these objectives. The wealthy alumni of the IIMs and IITs send funds for the institutions where they were trained as a gesture of appreciation. It has been proposed that such funds should now be channeled through the central Bharat Shiksha Kosh, so that the funds can be used anywhere and not necessarily on the institutions for which they were intended.

At the level of research there has been the virtual banning of two major publications putting together documents taken from the National Archives pertinent to the two decades prior to Indian independence. From 1970 to 1983, documents from the Archives in Britain referring to these events were published under the title of *The Transfer of Power*. Indian historians decided to publish documents from the National Archives in India on the same period in a multi-volume project. Some volumes had already been published but another two sets of volumes had just reached the press when the present government decided to prohibit their publication, with no reasonable explanation for this action. The government, it would seem, can ban the publication of documents from the National Archives, even when they are not time-barred.

An atmosphere has been created in which any group can object to a book, and threats can lead to the banning or the withdrawal of such books. Organizations claiming the right to arbitrarily decide what is intellectually and culturally permissible now resort to physical attacks on persons and books. The recent incident when the major Sanskrit library, the Bhandarkar Oriental Research Institute was ravaged by such an organization, has received little condemnation by the self-appointed protectors of Sanskrit and the Vedic tradition. Books are banned because they question the political agendas of certain groups, and the banning becomes a demonstration of power. The other side of this is that these books continue to be published outside India. If the banning of books becomes a habit in India there will be different histories read inside and outside India. The difference will not be because of academic views but because of the dictate of politics and the suppression of free expression.

We may well ask why there should be a fear of independent historical writing. The reasons behind the fear need investigation. Reducing history to the lowest and most doubtful common denominator means that this is not only an attempt to wreck the discipline, but has wider social implications. Since the earlier textbooks are dismissed because they are said to be not only Marxist in their orientation but also anti-national, an understanding of this allegation has to begin by briefly reviewing the history of nationalisms in India.

Nationalisms sometimes require a demarcation between the Self and the Other through constructing narratives that define each. These are not permanent categories but are projected as such. The reformulation of cultural idioms creates a contest over who does the reformulating and with what intention. Defining the Self and the Other is a complex process and inevitably varies in time and in the requirements of the particular nationalism. It is also worth investigating the point at which the Other becomes the Enemy.

Colonial societies, emerging from colonial experience and its policies, have known more than a single nationalism. In India there were two recognizable forms generally distinct but occasionally overlapping. One was inclusive nationalism dating from the late nineteenth century. This kneaded together the segments of Indian society and opposed colonial power. For this anti-colonial nationalism, the Other—the one to be contested —was the colonial power. The focus was on the sovereignty of an Indian identity, based on democratic and secular institutions.

Nationalism attempts to knead together the segments of society that were characteristic of earlier times. This gives primacy to particular features. Anti-colonial nationalism also focused on what shape the future society should take after independence. Implicit in this was a liberal, secular, democratic society, although what this entailed in terms of reorienting society was not worked out in any detail. But there were other kinds of nationalism that made religion the keystone. There was an assertion that there should be a return to 'traditional culture'. But this in effect did not and cannot happen. The encounter with Orientalism, produced a new interpretation of Indian history, religion and culture, reflecting in part the perspective of Orientalism and in part a reaction against some of these perspectives. The Indians that dominated intellectual life in the nineteenth century were responding to both a colonial discourse about India and a nationalist construction of what was viewed as a traditional discourse. The colonial discourse gave primacy to history as a component of that reformulation.

In the early twentieth century to new nationalisms acquired visibility. The earlier nationalism was contesting aspects of current imperial views of history, whereas these later forms were more rooted in the colonial discourse. These were groups drawing on a religious identity—either Hindu or Muslim—and for whom the identity of an independent nation-state derived from the religion of the majority community in the proposed state. This kind of nationalism drew substantially on the inheritance of identities moulded by colonial policy and the colonial interpretation of Indian history. Discussions in this context highlighted formulations equating community and religion. These nationalisms projected imagined, uniform, monolithic religious communities and imbued them with a political reality. Both nationalisms took shape almost simultaneously in the early twentieth century and have become virtually mirror images of each other—each maintaining the viability of separate nation-states. For religious nationalists, the Other, the one to be contested, was not the colonial power, to which they pledged loyalty, but the followers of the other religion, as also those who opposed religious nationalism, such as Mahatma Gandhi whom they assassinated. Political parties propagating this nationalism claimed to speak for communities as defined by religious labels—either Hindu or Muslim. The focus on the Indian citizen faded in their vision.

Muslim religious nationalism aspired to and eventually succeeded in establishing a Muslim majority state, Pakistan. India was not intended as a state to be ruled by a Hindu majority but influential Hindu opinion now seems to be seeing it as the Hindu counterpart to Pakistan. Such a change would meet the ultimate intentions of colonial policy aimed at creating two nations identified by majority religions. The two-nation theory was essential to both Hindu and Muslim nationalisms and in the early twentieth century was spawned by each.

Prior to the recent past, Indian historians were in dialogue with colonialism and mainstream nationalism. It has been said that post-colonialism is not only a dismantling of colonial institutions but an ongoing dialogue with the colonial past. History becomes an avenue for such a dialogue. Mainstream nationalism was critical of some negative colonial theories about the Indian past, but it did not replace these with alternate theories to explain the past. Thus the colonial argument that the pre-modern Indian polity was based on "Oriental Despotism" was rejected, but the rejection was not replaced by alternate equivalent theories of how the pre-modern Indian polity may have functioned. These explanations came from a later generation of historians in the last half-century. Mainstream nationalism was distanced from the religious variety, although there was some overlapping, as for instance, in the delineation of the ancient 'golden age' being viewed as the renaissance of Hinduism.

These trends have been recognized as common to nationalisms confronting colonization in other parts of the world, as for example, the role of Negritude in African nationalism. Nevertheless mainstream nationalism was different from the religious nationalisms, more frequently referred to as Hindu and Muslim communalism, which justified the exclusion of the Other by resort to history. History textbooks in Pakistan assert the superior claim of a Muslim presence over the Hindu Other, and the new textbooks in India project the reverse but the nature of the projection is similar.

The insistence of this new identity undermines the values that were sought in India after independence. Democracy is now threatened by religious majoritarianism, claiming that the basic definition of Indian society derives from religious communities, therefore, the wishes of the religious community that forms the majority, should prevail. This is a denial of the equal status of other religious groups. The secularizing of Indian society as a necessary part of modernization is described as alien to Indian civilization and therefore to be discarded. If secularism is alien so too are its essentials, namely, the ensuring of human rights and the equality of all citizens.

A pertinent question would be to ask what makes a religious identity seem necessary to the politics of the present. A possible reason is that a new middle class has replaced the old middle-class that had emerged from the colonial experience. Its expanded social base brings in middle-castes and others that had a lesser status earlier and are now moving towards center-stage. New elites require legitimating and this takes the form of a new identity validated by a new interpretation of history.

Globalization as a dominant mode of capitalism has created community interests in India that are a departure from earlier ones. A small but strikingly wealthy fraction within this middle-class is now the role model. The aspirations and frustrations among those still at the margins, intensifies into competition, insecurity, and aggression. When unemployment is aggravated, it is diverted into an attack on what is perceived as the enemy within, namely the minorities. This condition is common to the countries of South Asia. The culture of the economy that controls the Market imposes its imprint, sometimes to the discomfort of subordinated economies. Current nationalisms—ethnic, religious, linguistic—cannot be entirely isolated from globalization.

Anti-colonial nationalism had a strong economic component and a vision of converting the colony into an independent nation-state with a well-delineated economic structure. Attention to the prevalence of poverty, disease, ignorance and inequality were concerns at the forefront of the movement and in the immediate post-independence decades. They were values for their own sake and allowed us to live lives of greater freedom. These have now faded. With globalization trying to control the economies of developing countries, nationalist ideologies in these countries focus on other identities. It is not pure coincidence that Hindu nationalism has become increasingly visible and assertive over the last decade with globalization making inroads into the Indian economy.

Religious nationalism gives the illusion of a developing country asserting its independence against globalization. But in fact it builds up a dominant group that controls the new economy whilst speaking in the voice of religion and that can ride safely on globalization. The success of nationalism with a single identity is then used to validate the curtailing of the freedom of expression, through arguing that other identities and opinions are subversive. This is demonstrated by banning books and by assaults on films, art galleries and libraries, claiming that these methods are justified as a mechanism of keeping the culture pure and uncontaminated. Where humans are declared as subversive, curbing this supposed subversion often takes the form of organizing riots or terrorism.

Not unconnected with aspects of globalization is the increasing frequency of terrorism which has intensified prejudices, especially where identities of terrorist groups and of particular religions, are seen as coinciding. The patriot and the nationalist are redefined in keeping with the ideology of those in power, as we saw in Guiarat. The slogan of the war against terrorism has focused on Islam and the West as counterweights drawing also on the theory of the clash of civilizations. This conveniently overlaps with ideologies that see their own backyards threatened by Islamic militants, as in India. Few in India pause to count the number of militant groups, that are terrorizing areas of the sub-continent and are not concerned with matters of Islam, such as the PW, the Naxalites, the BODO, the ULFA, a variety of groups in the north-east some of whom go back fifty years, and various mafias acting like private militias. Yet the image of the terrorist is predominantly that of the Islamic militant. And fewer still give thought to why terrorist groups emerge or question the validity of the argument that religion is the most important defining feature of terrorism and militancy.

State terrorism of considerable magnitude has also become a feature of our times. There is a thin line between agencies of law and order providing protection to citizens, and the same agencies being diverted by the state to participate in what would otherwise be called acquiescing in terrorist activities. Such seeming ambiguities threaten human rights but are sought to be justified by resort to nationalism, and in turn to history, and both bring in the support of sections of the middle-class.

Combined with this, the fears of the middle-class are increased by movements surfacing from within the society but from below, in the form of Dalits and Backward Castes asserting rights. The middle-class that remains unsuccessful feels trapped. There are perhaps echoes of the anti-Brahmin movement of a century ago.

The lowering of the standards of education places the Backward Castes and the Dalits at a further disadvantage. The introduction of a non-pedagogically approved curriculum could well be a move to exclude such groups from the better jobs. The solution in relation to high quality specialized training is not to dilute education but to increase the number of scholarships and provide for better training in schools. Politicizing religion creates an over-arching identity. This seems to marginalize social inequalities, but nevertheless, the inequalities remain. The empowerment of the weak has no place in this ideology. The constant projection of the Muslim and the Christian as the Other diverts attention from the inequities of society.

In creating a religious nationalism many aspects of a religion have to undergo the kind of restructuring that allows a religion to lend itself to a political ideology, generally of a fundamentalist kind. Since religions have an extensive social function, apart from the belief and practice that they endorse, they have had multiple social roles, some tolerant and some intolerant. But such variant histories are seldom referred to when the claim is made that every religion is inherently tolerant. The introduction therefore, of social and political configurations, as for instance, a modern fundamentalist form, is always possible but requires some reformulation of the religion.

A new faction of Hinduism labeled Hindutva *or* "Hinduness," is a reformulation. To quote a founding statement, the aim is "to Hinduize all politics and to militarize all of Hindudom". In order to be effective, this change requires political support. Hindutva has taken on many meanings, varying according to occasion. It is also equated with Hindu Rashtra or else with what is called "cultural nationalism". This involves choosing and defining a single culture—in this case that of upper caste Hinduism. But equally important is the question of who defines it, how is the choice made, what is its agenda, and what happens to the marginalized or discarded cultures. This is of central importance not only to non-Hindus but also to the Backward Castes, Dalits and *adivasis*. Setting itself up as the sentinel of Hinduism, Hindutva is not sympathetic to views on Hinduism other than its own rather trivial assertions about the religion, bereft of the creativity of intellectual and aesthetic exploration. That which has often given Hinduism its sensitivity to the acceptance of unbounded belief systems, is reduced to a lifeless ordering of religiosity. When this reductionism is challenged, a claim is made that religious and cultural sentiments have been hurt, and violence is resorted to in the guise of defending religion and tradition.

Interestingly, this reformulation, of Hinduism, also borrows from certain aspects of Islam and Christianity, aspects that were previously not regarded as essential to Hinduism, such as, emphasizing historicity—preferably of a founder, locating a sacred topography, adopting a sacred book, and simulating an ecclesiastical authority. I have elsewhere referred to this as Syndicated Hinduism.

Hindutva promises empowerment through its organizations at various levels and encourages political mobilization directed towards the creation of a state dominated by a religious majority. The cadres of the RSS are trained in military fashion, attend schools, youth clubs and institutions associated with this ideology, and work in unison with the Akhil Bharatiya Vidyarthi Parishad (ABVP), the Vishva Hindu Parishad (VHP), the Bajrang Dal and the political party currently in power—the BJP, the Bharatiya Janata Party.

To be effective as a political ideology Hindutva has to redefine Hindu identity. Such a redefinition is rooted in ideas of origins. This focuses on history as was recognized by one of the founding ideologues of Hindutva. V.D. Savarkar, writing in the 1920s, stated that an Indian could be only that person who could claim that the land of his fathers, *pitribhumi,* and the land of his religion, *punyabhumi,* both lie within the territorial boundaries of British India. Furthermore, there had to be a commitment to a common Indian culture, inevitably defined by Hindutva. These qualifications automatically led to Muslims and Christians, being regarded as foreigners. Subsequently, Communists were added to this list! Issues of race and language that dominated contemporary European fascist movements were introduced as further qualifiers. And, as we know, in periods of confusing change, the preference is for a theory that simplifies the social world into 'us' and 'them'.

The rewriting of history is intended to bring about a new bonding by privileging the identity and origins of the majority community, and by the same token, indicating that religious minorities are foreign. I would like to refer to two examples of how attempts are being made to establish this.

The ancestry of the Hindus is to be linked to a lineal descent from the Aryans. 'Aryan' was initially a language label but it is often used indiscriminately to refer to race, peoples and ethnic groups. Aryan culture is now projected as the oldest and is assessed as superior to all others. This argument draws on nineteenth century ideas on the superiority of Aryan culture and its genesis from a single, unadulterated source—the Vedic corpus. The date given by most scholars for the earliest section of the Vedic corpus, the *Rigveda,* is around 1500 B.C. But in order to maintain that it is the oldest culture, the authorship of the earliest urban civilization in India that of the Indus, generally regarded as pre-Aryan and dating to the third millennium B.C., is also being declared as Aryan. The attempt therefore is to take back the date of the *Rigveda,* to 3000 B.C. or even earlier, and to read it into the archaeology of the Indus civilization. Attempts are being made to change the label for the Indus civilization to 'Sarasvati Civilization' thus evoking the *Rigveda* and Hindu connections. It is further held that the Aryans were indigenous to India. This strengthens their role as the founders of Indian civilization and ancestors of the Hindus. Aryanism and Vedic culture are projected as the foundational culture of Indians.

Historians who contest this formulation are described as anti-Indian, anti-national, and of course, "Commies". Yet historians have argued that such a chronology is difficult to reconcile with the archaeological and linguistic evidence. It is at least fifteen hundred years too early and there is little in common between the sophisticated urbanism of the Indus civilization and the agro-pastoralism of Rigvedic society. The two cannot be equated. At most it can be considered that some elements of the former may have found their way into the latter but such statements would have to be supported with firm evidence. That there was a graduated migration of Aryan speakers from across the Indo-Iranian borderlands and an inter-weaving of cultures remains a viable argument.

The Aryan theory when it was first promulgated in the late nineteenth century, was taken up in India by a range of people of different social backgrounds, each group seeing in it those perceptions of the past that were suitable to its own concerns. Thus, Jyotiba Phule writing in Marathi and in support of the lower castes and Dalits had an entirely different take on the theory. He maintained that there was an invasion of alien, Aryan *Brāhmaṇs* as a result of which the indigenous inhabitants were subjugated, oppressed and relegated to lower caste status. The conflict therefore was over the establishment of caste identities and not religious identities and there was an inversion of the present idea of who was indigenous or alien. Aryanism supports the notion of upper caste Hindus being racially and culturally superior to lower castes, Dalits and *adivasis,* and concedes the legitimacy of the dominance of the upper castes.

Theories of Aryan arrival from across the borderlands or alternatively those proposing indigenous origin have been debated for over a century. If Aurobindo supported indigenous origin Tilak argued for the long march from Arctic lands. The central question today is not whether 'the Aryans' were indigenous or foreign. Historians have moved on from this to analyses, seeking insights into the interface of the many cultures and societies, old and new, of this period and of their evolution. The complexity of cultures is being analyzed as also of the various societies that went into the making of the dominant cultures, such as those featured in Vedic compositions. The Vedic corpus makes a distinction between the *arya* and the *dasa* and various other communities—a distinction that is also reflected in the non-Aryan linguistic elements in Vedic Sanskrit. The interface between diverse societies and cultures means that not all of them conformed to the current, popular definition of "Aryan." The existence of diversities involves analyzing the varying processes from which these societies evolved, such as how-languages mutate and spread, populations move, myths and rituals encapsulate changing ideas, economies evolve, social hierarchies are established, dominant groups emerge and state-systems become visible. Historical processes have also to be differentiated. Thus, invasions or migrations are not identical processes and they differ in origin, intention and impact. Ascertaining these variations is crucial to understanding cultural evolution and change through interaction among and between societies, both in this period and in later times. A more meaningful debate would be to examine the validity of the received version of what is meant by 'the Aryan'.

The concept of civilization as a stage of socio-economic change remains an acceptable idea. But the nineteenth century definition of the term as a territory within the boundaries of which there was a single religion and language of significance is open to question. Now we know that each civilization is not only diverse within itself, but that its characteristics often emerge from an intersection with cultures beyond its geographical boundaries. The northern areas of the sub-continent have repeatedly been host to large numbers of settlers from central and western Asia throughout the centuries. Migrants coming by sea were common to the coastal areas of the peninsula. The debate therefore about defining who is indigenous and who is foreign, spanning five millennia, is a spurious debate.

Insisting on a single source for Indian civilization, such as the Vedic corpus, excludes the many facets of thought and structures that went "into its making and into subsequent philosophies. The rich tradition of perceptions, rationality, logic and dialectics, also get excluded since these often draw on the intellectual controversies of various times. Some of the most thought-provoking insights into early Indian social ethics come from comments not only in Buddhist and Jaina texts, but also from other sources, and these were often initiated by questioning the dominant culture. Even dominant cultures themselves evolve from such questioning. The marginalization or negation of controversy obstructs the understanding of cultures.

Controversies were recorded not only in pre-Islamic India but also after the arrival of Islamic schools of thought. These included the ideas within a tradition, and also those that emerged when the formal boundaries of Hinduism and Islam were transgressed at various levels, as in some Bhakti, Shakta, Natha and Sufi thought of the second millennium A.D. Such crossings of boundaries have been seminal to many contemporary Hindu and Islamic beliefs and practices. At the other end of the spectrum there was dialogue between and among scholars of Sanskrit, Persian and the regional languages. The fading of formal religious boundaries was particularly evident in the non-elite sections of society—in effect the majority of people.

The second focus in the rewriting of history relates to the role of Muslims or of Islam in Indian history, where the past is again used to justify an ideology of the present. It is argued that the arrival of Islam, resulted in two distinct and separate nations in the Indian sub-continent whereas earlier there had been only one, the Hindu; further, that the coming of the Muslims was a disaster because they oppressed the Hindus and caused the decline of Hinduism.

The history of the second millennium A.D. is therefore viewed as the history of two communities—Hindu and Muslim, each represented as uniform, monolithic, mono-cultural, right across the subcontinent, and each hostile to the other. Yet actually each was constituted of multiple communities of varying identities and diverse relationships. Some relationships led to conflicts, others were friendly, depending on the requirements of each. Groups identified themselves by caste, occupation, language, region and religious sect. Even labels such as 'Hindu' or 'Muslim' were not widely adopted until some centuries later. Among the many forms in which Islam arrived in the sub-continent—through pastoralists, traders, armies, migrants and religious sects—and even where conquest was the mechanism of control, relationships required social negotiations. But the study of such negotiations and the articulation of ensuing relationships have no place in the new history. It excludes the presence of plural relationships and multi-cultural societies. This would require conceding that such groups not only contributed to the making of Indian identities in the past, but equally important, that identities change over time.

Conversion is frequently referred to in this history. Even where it is said that some percentage of Muslims and Christians were converts from Hinduism, conversion is viewed only as the change from the formal manifestation of Hinduism to the formal definition of the other religions. There is little recognition that conversion is not a complete break from the previous way of life. The vast majority of Christians and Muslims who were converted from

Hinduism tended to carry their customary law and their cultural ways with them, introducing innovations in the practice of the religion to which they converted. This is recognized as part of the process of the conversion of large groups in the history of any religion. In India conversions were frequently by *jāti*/ caste or by a segment of the caste, and therefore caste practices were not easily shed. These relationships need to be explored so as to understand the link between religion and social forms. Nor did conversion by itself change the social status of a caste. The inequality of caste, although denied in the theory of Islam and Christianity, was effectively incorporated into Muslim and Christian society, with predictable variations.

Regional cultural norms tended to segregate groups even if they belonged formally to the same religion, whether Hinduism or Islam or any other. There were differences in social practices relating to caste, language, custom and sect. There were differences in food taboos, rules of kinship and marriage, access to property, language, between, for instance, the Meos of Rajasthan, the Khojas of Gujarat, the Navayats of the Konkan and the Mapillas of Kerala, all officially Muslim. Such differences often made them more akin to local non-Muslim communities than to each other. In recent times however, with attempts to homogenize such groups through Islamization or through the threat of the erosion of their culture, the differences are being erased. 'Among Hindus too such differences kept segments segregated. The intersections among these groups and their study are an ongoing process in the history of regional culture, and the latter are obviously ancestral to the Indian present, and more immediate than the 'golden ages' of the remote past.

The new history presents the arrival of Islam as that of the Muslims conquering the Hindus and the Hindus resisting them. Reference had earlier been made to Muslim epics of conquest in Persian and Hindu counter-epics of resistance in Hindi, creating two antagonistic communities in conflict. This view is now shared by the official histories of India and Pakistan. It is of course to be expected, that conquest will be met with resistance in all periods of history, but the purpose of both have to be viewed in greater depth. Resistance was more frequently over territory, political power and status, although references to religious differences were not excluded. Alliances and enmities were known to cross religious loyalties and pragmatic concerns in such cases had priority.

This becomes evident from what are cited as 'Hindu' epics, as for example, the court literature of various Chauhan Rajputs facing Mohammad Ghuri and Allah-al-din Khalji. Far from being concerned only with Hindu resistance to the Muslim, their narratives focus on court intrigue, and campaigns against neighbours who were almost hereditary enemies, issues of competitive status, political legitimacy and marriage alliances. Religious difference is not absent but is only one among many other factors. One such epic has a long peroration on a Khalji princess wishing to marry the Rajput prince of Jalor. She recalls their many previous births when they were husband and wife. He rejects her, arguing that such a marriage would be unacceptable to a Rajput, but it is unclear whether this was because of the difference in caste or in religion? In another such epic, when Ranthambor, the capital of the Rajput raja Hammira was besieged by the Khalji Sultan, the raja was deserted by most of his Rajput ministers and courtiers, but his Muslim advisor, Mahimashahi, remained loyal to him till the last.

It is claimed that the new history now being imposed has been constructed from an entirely indigenous, Indian point-of-view. It is therefore hailed as a departure from the earlier writing of Indian history, condemned as Eurocentric and written from a western perspective, even by Indian historians. But actually this history has no new theories of historical explanation, Indian or other. Such explanation would be expected normally from a historiography claiming to change the paradigm. This history merely repeats the theories of nineteenth century colonial history, some of which had been rejected even a century ago by nationalist historians. This is not a dialogue with the colonial past, but merely a fresh dressing up of the colonial view.

The two central themes namely, the Aryan foundations of Indian civilization and the nature of Muslim rule in India are taken from European and colonial writing. It is well known that Friedrich Schlegel in 1808 maintained that Sanskrit was the ancestral Indo-European language, isolated and unique, a view now regarded as outdated. He deduced from this that those who spoke it were imbued with the deepest wisdom. The genesis of language, whether from a single source or from many, dominated the nineteenth century debates among European Orientalists and in the German Romantic movement in particular. The sub-texts of these debates were often related to European self-perceptions especially in the heyday of imperialism. Language was assumed by some to be the collective creation of a national culture, and when race—and the Aryan race in particular—was added to this as another determining feature of culture, the combination as in Germany, was to be volatile.

It was also the century when 'the Aryan' as an entity came to be defined and established in Europe. The invention of the Aryan race and the superior Aryan culture was the outcome of what in Europe was called, 'race-science'. It had an impact on current social theories in Europe and on socio-religious reform movements in India. The prominence of Sanskrit and of the Vedic corpus in the elite cultures of India, draws on a continuing brahmanical tradition that gives it priority, although others such as the heterodox sects and those articulating regional cultures and languages, had contested this even in earlier times. However, the Vedic corpus as initiating Indian history is the contribution of nineteenth century Orientalism. Max Mueller popularized the term 'Aryan' in the Indian context linking it closely to the Vedic corpus. He argued that this was the most creative period of the Indian past. But he also maintained that the Aryans came from outside India and had links with the speakers of Indo-European. So half his thesis has been accepted and the other half turned outside in!

The currency of these ideas also influenced nineteenth century Indian thinkers such as Swami Dayanand, Shri Aurobindo and Swami Vivekananda. Their intellectual context was both the debate with European Orientalism on the Hindu religion and on Hindu culture and tradition, as well as the attempt to revive earlier debates in Indian thought. Their construction of Hindu civilization therefore, needs to be seen both in terms of their intention of evoking a pristine, original civilization, and at the same time having to react to Orientalist views. The nature of the colonial impact was such that in the nineteenth century the reconstruction of an indigenous culture was inevitably also responding to this impact.

In 1875, the colourful Mde Blavatsky founded the Theosophical Society, with Col. Olcott, among others. Olcott was closely connected with the shortlived merger of the Theosophical Society and the Ārya Samaj. He and many Theosophists maintained that the Aryans were indigenous to India and that they civilized the rest of the world. A much-discussed question at that time was whether the British and the Indians could be related by blood, since they both belonged to the Aryan race! Religion was clearly less important as a marker of identity than race in these discussions. Needless to say, contrary views such as those of Jyotiba Phule, which made caste the primary identity, were ignored.

The second theme, of the antagonism between the Hindu and the Muslim in Indian history, is closely linked to colonial interpretations of Indian history. That all Muslims were foreigners was stated in late eighteenth century Orientalist writings. In the nineteenth century, James Mill's *History of British India,* expounding this theory, became a hegemonic text. Mill divided Indian history into three periods: Hindu civilization, Muslim civilization and the British period. The use of the label 'civilization' for Hindu and Muslim with its focus on religion and language demarcating civilizations intensified the divisions. We have lived with this periodization for almost two hundred years. Although historians in the last fifty years have questioned its viability, it is now again being reinforced.

Mill argued that Hindu civilization was stagnant and backward, and Muslim only marginally better. Governance prior to the coming of the British was that of Oriental despots. British rule was an agency of progress because it could legislate change for the improvement of India. Mill's projection was that the Hindus and Muslims formed two uniform monolithic communities, permanently hostile because of religious differences, with the Hindus battling against Muslim tyranny and oppression. This view was an assumption in much of colonial writing on India.

H.M. Elliot and John Dowson in their multi-volume, *History of India as Told by Her Own Historians,* state that Muslim rule had to be depicted as oppressive and tyrannical in order to convince Hindus that they were better off under British rule. The dichotomy was cut deeper by the colonial emphasis on legal systems defined by religious codes, and community numbers measured through the census. The subsequent introduction of separate electorates validated the divide. The colonial view held that the Muslims of India were largely foreign, because of their supposed descent from immigrants. That the majority of those constituting various Muslim communities were converted from Hinduism was conveniently ignored. The dichotomy created by colonial perceptions was useful to both Hindu and Muslim religious nationalisms.

One may well ask why are the proponents of this new history repeating the colonial history of the nineteenth century and claiming it not only as new but indigenous? It should be recognized that since the political ideology derives from a colonial source, it is not surprising that the historical interpretation it wishes to project, does the same. If a claim is made to shifting the paradigm in history, then a way of explaining the past has to be constructed that is significantly different from previous attempts. It must provide new perspectives of the nature of the data and its comprehension. It must be accompanied by a viable theory of explanation relating to the new paradigm. But the supposed new history neither addresses the questions and the concepts that other historians are addressing, nor does it raise fresh ones.

Obviously history has to be rewritten from time to time since it is not a frozen body of information. Like all knowledge it has to be continually updated through advances in data and methods of analyses. This process is part of a critical enquiry, on which the historical method is founded. The assumption that such a method is not required in the reinterpretation of history is a premise that is disputed by those opposing the supposed new history.

In the last half-a-century, historians of India have moved away from the rather limited debates of colonial and nationalist interpretations, towards more precise methods of enquiry and a more critical use of sources and interpretations. Most of the changes are obvious and are observed by historians working on any aspect of history in any part of the world. Nevertheless they need to be reiterated where they are not being observed in claims made to historical writing. An awareness of updated information and readings is essential.

In speaking of a historical method a number of features of historical research are essential. Historical evidence consists of artifacts and texts in the main. The oral tradition is included but has its own methods of testing for reliability or assessing its intentions. Artifacts include visible remains such as architecture and icons from past periods as well as those that have to be excavated. Artifacts and texts have to be interpreted by historians and this raises the question of the basis on which interpretations are made. These are determined by the readings which when they depart from earlier accepted ones have to be justified. This was known to earlier historical research but now there are many more techniques of analyses that can bring variant readings. The many debates on the date of the *Arthashastra* are a case in point. Earlier views drew on arguments based on internal evidence and corroboration from other sources. More recently the text was subjected to a computer analyses based on linguistic forms. Concordances of the symbols on the seals from the settlements of the Indus civilization were also facilitated by the use of a computer. Similar techniques and analyses have been made of titles and designations from Chola and Vijayanagara inscriptions and these studies have enhanced our understanding of the structure of administration in south India.

Interpreting a period of history means viewing it from the perspective of various social groups: the many voices of a history. Historical evidence is no longer limited to the narrative of the victorious alone. Narratives also draw from and speak to the Other, and historians now seek the voice of the Other. But fantasy has to be differentiated from demonstrated evidence.

Sources therefore are questioned before their versions are accepted. There has been a further fine-tuning of the chronology of texts, using internal criticism or even new technical aids. A random use of sources ranging over five centuries to make a point is no longer acceptable. Where chronology is under discussion, precisely dated sources are given priority over evidence that comes from texts extending over large periods of time, as for example the *Mahābhārata* and the *Rāmāyana.* The latter constitute a different aspect of historical investigation.

A significant change of the last few decades has been that of viewing history as a process and not merely a narrative of events. This involves discussing concepts from comparative history and from other disciplines that often leads to a better-defined investigation and encourages more pertinent questions. The emphasis on historical context is a major methodological departure, very different from isolating evidence and treating it as individually self-sufficient as was done earlier. Not only are the contents of texts studied but also their context in terms of the author, the audience, the purpose and the genre. This has enriched our understanding of texts and provides greater precision.

The scope of history has widened enormously to include the study of changing forms of caste, gender studies, diverse economies of various periods, the role of technologies, processes of state-formation, the social context of religious sects, the history of ideas, the impact of environment and ecology on human activity and vice versa—in fact the normal components of what today is regarded as appropriate to historical investigation. The much wider range of causal analyses resulting from the broadening of the scope of history now requires a discussion of priorities in ascertaining causes. Over and above this, the historical context of ideas and historiography—the history of historical ideas—has become a prerequisite for historical research. The historian is not creating a belief about the past, but is attempting to understand the past through a logical analysis of the evidence.

Those who promote the new history, object to much of the history that has been written in recent decades. It is persistently referred to as anti-national and Marxist on the assumption that this in itself will discredit it. The label of Marxist has become a catchall for any kind of history that now is disapproved of by religious nationalism, whether of the Hindu or the Muslim variety, or any other. This is because such histories often incorporates a range of opinions enrich the understanding of the past by extending causal analyses, question popularly accepted or received notions and encourage an awareness of historical method and critical enquiry as the basis of research.

Historians in the last fifty years have made extensive analyses of the themes initiated by colonial historiography. Mill's periodization and the concept of Oriental Despotism have been set aside. Marxist historians have criticized Karl Marx's Asiatic Mode of Production, as the dominant political economy of pre-modern India; and instead of directly applying familiar theories, there is a greater interest in the range of Marxist methodologies used in historical analyses. The notion of a "Golden Age" has also been questioned, as it has in the current historical writing on virtually all civilizations.

Recent studies have made visible the multiple cultures that are essential to understanding the Indian past and present. The boon to the Indian historian is the continuing presence of what has been called "the living past", which has sensitized historians to one kind of comparative method. A view of history from the perspective of under-privileged groups that this provides, presents a more complete picture of society than was known in earlier studies. Above all, this kind of history cannot be controlled by a single ideology.

Yet such a control over knowledge is now being attempted. Issues relating to culture, aesthetics and philosophy have also to conform to the formulaic projection of what is referred to as "the Indian tradition". It is argued that Indian civilization has been continuous and without rupture, and that this is unlike the experience of western civilization that is seen as having broken with Greco-Roman Classicism and Medieval Christianism to arrive at Modern Enlightenment. It is maintained that the Indian reality of the past and the present, can only be understood through Indian theoretical constructs contained in Sanskrit texts. This is said to be the Indian cultural continuity. If taken literally this would in effect be the end of history. It is legitimate to base theories of Indian culture and tradition on textual sources—which is precisely what historians do. But it is intellectually illegitimate to ignore what one might call the double agenda of history: that each text has a historical context and an intention in the act of its composition; and that each subsequent reading of a text or of an event, is also conditioned by the context of the event and of the person writing about it and the audience for whom it is intended. Obviously texts from the past must be read, but they must be read with a comprehension of their time and function, which in turn requires that the reading be analytical. This is recognized in the methods basic to the humanities and the human sciences, where these are part of the larger discourse.

There is yet another aspect that has to be brought into the discussion of the role of religious nationalism in the discipline of history. This involves the attempt by Indians who live outside India to introduce belief into the construction of Indian history. Nationalism focuses on the link between power and culture and seeks to use culture in its access to power. Culture becomes a euphemism for power. The redefinition of Indian culture as essentially Hindu, and preferably of the upper caste, has also become the ideology of a section of the Hindu diaspora. This diaspora, among the richest in many parts of the world, is a wealthy patron of the politics of religious nationalism in the homeland, and like all wealthy patrons intervenes in these politics. Some have called such activities, 'long-distance nationalism', and others have maintained that distance is not a safety zone but a field of tension.

Where nationalism moves beyond the boundaries of the nation-state, culture becomes an abstract construction. It grows out of the fantasies about the past of the home country and these also form part of the response to confrontations with the culture of the host country. There is a tendency towards conservatism and a drawing on the earlier debates emerging from colonialism and nationalism. To the degree that the rewriting of history is a political act, history inevitably becomes the ground for contestation. The contest is over the shape and the intention of reformulating history.

The ministers of the Government of India, publicly abuse those of us who as historians are opposed to the current official view of Indian history. But the more sustained, vitriolic attacks come interestingly, from a section of Hindus in the diaspora and more particularly those in the United States. The experience and articulation of the diaspora has now become a subject of study among sociologists and political analysts and various reasons have been suggested to explain the forms of its articulation. It is being suggested that these arise from problems of self-projection. Many persons in the diaspora come from the middle class in India and experience cultural alienation in the host country. Whereas in the homeland they are part of the majority community and have therefore had a dominant status, in the host country however, they have to come to terms with being a minority, and that too, one among many others. They too are seeking an identity and a bonding as well as asserting a status. If the bonding has to derive from religious nationalism, they disallow any critique of the Hindu past since for them this is a romanticized golden age.

It has also been argued that the endorsing of an upper-caste Hinduism is an attempt at 'sanskritization' by various castes both in the homeland and in the diaspora. Middle incomes in the diaspora become the equivalent of accelerated upward mobility when compared to the economic index and life-style in the home country. This then is taken as the cue for an appropriate middle-class/upper caste pattern of living as well. Social anthropologists and historians have debated the concept of 'sanskritization' as a social process in various periods of history where some castes claimed higher status and adopted the lifestyle of upper castes. In contemporary society the claim is less to a higher caste and more to acceptance of status through lifestyle.

An argument frequently made in the home country is in the nature of a complaint: that there is perhaps an element of guilt among those who have migrated from the homeland into a society with a higher living standard, leaving the extended family to fend for itself against the overwhelming odds involved in attempting upward mobility in India.

Some members of the Hindu diaspora who are given to attacking academics and others not sharing their views, are generally in professions related to management and businesses or in technical fields. There seems to be an assumption among many of them that a proficiency in technical professions gives one the right to define all knowledge, even that of the humanities and social sciences. The attempt to claim this right takes the form of aggressively critiquing those scholars who do not support Hindu nationalist views. Most of what is stated by these critics contradicts the professionally accepted view—to put it mildly. It is not surprising that the impressive defense of the targeted scholars has come largely from academics and others working in the humanities and the social sciences.

Running through the critiques like a chorus is the familiar accusation that the liberal historians are communists and an appeal is made to the ghost of McCarthy to rescue Indian history. Such critiques often descend into hatchet jobs, layered with political invective and personal vilification. If the intention is to expose a lack of scholarship, as is also claimed, this has to be demonstrated through scholarship and not through political polemics. Had the intention been to advance scholarship, technical expertise might have been used in various ways, as for instance, in computer-aided analyses of archaeological and historical artifacts, or scientific investigations of material remains, rather than lengthy statements that read like period pieces of a century ago. Admittedly however, there is also a need for recognizing the possible misuse of modern technologies that are used to authenticate dubious claims, such as the so-called Harappan horse seal, now notorious as "the Piltdown seal", which was exposed as a computer manipulation.

The authors of these critiques are also increasingly claiming the authority to intervene in academic decisions taken by universities and research institutions in North America, in effect to threaten academia through marshalling numbers and claiming that their religious sentiments have been offended. The model seems to be that of some sections of the host country. Obstructing free discussion has antecedents in the United States, one aspect of which is, for instance, the contest between creationism and evolutionism in the educational curriculum in some states of the Union.

With the passing of time the culture of migrant groups has to adjust to the new environment of the host country, however much they may wish to 'freeze' the culture with which they arrived, and which they assume remains relatively unchanged in the homeland. But the latter changes and currently this is happening in India at an accelerated pace. There is therefore a gradual divergence in culture and thinking between migrant settlers and their homeland. This is perhaps most poignantly evident in the use of the original language of a migrant community after a few generations.

The point in time when certain historians are projected as anti-national is linked to the assertion of particular religious identities and their political potential, as was the case with some working on the history of the Sikhs at the time of the Khalistan movement. The assertion of a new political ideology in the home country, supporting religious nationalism, might well explain the present activity in the diaspora. What this underlines is the link between religious nationalism in the home country and its manifestation in the diaspora. At some point therefore the politics of the host country will also have to take into account the politics of such minority groups—and this may well be part of the intention.

And what of the future? At the level of pedagogy, the monitoring of curriculum procedures and the quality of textbooks will have to continue, with a constant effort to keep the discussion on these, open and active. Attitudes to the content of textbooks, is reflective of how the discipline of history is viewed at particular times. It becomes relevant therefore, to understand this activity in the context of the present, and not only as an exercise in constructing the past. The centrality of history to the present is that although its concerns are with the past of the society, it is also an effective means of moulding the present in terms of how societies perceive themselves and their identities.

There is some urgency for historians to continue to explore the history of religion and what is broadly called 'culture'. These are significant aspects of historical discourse and it must be expected that there will be innovative, even if controversial, explorations. This will also demonstrate how such concepts can be and are being hijacked for political purposes. Such explorations do not mean a return to something pristine called 'religion' or 'culture'. It would mean teasing out the historical strands and linking them to their social roots and contexts, and their actual and ideological roles in different social landscapes. Since they are part of a historical process they cannot be unshackled from their time. Definitions of religion have tended to suppress the role of popular religion—the religion of the majority. This will not only have to be made visible but take its rightful place in redefining the religions of India. Those that have been excluded as having no history—women, Dalits, lower castes and people of the forests—their history will be essential to explaining the past. These explanations will lead to fresh readings of the past.

The discourse on Indian history among academics both in India and elsewhere will have to be maintained through protecting the right to free expression. This will involve resisting attempts by various organizations in India and in the Hindu diaspora to silence divergent views; a silencing that now resorts not only to abuse but even to physical assaults. Historical writing across the intellectual and academic spectrum has to be available to whoever wants to read it. There will be those who will continue to polemicize rather than problematize, but their obstruction of independent historical writing will remain marginal. The intellectual maturity now demanded in the discipline of Indian historical writing has, and will continue to have, its practitioners in India and elsewhere.

However, the apprehension is that the discipline of history in India at a broader level may be forced to go into reverse, in an effort to instill an ideology of religious nationalism. The justification for this will be sought in the claim that the religion and culture of India are being protected. But there can be no concession to the claim that a history propagating religious nationalism is the way to protect the religion and culture of Indian society. There can be no justification for abuse and violence against the books and the authors that one disagrees with. Protection lies in the right to free debate, dialogue and discourse, as has been the tradition in the past. Protection lies in preventing the closing of the Indian mind.

Recognizing Historical Traditions In Early India

A couple of hundred years ago it was stated that Indian civilization was unique in that it lacked historical writing and implicitly a sense of history. With rare exceptions there has been little attempt since to examine this generalization and it is taken as given. I would like to suggest that while there may not be a conventional form of historical writing in the early period there are nevertheless, many texts that reflect a historical consciousness. This subsequently came to constitute a historical tradition which in the first and second millennia A.D. is reflected in distinctive forms that approximate historical writing.

My intention in this paper is to argue that irrespective of the question of the presence or absence of historical writing as such, an understanding of the way in which the past is perceived, recorded and used, affords insights into early Indian society. It is worth investigating what was written on the past and why and what were the dialogues and debates that occasioned this writing. Ascertaining the degree of historicity would be the subsequent step.

Societies need to construct a past, or rather their many pasts, for the past has a social function. Such constructions narrated in sequential order claimed that what they narrated happened in the past, a claim that differentiates them from fiction. Communities have to constantly situate themselves in relation to the perceived past[1] which therefore becomes a dimension of social identity although its construction, form and content might change with new definitions of identity. This is sometimes demonstrated in variant readings of the past which indicate plurality and

From the Trautman Felicitation Volume, June 2008.

which is particularly apparent when there is an official version which can differ from other versions. New demands on power and legitimacy change existing forms. Thus, what came to be required of conventional history a couple of centuries ago was closely tied to nationalism which tends preferably to tidy up variety into a single identity within the nation. The recognition of plurality is more recent.

My concern therefore is less with whether or not early Indian society produced a specific historical literature of the conventional kind to record the past, but rather with trying to understand the variety of texts that purport to represent the past. This involves many questions: why they took the form they did; what from the past was of relevance to their authors; and why particular types of records were maintained. It seems to me that three aspects need enquiry. I would first like to ask why it was necessary to argue that Indian civilization lacked a sense of history. This was largely but not entirely a colonial argument with an emphasis that derived in the main from the way Enlightenment thinking defined history. The second aspect is to recognize that historical traditions emanating from diverse cultures will inevitably differ and comparisons have to be more precise than they have tended to be so far. The third, which is in effect the most substantial, is to enquire into the nature of the representation of the past in the texts that are linked to the early Indian historical tradition.

The search for indigenous histories of early India began in the late eighteenth century. European scholars conscious by now of historical literature as a distinct category recording the past, looked in vain for recognizable histories from the literature in Sanskrit. Indian culture and particularly the Sanskrit articulation of what came to be called Hindu culture, was therefore defined as a-historical. William Jones, the leading Indologist of the late eighteenth century, suspected that some texts, even if including the myths and legends of the Hindus, probably contained the core of a history.[2] Most scholars tended to disagree. But even Jones quotes only the *Rājatarangini* of Kalhana, as acceptable historical writing.

A century later McDonnell's searing remark that, "early India wrote no history because it never made any"[3] was modified by others such as Rapson who granted the making of history but regretted the absence of a systematic record.[4] Comparisons with the Chinese chronicles of Ssu-ma-ch'ien and the Arabic writings of Ibn Khaldun or even the Biblical genealogies, not to mention Greco-Roman texts, strengthened, if only in contrast, the axiom of Indian society denying history. Such comparisons made no reference to the historiographical contexts of any of the other histories.

The officers of the East India Company derived their data on law and religion from their *brāhmaṇ* informants so the centrality of the texts important to Vedic Brahmanism had priority. These were the *dharmaśāstras* and later the *Vedas,* and to a lesser extent, the *Purāṇas,* the last of which they regarded as second order knowledge. Other systems of knowledge—Buddhist and Jaina—assessed as inferior branches of Hinduism, were initially given little importance. That these might earlier have been alternate systems of knowledge was hardly conceded. Even with the prominence this gave to a limited upper-caste Hinduism there was little attempt at a discourse with Indian scholars on the wider context of the texts and their authors.[5]

Other theories emerged from the European excitement at discovering what many believed might be an Oriental Renaissance bringing innovative knowledge similar to the earlier revival of Classical European learning.[6] That religion and mysticism were characteristic of Indian culture to the virtual exclusion of rational ways of organizing knowledge, was reinforced by the ideas of German Romanticism.[7] The argument that in India caste, viewed as civil society overwhelmed the state further underlined the notion that without a state there could be no history. For Hegel therefore, India was a land without recorded history.[8]

The enthusiasm for Sanskrit literature in some circles fed into what was emerging in the nineteenth century as the influential theory of the origins of language and culture, and came to determine the ideological context of early Indian history. The theory of Aryan race was woven into the readings of the *Vedas* and history lay in the foundations of Aryan culture. This explanation of origins presupposed that Vedic Brahmanism was to be equated with Aryan culture and since Vedic Brahmanism has little concern for history, there was a general absence of a sense of history. The entirely different Puranic projection of historical beginnings was ignored.

A different reconstruction of Indian history in the nineteenth century drew on other premises deriving from Utilitarian thought. This precluded the need for a historical tradition or even a concern for the past in the indigenous tradition. It underpinned the requirements of colonial policy in a changing relationship between the colonial power and the colony.[9] A denial of a sense of history was implicit in the theory of Oriental Despotism articulated at length in what became the hegemonic text on Indian history, James Mill's *The History of British India.*[10] Mill's view was seminal to arguing that Indian society was static registering no change and therefore had no use for recording the past,[11] one of the functions of the past being to legitimize the present. This stasis could only be broken by British administration legislating change and thus introducing the notion of history. Mill's *History* was defining a new idiom for imperial control.

The argument was that if the past is not recorded then despotic power cannot be accused of violating tradition, nor can any appeal be made to thwart despotism in the name of the past. History was a record of change and its teleology lay in the notion of progress. India's endemic despotism governed by custom rather than law and lacking rationality as the motivating force, represented the reverse of progress. Since neither law nor rationality prevailed, history too was absent.

The absence of history had the practical advantage of allowing the formulation of a history for the colony that would underpin colonial policy. Colonial attitudes to knowledge pertaining to their colonies assumed that such knowledge was a form of control.[12] Thus William Jones wrote of the *itihāsas* and *purāṇas* being "in our power" and decades later Lord Curzon saw the intellectual discovery of the Orient as the necessary furniture of empire. History was the portal to knowledge about the colony. Every aspect of colonial activity was formulated as a history of that activity. This would be enhanced if it could be maintained that even the awareness of the colony's past had to be provided by the colonial power.

Assisting this process was the almost virtual obsession with the Orient being necessarily 'the Other' of Europe. Statements on 'Otherness' were foremost in the writings of Karl Marx and Max Weber. For Weber, part of the 'Otherness' was a lack of transition to capitalism which he attributed to a failure of economic rationalism. For Marx the static oriental society was characteristic of the Asiatic Mode of production and in this there was an emphatic denial of history.

Meanwhile throughout the nineteenth century, the collection of manuscripts and artefacts for the reconstruction of Indian history continued apace. Equally impressive were the results from the decipherment of the *brahmi* script which revealed the new resource of epigraphic data and from archaeology which was largely the collecting of artefacts and recording monuments. Both were essential to the construction of early history. However, in the reconstruction and interpretation of the larger flow of history, European models and preconceptions hovered and comparisons with Europe were unavoidable. But the comparison was superficial and even the changing historiography of European history was ignored by colonial historians. For European historians the past of the non-European world was, even metaphorically, another country. The intellectual intensity of the discussion on the nature of history in Europe in the nineteenth century had little impact on Indologists and colonial historians.

The interest in the largely oral compositions of the bards was actively pursued by James Tod[13] and Tessitori.[14] But understanding the status of the bard in Indian society was inadequate, a status that was special yet separate even when the *brāhmaṇ* took over the compositions of the bard.[15] That the recording of the past could be a separate occupational function within the parameters of a caste society was not fully recognized. The bardic keepers of the tradition were alien to modern historians.

Indian historians, by and large, initially subscribed to the colonial view and accepted that Indian society was a-historical. Their own social background did not encourage them to question the premises of the interpretations which followed largely from the perspective of the social elite.

The existence or not of a historical tradition in early India has been the subject of passing comments in recent times. One argument is that a historical tradition did exist but that it was a weak tradition and despite high intellectual levels in other aspects of thought, in this it never developed into a major tradition. This has been attributed to the decentralized nature of political institutions, to the role of the priestly elite in fabricating genealogies for rulers, and to the exclusive control of the *brāhmaṇs* over the transmission of the tradition.[16] Another explanation points to the bifurcation between the keepers of state records, largely the scribal castes, and the *brāhmaṇs* from whom a critical intellectual assessment might have been expected.[17] More defensive views maintain that history as a discipline has been formatted through modernization and Indian civilization has been unconcerned with this.[18]

Such explanations are hardly adequate particularly in light of recent historical research which has questioned the earlier stereotypes about the Indian past being that of a static society. Indian society was clearly subject to change although the nature of such change was not uniform in time and space. This constitutes a radically different view of the Indian past. Change is a nodal point in history when new identities can emerge and the past can be reformulated for the purposes of the present. Two historical processes were tied into the question of perceptions of the past. One was the mutation of clan societies into castes which was part of a bigger change of the assimilation of such societies into a state system, generally a kingdom. Kinship ceased to be crucial to the pattern of polities and new features emphasized social hierarchy and differential access to resources. The second process was the transformation of early kingdoms, into more complex state systems. Both processes are reflected in what is referred to as the *itihāsa-purāṇa* tradition and in the genres of texts that recorded its articulation. Some represent historical change in a covert manner, others do so more openly.

Detailed explorations of the texts which claim to incorporate historical perspectives are necessary. Some studies of this theme have been made but they tend to remain sporadic. An initial foray was a collection of essays, where there were a few fresh ideas although by and large the older thesis tended to be repeated.[19] An attempt was made later to introduce a category of texts as distinctively historical but without much discussion to support this claim.[20] An important discussion elsewhere of one category of such texts, the *cārita* literature of historical biographies, can be regarded as a study of substance relating to early Indian historical traditions, although limited to the one genre.[21]

But before I speak about forms of historical consciousness I would like to consider the second aspect that I mentioned earlier. This concerns our changed understanding of history itself and the centrality of historiography in this change. Let me go back a bit in time to the Enlightenment.

History as defined by the Enlightenment was thought of as central to civilization. Every branch of knowledge had to have a history. Consequently a people without history were a people without knowledge. The history of civilizations also derived from humanist traditions which maintained that for Europe there was a unified European identity, with continuity from the Greeks to modern Europe and was accessible in European literature.[22] The same was sought from other civilizations.

There emerged from this a rather literal view of Greco-Roman historical writing and a susceptibility to treating narrative accounts as historical. There were at the time no analytical studies such as those which have recently re-examined Greek and Roman historical writing. These have pointed to the interweaving of fiction and history in the representation of the past. The term *historia* in Greek referred originally to an enquiry into a matter and this could incorporate hearsay.[23] It has been said that, " ... if one starts by distinguishing between Oriental or mythical or mythologizing historiography and a rational and scientific historiography which strictly sticks to sources and facts, it is questionable whether Thucydides can be counted among the latter."[24] This may be too harsh a judgement, but Herodotus was frequently accused of lying perhaps because he drew heavily on oral data and later writers such as Manetho and Plutarch did not accept his statements.[25] History was a narrative of persons and events, some recalled from the past through oral and written sources and some witnessed in the present.

Parallel to the late Greco-Roman notion of history was the altogether different Jewish tradition, antecedent to the Christian.

The Greco-Roman notion was virtually set aside with the coming of history infused with Judeo-Christian views. This began with Jerome and culminated in Augustine. History was no longer just a narrative of the past. It was now the record of the power of God and of Christ as reflected in the actions of the Christian Church. This was a departure which was contrasted in Renaissance writing drawing on Greek and Latin texts. It took a more secular form with the Enlightenment explaining human activity as the pivot of society. Historiography became decisive to Europe with the Judeo-Christian religions claiming the historicity of persons and events. History also provided a community identity for the nations of Europe as they emerged in recent centuries.

The recognition of historiographical mutation is a necessary part of history. Apart from the narrative of events, the explanation of events as forming a causal pattern ranges from commonsense observations to ideological perspectives. The change in European historiography needs underlining. Generalizations can hardly be made about the single, unified sense of history of the West. In Europe the change was from the Greco-Roman to medieval Christianity to the Enlightenment, each born of distinctly different historiographies and formulating diverse historical traditions. Some attempts were made to associate antiquity with new historiographies and to re-orient Greco-Roman ideas. Arnaldo Momigliano writes that Greek models became transformed into a Jewish apocalypse.[26] Historical consciousness is understood in a different sense now as compared to a century ago.

Islamic historiography is also treated as uniform and seen from the perspective of religious texts. Yet there are distinct ideological variations that gave shape to the writings that emerged. The Arab discourse was imprinted with facets of Judaism and Christianity, even if what eventually emerged was the distinctive ideology of Islam. The Persians internalized their legacy of Zoroastrianism and Manichaeism. The difference within the Islamic tradition is apparent if one compares the representation of the past in Firdausi's *Shah-nameh* or the writings of the Ghaznavid scribe, Baihaqi, with Ibn Khaldun's *Muqadimmah*. Such diversity would have produced histories with variable nuances.

The historiography most frequently taken as the measure of

historical writing is the Judaeo-Christian and Islamic. This has a clear eschatology narrating the beginning and end of humankind with a teleology built into it, and time is seen largely as linear. Other historiographies where this is not so evident are the Greco-Roman, the Chinese and the Indian. Eschatology in these traditions is not definitive. Time concepts takes various forms—linear, spiral, and cyclic. The Greco-Roman is treated as foundational to European historiography yet it has little in the way of common premises with the Judaeo-Christian.

We now recognize that history lies not just in a sequential narrative set in a chronological framework but also in enquiry and explanation. This implies that a comment on the presence or absence of a sense of history in a particular society also requires some familiarity with the genres of texts incorporating historical consciousness and these are not identical across its constituent cultures. Thus Al-Biruni visiting India in the eleventh century writes that Hindus do not pay much attention to the historical order of things and are careless in narrating the historical succession of their rulers.[27] Al-Biruni appears to be unaware of any Indian historical tradition and was probably seeking a parallel to the Islamic. His comments seem to follow from partial information and that too from brahmanical sources.

Al-Biruni came from a society in central Asia familiar with Buddhist thought and he mentions the importance of the *shramanas/ shamaniyyas* to Indian religion, noting the hostility between them and the *brāhmaṇs*. Yet his informants seem to have been *brāhmaṇ* ritual specialists and a few others knowledgeable about astronomy and the calendar. He was aware of Puranic chronology being unreliable but he also knew of the calculation of some aspects of historical chronology which was reliable. What were missing for him were possible parallels with Islamic historiography. Had he conversed with other scholars or with court scribes he might have come to know about inscriptions as annals and their focus on dynastic events and succession not to mention their calculation of chronology, or epics such as the Gaudavadha of Vakpatiraja.

In a sense, Al-Biruni was the forerunner of the seventeenth century Indian historian Firishta who perhaps initiated European comments on a lack of history. Firishta's dismissal of historical writing from the earlier period was a view that contributed to the colonial writing on India and was quoted through Alexander Dow's rendering of Firishta in the *History of Hindostan*. However, the more interesting question is why, in each case, were they so selective about whom they consulted.

Diverse historical traditions have narratives relating the past. The way the narrative is formulated reflects not just a curiosity about the past but also has to do with the historiography that it represents. This draws from the tradition and from political economies and religious-ideological concerns that had currency at the time. The form of the narrative changes when political economies and religious concerns change and therefore there is more than one genre of text encapsulating the past.

The context is what allows us today to observe the complexities of the past looking at its own earlier past. We need to be aware of what is selected and what is left out, of the audience directly addressed and the presumed audience, of the awareness of political organization and its possible collaboration with the author and finally, knowing whose cultures are being discussed.[28] Narratives claiming that the events they relate happened in the past make for historical consciousness but historical writing requires more than just this claim.

Essential to history is the shape and accounting of time. A distinction can be made between the past and the present which is initially often through symbols but gradually comes to incorporate measurements of time. Much has been made of the lack of history in India being tied to a cyclic concept of time, an insistence which continues despite research to the contrary.[29] This is contrasted with the linear time of the Semitic tradition which is said to provide a necessary factor for historical thinking. Yet linear time in India is manifested in the extensive incorporation of genealogies, in the use of the *samvat* (eras) and in the precise dating of inscriptions; and even more so in the shift in astronomy from lunar to solar reckoning. Stating in detail the time of an action is essential to recording gifts of land, rituals, accessions, and such like, as is evident in the many inscriptions intended for this purpose.

A sharp dichotomy between linear and cyclic time is not feasible since some elements of each are often parallel although pertaining to different functions. The Greeks observed categories of time in cycles as did the Indians and the form of time varied according to its function. Cyclic time is often viewed as cosmological time whereas the more measured time in human terms is linear and records generations and individual chronologies. Where cyclic time takes a spiral form, it can be seen as almost linear when sufficiently stretched. These variations are present in Indian texts and suggest an almost heterogeneous time calculation. Even in cyclic time the present is not a repetition of the past as has been maintained. The end of one cycle bypasses its beginning when transmuting into the next cycle. Each cycle records change and this too is represented in various ways. The notion of a past that is different from the present also assumes a future that is different from both.

Eschatology, both Buddhist and Puranic, is inherent in cyclic time but the pattern is unlike the more linear eschatology of the Judaeo-Christian tradition. The perfection of the first of the four *yugas,* cycles or ages, gradually degenerates, largely because of the distancing from norms and beliefs and the increase in non-meritorious behaviour. Eventually the catastrophic end is so imminent that it requires the saviour figure. This was the *brāhmaṇ* Kalkin—the final incarnation of Vishnu, or Maitreya—the Buddha to come, who would in each case restore the universe or the faith to its pristine condition. Even when a catastrophic end is spoken of, it is the precondition to the return of the first cycle, 4,320,000 years, a time period that is more suggestive of the end of history rather than a repetition.

Let me now turn the focus away from the rather dog-eared arguments about the absence of historical writing in early India and consider what I regard as the more relevant question of how the past was perceived and recorded. Answers to this question even if partial, might provide insights into early Indian society. Such a perspective is possible now that the understanding of history has itself undergone change.

The early Indian historical tradition has two distinctly different historiographies. One emerges from what might be called a

Puranic framework. This draws on narratives and ideologies deriving from Vedic sources and the emergence of new sects and social movements on the first millennium C.E. These historical traditions are encapsulated in one section of the early *Purāṇas*. The second historiography draws from ideologies that evolved from a questioning of if not opposition to Brahmanism, such as the Buddhist and the Jaina and what are included under the umbrella term of Shramanic. The ideological underlining of each was different as is reflected in the choice and representation of events and personalities that each highlight from the past or else represent in different forms. Alternate positions although not always stated as such, are nevertheless, reflected either in diverse formulations or in contradiction.

The awareness of the past seems to be represented in two forms suggesting perhaps a differentiation between historical consciousness and historical traditions. The first I would like to refer to as forms in which historical consciousness is embedded. Here the historical consciousness is subterranean as it were, being subordinated to other functions, as for example, references to events which occur in ritual hymns. The second category is forms that embody this consciousness and give expression to it as overt historical traditions. These occur in genres of texts, specific to this category. The forms are therefore embodied or externalized and recognizable as such. The texts themselves constitute new genres and their primary function is as expressions of a historical tradition. There is a shift from a representation of historical consciousness to the externalizing as it were, of this consciousness in specifically historical traditions. This allows us to ask why there was a shift and what were the new genres required in the writing of history.

The two terms associated either separately or conjointly with traditions relating to the past are, *itihāsa* and *purāṇa*. *Itihāsa* literally means, "thus indeed it was" and has come to be used now to mean history, but earlier it was not history in any modern sense of the term. *Puraṇa* refers to that which belongs to ancient times and includes a medley of events and stories believed to go back to the early past and some that we would now call myths. *Itihāsa-purāṇa* taken together is described as the fifth *Veda,* as also is the *Natyashastra* and the *Mahābhārata,* a phrase that refers to knowledge that is outside the *Vedas* but nevertheless important.[30] The label carries an oblique reference to divine sanction and constant recitation.[31] The embodied forms are not Vedic categories.

The origins of the Puranic framework of the *itihāsa-purāṇa* tradition go back to forms that are embedded in various texts such as, the *dāna-stuti* hymns in the *Ṛg Veda.* These have little ritual function *per se.* They are in praise of contemporary heroes and chiefs of clans and their generosity in giving gifts to the composers of the eulogies celebrating a successful raid or victory. Association with the sacrificial ritual perhaps gave these hymns greater credence, and certainly ensured their continuity. They could well have been inserted at a later stage of the compilation of the hymns.

The context for these compositions was clan societies and the narratives associated with them are more extensive in the epics, the *Mahābhārata* and the *Rāmāyana.* Action moves from raids and skirmishes to the formal battle and the politics is complicated by the incorporation of new societies. The epics introduce new features since the appeal to the past can be to fix a precedent for action in the present. The *Mahābhārata* as *itihāsa* was used on occasion for this purpose to legitimize the induction of hitherto unknown clans and their social custom.[33] The central narratives described the confrontations between clans some of which were older confederacies and some new upstarts. The *Rāmāyana* differs in as much as the conflict is between a newly emerging kingdom of Kosala with its capital at Ayodhya and the clan society of Lanka, the latter demonized as *rāksasas.*[34]

Interestingly, both epics are recited at a sacrificial ritual, almost as if the earlier tradition was being continued even if the compositions themselves did not initially have the status of ritual texts.

The embedded history in these texts relates to the first process of change that I referred to earlier. They represent clan societies and the epics register the gradual coming of kingdoms. Could we ask whether for historical purposes this might have been the function that had priority and persons and events helped to remember this past? There is some awareness of the difference between *itihāsa,* that which is claimed to have happened, and narratives that are fictional, but the difference is not deeply impressed. The authors are looking back nostalgically to the past. Perhaps for historical purposes this might have been the priority in the function of the compositions. Historicity of person and event was less the essential concern where the intention was rather to evoke a past society. Composed as oral traditions they are now seen as repositories of historical consciousness whereas earlier, societies without literacy were said to be without history.[35]

This was the raw material that was reformulated into a long-distance view of the past as in the *vaṃsānucarita*—succession lists—of the *Viṣṇu Purāṇa.*[36] As a section of the *Purāṇa* it is ill-suited to the Puranic format of being a sectarian text and could again have been an insertion into such texts to ensure centrality and continuity. Scattered material from Vedic and epic sources and possibly other oral traditions was drawn together and a pattern worked out. This was marked by distinctive phases in the mapping of the lineages and their genealogies to which were then attached lists of dynasties from the sixth century B.C.E. up to the Gupta period in the fourth century C.E. The latter are largely historically attested. Clan societies, recorded as *vamśas,* lineages, succeeded by dynasties, would appear to have been a way of representing the mutation of clan societies to kingdoms.

Another indicator of the transition from clan to kingdom was the change from *ksatriya* lineages to *non-ksatriya* dynasties described as either *śūdra* or *brāhmaṇ.* What is perhaps being stated in this format is that the legitimacy of kin relations among *ksatriya* chiefs had been undermined by upstarts of low status such as *śūdras* appropriating power through a change in the priority from chiefship to kingship. The *ksatriyas* of earlier times were the logical ancestors to royal dynasties but there seems to have been a break, perhaps encapsulated in the battle at Kurukshetra where the *ksatriya* clans destroyed each other and there was the subsequent emergence of political authority in the form of dynasties. These should have been of the *ksatriya* caste according to the normative codes but frequently were not.

The *vaṃsānucarita* was essentially history in a genealogical mode of thinking with the recording of succession and caste. It becomes a data-bank for families of obscure origin in post-Gupta times wishing to latch themselves onto a lineage and thereby claim *ksatriya* status. It was not intended to be taken literally, generation by generation, nor to be interpreted as racial identities as was done by modern scholars.

From the perspective of the *itihāsa-purāṇa* tradition the Gupta period starting in the fourth century C.E., marks a watershed between history that is embedded and differs from the articulation of the historical tradition in the post-Gupta period in embodied forms. The hint of historical consciousness is now embedded less in ritual texts and more in creative literature, as in some of the works of Bhasa and Kalidasa, or the more overtly historical play, the *Mudra-rāksasas* of Vishakhadatta. This is the prelude to more specifically historical genres. The occasion is now the court and not a ritual or the gathering of the clan. This historical consciousness is made apparent in other more striking ways, for example in the re-use of objects from the past known to have had historical value.

The most dramatic example of such re-use is the pillar erected by Ashoka Maurya now located in the Allahabad fort. It carries a series of inscriptions each of a different millennium and in a different language—the Pillar Edicts of Ashoka, the long *prashasti,* eulogy, on the Gupta emperor Samudragupta, and an inscription of the Mughal emperor Jahangir. Evidently there was a perception of its encapsulating history and the legitimacy that history provides, hence the deliberate choice of the pillar even though the reasons for eulogizing Samudragupta's fiercely violent campaigns were contrary to the ethics of the Ashokan edicts which endorsed non-violence. Gupta *brahmi* was probably still close enough to Ashokan *brahmi* for the earlier inscriptions to be read. Was it a response to the mute testimony of an earlier *cakravartin,* universal monarch, or was it the claim of a Gupta king to greater authority and the establishing of a new ideology?

The construction of the past now moved out of the chrysalis of embedded form whether ritual or literary and came to be expressed in genres specifically recording history. These were the embodied forms—the *cāritas* or biographies of kings and ministers, the *vamshavalis* or regional chronicles, and royal inscriptions some of which are in effect dynastic annals. The change of forms, information on authorship, and distinct ideological perspectives, signal the importance of the historical tradition to post-Gupta society. There is an awareness of sources in varying degrees and the specificities of space and time. What was subterranean now surfaces and takes visible new forms.

Kingdoms, of which there were many more, were being transformed into more complex state systems and their take on the past was necessarily different from before. A new form of kingship was symbolic of the polity requiring additional mechanisms of legitimacy and representations of state power. Kings are occasionally said to be incarnations of deity but as such they were not even a pale shadow of the articulation of Divine Will familiar to us from other historiographies. Incarnations did not direct events; they shored up the claims of the ruler. The role of human agency remains primary. Association with deity enhanced the value of the *prashasti,* eulogy, and the early *prashastis* were included in inscriptions since such inscriptions were in effect annals.

Inscriptions, and particularly the *shasanas*—orders of the king—have their own format. The *prashasti,* in Sanskrit, is largely formulaic: the opening benediction is followed by a statement on the origins and achievements of the dynasty and of the reigning king, followed by stating the purpose of the inscription and concluding with the name and designation of the official who composed it, the scribe who wrote it and the engraver. The precise date of the king's order is given in detail in the prevailing era, generally the Vikrama and Shaka *samvats.* Inscriptions recording grants of land provide qualifications of the donee and the details of the land granted. Ministers and wealthy householders also issued votive and other inscriptions but less frequently than royalty. Genealogies move from desirable links to actual descent. Some statements are rhetoric but some allow of a historical narrative, set for the most part in a precise chronology. The section in the regional language addresses the legal aspects of the donation and the local administration. These could probably be read with profit in a comparative manner with texts in the same language claiming to be histories.

The *cāritas,* biographies, are of contemporary kings but include the historical antecedents of both subject and author. The focus is on a particular problem, such as an aspiration to spectacular power as can be argued for Banabhatta's *Harsā-carita,* a biography of the seventh century king of Kanauj, Harshavardhana; or quelling a revolt of the *samantas,* feudatories, as in Sandhyakara-nandin's *Ramacārita,* a similar work on the Pala king, Kampala. The intention is to give the official version justifying the king's action. This could have been a response to the questioning of the action. This becomes more likely in view of the biographies not being a narrative from birth to death but focussing on specific events of contemporary interest and how they evolve. The response would be relevant even to future readers. New powers claimed by kingship in new societies are being invoked and justified.

The *vamshavali,* chronicle, of which the finest example is the twelfth century *Rājatarangini* of Kalhana, was the document establishing the legitimacy of the kingdom and its rulers. As such they were composed in various kingdoms and some continued to be updated into later centuries. Origins tend to be linked to the Puranic *ksatriya* descent lists. But there is much that accounts for persons and events, largely of the past and some of the present, that approximates historical writing. They are valuable in tracing the process of state-formation and the establishing of kingdoms and the nature of the dynasties to which they refer as for example, the *vamshavali* from the kingdom of Chamba in Himachal Pradesh.[37] As a genre of historical writing it continues to be written in the regional languages when chronicles became a necessity in every new kingdom. Comparisons can be suggested with Buddhist monastic chronicles and medieval European chronicles.

These perceptions were predictably different in the parallel Jaina and Buddhist writing although the difference narrows in later times. Texts from these traditions were regarded as heterodox by *brāhmaṇ* authors of the Puranic tradition. The Shramanic tradition sometimes contested the representations from *brāhmaṇ* authorship.

For example, the earliest Jaina version of the *rama-katha,* Vimalasuri's *Paumachariyam,* of about the third century A.D., contradicts other versions and insists on its historicity. A political dialogue is implied in these confrontations. The choice of subject in later Jaina biographies and chronicles highlights those who were their patrons and the style is not too dissimilar from other biographies and chronicles. The writing of *prabandhas* in the Jaina tradition was similar to chronicles. A clearly historical example is Merutunga's *Prabandhachintamani* which follows the format of the chronicle but with a distinctly Jaina view of the Chaulukya dynasty of Gujarat.

The Buddhist narratives of the history of Sri Lanka in the monastic chronicles of *Dipavamsa* and *Mahavamsa* of the fifth and sixth centuries C.E., begin with the earliest kingdoms in the Ganges plain and continue to draw on the history of the sub-continent up to the end of the Mauryan Empire. The Indian link is because of the Buddhist connection. These chronicles have a different focus on events and personalities from those in the Puranic king-lists. For example, Ashoka is a mere name in the latter but in the chronicles he is both a powerful monarch as well as the exemplar of a royal patron to the Buddhist Sangha.[39] The reason for the difference is ideological. For the pre-Buddhist period the narrative draws on some sources that were common to the *itihāsa-purāṇa* traditions. Subsequent to the establishment of Buddhism, history is determined by persons and events in relation to the Buddhist Sangha. The interface between political authority and the Buddhist Sangha has no echo in the Puranic perspective. The Sangha's attempt to ensure authority included co-relating the succession of monastic elders to successive rulers.

These heterodox traditions, as they have been called, have a sharper understanding of the centrality of a historical perspective. The reasons can be many. Literacy for them meant not only writing and copying the Pali, Prakrit and Sanskrit Canons but also commentaries on the Canon, on the monastic chronicles that record sectarian developments and dissidence, as well as the biographies of the founders and the Elders who were historical figures. The records of monastic properties had also to be maintained. Events were generally related to the central date commanding their chronology, the date of the *mahaparinirvana*—the death of Buddha (486–483 B.C.E.)—or in the Jaina tradition the date of the death of Mahavira (527 B.C.E.). Within their own chronological structure their dates are consistent even if modern scholars argue that the actual date may not be precise.

A new and distinctive kind of historical consciousness emerges with these changes of form. Some links with the embedded tradition are present but their role is different. Forms such as *cāritas,* biographies, and *vamshavalis,* chronicles, carry traces of the Shramanic tradition with its biographies of Elders of the Sangha and of patrons, and narratives of sectarian movements. Emergent Puranic sectarianism may have noticed the effectiveness of such literature in claiming a past to assert a particular present. At the same time inscriptions issued by Jaina patrons imitated the *prashasti* style and adopted the calendar of the *samvat.* To some extent therefore, there is a coming together of the forms, although the ideologies remain demarcated. These were forms that continued into medieval times—inscriptions, biographies, chronicles—claimed by various dominant social groups and often written in the regional language. Their assessment as history draws on both the *itihāsa-purāṇa* tradition and Sultanate and Mughal historiography. To these were added the epics of local heroes which were indirectly a commentary on local rulers and had perceptions that were different from the official version of events.

All these texts can be looked at afresh and in a comparative way because historians are now turning to themes which had earlier been precluded from history.[40] It is recognized that groups in society have their own versions of history which reflect the perception of their past as viewed by particular authors. Even what we regard as a fabricated version, claiming to be historical is of historiographical interest. Fabrication is often the rhetoric of ideology, therefore the reason for the fabrication has to be sought[41] as indeed the degree to which it is also an attempt to bypass the problematic.

A view of the past becomes pivotal at times of transition when the past can either be rejected or can be used to legitimize the changing present. A significant function of history has been to legitimize those in power by providing origins and antecedents. What others had to say has largely to be extrapolated from these statements or from alternate sources where they exist.

Any codification of the past tends to be selective and the reasons for making a particular selection are significant. The *itihāsa-purāṇa* tradition in both its Puranic and Shramanic forms came to constitute the core of the constituents of historical thinking. A heroic phase moved to a courtly phase, or a king had an interface with the Sangha. The ideology of the Shramanic perspective was different from the Puranic although some of the data could overlap. Other parallel traditions incorporating a historical consciousness took other forms. The bardic tradition, the retrieval of which is problematic, was among these and the tension between the brahmanic and the bardic remained an undercurrent.

In looking at the *itihāsa-purāṇa* tradition my intention is not to try and reinstate an indigenous interpretation of early Indian history or to argue that there is an 'authentic' version of Indian history, an Indian view of India, in such sources. I am arguing that an awareness of the perceptions which earlier authors had of the past could be a way of illuminating our understanding of early society. Such perceptions would relate to the creation of variable identities, and to social hierarchies of dominance and subordination that involved differentiated access to economic resources as well as claims to ritual status. It is for us as historians to recognize the manner in which these early writings record and explain how their authors perceived the processes of historical change. What I am arguing for is that we interrogate earlier traditions to ascertain if there is a coherent view of the past, analyze their constituent forms, and perceive the relation that these have with the society from which they emerge. Such an interrogation might help us recognize the nature of historical consciousness that went into the making of historical traditions and in some instances of historical writing.

NOTES

1. E.J. Hobsbawm, "The Social Function of the Past: Some Questions", *Past and Present,* (1972), vol. 55, pp. 3-18.
2. "On the Chronology of the Hindus", *Asiatic Researches,* (1790), vol. 2, p. 111 ff.
3. A.A. MacDonell, *History of Sanskrit Literature,* (London, 1900), p. 11.
4. E.J. Rapson, *The Cambridge History of India,* vol. I (Cambridge: University of Cambridge Press, 1922), p. 57.
5. The Asiatic Society founded in 1784 to encourage Indological research remained closed to Indians for almost half a century. O.P. Kejriwal, *The Asiatic Society of Bengal and the Discovery of India's Past,* (Delhi: Oxford University Press, 1988), p. 153.
6. R. Schwab, *The Oriental Renaissance,* (New York: Columbia University Press, 1984(tr.))
7. W. Halbfass, *India and Europe,* (Albany: SUNY, 1988)
8. G.W.F. Hegel, *The Philosophy of History*, (New York: Dover Publications, 1958) pp. 140-41; pp. 162-64.
9. R. Thapar, "Ideology and the Interpretation of Early Indian History", *Interpreting Early India*, (Delhi: Oxford University Press, 1997), pp. 1-22
10. J.Mujeeb, *Ungoverned Imaginings: James Mill's The History of British India and Orientalism,* (Oxford: Oxford University Press, 1992), p. 4 ff; R. Inden, "Orientalist Construction of India", *Modern Asian Studies,* (1986), vol. 20, no. 3, pp. 401-446; *Imagining India*, (Oxford: Oxford University Press, 1990).
11. J. Mill, *The History of British India*, vol. I (New York: Chelsea House Publishers, 1968 reprint), p. 33 ff.
12. E. Said, *Orientalism*, (New York: Pantheon Books, 1978).
13. J. Tod, *Annals and Antiquities of Rajasthan*, (London: Routledge and Kegan Paul, 1829-32; 1960, reprint).
14. L.P. Tessitori, "A Scheme for the Bardic and Historical Survey of Rajputana," *Journal of the Asiatic Society of Bengal,* (1914), vol. 10, pp. 373-86; (1919), vol. 15, pp. 5-79; (1920), vol. 16, pp. 251-79.
15. S. Havale, *The Pradhans of the Upper Narbada Valley*, (Bombay: Asia Publishing House, 1946); N. Zeigler, "Mewari Historical Chronicles", *Indian Economic and Social History Review,* (April-June 1976), vol. 13, no. 2, p. 219 ff.
16. B. Stein, "Early Indian Historiography: A Conspiracy Hypothesis", *Indian Economic and Social History Review,* (1969), vol. 6, no. 1, pp. 41-60.

17. H. Kulke, "Geshicteschreibung und Gesichichtsbild in Hinduistechen Mirtelalter", *Secculum*, (1979), vol. 30, pp. 100-113.
18. A. Nandy, "History's Forgotten Doubles", *History and Theory,* (1995), vol. 34, no. 2, pp. 44-66; V. Narayan Rao, D. Shulman and S. Subrahmanyam, *Textures of Time*, (Delhi: Oxford University Press, 2000); Praci Deshpande, *Creative Pasts: Historical Memory and Identity in Western India, 1700-1960*, (Delhi: Oxford University Press, 2007); S. Guha, "Speaking Historically: The Changing Voices of Historical Narration in Western India, 1400-1900", *American Historical Review,* (2004), vol. 109, no. 4, 1084-1103; Vinay Lal, *History of History*, (Delhi: Oxford University Press, 2002), pp. 14-16; pp. 58-60.
19. C.H. Philips (ed.), *Historians of India, Pakistan and Ceylon*, (London: Oxford University Press, 1961).
20. A.K. Warder, *An Introduction to Indian Historiography*, (Bombay: Popular Prakashan, 1972).
21. V.S. Pathak, *Ancient Historians of India*, (Bombay: Asia Publishing House, 1966).
22. Aijaz Ahmad, *In Theory: Classes, Nations, Literatures*, (London: Verso, 1992).
23. F.M. Cornford, *Thucydides Mythistoricus*, (London: Lawrence and Wishart, 1907).
24. W. den Boer, "Greco-Roman Historiography in its relation to Biblical and Modern Thinking", *History and Theory,* (1968), vol. 7, pp. 60-75.
25. A. Momigliano, "The Place of Herodotus in the history of Historiography", *History,* (1958), vol. 43, pp. 1-13.
26. Quoted in J. Weinberg, "Where Three Civilisations Meet," *History and Theory,* Beiheft 30, (1991), p. 19.
27. E. Sachau, *Alberuni's India*, vol. II (Delhi: Chand and Co., 1964 reprint), pp. 10–11.
28. A. Momigliano, "Polybius and Posidonius", *Alien Wisdom: The Limits of Hellenisation*, (Cambridge: University of Cambridge Press, 1975); *Historicism Revisited,* MKN, Akademie van Wetenschappen, Aftd. Letterkunde, Nieuwe Reeks, Deel 1974, vol. 37, no. 3, pp. 63-70.
29. M. Eliade, *Cosmos and History: The Myth of the Eternal Return*, (New York: Bollingen Series, 1959); R. Thapar, *Time as a Metaphor of History*, (Delhi: Oxford University Press, 2000).
30. *Chandogya Upanishad*, 7.1. 2. 4.
31. S. Pollock, "The Theory of Practice and the Practice of Theory in Indian Intellectual History," *JAOS,* (1985), vol. 105, no. 3, pp. 499-519.
32. R. Thapar, "*Dāna* and *Dakṣiṇā* as forms of Exchange," *Cultural Posts*, (Delhi: Oxford University Press, 2000), pp. 521-35.

33. R. Thapar, "The Historian and the Epic", Ibid., pp. 613-29.
34. R. Thapar, "The Rāmāyaṇa: Theme and Variation", Ibid., pp. 647-79.
35. J. Vansina, *Oral Tradition*, (Chicago: University of Chicago Press, 1965); *Oral Tradition as History*, (London: James Curry, 1985); D.P. Henige, *The Chronology of Oral Tradition*, (Oxford: Oxford University Press, 1974); *Oral Historiography*, (London: Longman 1982); A.M. Shah and R.G. Shroff, "The Vahivanca Barots of Gujerat: A Caste of Genealogists and Mythographers," in M. Singer (ed.), *Traditional India*, (Chicago: University of Chicago Press, 1959), pp. 40-70 ; N.P. Ziegler, "The Seventeenth Century Chronicles of Marvara: A Study in the Evolution and Use of Oral Tradition in Western India," *History in Africa,* (1976), vol. 3, pp. 127-53.
36. *Visnu Purana,* H.H. Wilson, The Visnu Purana, (Calcutta: Punthi Pustak, 1961), Book IV; R. Thapar, "Genealogical Patterns as Perceptions of the Past", *Cultural Pasts*, (Delhi: Oxford University Press, 2000), pp. 709-53.
37. R. Thapar, "The Vamshavali from Chamba: Reflections of a Historical Tradition", D. Bhattacharya (ed.), *India and Indology, The Professor Sukumari Bhattacharya Felicitation Volume*, (Kolkata: National Book Agency, 2008), pp. 581-94.
38. H. Jacobi, (ed.), *Paumachariyam of Vimalasuri*, (Varanasi: Prakrit Text Society, 1914, 1962 reprint); R.K. Chanda, *A Critical Study of the Paumachariyam*, (Muzaffarpur: Prakrit Research Institute, 1970).
39. W. Geiger, *The Mahavamsa*, (London: Luzac and Co., 1964); H. Oldenberg, *Dipavamsa*, (New Delhi: Asian Educational Services, 1992); J. Strong, *The Legend of King Ashoka*, (New Jersey: Princeton University Press, 1983).
40. J. LeGoff and P. Nora (eds.), *Constructing the Past*, (Cambridge: Cambridge University Press, 1985).
41. E.J. Hobsbawm, op. cit.; S. Errington, "Style in the meaning of the Past", *Journal of Asian Studies,*(1979), vol. 38, no. 2, pp. 231-44; J. Siegal, *Shadow and Sound: The Historical Thought of a Sumatran People*, (Chicago: University of Chicago Press, 1979); M. Sahlms, *Islands of History*, (Chicago: University of Chicago Press, 1985).

REFERENCES

A. Ahmed, *In Theory: Classes, Nations, Literatures*, (London: Verso, 1992).

D. Bhattacharya (ed.), *India and Indology, The Professor Sukumari Bhattacharya Felicitation Volume*, (Kolkata: National Book Agency, 2004).

W. den Boer, "Greco-Roman Historiography in its relation to Biblical and Modern thinking", *History and Theory*, vol. 7, (1968), pp. 60-75.

R.K. Chanda, *A Critical Study of the Paumachariyam*, (Muzaffarnagar: Research Institute of Prakrit, 1970).

S. Radhakrishnan, "Chandogya Upanishad" in *The Principal Upanisads*, (London: George Alien and Unwin, 1953)

F.M. Cornford, *Thucydides Mythistoricus*, (London: Lawrence and Wishart, 1907).

P. Deshpande, Creative Pasts: Historical Memory and Identity in M. Eliade's *Cosmos and History: The Myth of the Eternal Return*, (New York: Bollingen Series, 1959).

S. Errington, "Style in the meaning of the Past", *Journal of Asian Studies*, (1979), vol. 38, no. 2, pp. 231-44; W. Geiger, *The Mahavamsa*, (London: Luzac and Co., 1912).

S. Guha, "Speaking Historically: The Changing Voices in Historical Narration in Western India, 1400-1900," *American Historical Review*, vol. 109, no. 4, pp. 1084-1103.

W. Halbfass, *India and Europe*, (Albany: SUNY, 1988).

S. Havale, *The Pradhans of the Upper Narbada Valley*, (Bombay: Asia Publishing House, 1946).

G.W.F. Hegel, *The Philosophy of History*, (New York: Dover Publications, 1847, 1958 (tr.)).

D.P. Henige, *Oral Historiography*, (London: Longman, 1982).

D.P. Henige, *The Chronology of Oral Tradition*, (Oxford: Oxford University Press, 1974).

E.J. Hobsbawm, "The Social Function of the Past: Some Questions," *Past and Present*, vol. 55, (1972), pp. 3-18.

R. Inden, *Imagining India*, (Oxford: Oxford University Press, 1990).

R. Inden, "Orientalist Construction of India", *Modern Asian Studies*, vol. 20, no. 3, (1986), pp. 401-46.

H. Jacobi, *Paumachariyam of Vimalasuri*, (Varanasi: Prakrit Text Society, 1962).

William Jones, "On the Chronology of the Hindus," *Asiatic Researches*, vol. 2, (1790), p. 111 ff.

O.P. Kejriwal, *The Asiatic Society of Bengal and the Discovery of India's Past*, (Delhi: Oxford University Press, 1988).

H. Kulke, "Geshicteschreibung und Gesichichtsbild in Hinduistechen Mittelalter", *Secculum*, vol. 30, (1979), pp. 100-13.

J. LeGoff, and P. Nora (eds.), *Constructing the Past*, (Cambridge: Cambridge University Press, 1985).

A.A. MacDonell, *History of Sanskrit Literature*, (London, 1900).

J. Mill, *The History of British India*, (New York: Chelsea House Publications, 1818-23, 1968).

A. Momigliano, "The Place of Herodotus in the History of Historiography", *History*, vol. 43, (1958), pp. 1-13.

A. Momigliano, "Polybius and Posidonius", *Alien Wisdom: The Limits of Hellenisation*, (Cambridge: University of Cambridge Press, 1975).

A. Momigliano, *Historicism Revisited*, MKN, (Akademie van Wetenschappen, Aftd. Letterkunde, Nieuwe Reeks, Deel 1974), vol. 37, no. 3, pp. 63-70.

J. Mujeeb, *Ungoverned Imaginings: James Mill's The History of British India and Orientalism*, (Oxford: Oxford University Press, 1992).

A. Nandy, "History's Forgotten Doubles", *History and Theory*, vol. 34, no. 2, (1995), pp. 44-66.

V. Narayan Rao et al., *Textures of Time*, (Delhi: Oxford University Press, 2000).

H. Oldenberg, *Dipavamsa*, (Delhi: Asian Educational Service, 1879, 1992 reprint).

V.S. Pathak, *Ancient Historians of India*, (Bombay: Asia Publishing House, 1966).

C.H. Philips (ed.), *Historians of India, Pakistan and Ceylon*, (London: Oxford University Press, 1961).

S. Pollock, "The Theory of Practice and the Practice of Theory in Indian Intellectual History," *JAOS*, vol. 105, no. 3, (1985), pp. 499-519.

E.J. Rapson, *The Cambridge History of India*, vol. I (Cambridge: Cambridge University Press, 1922).

E. Sachau, *Alberuni's India*, (Delhi: Chand and Co., 1964 reprint).

M. Sahlins, *Islands of History*, (Chicago: University of Chicago Press, 1985).

E. Said, *Orientalism*, (New York: Pantheon Books, 1978).

R. Schwab, *The Oriental Renaissance: Europe's Rediscovery of India and the East 1680–1880*, (New York: Columbia University Press, 1984 (tr.)).

J. Siegal, *Shadow and Sound: The Historical Thought of a Sumatran People*, (Chicago: University of Chicago Press, 1979).

M. Singer, (ed.), *Traditional India*, (Chicago: University of Chicago Press, 1959).

B. Stein, "Early Indian Historiography: A Conspiracy Hypothesis", *Indian Economic and Social History Review*, vol. 6, no. 1, (1969), pp. 41-60.

J. Strong, *The Legend of King Asoka*, (New Jersey: Princeton University Press, 1983).

L.P. Tessitori, "A Scheme for the Bardic and Historical Survey of Rajputana", *Journal of the Asiatic Society of Bengal*, n.s. vol. 10, (1914), pp. 373-86; vol. 15, (1919), pp. 5-79; vol. 16, (1920), pp. 251-79.

R. Thapar, *Time as a Metaphor of History*, (Delhi: Oxford University Press, 1998).

R. Thapar, *Cultural Pasts*, (Delhi: Oxford University Press, 2000).

R. Thapar, *Interpreting Early India*, (Delhi: Oxford University Press, 2000).

J. Tod, *Annals and Antiquities of Rajasthan*, (London: Routledge and Kegal Paul, 1829-32, 1960 reprint).

J. Vansina, *Oral Tradition*, (Chicago: University of Chicago Press, 1965); J. Vansina, *Oral Tradition as History*, (London: James Curry, 1985).

A.K. Warder, *An Introduction to Indian Historiography*, (Bombay: Popular Prakashan, 1972).

J. Weinberg, "Where Three Civilizations Meet", *History and Theory*, Beiheft 30, (1991), p. 19.

Western India, 1700–1960, (Delhi: Oxford University Press, 2007); H.H. Wilson, *The Visnu Purana*, (Calcutta: Punthi Pustak, 1961 reprint).

N. Zeigler, "Mewari Historical Chronicles", *Indian Economic and Social History Review*, April-June 1976, vol. 13, no. 2, p. 219 ff.

N.P. Ziegler, "The Seventeenth Century Chronicles of Marvara: A Study in the Evolution and use of Oral Tradition in Western India", *History in Africa*, vol. 3, (1976), pp. 127-53.

Index